Graedons' Best Medicine: From Herbal Remedies to High-Tech R$_X$ Breakthroughs

Also by Joe Graedon and Teresa Graedon

50+
The Graedons' People's Pharmacy for Older Adults

The People's Pharmacy: Totally New and Revised

Joe Graedon's The New People's Pharmacy #3:
Drug Breakthroughs of the '80s

The People's Pharmacy-2

The People's Pharmacy

Graedons' Best Medicine:
From Herbal Remedies
to High-Tech R$_X$ Breakthroughs

By Joe Graedon
and
Dr. Teresa Graedon

A
BANTAM
TRADE
PAPERBACK

BANTAM BOOKS
NEW YORK · TORONTO · LONDON · SYDNEY · AUCKLAND

GRAEDONS' BEST MEDICINE: FROM HERBAL REMEDIES TO HIGH-TECH RX
BREAKTHROUGHS
A Bantam Book / February 1991

ISBN 0–553–07232–3 (Hardcover)
ISBN 0–553–35274–1 (Paperback)

Published simultaneously in the United States and Canada

PRINTED IN THE UNITED STATES OF AMERICA

0 9 8 7 6 5 4 3 2 1

THIS BOOK IS DEDICATED TO:

DAVID AND ALENA
Two wonderful children who have been
patient and understanding

DR. EVA SALBER
A friend and inspiration as well as a physician who believes
in people's ability to take care of themselves

DR. TOM FERGUSON
A friend who has led the self-care revolution

TONI BURBANK
A wonderful editor whose enthusiasm
kept us going

PEOPLE WHO ARE COMMITTED
To taking an active role in their own health care

Acknowledgments

Leo Ars, who truly represents self-care committment.

George Brett, a great friend who keeps us humming.

Cliff Butler, the best pharmacist we know.

Keith Cassell, a creative genius who made this book possible with his design skills.

Bruno Cortis, the most caring, loving cardiologist we have ever met.

Harrison Dekker, a perfect assistant who understands libraries and computers better than anyone we know.

Andi Frost, a great sister and super artist who made our book look better with her illustrations.

Betty and Bonnell Frost, parents who just keep getting better.

Robert Gilgor, a gentleman and a dermatologist who cares about effective communication.

Helen Graedon, a wonderful mother who helps in so many ways.

Marcia and Ricardo Hofer, who always provide support, encouragement and love.

Stan Levy, a great tennis partner and one of the country's leading cosmeceutical dermatologists.

Henry Myers, a selfless friend who cares.

Gail Schmidt, an enthusiastic supporter of self-care and a great friend.

Brian Weiss, who came through in the crunch once again.

Michael Woyton, a quick study and a wizard with words.

Attention

Table of Contents

Take Charge 1

Join the revolution! All around you people are taking charge of their health care as never before. In our do-it-yourself society, men and women want to be involved in every aspect, from monitoring blood pressure and glucose to choosing an effective over-the-counter drug or getting the prescription that is best for them.

People are selecting from a wide range of options. Some start with home remedies, herbs, vitamins, minerals, or amino acids, while others turn to an increasingly powerful selection of nonprescription products. The explosion in over-the-counter (OTC) medications and devices is being fueled in part by the manufacturers' recognition of public interest in new and better self-care products. Some of the most successful

OTC brands required prescriptions only a few years ago: **Advil**, **Motrin IB**, and **Nuprin** are all ibuprofen, which as **Motrin** was once a best-selling prescription-only arthritis medicine. The decongestant **Actifed** and antihistamine **Benadryl** have moved off prescription pads to pharmacy shelves, to the relief of countless allergy sufferers. Sales of such drugs have been spectacular, with **Benadryl** pulling in five times more after it went nonprescription. We expect this trend to continue, with even more powerful and popular prescription drugs jumping the pharmacy counter. **Seldane** for allergies, **Carafate**, **Tagamet** and **Zantac** for ulcers, and **Naprosyn** and **Feldene** for arthritis are all targeted for OTC status.

Biotechnology and microelectronics have allowed for the creation of highly accurate home tests that are easy to use. People now take for granted the diagnostic kits that allow women to determine when they are ovulating, for the best chance of becoming pregnant, and then to confirm their pregnancy, both with home tests. Blood pressure monitors for home use are no longer news, although today's digital equipment self-inflates over a finger instead of the whole arm and fits in a pocketbook for easy access. Blood sugar monitors no bigger than a pen have enabled diabetics to achieve better control of their disease than was ever possible before. Future diagnostic tests may allow people to detect strep throat or urinary tract infections without leaving home. Simple systems for determining blood levels of therapeutic medications such as digitalis or epilepsy medicine should soon take some of the guesswork out of these therapies, so that they will become both more effective and safer.

Doctors are finding that their patients have become more sophisticated and are now eager to understand their conditions and participate as partners in their management. The pharmaceutical companies have been quick to realize the potential of this expanding market and are beginning to target advertising for prescription medicines directly to consumers, on television and in print. These developments can be positive, but they do require more effort and responsibility from all of us. To participate effectively in your own

health care, information is essential.

This book is your field guide to the best therapies available for many common health problems. It covers a wide variety of alternatives, from exercise and amino acids for depression to herbal remedies and over-the-counter analgesics for pain relief. You will find information to evaluate many of the most important prescription drugs on the market. In addition, you will learn about experimental breakthroughs being developed for a wide range of medical conditions from Alzheimer's disease, enlarged prostate, and migraine headache, to heart disease, ulcers, and osteoporosis. We have done our best to peer into the crystal ball and determine which medicines under development offer the greatest promise for the future.

The Food and Drug Administration has loosened its regulations covering access to unapproved medicines for "immediately life-threatening" or "serious" disease. So if an important new AIDS therapy or cancer treatment were to become available in Europe or Japan, it would be legal for an individual or family member to import small quantities of that drug for personal use. Other conditions the FDA considers serious include Alzheimer's disease, advanced Parkinson's disease, advanced multiple sclerosis, and some forms of diabetes and epilepsy. A note from the supervising physician will make customs easier. People who decide to take a medication the FDA has not approved are taking an extra risk and need to assume far greater responsibility. They also must work closely with their doctors to monitor progress and potential side effects.

There have been so many recent advances that it is hard for anyone to keep up with all the latest treatments. That's why we've provided an evaluation that will help patients and physicians to figure out what's best. So many factors enter into consideration when someone seeks relief that the decisions need to be made on a very individual basis. There is rarely a single approach that fits everyone. If you feel more comfortable starting with herbs and vitamins as initial therapy, you will find facts that can be put to practical use. Keep in mind that if the remedy you try first doesn't work, you may need to continue stepping up the ladder of therapeutic options. We have flagged

the over-the-counter remedies that are most useful and have alerted you to potential pitfalls.

If you need a prescription, you will want to know the safest and most effective compounds available. Choosing the best medicine is a balancing act between many different factors. Everyone's response to medication differs. The arthritis remedy or blood pressure pill that works for you may be ineffective or toxic for your spouse. (Some people can't bear nausea; others don't mind it, but are driven to distraction by itching.)

You must learn to pay attention to your body, so that you will know how it is responding. Sometimes side effects can be subtle and slow in onset. If you begin to suspect that you are becoming forgetful or depressed, or if your hair starts to fall out, you'll need to communicate your findings to your doctor. He can't help you adjust your treatment unless he knows how you're doing with it. Convenience (once a day versus several times daily) also needs to be taken into account when a medication is chosen. No doctor can possibly know all these details about you without input; that is why a partnership is critical. To live up to your responsibility, you need knowledge as well as commitment.

Inform Yourself

Sometimes there are no clear answers. Controversies abound in medicine, which is more of an art and less of a science than most of us appreciate. For example, do birth control pills and estrogen replacement therapy increase the risk of breast cancer? Even after thirty years we still do not know. Each woman must decide with her doctor whether the risk for her individual situation is balanced by the benefits.

If you can't get the information you need from your physician, pharmacist, or a popular reference book, another source you might consider is a medical library. Once upon a time, the public wasn't allowed into these temples of medical knowledge. Now, however, most medical libraries permit free access. Ask the reference librarian for assistance in learning to search the

available resources. The library should have a printed copy of the *Index Medicus*, which is one place to start hunting. You may also be able to request a computerized literature search to help you locate the appropriate articles and journals.

If you have a personal computer and a modem in your home, you can access the National Medical Library directly through a database service such as Dialog Information Services or BRS Colleague. Learning to use these services takes some time and effort, but will allow you to follow the most recent medical research. You can obtain abstracts from most of the world's medical literature and even get complete articles from selected journals without leaving your chair.

If doing it yourself sounds too overwhelming, we have good news. A marvelous service exists in San Francisco called Planetree Health Resource Center. If you are in the Bay area, you can visit their complete medical library and bookstore. If you live out of town, you can call them and request any of three information packets:

(1) **PDQ (Physician's Data Query)** costs $15. If you have cancer and would like facts about your particular type of cancer and the latest treatment for it, this packet will provide you with current information from the National Cancer Institute.

(2) **The Computer Search** for $25 provides you with a "Medline" bibliography on the health topic or treatment you request. Abstracts of articles are provided when they are available.

(3) **The In Depth Packet** at $75 is the most comprehensive. It will include a forty- to fifty-page review of the areas of your concern with actual articles and bibliography.

How to Use This Book

Scattered throughout the book are thumbnail summaries of treatments, from home remedies to experimental new agents. They represent our evaluation, from moderately useful, one-star (★) medicines to spectacular, five-star (★★★★★) compounds. For example, chamomile tea and

Here is an example of the Therapy Thumbnail:

Wellbutrin
(bupropion)
A unique new antidepressant with fewer side effects than traditional antidepressants. Can have the added bonus of helping people lose weight and may also stimulate sexuality. People tend to feel energized rather than sluggish. Side effects: agitation, insomnia, tremor, headache, and dry mouth. Seizures are a rare but worrisome possibility.

★ ★ ★

Pepto-Bismol rate ★★★★ for tummy trouble, whereas niacin rates ★★★ for high cholesterol. **Rogaine** only rates ★ for baldness, while **Eldepryl** gets ★★★★ for the treatment of Parkinson's and the possibility of Alzheimer's prevention. We have been parsimonious with our ★★★★★ rating. Just as very few restaurants deserve ★★★★★, few medicines merit such an accolade. Aspirin is a clear winner in this category since it provides so many new benefits—heart attack, stroke, migraine, and multi-infarct dementia prevention. These are general guidelines and represent only our perspective. Although we have reviewed the scientific literature and consulted experts, there are honest differences of opinion even among specialists about which treatments are best. Only you and your physicians will be able to determine which is most appropriate for your condition.

Your doctor can't prescribe experimental compounds that are not yet approved in this country. However, we recognize that desperate situations sometimes call for heroic measures. Someone who is drowning may be willing to take a chance on a life preserver that has not yet been fully tested for safety or effectiveness. Alzheimer's disease is one example. If you are considering such action, we urge you to do so only with the full knowledge, cooperation, and supervision of your physician.

We have tried to identify promising new drugs, which company is testing them, and where they are available if they have been approved elsewhere. But not everyone can manage to travel abroad to obtain such state-of-the-art therapies. To participate in a clinical trial of an experimental compound in this country, you should ask your doctor to contact the medical director of the pharmaceutical firm in question. That individual will be able to refer her to one of the clinical investigators who is conducting studies. Medical centers and teaching universities are usually strong bets for such clinical investigation. They often advertise for subjects in local newspapers or over the radio. One woman managed to get her father into an experimental Alzheimer's program just by calling the Duke University operator and asking for the person in charge of Alzheimer's research.

You may have to be assertive, but when lives are at stake, being a little pushy can get a lot accomplished. There are, of course, risks in volunteering to be a human guinea pig. Serious or unexpected side effects may occur. On the other hand, you should be informed of the anticipated risks and benefits, and the medicine should be provided free of charge along with medical supervision. In some cases you may even be paid to participate in such a clinical trial.

Self-help groups and specialized agencies may be a good source for finding out about experimental therapies and who is studying them. In addition they can provide practical information on a variety of issues related to the condition. Besides psychological support, which can be very important, they may be able to offer information on tools for medical management or day-to-day living, advice on legal or financial questions that commonly arise, and updates on research advances. One such organization is the National Cancer Institute (NCI). Their cancer information service has trained professionals answering their information hotline (800) 4-CANCER. In addition to fielding a range of questions, they can create a customized computer search for appropriate clinical trials based on the specific diagnosis and history provided by the caller.

Local self-help chapters may differ somewhat in the services they offer; the only way to find out for sure is to get in touch. You will find the national headquarters for many of these organizations listed at the end of this chapter, along with other sources for up-to-date drug information. (Helpful as they are, please remember that no telephone information service can offer diagnosis or prescribe treatments tailored specifically to your situation.)

In this book we have tried to gather together the best remedies available. We would want to take them along as a sort of ultimate medicine chest if we were going to be stranded on a desert island. This collection can be tailored to your individual

---

Volunteering for Experimental Drugs

Before participating in a clinical trial of an unapproved medicine

- Know the name of the medication being tested.
- Check the informed-consent form carefully. It should tell you about potential benefits and risks and explain the study in clear language.
- Ask lots of questions. The investigators must answer all your queries, but they won't be able to tell you if you will get the active medicine or the look-alike placebo.
- Never give up your rights to legal recourse if the drug harms you.
- Get an emergency phone number in case of an adverse reaction.

needs and circumstances, but we hope that in the process of reading and referring to the following pages you will be empowered to participate in the self-care revolution.

Information Resources

National Health Information Clearinghouse   (800) 336–4797 (This hotline, run by the department of Health and Human Services, can give you phone numbers for information on almost any health topic.)

AIDS

National AIDS Hotline   (800) 342–AIDS
　　　　[to converse in Spanish, dial **(800) 344–SIDA**]
　　　　[deaf callers may dial **(800) AIDS–TTY** for keyboard technology]

Allergy & Asthma Organizations

American Academy of Allergy   (414) 272–6071
　　　　& Immunology
Mothers of Asthmatics   (703) 385–4403
National Asthma Center   (800) 222–5864
National Institute of Allergy   (301) 496–5717
　　　　and Infectious Diseases

Arthritis

Arthritis Foundation   (404) 872–7100
Arthritis Medical Center   (800) 327–3027
　　　　[in Fort Lauderdale, Florida, dial **(305) 739–3202**]

Cancer

Cancer Information Service   (800) 4–CANCER
　　　　[in Oahu, Hawaii, dial **(808) 524–1234**]

Y-Me Breast Cancer Support Program   **(800) 221–2141**
     [in Chicago, dial **(312) 799–8228**]

Child Abuse

National Child Abuse Hotline   **(800) 422–4453**
Parents Anonymous Hotline   **(800) 421–0353**
     [in California, dial **(800) 352–0386**]

Drug Abuse

National Drug Abuse Treatment Referral   **(800) COCAINE**
National Institute on Drug Abuse   **(800) 662–4357**

Handicaps

American Council of the Blind   **(800) 424–8666**
Association for Persons with   **(206) 523–8446**
     Severe Handicaps
Dial-a-Hearing Screening Test   **(800) 222–EARS**
     [in Pennsylvania, dial **(800) 345–3277**]
National Association for Hearing   **(800) 638–8255**
     & Speech Action
National Center for Stuttering   **(800) 221–2483**
     [in New York, dial **(212) 532–1460**]
National Society to Prevent Blindness   **(312) 843–2020**

Mental Illness

American Psychiatric Association   **(202) 682–6000**
Bulimia and Anorexia Self-Help   **(800) 762–3334**
     [in St. Louis, dial **(314) 768–3838**]
National Alliance for the Mentally Ill   **(703) 524–7600**
TERRAP (Agoraphobia and Panic Attacks)   **(800) 2–PHOBIA**

Nutrition & Vitamins

American Society for Clinical Nutrition	(301) 530–7110
Food and Nutrition Information Center	(301) 344–3719
Institute of Human Nutrition	(212) 305–6991
Nutrition Foundation	(202) 659–0074
USDA Meat and Poultry Hot Line	(800) 535–4555

Sexually Transmitted Diseases

Herpes Resource Center Hotline (eastern)	(919) 361–2120
[western (415) 328–7710]	
Sexually Transmitted Disease Hotline	(800) 227–8922

Skin

Acne Help Line	(800) 222–SKIN
[in California, dial (800) 221–SKIN]	
American Society for Dermatologic Surgery	(800) 441–ASDS

Other Health-Related Organizations

Alzheimer's Disease and Related Disorders Association	(800) 621–0379
[in Illinois, dial (800) 572–6037]	
American Association of Retired Persons (AARP)	(202) 872–4700
American Heart Association	(214) 373–6300
American Lung Association	(212) 315–8700
American Parkinson's Disease Association	(800) 223–2732
Endometriosis Association	(800) 992–3636
Epilepsy Foundation of America	(800) EFA–1000
FDA Consumer Inquiries	(301) 443–3170
Heartlife	(800) 241–6993
[in Georgia, dial (404) 523–0826]	
Juvenile Diabetes Foundation International	(800) JDF–CURE
National Chronic Pain Outreach Association	(301) 652–4948
National Foundation for Ileitis & Colitis	(212) 685–3440

National Headache Foundation   **(800) 843–2256**
National Kidney Foundation   **(212) 889–2210**
National Multiple Sclerosis Society   **(212) 986–3240**
National Parkinson Foundation   **(800) 327–4545**
National Reye's Syndrome Foundation   **(800) 233–7393**
National Scoliosis Foundation   **(617) 489–0888**
National Stroke Association   **(303) 762–9922**
National Women's Health Network   **(202) 347–1140**
Organ Donor Hotline   **(800) 24–DONOR**
Second Surgical Opinion Hotline   **(800) 638–6833**
Sudden Infant Death Syndrome Hotline **(800) 221–7437**
     [in Maryland, dial **(301) 459–3388**]

Heartburn and Indigestion	Irritable Bowel Syndrome (IBS)
Ulcers	Constipation
Gassiness and Flatulence	Itchy Bottom
Diarrhea	

Gut Issues | 2

Nothing gets your attention like a belly-ache. The pain may result from something as simple as dietary indiscretion or as serious as appendicitis or an ulcer. The trouble is that there's usually no quick and easy way to tell what's going on inside. Of course, if you just indulged in a monster pizza with pepperoni, onions, and anchovies or a triple-scooper hot fudge sundae with whipped cream, you probably don't need a fancy medical workup to figure out the culprit. And you may not need a powerful drug to cope with the problem.

There are lots of simple tricks and herbal medicines that can help with digestive tract woes. Would you believe that licorice can do a lot more than tickle your taste buds? Sucking on a piece of hard candy may stimulate the body's own natural defenses against heartburn. And if you love spicy foods, have we got good news for you! **Tabasco** for tummy trouble may sound heretical, but animal research backs up the benefits of hot peppers against aspirin-induced stomach irritation.

Selecting the right digestive aid from the pharmacy isn't easy. Should you worry that the aluminum in your antacid might be linked to Alzheimer's disease? Is **Pepto-Bismol** better for ulcers than prescription drugs like **Tagamet** (cimetidine), **Zantac** (ranitidine), **Axid** (nizatidine) or **Pepcid** (famotidine)? And with its aspirinlike ingredient, is **Pepto-Bismol** too dangerous for children?

If you suffer from the aches and pains of arthritis or tendonitis, what pain reliever will spare your stomach? Is ibuprofen (**Advil**, **Motrin IB**, **Nuprin**, etc.) really easier on the tum than aspirin? Those who must take an anti-inflammatory agent like **Clinoril** (sulindac), **Dolobid** (diflunisal), **Feldene** (piroxicam), **Indocin** (indomethacin), **Nalfon** (fenoprofen), **Naprosyn** (naproxen), or **Voltaren** (diclofenac) need to know what signs of digestive tract damage to watch for, and which medications can protect the stomach from these irritating compounds.

It's quite likely that the acid-fighting drugs **Tagamet** (cimetidine), **Zantac** (ranitidine), and **Carafate** (sucralfate) may soon become available without prescription. Whether you are taking these medications on your own or under a doctor's supervision, you will need inside information to use them wisely. We'll also tell you what's best for problems like constipation, colitis, diarrhea, and gas, whether it's a simple home remedy or a potent new prescription drug.

Heartburn and Indigestion

CAUSES

Diet

If only our stomachs could talk, imagine the horror stories they would tell. First we'd hear a cry of anguish at breakfast as we pour hot coffee down the hatch. That insult stimulates an incredible outpouring of stomach acid (even if it's decaf). We follow up with eggs, greasy sausage or bacon, and toast slathered with butter. And what about lunch at the ball park—the great American hot dog heaped high with sauerkraut, mustard, and onions—washed down with a beer. Ouch! It's hardly surprising that sometimes our stomachs bark back. A loud belch is a perfectly reasonable response to such an assault. (By the way, the baking soda burp is a direct result of carbon dioxide gas created in the stomach after sodium bicarbonate mixes with stomach acid.)

Sphincters

Dietary indiscretion is not the only cause of indigestion and heartburn. For many people the trouble lies at the bottom of the eating tube, or esophagus, where a small ring of muscle separates it from the stomach.

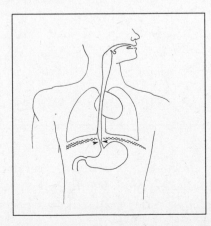

To understand the problem, think of the stomach as if it were an inflated balloon. As long as you pinch the end tightly closed, no air can escape. But relax your fingers and whoosh, the air will come racing out.

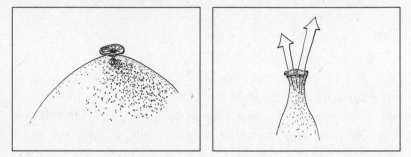

Like an inflated balloon, your stomach also has greater pressure inside than out. Stomach acid and partially digested food would tend to escape back up into the gullet were it not for that ring of muscle. Just as your fingers around the end of the balloon keep the air in, so too increased pressure at this sphincter keeps stomach acid where it belongs. But let that muscle get lazy or weak and watch out; when it starts to leak, heartburn may not be far behind. Doctors call this gastroesophageal reflux disease—GERD for short.

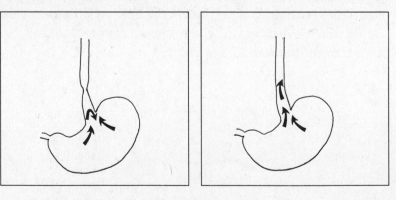

Things like chocolate, peppermint, cigarettes, alcohol, and even some medications can lower the pressure at the bottom end of the esophagus. They may make a weak sphincter even more vulnerable to splashback.

REMEDIES

Candy and Spit

In truth, it's not unusual to have some stomach acid splash back up into the esophagus a few times during the day, especially after eating. But usually it's temporary and painless. Swallowing and saliva normally wash any residual acid back down where it belongs in the stomach. Saliva, after all, is the body's own natural fire extinguisher.

Amazing stuff, spit. On average we swallow saliva once a minute throughout the day. It rinses and buffers the gullet from acid and, along with our sphincter, represents another line of defense against reflux. As we get older, we may make less saliva, which in turn can increase our risk of heartburn. Drugs like **Pro-Banthine** and **Norpanth** (propantheline), which are often prescribed for digestive tract woes, may actually be counterproductive because they dry out the mouth.[2] On the

---

Herbs Reported to Calm Upset Stomach

anise seeds	*Pimpinella anisum*
caraway seeds	*Carum carvi*
catnip	*Nepeta cataria*
chamomile	*Anthemis nobilis*
cinnamon	*Cinnamomum spp.*
dandelion leaves	*Taraxacum officinale*
dill	*Anethum graveolens*
ginger root	*Zingiber officinale*
goldenrod	*Solidago spp.*
lemon balm	*Melissa officinalis*
licorice	*Glycyrrhiza glabra*
peppermint	*Mentha piperita*
sage	*Salvia officinalis*
spearmint	*Mentha spicata*
summer savory	*Satureia hortensis*
wild geranium root	*Geranium maculatum*
wild mint	*Blephilia, Monarda, or Pycnanthemum spp.*
yellowroot (goldenseal)	*Hydrastis canadensis*

other hand, anything that stimulates saliva and swallowing could help dramatically,[3] so a simple home remedy for heartburn includes sucking on lozenges or hard candy. Even chewing gum might be helpful.

Herbal Tea

Another first-line approach for indigestion, stomach upset, and heartburn could be a spot of tea. Chamomile *(Anthemis nobilis)* is our first choice. It has been used for centuries by people all over the world to relieve stomach distress. Sipping an herbal tea may in itself stimulate saliva and help wash acid back into the stomach.

Many other herbs have also been tried as treatments for upset stomach. For many of these remedies from fields and gardens, the evidence of effectiveness is based more on the say-so of grandmothers in various cultures than on solid scientific tests. And at least one favorite herbal treatment, comfrey, has been proven dangerous and is to be avoided at all costs. Comfrey has been associated with liver damage and possibly even cancer. People with hay fever brought on by ragweed should also avoid chamomile (from the same plant family), as it may trigger a severe allergic reaction.

Bananas

Believe it or not, bananas may be great for your stomach. Physicians in India have been using bananas and banana powder for years as a treatment of ulcers and indigestion. They have found that bananas also work against aspirin-induced ulcers. A recent study proved that dried banana powder relieved indigestion in three-quarters of the treated patients.[4] Perhaps a banana a day will keep heartburn away.

Nondrug Approaches

There are several other steps you can take to control heartburn before resorting to drugs. First, watch what you eat. Stay away from fatty foods, chocolate, and peppermints. Chocolate and peppermint oil both relax the lower esophageal sphincter, increasing the risk of reflux. Don't be a couch potato,

Chamomile
Used for centuries around the world to relieve stomach distress.
★ ★ ★ ★

Comfrey
May cause liver damage and cancer; should not be swallowed.

especially after eating. Give gravity a chance to get some of that food out of your tum by taking yourself out for a walk, or at the very least, sitting upright. Cutting back on cigarettes and losing weight (if you are carrying extra pounds) can also be beneficial.

If heartburn bothers your sleep, try lying on your left side. That may help keep acid from creeping back up into your gullet. You can also raise the head of the bed about six to ten inches. Finally, give self-hypnosis a try. New research shows that your mind can have a profound influence on stomach acid secretion. Researchers discovered that when they asked hypnotized subjects to imagine eating their favorite foods, there was an outpouring of acid—an 89 percent increase. When they had the subjects concentrate on a relaxing scene, such as lying on a beach or watching a sunset, acid output declined 39 percent.[5] For a discussion of audio relaxation tapes turn to page 168.

> ### *Avoiding Heartburn*
> - Stay away from fatty foods like chips, dip, and cheese.
> - Don't indulge in coffee or alcohol, especially after dinner.
> - Don't lie down after eating.
> - Watch out for bedtime snacks.
> - Cut back on smoking.
> - Lose excess weight.

DRUG TREATMENTS

The mainstay in the treatment of heartburn, indigestion or "sour stomach" is medication that neutralizes or suppresses acid. If you can make the contents of the stomach less corrosive, then discomfort or damage are less likely even when a little backs up into the esophagus.

The same principle holds for gastritis (irritatation of the stomach lining) or stomach ulcers. For decades the dogma "no acid, no ulcer" represented standard medical wisdom. We now know that ulcers are a lot more complicated than that, but it is certainly true that many people do benefit from either antacids or drugs that reduce acid secretion: **Tagamet** (cimetidine), **Zantac** (ranitidine), **Axid** (nizatidine), **Pepcid** (famotidine) or **Prilosec** (omeprazole).

Before the first of these, **Tagamet,** entered the American marketplace in 1977, antacids ruled the roost. Ulcer patients were encouraged to chug quarts of the stuff. Ad agencies came up with catchy slogans like the "**Maalox** moment," a euphemism for a stressful situation.

Doctors almost inevitably recommended aluminum and magnesium-based products because they provided the most cost-effective acid neutralization. Some of the favorites included **Aludrox, Gaviscon, Gelusil-II, Delcid, Di-Gel, Maalox TC** (therapeutic concentrate), and **Mylanta-II**.

There are a couple of problems with these products, however. Magnesium has a laxative action, whereas aluminum tends to be constipating. In theory, the combination is supposed to balance out any such GI problems. In reality, though, people who take big doses often complain of diarrhea.

The Aluminum Question

There's another problem with aluminum. As widespread as this metal is in our environment, it's disturbing that there are still questions about safety. Although there is no absolute proof that aluminum contributes to Alzheimer's disease, this is one controversy that refuses to disappear.

When it is injected into the brains of animals, aluminum produces tangled brain cells that are somewhat similar to changes seen in human patients.[6] And scientists have long known that aluminum accumulates in the brains of people with Alzheimer's. For years we were reassured by neuroscientists that this was a result of the disease rather than a cause. Granola gurus, on the other hand, warned that aluminum was unsafe in any form (antiperspirants, aluminum cans, processed cheese, buffered aspirin, baking powder, and pots and pans) and should be avoided at all costs. It was a classic standoff.

We waited for further data, since there was no way to determine the actual risks of aluminum to the brains of normal people. We simply warned friends not to cook acidic or salty foods in aluminum pots and pans, but

Evidence Against Aluminum

- Natives of Guam get lots of aluminum from their water and locally grown food. They have a high incidence of Lou Gehrig's disease (ALS) and Parkinson's dementia, and excess aluminum in the brain at autopsy.[7]
- British and Norwegian researchers have found an increased risk (50 percent higher) of Alzheimer's disease among people whose drinking water is high in aluminum. The authors' stunning conclusion: "*The results of the present survey provide evidence of a causal relation between aluminium and Alzheimer's disease.*"[8]
- Other investigators have carefully measured neurologic performance of kidney dialysis patients. Patients who took aluminum-based antacids experienced impaired psychological function.[9]
- British researchers hypothesize that some people are less capable of handling aluminum in the body. Defective transfer enzymes may allow aluminum to accumulate and get into the brain, where it can do damage.[10]

did not worry too much about antacids. But now the circumstantial evidence against aluminum is mounting and we're getting nervous.

Scientists who have studied aluminum toxicity in kidney dialysis patients (who can't eliminate the mineral) discovered that treating these patients with a chelating agent called deferoxamine, which helps absorb and eliminate excess aluminum, improved test performance. These physicians labeled aluminum a neurotoxin and admonished kidney dialysis patients to restrict their exposure to aluminum "as much as possible."

Although it's true that kidney damage makes such patients much more vulnerable to aluminum-induced dementia, perhaps it's time for the rest of us to be a little more cautious also. Until researchers can prove beyond a shadow of a doubt that aluminum is absolutely safe over the long haul, we are looking for alternatives. Since calcium carbonate is a perfectly reasonable antacid and offers the added benefit of supplying extra calcium to the diet, we think that such products offer a wise choice in the treatment of indigestion or heartburn.

Tums Extra Strength tablets represent a cost-effective and readily available product. Also at the top of our list is **Titralac** liquid. Each teaspoon delivers 1000 mg of calcium carbonate, making it one of the most potent brands of calcium antacid on the market.

As effective as antacids are in neutralizing stomach acid, the so-called H_2 (histamine) antagonists are even better at controlling excess acid. If the ulcer-fighting prescription medicines **Tagamet**, **Zantac**, **Pepcid**, and **Carafate** become available over the counter, a whole new era in stomach treatment will begin.

Ulcers

Judging from the incredible success of **Tagamet** and **Zantac** (each brings in more than $1 billion every year), an awful lot of people are suffering from ulcers. Seeing how common this condition is, it's surprising how much we don't know about how

---

Calcium-containing Antacids

Advanced Formula Di-Gel
Alka-Mints
Alkets (plus magnesium)
Amitone
Bisodol tablets
Chooz
Dicarbosil
Equilet
Genalac
Mallamint
Marblen (plus magnesium)
Titralac liquid
Titralac tablets
Tums
Tums Extra Strength

Tums Extra Strength

Cheap, effective, contains calcium instead of aluminum.

How Can the Stomach Stand the Acid?

When you consider that the stomach is normally filled with acid strong enough to burn your skin, the question is not why ulcers occur, but rather, why aren't they the norm? The stomach lining appears to protect itself in several ways:

- It actively produces mucus, which keeps the acid from directly touching the cells in the stomach wall.
- It secretes bicarbonate, which helps to neutralize the acid next to the lining.
- The cells in the stomach wall are constantly renewing themselves.
- Adequate blood flow to the stomach wall helps keep cells healthy.

All of these protective actions are influenced by natural chemicals produced by the body, called *prostaglandins*.

these lesions of the stomach or intestinal lining develop.

The myth that the hard-driving workaholic is somehow more prone to ulcers has been discredited, but is still widely believed, even by some doctors. Stress is the great American bugaboo. When we can't figure something out, we blame it on psychological stress. Scientists haven't pinned down the actual relationship between emotions and the development of ulcers. Although stress may play a role, it is increasingly clear that many ulcers are not spontaneous, but are due to drugs or possibly even bacteria that damage the stomach lining or interfere with the body's natural repair processes.

THE HELICOBACTER CONTROVERSY

What is Hel?

One of the hottest debates in gastroenterology these days centers around the role of a spiral-shaped germ called *Helicobacter pylori* (formerly known as *Campylobacter pylori*). We abbre-

Helicobacter pylori

viate it HP or call it *Hel* for short. The questions center around the role of HP in the development of ulcers and stomach inflammation. Reluctantly, many physicians are beginning to accept the fact that this bacterium may be a direct cause or contributor to ulcer disease.[12–17]

The idea that ulcers might be caused by an infection is truly revolutionary. No one yet seems to know where HP comes from or how people "catch" or spread it. We do know that this little beastie is found in around 70–75 percent of patients suffering from stomach ulcers and 90–100 percent of those with duodenal ulcers (ulcers found in the first part of the intestine, leading from the stomach).[18,19] There is growing evidence that there is a "clustering" effect within families. When children have gastritis and *H. pylori*, there is a good chance that their parents and brothers and sisters will also have the bugs, suggesting that this organism can be spread when there is close family contact.[20]

Hel burrows into the tight junction between stomach mucosal cells. It makes an enzyme (protease) that destroys the mucus protecting our stomach lining, and also indirectly stimulates excess stomach acid.[21] Inflammation, indigestion, gastritis, and ulceration can all follow.

Drug Treatment

The usual treatment of ulcers relies mainly on neutralizing or suppressing acid. Although pain is often well-controlled with antacids or drugs like **Zantac** and **Tagamet**, relief is at best temporary. Whatever the drug, ulcers heal in 70-95 percent of patients within one to two months of treatment. We find it fascinating that almost half the patients treated with a sugar pill (placebo) also heal within a few months.

As long as people keep taking their **Zantac**, **Tagamet**, **Pepcid**, or **Axid**, they do quite well. But when they stop the medicine, the ulcers often come back. Anywhere from 66-90 percent of the patients who take such drugs and then discontinue them will have a relapse within a year.[22,23]

Now you begin to understand the incredible popularity of these drugs. Since they don't offer a permanent cure but only a holding action, millions of people have become dependent on a daily "maintenance" dose of ulcer medicine just to stave off stomach pain. No wonder **Zantac** and **Tagamet** are the two most successful drugs in the history of the pharmaceutical industry.

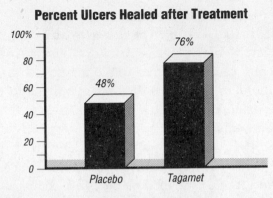

(Source: Moermann, Daniel E. "General Medical Effectiveness and Human Biology: Placebo Effects in the Treatment of Ulcer Disease." Med. Anthro. Quart. 1983; 14(4):3-16.)

Is Bismuth (Pepto-Bismol) Better?

Wouldn't it be nice if you could get rid of ulcers once and for all? There may be a way. Just as you treat an ear infection with antibiotics to produce a lasting cure, it may be possible to wipe out the bacteria that breaks down the protective lining of your stomach. Preliminary results suggest that killing *Helicobacter pylori* is a more effective and long-lasting solution to gastritis and ulcers than suppressing acid is. Dr. David Graham is chief of gastroenterology at the Houston Veterans Administration Medical Center and a

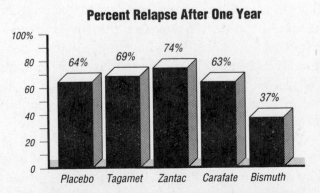

(Source: Lane, Mark R. and Lee, Sum, P. "Recurrence of Duodenal Ulcer after Medical Treatment." Lancet 1988; 1:1147–1149.)

professor at Baylor College of Medicine. He describes the situation this way: "Genetics is the gun, and *H. pylori* is the bullet. Remove the bullet from the gun and you don't develop ulcers."[24]

Dr. Graham has had impressive success with "triple therapy." When he compared a short course of **Zantac** alone to **Zantac** plus tetracycline, **Flagyl** (metronidazole), and **Pepto-Bismol** (bismuth subsalicylate), all the patients on triple therapy healed, compared with only 83 percent of those on **Zantac** alone. But the real story was revealed six months later. Of those ulcer patients who had received only a short course of **Zantac**, 80 percent had suffered an ulcer relapse. Only 6 percent in the triple-therapy group had their ulcers return.[25] Dr. Thomas Barody of the Center for Digestive Diseases in Sydney, Australia, has reported even longer-lasting benefits. Fifty out of fifty-three patients treated with triple therapy (bismuth, tetracycline or amoxicillin, and metronidazole) were cured of their ulcers for sixteen months.[26]

> ### Killing Hel with Drugs
>
> According to Dr. Harris S. Clearfield, Director, Division of Gastroenterology, Hahnemann University School of Medicine, there may be a time when antibiotic therapy is called for: "Because current therapy for *H. pylori* is not benign, specific treatment is limited to patients with confirmed infection whose ulcers have not healed with appropriate administration of a histamine H_2-receptor antagonist or sucralfate (**Carafate**). Several regimens are in use; one includes amoxicillin (**Amoxil**, **Trimox**, **Wymox**, etc.) 250 mg qid [four times a day], metronidazole (**Flagyl**, **Protostat**) 250 mg qid, and bismuth subsalicylate (**Pepto-Bismol**) 5 mg [one teaspoonful]. A histamine H^2-receptor antagonist is also included in this regimen. Treatment continues for three weeks."[29]

You can't count on **Pepto-Bismol** to knock out an ulcer all by itself, although it may work at least as well as **Tagamet**.[27] Bismuth, by the way, has been used for over two hundred years to treat a wide variety of digestive disorders. It also seems to zap the outer coat of the *Helicobacter pylori* bacterium and cause its destruction.[28] But antibiotics seem to be essential to deliver the extra one-two punch once bismuth has softened up the opponent.

Many physicians still think it is too early to prescribe medications like amoxicillin, tetracycline or **Flagyl** for ulcer patients. But the trend is definitely in the direction of attacking the root cause of gastritis rather than treating symptoms. No one in his right mind would treat a strep throat or cystitis with pain killers alone. If ulcers are caused by an infection too, then appropriate antibiotic therapy is clearly the wave of the future.

Pepto-Bismol

The active ingredient in **Pepto-Bismol** is bismuth subsalicylate. It can interact with a number of prescription and over-the-counter medications. *Do not take* the following in combination with **Pepto-Bismol**:

- aspirin (in any form)
- anticoagulants (**Coumadin**)
- **Benemid** (probenecid)
- **Anturane** (sulfinpyrazone)
- **Achromycin** (tetracycline)
- **Methotrexate**

Bismuth can darken the tongue and turn the stool black. Nothing to worry about. But other side effects may be a problem after prolonged use. They include:

- constipation
- confusion
- drowsiness
- headache
- hearing difficulty
- muscle twitches and uncontrolled movements
- light-headedness
- anxiety and slurred speech

DRUG-INDUCED ULCERS

Causes

Drugs cause ulcers. It's surprising how many things can be irritating to the digestive tract. Alcohol and cigarettes are nasty and increase the risk of ulcer relapse. But medically useful drugs, especially those used to relieve pain and inflammation, are the worst culprits.

Almost forty million people with arthritis are caught in a cruel double bind. It is terrible to have to choose between the crippling symptoms of arthritis and the risk of a perforated ulcer. Yet doctors and patients alike are well aware that aspirin (acetylsalicylic acid), the cheapest and one of the most effective of the nonsteroidal anti-inflammatory drugs (NSAIDs), has the disadvantage of causing stomach bleeding in most of those who take it on a daily basis. It leads to ulcers, sometimes life-threatening perforated ulcers, more frequently than anyone would wish.

Nonsteroidal Anti-Inflammatory Drugs

Brand name	Generic name
—	aspirin (acetylsalicylic acid)
Aches-N-Pain	ibuprofen
Advil	ibuprofen
Anaprox	naproxen
Ansaid	flurbiprofen
Azolid	phenylbutazone
Butazolidin	phenylbutazone
Clinoril	sulindac
Dolobid	diflunisal
Feldene	piroxicam
Froben	flurbiprofen
Haltran	ibuprofen
Ibuprin	ibuprofen
Ifen	ibuprofen
Indameth	indomethacin
Indocin	indomethacin
Meclomen	meclofenamate
Medipren	ibuprofen
*Mexicam	isoxicam
Midol 200	ibuprofen
Motrin	ibuprofen
Motrin IB	ibuprofen
Nalfon	fenoprofen
Naprosyn	naproxen
Nuprin	ibuprofen
Orudis	ketoprofen
Pamprin-IB	ibuprofen
Ponstel	mefenamic acid
Rufen	ibuprofen
Tolectin	tolmetin
Trendar	ibuprofen
*Ultradol	etodolac
Voltaren	diclofenac

*approval pending

Other NSAIDs may be a little less harmful than aspirin, but they are far from safe. A recent study of people taking such medication found they were almost three times as likely to develop gastric ulcers as similar patients who did not take NSAIDs.[30] According to Dr. Ross Hall of the University of Virginia, as much as $130 million is spent in this country each year trying to treat the gastrointestinal damage caused by NSAIDs. Other experts estimate that twenty-six hundred deaths and twenty thousand hospitalizations each year can be directly attributed to NSAID-induced ulcers just among patients with rheumatoid arthritis.[31] That's more people than die each year from cocaine abuse. If you want to know whether you are taking an NSAID, check the list on page 27.

There is no simple solution to the arthritis drug dilemma. These medicines work by suppressing the synthesis of prostaglandins. These hormone-like chemicals are responsible for much of the pain and inflammation associated with arthritis, sprains, and strains. But prostaglandins also help protect the stomach from irritation. That's why drugs that knock out prostaglandins often cause ulcers.

PREVENTION

Some people can get by without NSAIDs. Others may be able to take their medicine intermittently, several days on and several days off, to give the stomach a chance to recover a bit. Two rheumatologists, Dr. Louis A. Healey, at the University of Washington, and Dr. Sanford Roth, of the Arthritis Center in Arizona, offer various suggestions for minimizing damage from NSAIDs.[32, 33] Other medications may be appropriate for certain patients, depending on their diagnosis. For example, if the problem is osteoarthritis, acetaminophen (**Tylenol**, **Anacin-3**, **Panadol**) can offer pain relief. It does not promote ulceration, but daily use over the long term may contribute to kidney damage.

Drs. Roth and Healey occasionally prescribe low-dose cortisione-type medications (such as prednisone) for patients with rheumatoid arthritis. Such corticosteroids can reduce inflammation with a slightly lower risk of ulcers. Dr. Roth is a big booster of salsalate (**Disalcid**), an aspirinlike drug less likely to irritate the GI lining. Other salicylates that may also be a little easier on the stomach lining include choline salicylate (**Arthropan**), sodium salicylate (**Uracel 5**), choline magnesium trisalicylate (**Trilisate**) or sodium thiosalicylate (**Tusal**).[34] Although these drugs are pretty good at relieving inflammation, they may not be quite as strong as aspirin when it comes to pain relief.

If an NSAID is essential, it may be better for older people to use shorter-acting arthritis drugs (**Nalfon**, **Naprosyn**, **Motrin**) rather than long-acting medications like **Feldene**. A drug to protect the stomach lining, such as **Carafate** or **Cytotec,** may also be appropriate (see pages 32 and 33).

One of the trickiest problems of taking an anti-inflammatory agent on a regular basis is that you can't always tell when you are damaging your stomach lining. Sometimes indigestion, pain, or diarrhea will warn you. But for many people, there are no clear early-warning symptoms, and the first sign may be a health crisis associated with a bleeding or perforated ulcer. This is especially dangerous in older people.

If you've noticed any of the signs of a silent ulcer and you are taking an NSAID, whether it is an over-the-counter medicine like aspirin or ibuprofen (**Advil**, **Ibuprin**, **Medipren**, **Motrin IB**, **Nuprin**) or a drug your physician prescribed, it's time to check in with your doctor and make sure you are not headed for serious ulcer trouble.

GI problems like indigestion and constipation are uncomfortable, but not really life-threatening. They can usually be treated at home with simple remedies, especially at first. Ulcers caused by medication are big-time trouble. Because they can kill people, these ulcers deserve a gastroenterologist's supervision, even if the medication that caused the problem was nonprescription.

The first logical step in healing the stomach when it has been harmed is to stop the drug responsible for the damage. (It

---

Signs of a Silent Ulcer

- Do you feel full before you've eaten the usual amount?
- Have you lost weight without trying?
- Do you frequently experience indigestion and heartburn?
- Are you anemic? (This requires a blood test.)
- Are you feeling unusually tired and under the weather?

may take at least six weeks for complete healing.) In healthy people, the stomach lining often recovers from ulcers on its own. But people who continue to take a drug (including alcohol) that harms the digestive tract are less likely to heal spontaneously. Remember, though: *never stop or start any medication without consulting with the doctor who prescribed it.*

DRUG TREATMENT

H$_2$ Antagonists

> **Axid** (nizatidine)
> **Pepcid** (famotidine)
> **Tagamet** (cimetidine)
> **Zantac** (ranitidine)

As we have already noted, the most popular prescription drugs to treat ulcers are the H$_2$ antagonists: **Axid** (nizatidine), **Pepcid** (famotidine), **Tagamet** (cimetidine), and **Zantac** (ranitidine). All of these medicines act in a similar manner, by reducing the acid the stomach produces. But if the ulcer is caused by an infection or an irritating drug, cutting back on acid may reduce the pain and even heal the lesion temporarily, but won't remove the source of the problem. Relapses are common.

Bugs in the Belly

One thing that continues to concern us about the acid-suppressing drugs is the possibility that they allow bacteria to grow in the stomach.[35] Normally the stomach is far too acid for any germs to thrive. But there have been hints in the medical literature that reducing acid makes for a more hospitable environment for foreign bugs, which may in turn produce harmful nitrites and nitrosamines. These potent cancer-causing chemicals could increase the risk of stomach cancer. We always recommend that anyone taking drugs like **Zantac** or **Tagamet** , **Axid** or **Pepcid** should supplement his diet with extra vitamin C and E to prevent the formation of

---

Zantac
(ranitidine)

One of the best-tolerated and most effective ulcer treatments. As with all H$_2$ antagonists, we suggest also taking 500 mg of vitamin C four times a day and at least 400 IUs of vitamin E.

The biggest downside to this medicine is its high cost.

Side effects, while rare, include nausea, headache, depression, and insomnia.

★ ★ ★

Side Effects Reported for Common Ulcer Drugs

Axid (nizatidine)
   Possible problems: sleepiness, sweating, and itching
   Rare: elevated liver enzymes, rash, and uric acid buildup
   Interacts adversely with: aspirin

Pepcid (famotidine)
   Possible problems: headache, diarrhea, dizziness, constipation
   Rare: nausea, vomiting, loss of appetite, dry mouth, elevated liver
      enzymes, joint or muscle pain, depression, anxiety, insomnia,
      sleepiness, breathing trouble, hair loss, itching, rash, ringing in the
      ears, palpitations, loss of taste, swollen eyes
   Interacts with: no other drugs tested

Tagamet (cimetidine)
   Possible problems: diarrhea, constipation, dizziness, sleepiness, breast
      enlargement, mental confusion (especially in elderly or very ill
      patients)
   Rare: headache, dry mouth, impotence, decreased white blood cell
      counts, elevated liver enzymes, pancreas inflammation, depression,
      fever, joint pain, muscle aches, hair loss
   Interacts adversely with: alcohol, antacids, antianxiety agents,
      anticonvulsants, antidepressants, caffeine, cigarettes, diabetes pills,
      heart medicines (calcium channel blockers, digoxin, labetalol,
      lidocaine, metoprolol, procainamide, propranolol, quinidine,
      warfarin), metoclopramide, metronidazole, morphine, theophylline

Zantac (ranitidine)
   Possible problems: headache, diarrhea, nausea, vomiting, rash
   Rare: dizziness, sleepiness, insomnia, mental confusion (especially in ill
      and elderly patients), depression, changes in heart rate, liver
      problems, joint pains, enlarged breasts, impotence, hair loss,
      allergic reactions
   Interacts adversely with: antacids, warfarin

Prilosec
(omeprazole)
The most potent acid suppressor. Side effects: headache, diarrhea, stomach pain. May heal ulcers resistant to conventional therapy but recurrences are high when **Prilosec** is stopped. Controversy about cancer potential has medical community arguing.

★

---

nitrosamines. Although the dose is debatable, 500 mg of Vitamin C taken three or four times a day and 400 units of Vitamin E have been suggested.[36]

The newest competitor in the acid wars is **Prilosec** (omeprazole), a completely different kind of ulcer medicine. It is one of the most potent drugs yet developed for suppressing acid secretion in the stomach. **Prilosec** works by zapping the proton pump, making it sound like some strange new weapon aboard the Starship Enterprise. Knocking out this acid pump produces anti-ulcer effectiveness that ranges from 88–100 percent. This makes it quite helpful against hard-to-treat ulcers and severe heartburn caused by acid reflux into the esophagus.

Some of the more common side effects of this new medicine include headache (in 6.9 percent of patients), diarrhea (3 percent), nausea (2.2 percent), vomiting (1.5 percent), and abdominal discomfort (2.4 percent). **Prilosec** can interact with **Valium** (diazepam), **Coumadin** (warfarin), and **Dilantin** (phenytoin), so doses of these medicines should be adjusted accordingly by a physician.

Unfortunately, there is also a cloud that hangs over the future of **Prilosec**. In animal studies, large doses were associated with an increased risk of stomach cancer.[38] Scientists at arch rival Glaxo (the manufacturer of **Zantac**) added fuel to this fire when they reported that "a new laboratory test shows **Prilosec** has a far greater potential for causing cancer in rats than previously believed."[39,40] No one knows whether **Prilosec** poses a cancer risk for humans, but until the dust settles it might not hurt to proceed cautiously, wait for up-to-date information, and perhaps even invest in some vitamin insurance just as you would with **Zantac** or any other H_2 antagonist (see page 30).

If you have to keep taking pain medicine, you may need a completely different approach. One choice is **Carafate** (sucralfate), a mixture of sulfated sucrose and aluminum hydroxide. It's an excellent prescription ulcer drug, at least as effective as the H_2

antagonists like **Zantac** and **Tagamet**. But unlike these medications, **Carafate** is barely absorbed into the body and does not increase the risk that bacteria will grow in the stomach. Thus, any concerns about stomach cancer should be allayed. Interactions with other drugs are rare, and side effects are, too. Occasionally, however, a person will experience nausea, constipation, or diarrhea on **Carafate**.

What makes **Carafate** unique is its ability to form a protective layer that coats the ulcer and speeds healing. In addition, **Carafate** offers cytoprotection, meaning that the drug can also prevent damage caused by other irritating chemicals. Because of this prophylactic power, some doctors prescribe **Carafate** along with an arthritis medicine to keep ulcers from developing. It is often helpful and usually easy to take. However, it may not produce the immediate pain relief H_2 antagonists offer. The manufacturer recommends that **Carafate** should be taken on an empty stomach to maximize effectiveness, but Dr. Sanford Roth, one of this country's leading rheumatologists, suggests that patients can obtain good results by taking their arthritis medicine and **Carafate** together at mealtime.

If and when **Carafate** becomes available over the counter (and there are rumors that this may happen), it may be the best choice for nonprescription treatment of ulcers, especially those caused by pain relievers. Taken for a short period of time (several weeks or months), the risks seem minimal.

Only one thing concerns us about **Carafate**. Aluminum makes up almost 20 percent of the drug. A daily **Carafate** dose of four grams (four tablets) would expose you to almost 800 mg of aluminum. There is evidence that some of that aluminum is absorbed into the body.[41-43]. People with kidney problems, especially those undergoing dialysis, could be at risk.[44] Whether long-term **Carafate** use poses any problems for people with normal kidney function remains an unanswered question at the time of this writing.

Another medication that a physician may want to use to prevent ulcers in patients taking NSAIDs is **Cytotec** (misoprostol). This prescription drug was developed on the theory that if you replace the prostaglandins that are depleted by

---

Carafate
(sucralfate)
Protects the stomach lining. Few side effects, but questions remain about aluminum absorption with long-term use.

★ ★ ★

Cytotec
(misoprostol)
Protects the stomach lining from irritation caused by arthritis medicines. Side effects: serious diarrhea, stomachache, dizziness, gas, headache, and nausea. Never take during pregnancy!

★

arthritis medicines, you can forestall much of the damage. **Cytotec**, a synthetic prostaglandin, prevents stomach-wall damage and helps ulcers heal, even in rheumatoid arthritis patients on high doses of aspirin, one of the most irritating of the NSAIDs.[45]

Drawbacks to **Cytotec** include the possibility of major-league diarrhea and stomachache. Up to 14 percent of the patients taking it experience serious diarrhea. It must *never* be taken by pregnant women, as its prostaglandin activity could trigger premature labor or abortion. Other side effects include dizziness, constipation, gas, headache, and nausea.

Some people may find **Cytotec**'s side effects worse than an ulcer. Others manage to adapt. Smaller doses taken more frequently may help a little. For people who don't experience bothersome adverse reactions and have to take aspirin, ibuprofen, or one of the prescription NSAIDs, **Cytotec** could make a difference in stomach protection.

You may find this very hard to believe, but can you imagine that hot sauce might be good for gastritis caused by arthritis meds? Most people believe that hot food should be avoided at the first sign of an ulcer. For decades doctors have admonished their patients to stick to a bland diet. New data, however, suggest that was entirely unnecessary. Dr. David Graham, a world-class gastroenterologist, offers the following observations:

> . . . when jalapeno peppers are administered with food there is no visible damage . . . Spicy food seems safe. We found no gastric mucosal abnormalities after ingestion of highly spiced foods, and previous studies have shown that the administration of large amounts of red peppers does not reduce the rate of healing of duodenal ulcers.[46]

Not only do hot peppers (capsaicin) appear harmless, there is some preliminary evidence that they may even help protect the stomach lining against assault. Dr. Peter Holzer conducted an intriguing experiment on rats. First he administered an aspirin solution into their tummies. Not surprisingly, the

---

Tabasco
(capsaicin)
Stimulates blood flow to stomach lining. Protects rats from intestinal damage due to aspirin and alcohol.

★ ★ ★

aspirin produced substantial damage to the stomach lining. When capsaicin was given along with the aspirin, the hot peppers offered incredible protection. There was 92 percent less bleeding in the tissue exposed to capsaicin than with aspirin alone.[47] Dr. Holzer has also demonstrated that this hot pepper extract can protect the rat stomach against damage caused by alcohol.[48]

Capsaicin appears to work its magic by stimulating nerves in the stomach wall. This in turn leads to dilation of blood vessels and improved blood flow. So far the experiments have been carried out only in rats. Whether people will benefit from it is anyone's guess. But wouldn't it be a hoot if hot peppers are proven to help prevent gastritis and ulcers caused by NSAIDs? At least the new research should reassure chili lovers that their favorite taste treat won't slow recovery from an ulcer.

If **Tabasco** turned you on, you'll love the lowdown on licorice. Here is a remedy that can be traced back to the Roman Empire. Chinese herbalists have used licorice root for centuries. And now modern pharmacologists and gastroenterologists are discovering that ingredients in licorice have a wide variety of fascinating effects, not to mention powerful protective actions in the digestive tract.

The Russians have reported that in rabbits, licorice root extract has an extraordinary ability to lower cholesterol and triglyceride levels.[49] Chinese scientists note antianxiety benefits along with strong cough-suppressant effects. Japanese microbiologists have discovered that a component in licorice is helpful against hepatitis B, perhaps by stimulating the immune system to produce interferon.[50] And research on rats has shown that licorice, like hot peppers, protects the stomach against aspirin-related damage.[51] The active ingredients in licorice seem to reduce acid, stimulate mucus secretion, and promote stomach-wall repair.[52–53]

As tempting as these results may appear, don't rush out and start overdosing on licorice sticks. There is a little-known danger to eating too much of this sweet treat. Side effects of regular licorice consumption (an ounce or more daily) can include fluid retention, potassium depletion, muscle pain and

> ### *Licorice*
> ### (Glycyrrhiza glabra)
> Reduces acid production and protects rat stomach linings from aspirin damage.
> Serious side effects include fluid retention, hormone and mineral imbalances, muscle weakness, high blood pressure, and heart trouble.
>
> ★

weakness, lethargy, high blood pressure, hormonal imbalance, and sexual difficulties. One woman lost so much potassium because of bingeing on licorice that her heart stopped.[54]

Most of these adverse reactions are caused by one active ingredient in licorice called *glycyrrhizin*. Investigators have developed "deglycyrrhizinated" licorice (**Caved-S**), a product that has most of the benefits and few of the risks of regular licorice. One study showed it to be as good as **Tagamet** at curing ulcers.[55]

Until **Caved-S** becomes widely available, however, we are stuck with good old-fashioned licorice. As long as you don't overdo, a couple of licorice twists or a cup of licorice tea might represent a nice, short-term treatment for tummy trouble that lasts less than a few days.

Gassiness and Flatulence

CAUSES

There's just no nice way to say this. Flatulence is on the rise. Our love affair with oat bran is a big part of the problem. Plain and simple, fiber makes you fart. If you have followed all the recommendations to eat heart-healthy foods, your digestive tract will pay a penalty. Gastroenterologists and family doctors candidly admit that excess gas heads the list of common patient complaints. According to experts, a "normal" person can produce up to fourteen farts a day, with a total gas output ranging anywhere from two to eight cups (400–1,600 mL).[56]

Beans of course are notorious. Any nine-year-old can recite the old refrain:

> **"Beans, beans, good for the heart**
> **The more you eat, the more you fart."**

Leave it to the doctors to try and prove what cowboys have known for a couple hundred years. Some researchers fed five

---

Foods that Lead to Gassiness

apple juice
apricots
bagels
bananas
beans
bran
broccoli
brussels sprouts
cabbage
candy with sorbitol
carrots
cauliflower
celery
eggplant
fiber cereal
fructose
milk
oat bran
onions
peas
pretzels
prunes
radishes
raisins
soybeans
sugarless gum
turnips
wheat germ

volunteers a diet made up of 56 percent beans. Gas production went from roughly three teaspoonfuls an hour (15 mL) to thirty-five teaspoonfuls (176 mL).[57]

It happens this way. Bacteria in the lower intestines attack the undigestible left-overs that comprise the outer coating of beans, bran, and lots of other foods. Complex carbos are great fuel for the bugs in your gut. Fermentation follows and that leads to flatulence. Think of it another way. If you were making beer or champagne, fermentation would lead to bubbles and foam. In the large intestine your belly brewery produces gas.

The Fart Chart

The only way to know what food is your nemesis is to keep what doctors call a flatulogram or flatographic record. We call it a fart chart. You have to be rather compulsive to keep this up for very long. First, you keep a detailed record of all the food you eat. Next, you note every time you pass gas. Keep in mind that it may take awhile for the food to do its dirty work.

You may be surprised with the results. Milk products are an often-overlooked culprit. One man went from thirty-four "flatus passages" per day to 141 when he was put on a straight-milk diet. At one point during this experiment this poor fellow had seventy "events" in one four-hour period.[58] Sometimes this lactose intolerance is accompanied by abdominal cramps and diarrhea. It can often be prevented if you take a lactase enzyme product to break down the milk sugar. **Lactaid** is widely available in tablet or liquid form and often allows people to enjoy dairy products.

> ### *Fighting Farts*
> - Avoid swallowing air—no water fountains, fizzy drinks, or gum chewing.
> - Be moderate with bran and fiber (especially beans).
> - Forgo fructose and sorbitol in "diet" candies or gums.
> - Soak beans and discard water before cooking.
> - Try **Charcocaps** (activated charcoal) when eating farty foods.

PREVENTION

If you are not prepared to give up an offending food, especially now that we know how healthy beans and onions are, what else can you do? Well, one option is to share your dietary indiscretions with a spouse or loved one who can then reciprocate without embarrassment. This uninhibited approach to intestinal gas may be fine at home, but at social events it could prove awkward.

Careful cooking may help to some extent. Undercooked beans seem to be much more potent than thoroughly cooked ones; presoaking beans at least four hours and throwing away the soaking water is often recommended to reduce their flatulence potential.

TREATMENT

Another option is activated charcoal (**Charcocaps**), the main ingredient in gas masks, water filters, and poison antidote kits. It is capable of absorbing great amounts of nastiness. One study demonstrated that when activated charcoal capsules are taken with a fartatious meal and again two hours later, they can dramatically reduce gas output.[59]

Simethicone is often promoted for relieving gas, but this defoaming agent appears to work better at the upper end of the digestive tract against belching. It may relieve feelings of gas pressure but cannot reduce gas output or absorb unpleasant odors. **Charcocaps** reduces gas at the lower end of the GI tract and may make social interactions more bearable for people who have a tendency to produce unpleasant smells.[60] A new product combining simethicone and activated charcoal, **Flatulex**, is available from Dayton Laboratories in Miami [(800) 446-0255]. The only major drawback to activated charcoal is its ability to absorb a wide variety of chemicals. Do not take **Charcocaps** or **Flatulex** within two hours of any other medication.

Diarrhea

CAUSES

Diarrhea is the body's way of saying "no thank you." It may occur after you eat something that doesn't quite agree with your system. One member of our family has to make quick trips to the bathroom after consuming onions in any form. Other people react the same way if they are exposed to milk sugar (lactose). Sometimes the problem can be traced to food that's gone bad. Or it may be a stomach "flu" that is going around.

When diarrhea lasts longer than two days or is accompanied by fever, abdominal cramping, or a bloody stool, don't mess around with do-it-yourself diarrhea remedies. Such symptoms suggest something serious and require a complete medical workup.

Usually, people can tough out a short case of the "trotskis." Extra fluids to prevent dehydration may be all that are necessary. But if you have to go to work, or you lose patience running back and forth to the bathroom, you might want to know about a new, over-the-counter, anti-diarrhea medicine that is our first choice.

DRUG TREATMENT

Once available only by prescription, loperamide finally received FDA approval for over-the-counter status. The drug works by slowing down intestinal contractions and reducing fluid loss. Side effects are rare and the drug can even be given to children six years and older. (Do not give to younger children without medical supervision. Poisoning is possible.) Potential adverse reactions include constipation, dry mouth, nausea, vomiting, drowsiness, and skin rash. Do not drive after taking **Imodium,** as alertness may be impaired.

Our second choice for mild diarrhea is polycarbophil (**Mitrolan**, **Equalactin**, and **Fibercon**). It actually does double duty for constipation or diarrhea. This paradox is easily solved when you understand that the drug works by absorbing water in the lower gut and adding bulk. It too can safely be given to children over two years of age and has few side effects. At worst, people report a feeling of fullness.

Imodium A-D (loperamide)

Stops diarrhea quickly. Not intended for diarrhea due to food poisoning or drugs. **Imodium A-D** should not be used when there is fever or bloody stool.

★ ★ ★

Traveler's Diarrhea

When you're on a business trip or that dream vacation, the last thing you want is to be stuck in a hotel room suffering with the trots for a few days. Researchers at the University of Texas, Houston, studied U.S. medical students studying at the University of Guadalajara, Mexico.

They found that the most rapid relief came from a three-day combination therapy of sulfamethoxazole-trimethoprim (**Bactrim** or **Septra**) and loperamide (**Imodium**), with "half of persons so treated passing their last unformed stool in less than 1 hour."[61] (**Imodium** should not be used if there is a fever or bloody stool. People with sulfa allergy must avoid these antibiotics!)

Kaolin and pectin are also supposed to absorb water, but results have been unimpressive. Perhaps that's why **Kaopectate** was recently reformulated. The ingredients for which this popular brand-name diarrhea medicine was originally christened have been replaced by an absorbent aluminum clay called attapulgite (also found in **Diar-Aid**, **Diasorb,** and **Rheaban**). We think it doubtful that the new ingredient will be dramatically more effective than the old ones.

Pepto-Bismol is another old standard in diarrhea treatment, especially for travelers in a foreign land. When taken as a preventive, **Pepto** (either liquid or tablets) works suprisingly well to ward off the vengeful bugs of *turista*. Why it works so well against traveler's diarrhea is not entirely clear, but the drug appears almost as good as high-potency, expensive, prescription antibiotics like **Vibramycin** (doxycycline) or **Bactrim** and **Septra** (sulfamethoxazole plus trimethoprim).

Anyone taking regular aspirin doses should stay away from the extra salicylate in **Pepto-Bismol**. It could add up to an aspirin overdose and ringing in the ears. Other medicines that shouldn't be combined with **Pepto-Bismol** include **Coumadin**, **Anturane**, **Benemid,** and **Methotrexate**. Children should never be given **Pepto-Bismol** if they have chicken pox or a case of the flu, because Reye's syndrome is a rare but real risk with any form of aspirin or salicylate.

> **Pepto-Bismol**
> *(bismuth subsalicylate)*
> Beneficial for traveler's diarrhea, ulcers caused by *H. pylori*, heartburn. Don't give to children with chicken pox or flu.
>
> ★ ★ ★ ★

Irritable Bowel Syndrome (IBS)

> **Clocking the Digestive Tract**
> To see if your digestive speed is normal, serve yourself a helping of whole-kernel corn. Write down the time and date you eat. Then watch to see when kernels show up in the stool. If you spot them in less than 36 hours, or more than 80 hours, your gut is marching to a different drummer. This isn't necessarily a problem, but it can contribute to symptoms of IBS.

When abdominal pain, gas, and bouts of diarrhea or constipation become a chronic problem, the diagnosis may be IBS. Of course, the doctor will need to rule out any serious illness that might account for the symptoms. Irritable bowel syndrome itself isn't dangerous, just uncomfortable. It appears to be due to an intestinal tract that works much faster or slower than normal, together with unusual sensitivity to GI pressure. Often people with IBS report that their symptoms worsen when they are under psychological stress.

The treatment of choice these days for IBS is fiber. That's a complete turnaround from a decade ago when bland, highly refined food was the prescription. Nowadays doctors often recommend psyllium (**Correctol** powder, **Metamucil**, **Modane**, **Naturacil**, **Perdiem** plain, **Serutan**) or polycarbophil (**Fibercon**, **Equalactin**, or **Mitrolan**). Such products may help to normalize GI tone. Do be sure to get at least six cups of water or juice if taking a bulk agent, as the last thing anyone needs is a solid mass of fiber solidifying in the intestine. If diarrhea is a major component, **Imodium A-D** can be helpful.

Constipation

Watch television and you will come away with the idea that regularity is a virtue right up there with cleanliness and chastity. Miss a bowel movement, and the ads would have you believe you are backsliding. But "regularity" is relative. Cousin Jane may be perfectly fine with three movements a day, while Uncle Charlie is healthy as a horse with three bathroom breaks a week.

It's best not to get too excited about someone (especially a child) being temporarily "stopped up" unless there are other problems. It can take kids a while to establish their natural rhythm, and even adults may be thrown off schedule by a change in routine or a shift in hormones as the menstrual cycle progresses, with no harm done.

PREVENTION

The first step against constipation is simple—**F** & **F** (fluids and fiber). It doesn't much matter what you pick, as long as you make sure a variety of high-fiber foods are a part of your daily routine. It's the insoluble fiber, like that in bran cereals, that wards off constipation and may protect against colo-rectal cancer. Soluble fiber, such as that in oats and barley, is more effective in reducing cholesterol and blood sugar.

As effective as fiber can be at fighting constipation, don't

High-Fiber Foods

All-Bran*
All-Bran with Extra Fiber*
apples
artichokes
bananas
blackberries
bran*
Bran Buds*
Bran Chex
Bran Flakes
broccoli
Brussels sprouts
carrots
dried figs
Fiber One*
lentils
lima beans
Nabisco 100% Bran*
peanut butter
pears
peas
raisins
Shredded Wheat'n Bran
winter squash

* Ultra-high-fiber, providing more than 10 grams per serving

OD. You kind of have to work up gradually or you will be fighting flatulence, not to mention bloating and abdominal discomfort. Too much fiber, especially if it's not washed down with enough liquid, can even get stuck in a solid lump somewhere in the digestive tract.[62, 63] This is rare, but when it happens, it may require surgery. So take it easy, increase fiber intake *gradually*, and be sure to get plenty of liquid into the system. Don't forget to exercise, too.

If all else fails, a bulk-forming laxative such as psyllium is the best bet. Other bulk-forming laxatives include **Citrucel**, **Cologel**, **Fibercon**, **Equalactin**, **Maltsupex**, and **Mitrolan**. There are many brands available, so you can pick the flavor—or price— you like best. If you have Crohn's disease or a narrowing of the intestine due to previous surgery, psyllium or other bulk agents could be dangerous, but for most people this is the top choice.

Laxatives aren't just for constipation anymore. Psyllium cereal is a hot item because of some research sponsored by Procter & Gamble (manufacturer of **Metamucil**). Scientists discovered that a teaspoon of this soluble fiber taken three times a day could lower cholesterol levels anywhere from 5 to 15 percent.[64, 65] Impressed with such startling results, the food giant General Mills rushed **Benefit** to market, claiming that the psyllium-containing cereal could lower cholesterol in conjunction with a low-fat diet. Kellogg wasn't far behind with its breakfast entry, **Heartwise**. (A new and "improved" **Bran Buds** formulation also contains some psyllium.) Whether such cereal will have the same benefits as **Metamucil**, or the same liabilities (bloating, gas, abdominal cramping, and fullness and extra bathroom visits), remains to be seen.

When fiber and fluid do not relieve constipation, where do you turn for help? Well, when we pin our experts to the wall, they admit that mom (milk of magnesia) does come through. This saline laxative contains magnesium hydroxide, which draws water into the intestines and pretty much guarantees a bowel movement. Don't let such "success" lead to a laxative habit, though. It can be hard to break.

Itchy Bottom

CAUSES

Television ads have brainwashed most of us to think of "pain and itching" as symptoms of hemorrhoids. But in truth, if hemorrhoids are bothersome, they are more likely to hurt than to itch. Figuring out the cause of an itchy bottom can require the concentration of a Sherlock, as the explanation might range from the simple—perfume in the toilet paper, say, or moisture-trapping pantyhose—to the serious, including infection, psoriasis, or fissures. Persistent itching deserves a doctor's exam to rule out any treatable disease. If there's no diagnosis, there may also be no cure, but there are some tactics that can help control the problem. Scratching is sure to make things worse. One drug company exec admitted to us that the "itch-scratch-itch" vicious cycle is responsible for much of the problem. As overpowering as the urge may be, don't scratch! Instead, reach for the witch hazel.

TREATMENT

Cleanliness is crucial in preventing itching, but scrubbing is only likely to make matters worse. Lacking a bidet, it's best to use cotton balls wet with water or witch hazel or a pre-moistened towelette such as **Preparation H Cleansing Pads, Tucks Pads**, or **Gentz Wipes** to cleanse the area gently and then pat it dry.

Some hemorrhoid remedies, such as **Tronolane**, **Anusol**, or **Proctofoam**, contain a local anesthetic which may provide some temporary relief from the itching. (They're handy for quelling mosquito bites on other parts of the body, too.) Hydrocortisone cream, whether in an OTC hemorrhoid treatment or simply as a first-aid cream such as **CaldeCORT, Cortaid, Corticaine** or **Lanacort,** may also be useful in relieving itching for a short time.

Certain hemorrhoid preparations contain zinc oxide, petrolatum, or some other substance that can act as a barrier against moisture and might help protect against irritating chemicals in the stool; chocolate, caffeinated beverages, and hot peppers are common culprits. So although these hemorrhoid remedies can't change a hemorrhoid—a physical outpouching of little blood vessels in the anal area—they might be helpful in some cases of itching. And **Preparation H** is gaining a reputation for its value in helping wounds (bedsores, mild burns, etc.) to heal, although this is still based mostly on individual anecdotes rather than on scientific studies.

Drugs of the Future

The revolution in GI drugs is far from over. The last decade has seen a complete change in the way ulcers and heartburn are treated with medications like **Tagamet**, **Zantac**, **Pepcid**, **Carafate**, **Cytotec,** and **Prilosec**. But the best is yet to come.

If you like **Pepto-Bismol**, you should love **De-Nol** (colloidal bismuth subcitrate, or CBS for short). It appears to be about as effective as **Tagamet** and **Zantac** when it comes to speeding healing of ulcers and somewhat more effective than good old **Pepto** in preventing ulcer recurrences.[66, 67] CBS kills that old bugaboo *Helicobacter pylori*, which is thought to be responsible for many ulcers in the first place. Procter & Gamble (maker of **Pepto-Bismol**) knew a good thing when they saw it. The company licensed the rights to CBS for North America (and subsequently sold them to Rorer). We can only hope Rorer gives it a sexier name than **De-Nol**.

Speaking of weird names, can you think of anything more repulsive than **Prepulsid**? It may sound bad, but this could be one of the most exciting new drug developments in years. Cisapride (marketed in the United Kingdom, Belgium, and Switzerland as **Prepulsid** and in Japan as **Risamol**) is a unique compound that works by normalizing muscular action throughout the digestive tract. That means it helps tone up the sphincter between the esophagus and the stomach and reduces the likelihood of acid reflux back into the gullet.[68] It is at least as good if not better than **Zantac** at healing lesions in the esophagus.[69] Besides relieving heartburn and indigestion, cisapride can help empty the stomach of food and ease chronic constipation that does not respond to other treatments.[70]

Cisapride offers tremendous promise for victims of heartburn. It contains no aluminum, does not change the acidity of the stomach or increase the risk of cancer, and has few side effects. About the only adverse reactions associated with this drug are abdominal cramping, stomach noises, and diarrhea (about 4 percent).

Another interesting new GI drug is **Motilium** (domperidone). Although somewhat similar to an existing drug called **Reglan** (metoclopramide), it does not cause the same nasty side effects (drowsiness, fatigue, dizziness, anxiety, insomnia, headache, depression, nausea, diarrhea, breast enlargement, and uncontrollable muscular movements of the eyes, face, hands, or legs). **Motilium** can ease nausea and vomiting after surgery, radiation treatment, or cancer chemotherapy. It also seems to relieve bloating and indigestion after eating. **Motilium** rarely produces side effects, but things to be alert for include skin rash, dry mouth, anxiety, thirst, and diarrhea.

People who suffer with inflammatory bowel disease (colitis, Crohn's disease) have some new medications to discuss with a gastroenterologist. Instead of **Azulfidine** (sulfasalazine) which often causes nausea, indigestion, headache, rash, fever, anemia, and arthritis-like pains, there are alternatives like **Dipentum**, **Asacol**, **Pentasa,** and **Rowasa**. All of the new compounds are similar, but work at different levels of the GI tract. Researchers hope they will be more effective and better tolerated than **Azulfidine**. As a last resort before surgery, **Sandimmune** (cyclosporine) shows some promise in controlling severe Crohn's disease.[71, 72]

Quick Takes

- Heartburn is often caused by stomach acid splashback into the gullet. Stimulating saliva by chewing gum, sipping tea, or sucking on hard candy can help ease mild irritation. Cisapride can tighten the sphincter between esophagus and stomach and prevent reflux in the first place.

- Until the questions about aluminum are resolved, double-duty antacids that contain calcium are preferable. Some of our favorites include **Titralac** and **Tums Extra Strength**.

- If ulcers are infectious, the best treatment will wipe out the bugs in the belly. There is growing enthusiasm about the combination of bismuth (**Pepto-Bismol** or **De-Nol**) with antibiotics such as tetracycline, amoxicillin, or metronidazole to heal ulcers with less likelihood of relapse.

- Arthritis medications are tough on the tummy. Silent ulcers can lead to hospitalization or death. Drug holidays may allow the stomach to recover partially, and medicines such as **Carafate** or **Cytotec** help protect the stomach lining from damage.

- **Cytotec** must *not* be taken by pregnant women. It can induce premature labor and miscarriage.

- If acid-suppressing drugs become available over the counter, our first choice will be ranitidine (**Zantac** by prescription). It is less likely than **Tagamet** to interact with other medications and can provide rapid pain relief for indigestion, heartburn, or even ulcers. Vitamin C (500 mg three or four times a day) and Vitamin E (400 units) should reduce possible long-term risks.

- **Tabasco** and licorice are not exactly ulcer therapies, but both may have a place when it comes to protecting the stomach from damage.

- Flatulence isn't funny—though kids seem to think so. Next

to dietary discretion, **Charcocaps** appears to be about the only product likely to offer any relief.

- **Imodium A-D** is the most effective OTC remedy for garden-variety diarrhea. Travelers will want to bring **Pepto-Bismol** tablets to keep Montezuma from wreaking his revenge. **Vibramycin** (doxycycline) and **Septra** (trimethoprim and sulfamethoxazole) are prescription alternatives for traveler's diarrhea.

- *F & F* is the key to controlling constipation—fiber and fluids. When diet doesn't do it, **Metamucil** is a triple threat. It works to control constipation, cholesterol, and irritable bowel syndrome.

- For itchy bottoms, cleanliness is the clue. Witch hazel or pre-moistened towelettes (**Preparation H Cleansing Pads, Tucks Pads**, or **Gentz Wipes**) can help here: scrubbing and scratching are out! A local anesthetic like that in **Tronolane** or **Anusol** offers short-term relief.

References

[1] Vitale, Gary C., et al. "The Effect of Alcohol on Nocturnal Gastroesophageal Reflux." *JAMA* 1987; 258:2077–2079.

[2] Jamieson, Glyn G., and Duranceau, Andre C. "The Defense Mechanism of the Esophagus." *Surgical Clinics of North America* 1983; 63:787–799.

[3] Helm, James F., et al. "Effect of Esophageal Emptying and Saliva on Clearance of Acid from the Esophagus." *N. Engl. J. Med.* 1984; 310:284–288.

[4] Arora, Anil, and Sharma, M.P. "Use of Banana in Non-ulcer Dyspepsia." *Lancet* 1990; 335:612–613.

[5] Klein, Kenneth, B., and Spiegel, David. "Modulation of Gastric Acid Secretion by Hypnosis." *Gastroenterology* 1989; 96:1383–1387.

[6] Klatzo, I., et al. "Experimental Production of Neurofibrillary Degeneration. I. Light Microscopic Observations." *J. Neuropathol. Exp. Neurol.* 1965; 24:187–199.

[7] Perl, D.P., et al. "Intraneuronal Aluminum Accumulation in Amyotrophic Lateral Sclerosis and Parkinsonism-dementia of Guam." *Science* 1982; 217:1053–1055.

[8] Martyn, C.N., et al. "Geographical Relation Between Alzheimer's Disease and Aluminium in Drinking Water." *Lancet* 1989; 1:60–62.

[9] Altman, Paul, et al. "Disturbance of Cerebral Function by Aluminium Haemodialysis Patients Without Overt Aluminium Toxicity." *Lancet* 1989; 2:7–12.

[10] Farrar, Gillian, et al. "Defective Gallium-Transferrin Binding in Alzheimer Disease and Down Syndrome: Possible Mechanism for Accumulation of Aluminum in Brain." *Lancet* 1990; 335:747–750.

[11] Aabakken, L., and Osnes, M. "Management of NSAID-induced Gastrointestinal Lesions." *Scand. J. Gastroenterol.* 1988; 23(Suppl. 155):106–116.

[12] Evans, Doyle J., et al. "A Sensitive and Specific Serologic Test for Detection of Campylobacter Pylori Infection." *Gastroenterology* 1989; 96:1004–1008.

[13] Graham, D.Y., et al. "Epidemiology of Campylobacter Pylori Infection: Ethnic Considerations." *Scand. J. Gastroenterol.* 1988; 23(Suppl. 142):9–13.

[14] Langenberg, W., et al. "Follow-up Study of Individuals with Untreated Campylobacter Pylori-Associated Gastritis and of Noninfected Persons with Non-ulcer Dyspepsia." *J. Infect. Dis.* 1988; 157:1245–1249.

[15] Rauws, E.A.J., et al. "Campylobacter Pyloridis-associated Chronic Active Antral Gastritis: A Prospective Study of its Prevalence and the Effects of Antibacterial and Antiulcer Treatment." *Gastroenterology* 1988; 94:33–40.

[16] Soll, Andrew H. "Pathogenesis of Peptic Ulcer and Implications for Therapy." *N. Engl. J. Med.* 1990; 322:909–916.

[17] Clearfield, Harris R., and Wright, Richard A. "Update on Peptic Ulcer Disease." *Patient Care* 1990; Feb.:28–40.

[18] Graham, D.Y., et al. "Effect of Age on the Frequency of Active Campylobacter Pylori Infection Diagnosed by the [13C] Urea Breath Test in Normal Subjects and Patients with Peptic Ulcer Disease." *J. Infect Dis.* 1988; 157:777–780.

[19] Simjee, A.E. "Campylobacter Pylori." *Scand. J. Gastroenterol.* 1988;23(Suppl.155):38–40.

[20] Drumm, Brendan, et al. "Intrafamilial Clustering of *Helicobacter Pylori* Infection." *N. Engl. J. Med.* 1990; 322:359–363.

[21] Levi, Sassoon, et al. "Campylobacter Pylori and Duodenal Ulcers: The Gastrin Link." *Lancet* 1989; 1:1167–1168.

[22] Van Deventer, Gary M., et al. "A Randomized Study of Maintenance Therapy with Ranitidine to Prevent the Recurrence of Duodenal Ulcer." *N. Engl. J. Med.* 1989; 320:1113–1119.

[23] Miller, J. Paul, and Faragher, E. Brian. "Relapse of Duodenal Ulcer: Does it Matter Which Drug is Used in Initial Treatment?" *Br. Med. J.* 1986; 293:1117–1118.

[24] Pollner, Fran. "Studies Back Campylobacter Link to Ulcer Recurrence." *Medical World News* 1989; June 26:9–11.

[25] Clinical News. "Antibiotics for Ulcer: Caution is Urged." *Modern Medicine* 1989; 57:20–23.

[26] Husten, Larry, and Haglund, Keith. "C. Pylori Jury Out." *Medical Tribune* 1989; June 29:4.

[27] Tytgat, Guido, N.J. "Bismuth is Better." *Scand. J. Gastroenterol.* 1988;23(Suppl. 155):16–17.

[28] Tytgat, Guido N., et al. "Campylobacter Pylori." *Scand. J. Gastroenterol.* 1988;23(Suppl. 155):68–81.

[29] Clearfield, op. cit.

[30] Bloom, B.S. "Risk and cost of gastrointestinal side effects associated with nonsteroidal anti-inflammatory drugs." *Arch. Intern. Med.* 1989; 149:1019–1022.

[31] Healey, L.A. "Rheumatology: reevaluate NSAIDs." *Medical World News* 1989; July:49.

[32] Ibid.

[33] Roth, Sanford. "NSAID and Gastropathy: A Rheumatologist's Review." *J. Rheumatol.* 1988; 15:912–919.

[34] Clearfield, op. cit.

[35] Driks, M.R., et al. "Nosocomial Pneumonia in Intubated Patients Given Sucralfate as Compared with Antacids or Histamine Type 2 Blockers: The Role of Gastric Colonization." *N. Engl. J. Med.* 1987; 317:1376–1382.

[36] Personal communication, Steven Tannenbaum, July 6, 1983.

[37] "Rx-To-OTC Switch Products in Gastric Market Could Generate $350 mil." *F-D-C Reports* 1989; 51(39):T&G15–16.

[38] Larsson, H., et al. "Plasma Gastrin and Gastric Enterochromaffin-like Cell Activation and Proliferation. Studies with Omeprazole and Ranitidine in Intact and Antrectomized Rats." *Gastroenterol.* 1986; 90:391–399.

[39] Lublin, Joann S. "Merck's Drug For Ulcers Faces Safety Concerns." *Wall Street Journal* 1990; Feb. 20:B4.

[40] Burlinson, B., et al. "Genotoxicity Studies of Gastric Acid Inhibiting Drugs." *Lancet* 1990; 335:419.

[41] Pai, S., et al. "Elevation of Serum Aluminum in Humans on a Two-Day Sucralfate Regimen." *J. Clin. Pharmacol.* 1987; 27:213–215.

[42] Robertson, J.A., et al. "Sucralfate, Intestinal Aluminum Absorption, and Aluminum Toxicity in a Patient on Dialysis." *Ann. Intern. Med.* 1989; 111(2):179–181.

[43] Burnatowska-Hledin, M.A., and Mayor, C.H. "The Effects of Sucralfate Ingestion on Serum and Specific Tissue Aluminum Concentration in Normal Rats." *Clin Tox.* 1984; 22(1):87–93.

[44] Withers, D.J., et al. "Encephalopathy in Patient Taking Aluminum-Containing Agents, Including Sucralfate." *Lancet* 1989; 2:674.

[45] Roth, S., et al. "Misoprostol heals gastroduodenal injury in patients with rheumatoid arthritis receiving aspirin." *Arch. Intern. Med.* 1989; 149:775–779.

[46] Graham, David Y., et al. "Spicy Food and the Stomach. Evaluation by Videoendoscopy." *JAMA* 1988; 260:3473–3475.

[47] Holzer, P., et al. "Intragastric Capsaicin Protects Against Aspirin-Induced Lesion Formation and Bleeding in the Rat Gastric Mucosa." *Gastroenterology* 1989; 96:1425–1433.

[48] Holzer, P., and Lippe, I.T. "Stimulation of Afferent Nerve Endings by Intragastric Capsaicin Protects Against Ethanol-Induced Damage of Gastric Mucosa." *Neuroscience* 1988; 27:981–987.

[49] Mezenova, T.D. "Hypolipidemic Activity of Licorice Root Extract." *Pharm. Chem. J.* (USSR) 1984; 17:275–277.

[50] Shinada, Masahiro, et al. "Enhancement of Interferon-√ Production in Glycyrrhizin-Treated Human Peripheral Lymphocytes in Response to Concanavalin A and to Surface Antigen of Hepatitis B Virus (42241)." *Proc. Soc. Exp. Biol. Med.* 1986; 181:205–210.

[51] Russell, R.I., et al. *Scand. J. Gastroenterol.* 1984; 19(Suppl. 92):97.

[52] Tarnawski, Andrzej, et al. "Cytoprotective Drugs; Focus on Essential Fatty Acids and Sucralfate." *Scand. J. Gastroenterol.* 1987; 22(Suppl. 127):39–43.

[53] Jun, Ren, and Zhengang, Wang. "Pharmacological Research on the Effect of Licorice." *J. Traditional Chinese Med.* 1988; 8(4):307–309.

[54] Bannister, B., et al. "Cardiac Arrest Due to Licorice Induced Hypokalemia." *Br. Med. J.* 1977; 2:738–739.

[55] Morgan, A.G., et al. "Comparison Between Cimetidine and Caved-S in the Treatment of Gastric Ulceration, and Subsequent Maintenance Therapy." *Gut* 1982; 23:545–551.

[56] Van Ness, Michael M,. and Cattau, Edward L., Jr. "Flatulence: Pathophysiology and Treatment." *American Family Physician* 1985; 31(4):198–208.

[57] Steggerda, F.R. "Gastrointestinal Gas Following Food Consumption." *Ann. NY Acad. Sci.* 1960; 150:57.

[58] Leavitt, M.D., et al. "Studies of a Flatulent Patient." *N. Engl. J. Med.* 1976; 295:260–262.

[59] Van Ness, op. cit.

[60] Jain, Naresh K. "Activated Charcoal, Simethicone and Intestinal Gas: A Double Blind Study." *Ann. Int. Med.* 1986; 105:61–62.

[61] Ericsson, Charles D., et al. "Treatment of Traveler's Diarrhea with Sulfamethoxazole and Trimethoprim and Loperamide." *JAMA* 1990; 263:257–261.

[62] Lee, Austin, et al. "Bulk Laxative Causing Esophageal Obstruction." *NCMJ* 1989;50:489–491.

[63] Cooper, Stanley G., and Tracey, Edward J. "Small-Bowel Obstruction Caused by Oat-Bran Bezoar." *N. Engl. J. Med.* 1989; 320:1148–1149.

[64] Anderson, J.W., et al. "Cholesterol-Lowering Effects of Psyllium Hydrophilic Mucilloid for Hypercholesterolemic Men." *Arch. Int. Med.* 1988; 148:292–296.

[65] Bell, Larry P., et al. "Cholesterol-Lowering Effects of Psyllium Hydrophilic Mucilloid: Adjunct Therapy to a Prudent Diet for Patients with Mild to Moderate Hypercholesterolemia." *JAMA* 1989; 261:3419–3423.

[66] Simjee, A.E. "Colloidal Bismuth Subcitrate." *SAMJ* (Suppl.) 1988; July 2:61–63.

[67] Pollner, op. cit.

[68] Gilbert, Richard J., et al. "Effect of Cisapride, a New Prokinetic Agent, on Esophageal Motor Function." *Dig. Dis. and Sciences* 1987; 32:1331–1336.

[69] Janisch, H.D., et al. "Cisapride Versus Ranitidine in the Treatment of Reflux Esophagitis." *Hepato-gastroenterol.* 1988; 35:125–127.

[70] Ducrot, R. Jian F., et al. "Symptomatic, Radionuclide and Therapeutic Assessment of Chronic Idiopathic Dyspepsia." *Dig. Dis. and Sciences* 1989; 34:657–664.

[71] Brynskov, Jorn, et al. "A Placebo-Controlled, Double-Blind, Randomized Trial of Cyclosporine Therapy in Active Chronic Crohn's Disease." *N. Engl. J. Med.* 1989; 321:845–850.

[72] Pollner, Fran. "Colectomy Alternative Outlined." *Med. World News* 1989; Jun. 26:16.

Heart Help

3

It all seemed so simple. Butter was bad, margarine was good. Salt raised blood pressure, oat bran lowered cholesterol. Type As were impatient and vulnerable to heart attacks, while Type Bs were laid back and protected. If we just ate less red meat and more fish we were almost guaranteed a healthy heart.

But the trouble with such conventional wisdom is that there are no guarantees; the more we know, the more complicated the question of heart disease becomes. Take salt, for example. Researchers have been debating the dangers of sodium for decades. Millions of dollars have been spent trying to determine whether a diet high in salt causes elevations in blood pressure.

SALT TALKS

To resolve this issue the Intersalt Cooperative Research Group enlisted over ten thousand participants from thirty-two countries trying to reach some definitive conclusion. The result—salt consumption has only minimal impact on hypertension.[1, 2] Experts for *Consumer Reports* acknowledge that "a growing body of scientific evidence indicates that the role of dietary salt as a threat to health has been greatly exaggerated."[3]

That doesn't mean you should immediately suck on a salt shaker or pig out on pretzels, pickles, and potato chips. Many people with mild high blood pressure can indeed control their hypertension by restricting sodium intake.[4,5] But if you don't suffer from high blood pressure, or if you are not salt sensitive, there is little reason to deprive yourself of some of life's little pleasures—like a delicious cup of chicken soup and a Saltine cracker.

TYPE A TRIUMPHS

Another sacred cardiac cow was slain when Dr. Redford Williams of Duke University discovered that so-called Type A personalities might not be more vulnerable to coronaries. In fact, Dr. Williams has gone so far as to suggest that some Type A traits may be generally beneficial—ambition, follow-through, and mastery. He doesn't worry about impatience or the work

drive. His research shows that other culprits—anger, hostility, aggression, and mistrust—may be the key elements that predispose to heart disease. So for the moment at
least, impatient, hard-driving Type As can
stop worrying, as long as they are trusting and
considerate.

CHOLESTEROL MYTH?

As if such contradictions weren't enough
to drive the cardiology community crazy,
along came Thomas J. Moore's "Cholesterol
Myth" in *The Atlantic*. Just when everyone had been told to get
total cholesterol levels to 200 or lower, Mr. Moore suggested
that dancing the lipid limbo (how low can you go?) might not be
the answer to heart attack prevention. His heretical book *Heart
Failure*, on which the article was based, proposed that "diet has
hardly any effect on your cholesterol level; the drugs that can
lower it often have serious or fatal side effects; and there is no
evidence at all that lowering your cholesterol level will lengthen
your life."[7] He even went so far as to suggest that there might be
dangers in lowering cholesterol too far. The fire storm of
controversy that erupted on the book's publication was bitter if
not bloody.

Europeans have observed the bickering with some amusement. They marvel over Americans' obsession with diet and
exercise. The French, in particular, still love their croissants,
Brie, and Camembert. Jogging is nowhere near as popular in
Paris as it is in San Francisco. Yet France has the lowest rate of
death from heart disease of all western countries.[8]

The cholesterol bandwagon that has been gathering mo-
mentum over the last several years has been fueled in large
measure by drug companies dazzled by dollar signs. The vision
of millions of Americans, each spending hundreds if not thousands of dollars on medicine every year for the rest of their lives,
has motivated manufacturers to increase cholesterol awareness. With so much money at stake, it is hardly surprising that
objectivity is hard to find these days, even among the scientists

---

Keys to a Trusting Heart[6]

- Turn off cynical thoughts—Just say "Stop!"
- Put yourself in the other's shoes.
- Laugh at yourself and learn to relax—eat dessert first!
- Practice trusting others; don't punish minor mistakes.
- Force yourself to listen, LISTEN, **LISTEN!**
- Substitute firmness for aggressiveness.
- Imagine that today is your last day on earth.
- Try to understand and forgive.

doing the research.

Given all the uncertainties and contradictions of the last decade, it might be tempting to throw your hands up in the air and say "the hell with it!" If the experts can't make up their minds, then bring on the butter and burgers, the shakes and the fries.

Hold on just a finger-licking minute here. True, there are unresolved questions, but we have a few tricks up our sleeves to help you reduce the risk of heart disease and high blood pressure, both with and without medicine. You don't have to suffer to improve your odds.

Cholesterol Control

GOALS

Over a short period of time people have become very sophisticated about lipids. "Good cholesterol" and "bad cholesterol" have become buzzwords. We've heard grandmothers comparing HDL (high-density lipoprotein), LDL (low-density lipoprotein), and triglyceride values.

But doctors are not unanimous about ideal lipid levels. For awhile the simplistic idea that everyone should get total cholesterol below 200 was appealing. It was a nice round number that was easy to remember. It was also misleading. Studies have *not* shown that older people or women over the age of forty-seven will live longer or healthier lives if they reach such a stringent target. So far the only people shown to improve their longevity by cholesterol reduction are middle-aged men with substantial elevations of cholesterol (about 290).[9]

Harvard researchers conclude that "For persons aged 20 to 60 years who are at low risk [nonsmokers with normal blood pressure], we calculate a gain in life expectancy of 3 days to 3 months from a lifelong program of cholesterol reduction."[10] Big deal! (By the way, they did find substantial impact on life expectancy from smoking cessation and blood pressure control.)

Total cholesterol may not be as important as we have been

led to believe. Scientists are now debating whether the good fat, HDL, is a better predictor of heart disease.[11] Researchers at Harvard and Johns Hopkins have pointed out that a surprising number of their patients with coronary artery disease (up to 40 percent) have cholesterol readings below 200.[12] Although such a low total cholesterol figure looks good on paper, these people apparently developed atherosclerosis because they were deficient in protective HDL. Their HDL levels were 35 or below. HDL levels over 45 may help protect against heart disease by removing bad cholesterol from the bloodstream where it can clog arteries.

One of the listeners to our radio show called recently to complain about the unfairness of life. He had been careful about his diet and had always maintained a total cholesterol level that he could be proud of—around 180. His doctor had patted him on the back and told him not to worry, even though his father, brother, and uncles had all died in their fifties from heart attacks. When our caller reached his late fifties, he too was found to have clogged coronary arteries and went through balloon angioplasty and eventually triple bypass surgery. No one had bothered to mention that his HDL levels were low and that might be even more important than his total cholesterol.

HDL and LDL may not be the last word in the cholesterol conflict. New research suggests that the blood fat lipoprotein(a), abbreviated Lp(a), may be the most important marker of coronary heart disease. Unfortunately, most of the lipid-lowering medications on the market do not affect Lp(a) levels. The only one that appears capable of reducing this artery-clogging compound is niacin, though fish oil may also be beneficial.[14,15]

TOO LOW CHOLESTEROL?

The idea that cholesterol could fall too low is hard for most people to imagine. The cholesterol craze has spawned the concept that if a little reduction is good, then more is better. But Goldilocks might have been on to something when she rejected both the porridge that was too hot *and* too cold. There might be an optimal cholesterol range that is not too high *or* too low.

Growing evidence suggests that there may be some risks

Things that Raise Good HDL Cholesterol[13]

Dilantin
(phenytoin)
estrogen
exercise
Lopid
(gemfibrozil)
moderate alcohol
intake
niacin
quitting cigarettes
weight loss

Things Associated with Lower HDL Cholesterol

beta-blockers
(**Inderal**,
Lopressor,
Corgard,
Tenormin, etc.)
diabetes
male hormones
(testosterone)
oat bran
obesity
polyunsaturated
vegetable oils
progestin
(progesterone)
smoking

associated with low cholesterol levels. Japanese researchers have found that people with low blood cholesterol are more susceptible to dangerous bleeding strokes (cerebral hemorrhage). In their study, men with cholesterol levels below 178 and women with readings below 190 were at greater risk.[16]

American researchers have also found that low cholesterol is linked to a higher incidence of stroke. In one big heart-attack prevention study, men with high blood pressure (diastolic above 90) and low cholesterol (below 160) were six times more likely to die from cerebral hemorrhage.[17] And the Honolulu Heart Project, a long-term study of Japanese-American men, discovered that men with cholesterol levels below 150 were at four times the risk of bleeding stroke than men with levels of 190 or above.[18] The Honolulu researchers determined that for these middle-aged men, the safest cholesterol range was between 200 and 220.[19]

For older women the ideal cholesterol level might be even higher. European researchers have discovered that elderly women have the lowest risk of death when their cholesterol levels are around 270.[20–22]

With all the negative publicity that cholesterol has received over the years, it is hard to realize that this substance plays an essential role in the body. Cholesterol is a necessary component of cell membranes. Scientists have speculated that if levels get too low, blood vessels may become fragile and prone to break under pressure.

French physicians suggest that "an increase in plasma cholesterol might be an adaptive process during aging, necessary to maintaining the physical or chemical characteristics of the cell membrane. If this hypothesis is true, a reduction of cholesterol, either by drugs or by a high intake of polyunsaturated fats, should not be advisable in the elderly, at least when total cholesterol value is not over 7 mmol/l (270 mg/dl)."[25]

Violence and Too Low Cholesterol?

One of the oddest findings from studies on lowering cholesterol is a consistent increase in deaths associated with violence and accidents.[23, 24] At first, physicians attributed this purely to chance and laughed about the strange coincidence. But this trend hasn't disappeared and scientists aren't laughing anymore. Cholesterol is essential to proper brain function and is a critical component of myelin, the insulation around nerves. If the insulation around an electric wire is faulty, you can end up with a short. Could inadequate cholesterol short circuit the central nervous system? No one knows, but until the bizarre relationship between violent or accidental death and low cholesterol is explained, we might want to be prudent in the crusade against cholesterol.

So where does this leave us? What are the optimal levels of cholesterol? Moderation has always made sense to us. We interpret the data that is currently available to mean that middle-aged men should aim for total cholesterol levels between 180 and 215. Women can probably feel reasonably secure

Cholesterol Quest	*Goal*[26]
HDL Cholesterol	45 or higher
Total Cholesterol (middle-aged men)	180–215
Total Cholesterol/HDL ratio	4.5 or less

if their cholesterol ranges between 190 and 230, especially if their good HDL cholesterol is 45 or higher. In our opinion, the ratio of total cholesterol to HDL cholesterol is the single most valuable number you can calculate because it is one of the best predictors of coronary artery disease.[27] Anything below 4.5 is good news.

DO-IT-YOURSELF MONITORING

Cholesterol measurement is notoriously unreliable. The American College of Pathologists surveyed five thousand clinical laboratories and discovered that nearly half produced results that were "unacceptable."[28] Public screenings at malls, work places, and pharmacies are even worse. Richard Kusserow, Inspector General of the Department of Health and Human Services, reported that many of these cholesterol screenings are improperly conducted, produce unreliable results, and are unsanitary. Far too often, equipment was calibrated by improperly trained personnel and poorly maintained.[29]

How can you tell what your cholesterol level really is? You are partially dependent on the quality control of your physician's laboratory. Some doctors have their own machine for measuring cholesterol, which may or may not be accurate. Others send blood samples out to commercial labs.

Calculating the Ratio

Take your total cholesterol (TC) reading:

_____

Take your HDL reading:

_____

Now divide your TC by your HDL. The answer:

_____

is your ratio of total cholesterol to HDL. If it's below 4.5, pat yourself on the back. Example: If your total cholesterol is 220 and your HDL cholesterol is 50, then 220/50 = a ratio of 4.4. Congratulations!

No matter how your blood is handled, it is important that you get at least three different analyses several months apart. And to ensure best results, do not eat for at least twelve to fourteen hours before blood is drawn.

If you would like to get even more involved, you can do your own cholesterol screening at home. This is not for the squeamish, however, since it will require a drop of blood. Just as diabetics can measure their blood glucose with a finger prick, people can get a rough idea of their cholesterol level with a credit card-sized test called Chemcard. You will have to ask your doctor to order you some Chemcards, as they are not yet available over the counter. (If your doctor is a nice guy, he shouldn't charge you more than $5.00 per card.) Have a nurse or lab technician demonstrate the proper technique.

Chemcard Cholesterol Test

Chematics, Inc.
P.O. Box 293
North Webster, IN 46555
(219) 834–2406

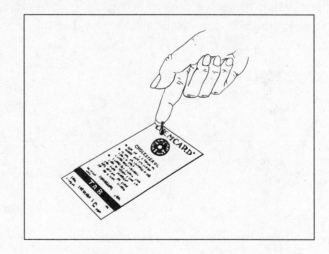

All you need is a sterile lancet to prick your finger and obtain a drop of blood. (Automatic devices can be purchased in most pharmacies.) The blood is placed on a pad about the size of an eraser tip. Chemicals in the pad then react with enzymes in your blood to produce a result in three minutes. You then peel back the paper and match a color chart to determine if your cholesterol level is 150, 175, 200, 225, 250, or greater than 300. Although not as specific as a quantitative blood test, the Chemcard produces results that are reasonably accurate for screening or monitoring general progress.[30]

REMEDIES

For years we were told that if we just ate enough soluble fiber we could lower cholesterol levels as much as 20 percent. People were urged to gorge themselves on oat bran in muffins, granola, and hot cereal. The Quaker Oats Company went from selling a million boxes of oat bran cereal a year in 1987 to a million boxes a month in 1989.[31] You could even buy bran-enriched potato chips, licorice, and beer.

Phooey! Oat bran tastes like ground-up shirt cardboard. And it gives you gas. Why fight flatulence, cramping, and diarrhea when there is nothing magical about oat bran? Despite the hype from cereal manufacturers, there is no evidence that oat bran has special power to lower cholesterol. Harvard researchers found that any benefit from oat bran probably comes mostly from substituting low-fat breakfast cereal for high-fat foods like sausage and fried eggs.[32] After all, if you walk around with that much oat bran in your belly you won't have room for much else. You can do just as well with low-fiber wheat flour, and it won't make you fart.

By the way, scarfing down low-fat muffins of any variety throughout the day could be a key element in lowering cholesterol. How you eat may be more important than what you eat. Gorging is out and nibbling is in. Canadian nutritionists have found that men who ate seventeen snacks a day instead of three big meals had total cholesterol 8.5 percent lower and bad LDL cholesterol almost 14 percent lower than the normal eaters.[33] For all practical purposes the diets were identical. It didn't matter what they ate so much as when they ate it. Nibbling small portions all day long apparently lowers insulin levels compared to gorging, and it is suspected that insulin stimulates the body to create cholesterol.

Psyllium

Should you give up on fiber completely? Perhaps not. Research indicates that psyllium can lower total cholesterol anywhere from 5 to 15 percent.[34, 35] Ispaghula, or blond psyllium seeds, are much higher in soluble fiber than oat bran.

Oat bran

No unique power to lower cholesterol.
Side effects: Cramping, bloating, loose stools, diarrhea, and flatulence.

Metamucil (psyllium)

One teaspoonful with eight ounces of water three times a day before meals.
Side effects: temporary fullness, bloating, and gas.

★ ★ ★ ★

**Sources of
Psyllium**

Correctol Powder
Fiberall
Hydrocil Instant
Konsyl-D
Metamucil
Modane Bulk
various house
    brands of
    psyllium
hydrophilic
    mucilloid

Subjects who took one teaspoon (3.4 grams) of **Metamucil** three times a day before meals instead of a similar-tasting placebo powder had a significant drop in total cholesterol and an even greater reduction in bad LDL cholesterol (up to 20 percent).

Although researchers don't know exactly how psyllium works, they suspect that this soluble fiber grabs on to cholesterol and bile acids in the intestines and then acts as a garbage-disposal system by carrying the bad guys out of the GI tract in the stool. Psyllium appears to be about as good as expensive prescription drugs like **Questran** (cholestyramine) when it comes to lowering cholesterol. Unlike harsh laxatives, psyllium is a bulk-forming agent that is not likely to cause a laxative habit or produce serious side effects.

Fish

If you could make only one change in eating habits, why not make it fish? The evidence keeps mounting that just adding fish to the menu can make a big difference in heart health. Welsh researchers studied 2,033 men who had suffered one heart attack. One group was encouraged to reduce total fat consumption and substitute polyunsaturated oil for saturated fat. Another group was told to increase fiber intake. The third group was advised to increase fatty fish consumption (two or three portions a week). If they just couldn't stand fish, these men were told to substitute three fish oil capsules a day (0.5 grams of **MaxEPA**).

Two years later the scientists counted the number of heart disease deaths and discovered something quite extraordinary. Much to everyone's surprise, subjects who were told to reduce fat or increase fiber experienced no signficant change in mortality. (They actually showed a slightly higher death rate.) The fish eaters, on the other hand, had impressive results. The authors concluded: "The results suggest that fatty fish (and fish oil) reduced mortality in men after MI [heart attack], by about 29 percent during the first 2 years."[36]

This latest study adds to the evidence that regular fish consumption reduces the risk of death from coronary heart

Fatty Fish

bluefish
herring
kipper
mackerel
salmon
sardines
trout
tuna

disease.[37–39] Although researchers are still debating what component of fish actually improves mortality, the assumption is usually made that the omega-3 fatty acids, EPA (eicosapentaenoic acid) and DHA (docosahexaenoic acid), are responsible.

Fish oils appear to thin the blood, make platelets less sticky, and reduce the risk of clots and certain kinds of irregular heart rhythms.[40–42] They may also reduce the levels of some dangerous blood fats, especially triglycerides.[43–45] They also appear to raise good HDL cholesterol, but unfortunately may increase LDL cholesterol as well. One group of physicians report that fish oil supplements may reduce the risk that plaque-narrowed arteries, once opened, will clog up again later,[46] although another group found no such benefit.[47] Pigs fed a diet guaranteed to produce atherosclerosis developed significantly less coronary artery disease when they were given cod liver oil as an antidote.[48]

Blood pressure may also be an important factor. Large doses of **MaxEPA** fish oil (50 ml per day) seem to lower blood pressure about as much as antihypertensive medications such as diuretics or beta blockers like **Inderal** (propranolol).[49] A recent Norwegian study has confirmed that fish oil (six grams daily) reduces elevated blood pressure significantly.[50]

Although it is still too soon to say whether fish oil will ever be recommended as a treatment for high blood pressure, these early results are tantalizing. There are also hints that fish oil may reduce redness, itching, and scaling in psoriasis and diminish morning stiffness and joint tenderness in rheumatoid arthritis.[51, 52] All in all, the benefits of fish and fish oil appear to be mounting, though there are still important questions to be resolved.

Lest you be tempted to start popping down dozens of little golden fish oil footballs, be aware that there are some side effects. Besides causing fishy burps, supplements may increase the risk of bleeding or bruising. (Greenland Eskimos eating a high-fish diet have less heart disease but more bleeding strokes.) Anyone with uncontrolled blood pressure, a tendency to hemorrhage, or who is taking anticoagulants

---

MaxEPA
(fish oil)
The optimum dose is still unclear. One or two capsules a day may provide some heart help with low risk.
Side effects: fish burp; bruising and bleeding;
Avoid if pregnant, child, diabetic, on other blood thinners, or if at increased risk of hemorrhage.

★ ★

should avoid fish oil. Aspirin may also interact adversely with fish oil to increase the risk of bleeding.

Although most physicians are not yet ready to prescribe fish oil, a recent analysis offered a cautiously optimistic overview:

> . . . a case could be made for providing low levels of omega-3 fatty acids (0.3 to 1 gram/day [1 to 2 capsules]) to any patient at increased risk for CHD [coronary heart disease]. This level in intake would provide as much omega-3 fatty acids as consuming three servings of salmon per week and would far surpass the omega-3 fatty acid intake associated with reduced coronary events observed in a recent epidemiologic study.[53] Although this low dose may have little, if any, measurable effect on serum lipid levels, it may in the long run help prevent complications of atherosclerosis. The potential risk from this intake should be minimal.[54]

THE GOOD FATS

No matter how much you cut back on meat and margarine, there is no way to completely eliminate fat from your diet. What's more, you may not even have to feel guilty, as

Canola oil (*Puritan* or other brands)

Lowest in saturated fat. High in monounsaturated fat. More omega-3 fatty acid (like fish oil) than any other cooking oil.

★ ★ ★ ★

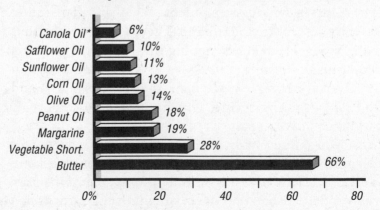

Comparison of Percent of Saturated Fat

Canola Oil*	6%
Safflower Oil	10%
Sunflower Oil	11%
Corn Oil	13%
Olive Oil	14%
Peanut Oil	18%
Margarine	19%
Vegetable Short.	28%
Butter	66%

0%   20   40   60   80

*Source: Canola Oil (*Puritan) Procter & Gamble data on file*
Other fats: Composition of Foods, US Department of Agriculture Handbook No. 8-4

Comparison of Percent of Monounsaturated Fats

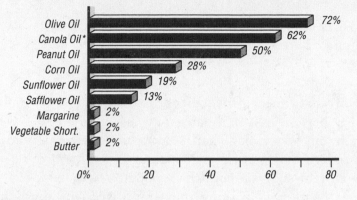

Adapted from the folllowing sources:
   Canola Oil (*Puritan) Procter & Gamble data on file
   Other fats: Composition of Foods, U.S. Department of Agriculture
      Handbook No. 8-4
   Council on Scientific Affairs "Saturated Fatty Acids in Vegetable Oils"
      JAMA 1990; 263:693–695.

long as you pick the right oil. Canola oil (Puritan and other brands) contains omega-3 fatty acids, similar to fish oil. One teaspoon of canola is roughly equal to two fish oil capsules (600 mg of omega-3 fatty acids).[55]

Canola oil has the lowest level of saturated fat of any vegetable oil (only 6 percent). Corn oil has twice as much nasty saturated fat (sat-fat) and peanut oil has three times more than canola oil. What this means is that "the cholesterol-raising potential of canola oil is very low."[56] .

Monounsaturated fat seems to be good for your heart, at least if you substitute it for saturated fat. New research shows that a diet rich in olive oil can actually lower total cholesterol 14.1 percent and lower bad LDL cholesterol almost 18 percent.[57] A lot of low-fat diets and even some cholesterol-lowering drugs don't have as strong an effect.[58] And like fish oil, monounsaturated fats also seem to help lower blood pressure.[59, 60] Olive oil is highest in monounsaturated fats (72 percent) and canola oil is not far behind (62 percent).

Olive oil

Highest in monounsaturated fat. Relatively low in saturated fat. Can lower cholesterol and blood pressure.

★ ★ ★ ★

Garlic, Onions, and Alcohol

Wel Loved he garleek, oynons, and eek lekes,
And for to drinken strong wyn, reed as blood,
—CHAUCER; *The Canterbury Tales*

Now that you have the right entree (fish) and the optimal oils (canola and olive), what about the extras? Well, we recommend you include garlic and onions with as many dishes as possible. There is an impressive amount of new research that suggests both these odiferous vegetables can help the heart. For one thing, they may lower cholesterol. It used to be thought you had to consume huge quantities of garlic to get any beneficial results. Some researchers reported that you would need up to twenty-eight cloves a day to experience any cholesterol-lowering impact.[61] At that dose you could kiss all social relationships goodbye. But new studies suggest that as little as one clove (600–900 mg of garlic powder) may reduce cholesterol and triglycerides roughly 10 and 13 percent, respectively.[62]

Of even greater interest is the ability of garlic and onions to prevent or dissolve blood clots. Some very respectable scientists, including Dr. Eric Block, Chairman of the Department of Chemistry at the State University of New York at Albany, have discovered ingredients in onions and garlic that thin the blood.[63] Because these chemicals may also make red blood platelets less sticky, blood is less likely to clot when it shouldn't and precipitate a heart attack or stroke.[64, 65] One to two cloves of garlic have a pronounced effect on clotting activity.[66]

There are still unresolved questions as to whether odorless garlic is effective.[67–69] Although some garlic powder preparations (especially those that are freeze-dried) maintain their potency and lower cholesterol,[70] scientists believe that it is the smelly, sulfur-containing ingredients in garlic and onion that work the magic. Until research proves otherwise, we recommend the real stinky stuff, cooked or raw, as often as social relations will allow.

As you sit down to your meal of broiled salmon (brushed

thoroughly with olive oil of course) accompanied by a salad liberally sprinkled with onions and doused with a garlicky vinaigrette, you might also want to pour a glass of wine. Evidence keeps mounting that moderate alcohol consumption is associated with an increase in good HDL cholesterol.[71-74] This beneficial effect appears to be more pronouced for people who exercise, especially if they are thin rather than overweight.[75]

One of the largest studies of its kind followed 16,349 men in Honolulu, Puerto Rico, and Framingham, Massachusetts, for six years to see what kind of diet was associated with coronary heart disease and heart attacks. The key factor was alcohol. The drinkers had substantially less heart disease.[76] This is not a recommendation to turn into a boozer, but if you like a glass of wine now and again with dinner, it might be helping your heart rather than hurting. Heavy drinking, on the other hand, is associated with hypertension and heart disease.

Coffee

The coffee controversy has been brewing for decades. Does it raise cholesterol and increase the risk of heart disease? Which is better, regular brew or decaffeinated? The problem is that different studies have produced conflicting results. Norwegian researchers have reported a strong relationship between coffee drinking and elevated cholesterol.[77] A study at Stanford University also noted an association between modest coffee consumption and cholesterol, but University of Pittsburgh scientists found just the opposite.[78] And the famous Framingham, Massachusetts, heart study showed no relationship between coffee-drinking and heart disease.[79]

The mystery may have been solved. Finnish and Dutch investigators have discovered that the Nordic brewing method may be the cholesterol culprit. Scandinavians apparently like to boil their coffee—either throwing the coffee grounds into the pot or pouring boiling water into a thermos on top of coarsely ground beans. This steeping process is apparently capable of raising cholesterol by liberating some nasty chemical (not caffeine). But when coffee is made by pouring boiling water over a paper filter instead, cholesterol levels do not go up, even when subjects drank as many as eight cups a day. [80–82] Perhaps the paper filters out whatever compound causes blood lipids to climb.

One cloud on the horizon, however, has to do with decaffeinated coffee. For years the commercials have told us to cut back on caffeine because it will make us jittery. Now researchers at Stanford have reported that in their experiments, decaffeinated coffee drinkers (three to six cups a day) experienced a slight rise in bad LDL cholesterol. The coffee was prepared with a drip-through filter method, leading the investigators to conclude that perhaps the robusta coffee bean usually used for decaffeinated coffee is the culprit.[83]

Where does this leave all of us coffee lovers? Well, once again moderation makes sense. A couple of cups of regular coffee prepared with a paper filter should do little if any harm. We would keep the decaf to a minimum, but if caffeine keeps you awake, then one cup of decaffeinated coffee in the evening probably won't be a big deal.

VITAMINS AND MINERALS FOR THE HEART

Millions of people will not be able to get their cholesterol into the desirable range even if they substitute fish for red meat, convert to canola and olive oil, increase intake of fruits and vegetables, and cut back on decaf coffee. For a surprising number of conscientious eaters, cholesterol levels just don't seem to play by the rules.

Niacin

Before resorting to expensive prescription drugs, though, it might be worth talking to a doctor about a vitamin. It's hard to imagine that vitamins could protect us from heart disease; yet there are few more effective cholesterol-lowering compounds than vitamin B_3 (known as niacin or nicotinic acid). A derivative of vitamin B_3 called niacinamide or nicotinamide is not effective against cholesterol.

This drug (and at the effective dose, niacin must be considered a drug) has been prescribed for high cholesterol since 1955. At doses of three grams or greater a day, niacin lowers bad LDL cholesterol between 15 and 40 percent and raises good HDL cholesterol 10 to 20 percent.[84] It also reduces triglycerides, making niacin a triple whammy against heart disease.

A long-term study called the Coronary Drug Project followed heart attack victims for fifteen years. Those men who had been on niacin had a significant reduction in repeat heart attacks and 11 percent fewer deaths, even nine years after they stopped taking niacin.[85]

Best of all, niacin is cheap. Whereas many of the newer cholesterol-lowering drugs can easily cost $100 or more a month, generic niacin runs $10 or less. There are, however, some important cautions. First and foremost, niacin is not a do-it-yourself project. You *must* be carefully monitored by a physician. It is thought that niacin works by somehow blocking the liver's production of bad cholesterol and boosting the good HDL; consequently, there is a risk of interfering with normal liver function.

The most common side effect is the niacin flush: uncomfortable burning, tingling, redness, and itching that often spreads down from the face and neck to the rest of the body. It may come on within fifteen minutes to two hours after swallowing a pill and can last thirty minutes or longer. As far as we know, this flushing reaction is not dangerous, but it can be darned annoying. Niacin should be taken with food to minimize the reaction. Some doctors also recommend an aspirin tablet half an hour before taking niacin to diminish the discomfort. Many people report that the flushing tends to disappear after several weeks of treatment.

Time-release niacin has become very popular in recent years because it is far less likely to cause the niacin flush. Physicians often prescribe this controlled-release type of product under the brand name **Nicobid.** This product is very expensive and there

---

Niacin

Lowers LDL, Lp(a), and triglycerides. Raises good HDL cholesterol. Proven track record against heart disease. Inexpensive. Monitor liver enzymes for potential liver damage. Not recommended for diabetics.

★ ★ ★

Niacin Side Effects

- Flushing, tingling, itching, nausea, stomach cramps, diarrhea, blood sugar fluctuations.
- Rare side effcts include aggravation of peptic ulcers, irregular heart rhythms, and elevation of liver enzymes.
- Do not take if you have a history of ulcers, liver disease, gout, glaucoma, or diabetes.
- Requires medical monitoring, especially liver function tests.
- Lower doses (1 to 1.5 grams/day) appear safer.

Niacin: Cheap & Effective

Time Release Niacin available from
Bronson Pharmaceuticals
4526 Rinetti Lane
La Canada, CA 91011-0628

Lower-Dose Niacin Treatment Regimen

Physicians have reported impressive results with fewer side effects on a lower-dose regimen like this:

100 or 250 mg twice a day for one week. Over the next month, the dose is increased gradually up to 1,000 or 1,200 mg total per day (divided doses, such as 400 mg three times a day or 500 mg twice a day).

If flushing is a problem, one aspirin thirty minutes to an hour before niacin dose is recommended. If side effects persist, niacin dosage is reduced.[92–94] Periodic monitoring of liver function is essential.

are now a host of cheaper over-the-counter varieties available. One time-release niacin, sold through the mail by Bronson Pharmaceuticals, has been found to be at least as good as, if not better than, the far more expensive prescription preparation.[86]

The problem with controlled-release niacin is that questions have been raised about its safety and effectiveness. One team of researchers found that regular (prompt-release) niacin was better at controlling cholesterol and triglycerides than time-release niacin.[87] Of far greater concern is the question of safety. Time-release niacin may be more likely to cause nausea, diarrhea, fatigue, and elevations of liver enzymes, especially when doses are increased from 1.5 grams to 3.0 grams a day.[88] Dr. Mack Mitchell, a physician at Johns Hopkins School of Medicine, has seen a number of patients develop liver toxicity after switching from regular niacin to time-release preparations. He speculates that "the additional time the sustained-release preparations spend in circulation increases liver toxicity. He recommends patients who take niacin stick with regular niacin preparations and be monitored for liver damage every three to six months."[89] Other physicians have also reported serious liver problems with sustained-release niacin that do not occur when the patients are switched to regular crystalline niacin.[90,91]

Despite the side-effect dangers, there is room for optimism. New research suggests that lower niacin doses can reduce the risk of adverse reactions and still improve total cholesterol/HDL ratios. Doses that range from 1 gram (1,000 mg) to 1.5 grams (1,500 mg) per day raised good HDL cholesterol up to 31 percent.[95] When coupled with a sensible diet, lower-dose niacin may represent one of the most cost-effective ways to control cholesterol.

Other B Vitamins

Niacin isn't the only B vitamin that offers help for the heart. Pantethine is a natural derivative of pantothenic acid. Numerous studies have shown that at doses of 600 to 1,200 mg daily, pantethine has an impressive ability to lower total cholesterol, LDL cholesterol, and triglycerides, while raising good HDL choelsterol.[96-98] This compound is relatively new to the U.S. health-food market and is still not widely available. The Japanese have been faster to recognize its potential effectiveness. Preliminary data suggest that pantethine is very well tolerated, with few if any of the adverse reactions associated with niacin.

Pyridoxine (vitamin B_6) may also be good for the heart. Two neurophysiologists at the Massachusetts Institute of Technology have presented a fascinating theory. They propose that "arteriosclerosis is caused by homocysteine [a compound produced during digestion of protein]. Low levels of dietary vitamin B_6, in conjunction with high intake of protein, lead to toxic levels of homocysteine in the blood. Arteriosclerosis can be prevented or possibly reversed by reducing protein intake and insuring an adequate level of vitamin B_6."[99] They suggest 10 to 25 mg of pyridoxine per day.

High doses of vitamin B_6 can be toxic (over 200 mg daily may lead to nerve damage; symptoms to be wary of include numbness or difficulty walking). But application of this novel theory appears reasonably safe. Most of us could certainly do with a little less protein, especially when it comes from animal sources. There is also some preliminary data that suggest vitamin B_6 may be helpful for a number of medical conditions including asthma, PMS, and carpal tunnel syndrome (a pinched nerve in the wrist that can lead to sensations of pins and needles, numbness, and pain.) When vitamin B_6 is taken in doses of 10 to 25 mg per day it appears quite safe. Anyone contemplating regular daily doses of 50 mg or higher should consult a physician.

Selenium

Selenium is a fascinating mineral that is found naturally in the ground and in the food we eat. It has antioxidant properties

Selenium
(organic form derived from brewer's yeast preferred over inorganic sodium selenite) Antioxidant, anticancer potential. May protect against heart disease. Dose recommended = 50 to 100 micrograms organic selenium/ day.
★ ★ ★

and many studies have suggested that selenium may be protective against cancer, especially of the breast, bladder, skin, and colon. There is also evidence that low selenium levels are associated with increased heart attack risk.[100]

Since the selenium content of the soil varies considerably by geographic area, epidemiologists have tried to correlate levels of this mineral with cardiovascular disease. They have found that heart attacks and strokes seem to go up as soil selenium drops. Although researchers are now considering the possibility that low selenium may be important in heart disease, it is probably premature to assume that supplements can reverse or prevent atherosclerosis. On the other hand, we favor moderate selenium supplements for their anticancer potential; if there are additional cardiac benefits, what a lovely bonus. Don't be tempted to overdo, though: at high doses, selenium can be toxic.

PRESCRIPTION DRUGS

What do you do if all the preliminary steps to control cholesterol fail? If your total cholesterol/HDL cholesterol ratio is still substantially above 4.5, what comes next? Chances are good that your doctor will reach for the prescription pad. But which medicines work best and still provide a reasonable margin of safety? There is an impressive array of prescription products on pharmacy shelves with more on the way. Drug companies have seen profits skyrocket so they willingly spend millions trying to convince physicians that they have a magic bullet to control cholesterol.

One friend told us about the New Orleans waiter who bragged about a new candy bar medicine called **Cholybar** (cholestyramine). According to the waiter you could eat all the eggs, prawns in butter, or cheesecake you wanted as long as you snacked on a **Cholybar** that would counteract such excess.

Sorry. There is no fairy godmother. There is no magic wand and there are no perfect cholesterol-lowering drugs that can act as antidotes to dietary disasters. The medications are all expensive, they all have the potential to cause some pretty unpleasant side effects, and to date none have been proven to actually prolong life.

Lopid

Of all the medications on the market, **Lopid** (gemfibrozil) is one of the more effective and better tolerated. A Finnish study followed 2,051 men between forty and fifty-five years of age who had high cholesterol levels. Except for their blood-fat problem they were healthy. **Lopid** lowered LDL cholesterol 11 percent and raised HDL cholesterol 11 percent. Triglycerides fell 41 percent. At the end of five years, the men on **Lopid** had 34 percent fewer heart attacks. [101]

Lopid does have a downside, however. It may increase the risk of gallstones. Periodic monitoring of gallbladder function is necessary and if stones are suspected, **Lopid** should be stopped immediately. The other concern is cancer. Animal studies have linked liver and testicular tumors to **Lopid**, but only at higher doses than those used in humans. Whether **Lopid** poses a risk of cancer in humans is still uncertain. Less serious side effects include indigestion (7 percent) and stomach pain (6 percent). Uncommon side effects include diarrhea, nausea, flatulence, dizziness, blurred vision, headache, numbness or nerve tingling, lowered libido, and impotence. Anyone with kidney, liver or gallbladder disease should avoid **Lopid**. Periodic blood tests are essential for liver function and glucose.

Mevacor

Mevacor (lovastatin) is the hottest cholesterol-lowering drug on the market. It was introduced with great fanfare and quickly became the most prescribed anticholesterol drug in the country. It has fewer side effects than most other medications in this class and is one of the most effective when it comes to lowering LDL cholesterol and triglycerides. But **Mevacor** does not raise good cholesterol the way niacin and **Lopid** do. And new research raises concern that in some people **Mevacor** may actually increase one important risk factor for atherosclerosis called Lp(a). [102] The drug may also raise liver enzymes and increase the risk of cataracts. The company recommends that "liver function tests be performed before treatment begins, every 4–6 weeks during the

Lopid
(gemfibrozil)
Does it all: Lowers total cholesterol, bad LDL cholesterol, and triglycerides. Raises good HDL cholesterol. Reduces heart attack risk.
Side effects: Uncommon. GI upset (nausea, stomach pain). Biggest concern is an increased risk of gallstones.

★ ★

first 15 months of therapy with lovastatin and periodically thereafter in all patients." Eye exams are also suggested early in treatment and annually thereafter.

We are somewhat concerned that certain animal species tested with large doses of **Mevacor** developed malignant tumors. A chemically similar drug, compactin, caused lymphomas in dogs. At this time it is unclear whether there is any risk of cancer in humans. Rare side effects include muscle pains, hepatitis, insomnia, numbness or nerve tingling, gas, stomach cramps, rash, headache, and blurred vision. At this writing, there is still no evidence that **Mevacor** reduces coronary heart disease or prolongs life, and long-term safety has not been established.

After all is said and done, the benefits of niacin as a cholesterol controller are hard to beat. It is more effective than most other prescription drugs when it comes to lowering all the bad lipids (total cholesterol, LDL, Lp(a), VLDL, and triglycerides). Niacin raises good HDL cholesterol 25–50 percent. It is also much less expensive than all the other

Other Cholesterol-Lowering Drugs [103–106]

Medication	Lipid Effect	Side Effects
cholestyramine (8–24 g) **Cholybar** **Questran**	⇓ Total cholesterol 8.5–20 percent ⇓ LDL cholesterol 12.6–30 percent ⇑ Triglycerides	Constipation (29%), Heartburn (17%), Belching (9%), Nausea (8%) Stomach pain, Bloating, Flatulence Block absorption of vitamins A, D, E, & K & folic acid
colestipol (10–30 g) **Colestid**	(These medications have been shown to lower coronary heart disease by one third or more.)	May ⇑ liver enzymes Unpleasant gritty aftertaste
probucol (1000 mg) **Lorelco**	⇓ Total cholesterol 10–15% ⇓ LDL cholesterol 10-40% ⇓ Good HDL cholesterol is reduced 8–30% (undesirable lipid effect)	Diarrhea (8–10%) Stomach pain Nausea Flatulence

(unique antioxidant action may make this drug more promising than previously anticipated in protecting against atherosclerosis) [107] medications on the market. Most important, it is the only drug that has actually demonstrated improved longevity over the long haul. And that's what this cholesterol craze is supposed to be all about.

Not everyone can handle the niacin flush (even when the drug is taken with food or when an aspirin is swallowed thirty minutes to an hour beforehand). Low-dose, time-release formulations (such as the one supplied by Bronson Pharmaceuticals) may offer an acceptable alternative as long as liver function is carefully monitored. Then again, some people should never take niacin. They include anyone with a history of stomach ulcers, liver disease, gout, diabetes, or glaucoma. If niacin is out, then **Lopid** is a strong second choice and if you can stand it, **Questran** has a proven track record, too. For really elevated levels, **Mevacor** does have its advocates. **Lorelco** may ultimately prove to be far more important than previously thought if its unique antioxidant action is proven to prevent atherosclerosis in humans. No matter which medicine is selected, medical supervision and follow-up is essential!

FUTURE DRUGS

As the cholesterol crusade gathered converts, drug company profits soared. The pressure to create ever more effective cholesterol-lowering drugs has picked up steam. Even though questions remain about safety and long-term survival benefits, we are destined to see more products hit pharmacy shelves in coming years.

The newest additions to the sweepstakes are related to **Mevacor** (lovastatin). They are pravastatin (**Pravachol**), simvastatin (**Zocor**), and fluvastatin (XU-62-320). These drugs are very good at reducing LDL and total cholesterol. **Pravachol** may have a slight advantage over **Mevacor** because it works more selectively in the liver instead of throughout the body. And fluvastatin does not appear to get into the brain as easily as **Mevacor** and thus may be less likely to cause any sleep disturbances. No matter what new advances the pharmaceutical industry is likely to develop, none will eliminate the need to eat wisely and get enough exercise.

Heart Disease and Angina

Even if you do everything right, there is no guarantee that you will avoid coronary artery disease. You can certainly cut your risks but sometimes even the best diet and drug treatment cannot overcome genetics. And that is why the lowly aspirin tablet gets our highest five-star rating. We are hard put to think of a more miraculous medicine than acetylsalicylic acid.

ASPIRIN FOR THE HEART

Willow bark, from which aspirin was developed, has been used at least since the fifth century B.C. when Hippocrates prescribed it to relieve pain. Although aspirin has been available for more than ninety years, it wasn't until the 1950s that doctors began writing about the drug's potential to prevent heart attacks. Even then, most health professionals discounted the early data and bad-mouthed the lowly aspirin tablet.

It took thirty more years before the medical establishment began to take aspirin seriously for heart-attack prevention. Three major studies proved that high-risk patients (such as those with unstable angina or previous heart attacks) could reduce the risk of a coronary by at least 50 percent with regular aspirin.[108] But even such good news did not convince doctors that otherwise healthy people would benefit the same way.

Logically, they decided to study themselves to find out once and for all how good aspirin really is. The Physicians' Health Study recruited 22,071 healthy doctors. Half (11,037) took one regular strength (325 mg) aspirin tablet every other day. The other 11,034 physicians took an identical placebo. After roughly five years, the researchers took a preliminary peek at the data to see how the docs were faring. The results were so startling they decided to halt this part of the experiment early (it was supposed to run at least three more years).

In July 1989 the final report announced that alternate-day aspirin had already reduced the risk of a heart attack by nearly half (44 percent).[109] The Steering Committee for the Physicians' Health Study felt it would be unethical to withold such informa-

Aspirin (acetylsalicylic acid)

The gold standard for minor pain and inflammation.
Reduces the risk of heart attack up to 50 percent.
Reduces the risk of thrombotic stroke (caused by a blood clot).
Common side effects: stomach irritation and ulceration. May slightly increase the risk of a bleeding stroke (hemorrhagic stroke).
Avoid if there is uncontrolled hypertension or a bleeding tendency. Potential adverse interactions with dozens of other drugs. Medical supervision appropriate.

★ ★ ★ ★ ★

tion, and indeed, 74 percent of the doctors taking placebo opted for aspirin once the benefit was revealed.

The only real negative findings were a slight risk of ulcers and a trend (not statistically significant) toward increased hemorrhagic (bleeding) stroke. Although aspirin reduces the risk of a thrombotic (clotting) stroke, there is a fear that when the blood is thinned, susceptible people may be more likely to bleed into the brain. That is why medical supervision is important to assess long-term risks and benefits. People with uncontrolled high blood pressure or a tendency to bleed should probably stay away from aspirin, as should those with asthma, ulcers, and of course those with an allergy to aspirin.

Children's Aspirin: Not Just for Children

One of the biggest debates about aspirin these days is how low you can go with the dose and still maintain benefits for the heart. Doctors used to think you needed at least one to four tablets daily to reduce the risk of cardiovascular disease. Now we know that half a tablet daily or one tablet every other day is extremely effective. Some data suggest that the optimal dose may actually be as little as 80 mg per day (a child's aspirin dose—one fourth of a regular-strength tablet).[110] This amount is as good as 600–1000 mg at blocking platelet aggregation, which is important in blood clot formation. It is now possible to buy **St. Joseph Adult Chewable Aspirin** (81 mg each). Until the final word is in, however, doctors may want to stick with one, tried-and-true, regular-strength tablet every other day in their healthy patients. People with angina may need one tablet daily.[111]

Halting a Heart Attack

Most people think it will never happen to them. "Me have a heart attack—no way! I eat oat bran, olive oil, and fish." When it actually happens, denial is the first reaction. "Oh, I'm just having a touch of indigestion, dear. Pass the bicarb." One poor fellow started experiencing chest pains at work in the middle of the afternoon and pretended it was heartburn. He drove all the way home during rush-hour traffic as the pain continued to get

What if You're Having a Heart Attack?

Symptoms that require immediate action:

- Deep crushing chest pain lasting more than two minutes.
- Pressure, fullness, aching or squeezing pain in the center of the chest.
- Pain that spreads to neck, jaw, shoulders, arms, or back.
- Sensation of weakness in left arm muscles.
- Heart attacks may be accompanied by shortness of breath, nausea, sweating, dizziness, fainting, and confusion.
- Older people may not experience chest pain.

Action:

- Call ambulance.
- One aspirin if not contraindicated by other medication.

worse. When he walked in the door and his wife took one look at him she knew something dreadful was happening. She insisted on calling an ambulance, even though her husband protested bitterly that he was fine. By the time he arrived at the hospital, over five hours had elapsed since his heart attack had begun.

In the bad old days it might not have mattered very much if people dallied. Before defibrillators, there wasn't a whole lot doctors could do if you had a heart attack except watch, wait, and give you morphine to ease the pain and oxygen to assist in breathing. Today, emergency medical personnel can defibrillate a heart that has stopped beating effectively and they can even reverse a heart attack in midstream with clot busters like **Activase** (alteplase), **Eminase** (anistreplase), and **Streptase** (streptokinase).

Clot busters work best if they are given as soon as possible after a heart attack. But even when someone responds immediately to chest pain, hospitals are not always prepared to react promptly. Between the admission forms, the initial ER workup (EKG and blood work), and pharmacy bureaucracy, hours can slip away before a patient actually gets the heart-saving medicine. Dr. Eric Topol, one of the country's most experienced clot-busting cardiologists, complains that "it's amazing that it takes so long. Typically, I will get a call at 10 p.m. about a 60-year-old man who has come in with an anterior MI [myocardial infarction or heart attack]. I'll say, 'Let's treat,' and the typical situation is that it's midnight before the patient is actually getting therapy."[112]

So what should you do if you suspect you are experiencing a heart attack? Don't waste a minute; call an ambulance. Even if it turns out to be a bad case of heartburn, there is no reason to gamble on what could be a life-and-death situation. You may also want to consider popping down an aspirin tablet or plopping and fizzing with **Alka-Seltzer** (for faster aspirin action) while you wait for the cavalry to arrive. Some doctors are starting to advocate one aspirin at the first sign of chest pain. A landmark study demonstrated that when aspirin is administered at the time of a heart attack and continued for five weeks it could dramatically reduce the death rate.[113] The authors suggest that if a heart attack is suspected, "it might well be appropriate to start it [aspirin] as soon as possible (in the home, ambulance, or emergency room) provided there are no clear contraindications."[114]

The anticlotting benefits of aspirin are measurable within five minutes of a 300 mg dose. This has led several physicians at the William Beaumont Army Medical Center to propose "the earliest possible use of aspirin in the face of probable ischemic chest pain. The on-site use of aspirin by the public in the hours to minutes of insidious pain before medical attention is sought has the potential to thwart thrombus [clot] development, slow propagation, delay infarction, and reduce the incidence of sudden death outside hospital and may further improve the prospects for patients who reach hospital. The risk of one-time aspirin use in this setting seems very small."[115]

ANGINA

Just as it's possible to have a heart attack even if you are careful about your diet, so too it is possible to develop atherosclerosis because of plaque buildup in the coronary arteries. Author James Fixx was a marathon runner who averaged ten miles a day. He ate sensibly, sticking to low fat foods and plenty of fiber. He died anyway at age fifty-two of a heart attack. His arteries were plugged with plaque. Once again the genes played a nasty trick. His father had suffered a heart attack at the early age of thirty-five and died at forty-three of heart disease. Even Fixx's extraordinary physical conditioning apparently couldn't overcome his genetic predisposition.

We don't know if James Fixx suffered with angina because he didn't volunteer that information. It would be surprising if he didn't occasionally suffer some chest pain with as many clogged arteries as he had. (Some people never do suffer chest pain even though their arteries are blocked.) Angina usually occurs when there is underlying atherosclerosis, or narrowing of the arteries that supply the heart with blood. If the heart needs extra oxygen (because of exercise or stress) and if the blood supply is limited because the pipes are corroded, the result is often a chain of events that leads to pain, fear, and more pain.[114] As the pulse quickens and blood pressure rises, extra demands are placed on the heart. If it can't cope with them, a vicious cycle is set in motion that brings on chest pain—Mother Nature's way of telling you to slow down and relax. When such symptoms first show up, it is essential to have a cardiology workup.

The Missing Mineral

Scientists have known for years that "hard" water (high in calcium and magnesium) is associated with a lower rate of heart disease and death.[117,118] Unfortunately, people often go to some expense and trouble to soften their water with special filtration units. Magnesium deficiency is probably far more common than most people realize. Our diets tend to be low in magnesium and thiazide diuretics like hydrochlorothiazide only make this problem worse.[119]

Magnesium supplementation could be one of the best things you can do for your heart and cardiovascular system. Not only does this mineral appear to help lower blood pressure, it may also be beneficial against certain forms of angina, congestive heart failure, and irregular heart rhythms.[120–123] People on thiazide diuretics or digitalis should make certain their magnesium and potassium levels are adequate, since a deficiency may predispose them to dangerous arrhythmias. One word of caution, though. People with kidney problems should probably steer clear of magnesium supplements, as should those with certain kinds of atrioventricular heart blocks. Check with a cardiologist.

NITROGLYCERIN

Treatment of garden-variety "stable" angina (as opposed to unstable, potentially life-threatening angina) is aimed either at preventing the cycle from starting or aborting an attack before it gets a foothold. The gold standard is still sublingual (under the tongue) nitroglycerin. This drug has been around since 1847, and although manufacturers have recently tried hard to modernize with nitro skin patches, there is some doubt that they have improved on the original version. Calcium blockers work very well, too, especially if angina is brought on by spasm of the coronary arteries (see page 86).

When a nitro pill is placed under the tongue at the first sign of chest pain it can dilate blood vessels, reduce oxygen demand on the heart, and abort an angina attack in one to three minutes. It can also be used prophylactically five to ten minutes before an activity that might bring on an attack. A hundred-pill bottle is incredibly cheap, costing less than $3.00, and can carry many patients a month or more.

Sublingual nitroglycerin has one major shortcoming, though—its benefits are short-lived, lasting only thirty to sixty minutes. Longer-acting oral formulations are also affordable and can provide more sustained relief (four to eight hours), but continued use day-in and day-out makes these drugs less effective. The problem is tolerance. The body adapts quickly to continuous nitro exposure and may no longer respond during an attack of angina.

Drug companies thought they had developed the ultimate in high-tech nitroglycerin when they introduced patches— adhesive strips that look a lot like bandages. They are usually placed somewhere on the chest and the medicine is supposed to slowly penetrate the skin. They are promoted for convenience. A television commercial that appeared on the Cable Health Network in the early 1980s pushed a patch from Ciba-Geigy. You see two men in a boat fishing. When the alarm goes off on one man's wristwatch the other fellow complains that the beeps are scaring the fish. The first man responds that the alarm reminds him to take his nitroglycerin pills. The second man then brags that he doesn't need nitro pills anymore, but instead relies on **Transderm-Nitro** nitroglycerin patches. The camera comes in a for a closeup of the patch on the man's chest while the announcer tells us, "Now there's **Transderm-Nitro**. A

simple ten-second application helps protect your angina patient, with twenty-four-hour sustained blood levels."[124]

The only trouble with nitroglycerin patches is that the idea is better than the reality. Tolerance is the problem. They "rapidly become ineffective for treatment of angina pectoris if they are left in place for twenty-four hours and reapplied daily, and remain ineffective even if the dosage is progressively increased."[126] So the convenience and expense (a month's supply can run $35 to $50—more than ten times the cost of nitro pills) may not be worth it.

The only way to get any benefit from a patch is to remove it for ten to twelve hours a day, usually at night. In this manner the body has a drug-free period in which to recover responsiveness. The problem with this approach, however, is that some people report increased angina while they aren't wearing the patch. Someone who puts the patch on at seven a.m. and has to remove it at seven p.m. may experience chest pain later in the evening. For someone who experiences angina only at night, the patch may be ideal, but all in all, we would have to conclude that these high-tech patches are a costly and controversial form of angina treatment.

Anyone on nitroglycerin, especially a long-acting formulation, should keep a diary of side effects and chest pain. This can help a doctor adjust the dose until it is just right. If pain lasts longer than usual, is unexpectedly intense, or occurs in an unusual circumstance, you should contact a doctor immediately, as it could be a warning of unstable angina, a condition that requires prompt medical attention.

Beta- and Calcium-Channel-Blockers

If nitroglycerin is not good enough, or if other medical conditions, such as high blood pressure or irregular heart rhythms, require supplemental medications, which drugs work

Beta-Blockers

Corgard (nadolol)

Inderal (propanolol)
Available generically at
1/5 the cost

Inderide (propanolol +
hydrochlorothiazide)

Lopressor (metoprolol)

Tenormin (atenolol)

Tenoretic (atenolol + chorthalidone)

Side Effects

- Beware the beta-blocker blues (fatigue, mental depression, lethargy).
- Shortness of breath; may make asthma worse. Asthmatics should avoid beta-blockers if possible.
- Cold hands and feet; nerve tingling.
- Heart failure and heart block.
- Insomnia, forgetfulness, nightmares.
- May mask symptoms of low blood sugar in diabetics.
- Reduced libido and impotence.
- Cholesterol and other lipid levels may be adversely affected. Measure lipids before and during treatment.
- Never discontinue beta-blockers

Calcium-Channel-Blockers

Calcium-Channel-Blockers	Common Side Effects	Price*
Adalat (nifedipine)	Flushing, low blood pressure	$33
Calan (verapamil)	Constipation	$29
Cardene (nicardipine)	Flushing, palpitations, angina, dry mouth, stomach upset	$26
Cardizem (diltiazem)	Abnormal ECG, flushing, frequent urination	$35
Isoptin (verapamil)	Constipation	$29
Procardia (nifedipine)	Flushing, low blood pressure	$35
verapamil (generic)	Constipation	$9–$33

*Source: The Medical Letter *1989; 31:42 and* Drug Topics Red Book *1989. These prices represent approximate cost to pharmacist in 1989 for one month's treatment. Add anywhere from 25–40 percent markup to calculate price to patient.*

best? This is a judgment call that only a physician can make. Someone with high blood pressure and a heart rate that climbs too high after exercise or stress might do best on a beta-blocker.

A person with asthma, elevated cholesterol, hypertension, or certain irregular heart rhythms may do better on a calcium-channel-blocker. These drugs have certain advantages over beta blockers, and may even be able to prevent atherosclerosis.[127] An international study recently showed that **Procardia** and **Adalat** (nifedipine) substantially reduced clogging of coronary arteries.[128]

Calcium-channel-blockers may also be effective against angina, hypertension, migraine headache, Raynaud's syndrome, and exercise-induced asthma. Many doctors now consider calcium blockers a reasonable first choice for either angina or high blood pressure. Side effects are generally mild. Many patients experience no, or minor, problems. Longer-acting, sustained-release formulations (**Cardizem SR**, **Procardia XL**, **Calan SR**, and **Isoptin SR**) are slightly more convenient and may be less likely to cause adverse reactions.

Physicians sometimes work on the principle that if one is good, then two might be better. Consequently, a low-dose beta-blocker is sometimes combined with a low-dose calcium-channel blocker in the hope that angina can be controlled with fewer side effects. But a review published in the *New England Journal of Medicine* suggests that putting these two kinds of medicine together rarely produces additional antiangina benefits and will likely increase adverse reactions (up to 60 percent for some combos).[129] The author concludes that most people do better if they receive optimal treatment with one or the other.

Cardizem
(diltiazem)
One of the best-tolerated drugs for high blood pressure and angina. Fewer side effects than other calcium blockers like **Procardia**, **Cardene**, **Calan**, or **Isoptin**.
★ ★ ★ ★

Heart Rhythms

An irregular heartbeat can be scary. Sometimes arrhythmias (abnormal heartbeats) are a sign of danger. At other times they are nothing to worry about. Healthy people with no symptoms of heart disease occasionally experience extra ventricular beats during exercise, but cardiologists have found that this is rarely cause for alarm.[130]

Assuming that there is no underlying heart disease (see your doctor and check your mirror for an earlobe crease), the first step in treating ventricular arrhythmias is to eliminate caffeinated coffee, tea, and any other caffeine-containing beverages or medicine (including over-the-counter pain relievers like **Anacin**, **BC Powder**, **Cope**, **Excedrin**, and **Vanquish**). Caffeine may make the heart more susceptible to irregular beats and giving up regular coffee is a small price to pay for relief. Don't forget to make sure your potassium and magnesium (see page 82) levels are adequate, since a deficiency in these minerals may predispose to arrhythmias.

If ventricular arrhythmias still don't go away, the cardiologist is faced with a terrible dilemma. Except in extreme life-threatening situations, most of the drugs that are prescribed for such irregular heartbeats have not been shown to prolong life.[132] These medications are expensive, they often cause unpleasant side effects (diarrhea, GI upset, rash, etc.), and ironically, they may even make the heart more vulnerable to abnormal beats.

A huge $45 million study of two antiarrhythmics, **Tambocor** (flecainide) and **Enkaid** (encainide), had to be terminated abruptly when it was discovered that the drugs were associated with a "substantial increase in the sudden-death rate" and a 200 percent elevation in mortality compared with placebo.[133,134] This led the FDA to limit use of these two drugs except in the case of life-threatening ventricular tachycardia.

Cardiologists that we have consulted candidly admit that if other antiarrhythmic drugs were submitted to the same scrutiny as **Tambocor** and **Enkaid**, they might well come out as bad. One told us, "I would be astonished if quinidine (**Cardioquin**, **Duraquin**, **Quinaglute**, **Quinidex**, **Quinora**) and disopyramide

Earlobe Crease and Heart Disease

As crazy as it sounds, researchers have been reporting for years that a diagonal earlobe crease which runs at a forty-five-degree angle is strongly associated with cardiovascular disease.[131] Don't panic if you find one, but check in with a cardiologist for a more scientific workup.

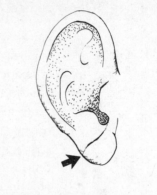

(**Norpace**) would not produce similar results if they were tested. We can make premature ventricular contractions (PVCs) go away—a splendid cosmetic effect—and still end up killing patients." A review of the scientific literature confirmed the view that except in special situations, many of the type I antiarrhythmic medications may not improve survival and instead could be lethal.[135] Experts for the respected *Medical Letter on Drugs and Therapeutics*, commenting on the new drug **Rhythmol** (propafenone), concluded

> Currently available data do not support use of any antiarrhythmic drug in asymptomatic or mildly symptomatic patients with non-sustained ventricular arrhythmias. In life-threatening ventricular arrhythmias such as sustained ventricular tachycardia, propafenone, like encainide and flecainide, is not particularly effective and may have a pro-arrythmic effect. When ventricular arrhythmias require continued oral treatment, many cardiologists prefer quinidine or procainamide, even though there is no evidence that these drugs decrease mortality in such patients, or that they are safe.[136]

Until we have newer, safer drugs, most cardiologists will continue to be very cautious when it comes to managing irregular heart rhythms, especially PVCs. One bright spot may be **Ethmozine** (moricizine), a brand new medication that is reported to have a better safety profile than previous drugs. Patients who have no other symptoms or underlying heart disease, however, may still be better served with conservative treatment.

Heart Failure

It sounds so ominous, almost like an imminent death sentence. And yet congestive heart failure (CHF) is a treatable condition that can often be well-controlled for many years. For reasons that are not always clear, the heart may begin to lose its ability to pump blood efficiently. Fatigue, breathlessness (especially after exercise), sensitivity to cold, and fluid retention in the legs and lungs are common symptoms. People often find they may start coughing and have difficulty breathing when they lie down at night. This is caused when excess fluid that has accumulated in the extremities during the day starts moving to the lungs when someone lies down.

Although deaths from strokes have dropped dramatically in recent years (down 43 percent over the last two decades) and mortality from clogged coronary arteries has also fallen (42 percent reduction), heart failure has surged (up 33 percent in adults).[137] It is estimated that over two million Americans suffer from heart failure. There are half a million hospitalizations each year.

The reason for this increase may paradoxically have to do with the improved lifestyle so many are adopting. As people cut back on fat, quit smoking, and exercise more, they reduce their risk of coronary artery disease and heart attack. The use of aspirin and other clot busters has also improved the odds of surviving a coronary. That means folks live longer. Heart failure appears to be a condition of aging. In most cases we haven't yet figured out a way to prevent it.

Coenzyme Q$_{10}$

One exciting new line of research in the treatment of congestive heart failure involves a fascinating vitaminlike nutrient called coenzyme Q$_{10}$ (CoQ$_{10}$) or ubiquinone. This substance is found naturally in your body and is essential for the smooth functioning of many biochemical reactions.

Preliminary research has shown that CoQ$_{10}$ may provide impressive improvement in the treatment of heart failure.[138–140] Not only does it seem to improve the pumping potential of the heart, it may enhance the effectiveness of traditional heart failure medications. Doses that have been employed range from 60 to 100 mg,[141] although anyone contemplating CoQ should first check with a cardiologist.

> ### *Sensible Steps*
> - Cut back on sodium.
> - Avoid alcoholic beverages.
> - Be sparing with caffeine: reduce coffee, tea, and cola consumption.

Coenzyme Q_{10} is still considered an experimental compound, but it appears quite safe, with far fewer side effects than many traditional heart medications. Nausea, although rare, is one of the few adverse reactions that has been reported. Coenzyme Q_{10} is available from many health food stores and mail-order vitamin catalogs. More research is certainly needed on this exciting substance, but respected cardiologists are beginning to consider it a viable treatment option.[142] If the preliminary research holds up, it could well become an important adjunct to traditional therapies and may even allow drugs like digitalis to be used at lower doses.

DRUG TREATMENT

Digitalis

Here is a drug that has been used for more than two hundred years for heart failure. It is still to this day harvested from the foxglove plant. The leading brand of digoxin, **Lanoxin**, is obtained from the leaves of a close cousin, *Digitalis lanata*.

Even though digoxin is one of the oldest and most commonly prescribed medications in the United States (eleventh on the doctors' hit parade), there is no proof that patients actually live longer because of this medicine. In recent years there has been a raging controversy over the benefits of **Lanoxin** versus its risks. This is a tricky drug. The therapeutic dose is very close to the toxic dose, which means it has to be monitored very carefully. Older people are especially vulnerable to serious side effects, often because of reduced kidney function.

The only consensus on digoxin treatment these days is that this drug is appropriate for an abnormal heart rhythm called atrial fibrillation. When patients have a normal heart rate and only mild-to-moderate heart failure, there appears to be a growing

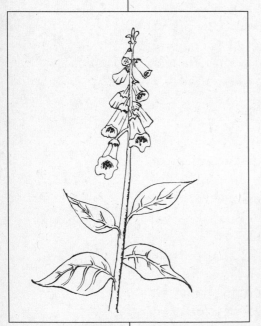

Foxglove

belief that digitalis use should be reevaluated and alternative medications considered, especially in older people.[143–145] Although digoxin can be taken safely at low doses when kidney function is normal, the drug does not appear to offer any advantage over a newer class of medications called ACE inhibitors. **Vasotec** (enalapril) and **Capoten** (captopril) appear better able to improve symptoms of heart failure and prolong life.[146–148]

Other alternatives include diuretics, such as furosemide (**Lasix**) or thiazides (hydrochlorothiazide), nitroglycerin-type medicines such as isosorbide dinitrate (**Isordil Titradose**, **Sorbitrate**, etc.), or a dilating drug like hydralazine (**Apresoline**). The successful treatment of heart failure requires that a doctor stay on top of a rapidly changing field and abandon old outmoded drugs and theories as new information becomes available. We still have a long way to go when it comes to improving the lot of patients with congestive heart failure (CHF). Dr. William Kannel, one of the country's leading cardiologists, sums it up this way: "The likelihood of reducing the incidence of CHF with new drugs, or of halting the disease's course in an individual patient, is as slim as trying to stop the polio epidemics of the 1950s by building a better iron lung. Medicine is still in the iron-lung phase where CHF is concerned."[149]

> ### *Lanoxin* (digoxin) *Adverse Reactions*
>
> - *Loss of appetite, nausea, diarrhea, stomach pain*, or *vomiting* are symptoms of digitalis overdose. If any occur, contact MD immediately!
> - *Headache, fatigue, malaise, drowsiness,* or *muscle weakness* are also early warning signs of danger.
> - Mental depression, personality change, disorientation, confusion, apathy, blurred or disturbed color vision (especially yellow or green), bad dreams, or hallucinations.
> - *Any* of the above symptoms must be brought to a doctor's urgent attention!
> - Premature ventricular contractions (PVCs) or other abnormal heartbeats can be caused by overdose. If digoxin poisioning occurs, it can lead to heart fibrillation and death.
> - Periodic blood tests for potassium and digoxin levels are an excellent idea.
> - In older people the typical daily dose is 0.125 mg tablet or 0.1 mg capsule.
> - Do not take any other prescription or OTC medication without first checking with a physician or pharmacist.

FUTURE DRUGS

The pharmaceutical industry has invested heavily in cardiovascular research. Heart disease and hypertension produce handsome profits because people have to take pills every day for the rest of their lives. Some of the most successful drugs of all time include **Capoten, Vasotec, Tenormin, Adalat, Cardizem, Mevacor, Procardia, Calan, Inderal**, and **Lopid**. The combined

ACE Inhibitors for Hypertension and Heart Failure

captopril (**Capoten**)

captopril + hydrochlorothiazide (**Capozide**)

enalapril (**Vasotec**)

enalapril + hydrochlorothiazide (**Vaseretic**)

lisinopril (**Prinivil**, **Zestril**)

lisinopril + hydrochlorothiazide (**Prinzide**, **Zestoretic**)

These medications have a number of desirable characteristics:

- They increase blood flow to organs such as brain, kidney, and heart.
- They tend to preserve potassium (except when combined with diuretics).
- They do not raise cholesterol or adversely affect other lipids.
- Patients who are susceptible to asthma, mental depression, or diabetes can tolerate these medications far better than beta-blockers.
- Sexual side effects appear to be less common with these medications than with many other antihypertensive drugs.
- Low doses are often effective, especially in older people.

Side Effects:

- Cough, especially a dry nighttime hack, can be extremely annoying. May be much more common than previously thought.
- Loss of taste or taste disturbances (more common with **Capoten**).
- Rash, often with itching.
- Kidney problems may occur. Kidney function *must* be monitored closely, especially BUN and creatinine tests. Liver enzymes should also be checked.
- Dizziness from too low blood pressure. May be a problem early in treatment or after exercise.
- Potassium buildup may occur. Potassium-sparing diuretics (**Aldactone**, **Dyazide**, **Maxzide**, **Moduretic**) should generally not be taken with ACE inhibitors. Low salt/no salt substitutes with potassium chloride, as well as potassium supplements (**K-Lyte**, **Kaon-Cl**, **Klorvess**, **Klotrix**, **Micro-K**, **Slow-K**) should also be avoided in most cases. Frequent monitoring of potassium levels is crucial.
- A rare but potentially life-threatening side effect is angioedema. The tongue and throat may swell and make breathing difficult. This is a medical emergency!

worldwide sales of these ten medications adds up to over seven billion dollars each year. It's no wonder, then, that as many of these compounds lose their patent protection to generic competition in the 1990s, companies will be anxious to replace them with newer drugs that cost even more.

At the time of this writing, it is too early to tell where the next breakthrough will come. Most of the new drugs undergoing testing and awaiting approval will be minor variations on an existing theme. We will undoubtedly see lots of new calcium-channel-blockers, such as **Baypress** (nitrendipine), **DynaCirc** (isradipine), and **Nivadil** (nilvadipine) for high blood pressure and angina. ACE inhibitors like **Accuprin** (quinapril), **Cardace** (ramipril), **Cetapril** (alacepril), **Inhibace** (cilazapril), and **Monopril** (fosinopril) will proliferate for high blood pressure and perhaps even heart failure. Most assuredly cholesterol-lowering drugs will continue to be hot items, with the addition of **Pravachol** (pravastatin) and **Zocor** (simvastatin). And companies are scrambling to come up with better rhythm regulators since existing agents are so problematic. It remains to be seen whether **Cipralan** (cifenline), **Decabid** (indecainide), and **Napa** (acecainide) are less likely to cause nausea, GI upset, dizziness, light-headedness, blurred vision, or arrhythmias.

Some of the new drugs will flame out before reaching market. Others will be widely prescribed until we uncover serious toxicity, as in the case of **Enkaid** and **Tambocor**. One new drug, **Primacor** (milrinone), was supposed to be safe and effective for patients with congestive heart failure. Many doctors were counting on it to replace **Lanoxin** (digoxin). But an important study found that old-fashioned digoxin, even with all its limitations, was better than **Primacor**, which had a tendency to cause irregular heart rhythms, palpitations, light-headedness, nervousness, and headaches.[150]

No matter what new and wonderful medications are developed for treating heart disease, there is little doubt that prevention will always be the best medicine. If we can control cholesterol without going crazy, we may be able to make a good first step toward reducing the risks of coronary artery disease and heart attacks.

Quick Takes

- Save your heart by trading in cynical mistrust for a little understanding. When you put yourself in the other person's shoes it's harder to be hostile. Appreciate your accomplishments, Type As, but don't bully.

- Cholesterol counts, but don't get carried away. The best single estimate of your risk appears to be the ratio of total cholesterol to HDL cholesterol. Anything below 4.5 is good news.

- There is a growing suspicion that very low cholesterol may increase the risk of a bleeding stroke. And we don't yet understand why so many of the people saved from heart disease by cholesterol-lowering drugs appear more vulnerable to violent or accidental death.

- Forget oat bran. Its only apparent cholesterol-lowering power is to fill you up so you won't have room for high fat foods. If you want soluble fiber, eat lots of fruits and vegetables or buy some psyllium (**Correctol Powder, Fiberall, Metamucil**).

- Nibbling is great for controlling cholesterol—the more snacks the better, provided you keep fat and calories within reason.

- Fish is fantastic! The more you eat the lower your risk of heart attack. Add onions, garlic, olive oil, and wine and you really can't go wrong.

- Give canola oil (Puritan or other brands) the blue ribbon for least saturated fat and most omega-3 fatty acids. It is also high in good monounsaturated fatty acids. This should be your number-one choice for cooking and baking.

- If you like coffee, be moderate. The latest episode in this ongoing saga suggests that regular filtered coffee does not raise cholesterol. Decaffeinated, on the other hand, may not be as good as most people think.

- If we could take only one cholesterol-lowering compound to a desert island, it would be niacin. This vitamin/drug is one of the cheapest and most effective agents on pharmacy shelves. It can, however, do nasty things to the liver so periodic liver tests are essential.

- Pantethine is growing in popularity. This vitamin derivative may be almost as effective as niacin and even safer. More research is needed but preliminary results are encouraging.

- **Lopid** looks good for cholesterol control, but you better watch your gallbladder. We wish the tumor studies were more reassuring. Ditto for **Mevacor**.

- Aspirin gets our highest rating—★★★★★! Studies have shown that either half an aspirin a day or one tablet every other day can lower the risk of heart attack by up to 50 percent. We can't think of cheaper life insurance. Not everyone should take aspirin, however, and if you are planning to follow this program for the rest of your life you definitely need a physician's supervision.

- If you think you're having a heart attack (see page 79), call an ambulance and ask about an aspirin. This may be the best home clot-buster you can get for emergency action.

- Nitroglycerin may be over two hundred years old, but it's still good for treating angina. The high-priced, high-tech patches lose their effectiveness if worn more than twelve hours at a time.

- **Cardizem** is one of the most effective and best tolerated drugs for both angina and high blood pressure. **Vasotec** is a strong contender for hypertension and congestive heart failure.

- Palpitations are scary, but unless the doctor thinks they are serious, conservative treatment is best. Many of the drugs used to control abnormal heart rhythms can themselves cause arrhythmias.

- Heart failure is a mystery. Doctors still don't know how to prevent it in most cases. **Lanoxin** (digoxin) is a tricky drug that requires frequent monitoring to avoid toxicity. Older people are especially vulnerable.

References

[1] Swales, J.D. "Salt Saga Continued: Salt Has Only Small Importance in Hypertension." *Br. Med. J.* 1988; 297:307–308.

[2] Intersalt Cooperative Research Group. "Intersalt: An International Study of Electrolyte Excretion and Blood Pressure: Results for 24 Hour Urinary Sodium and Potassium Excretion." *Br. Med. J.* 1988; 297:319–328.

[3] "Too Much Salt?" *Consumer Reports* 1990; 55:48–50.

[4] MacGregor, G., et al. "Double-blind Study of Three Sodium Intakes and Long-term Effects of Sodium Restriction in Essential Hypertension." *Lancet* 1989; II:1244–1247.

[5] Australian National Health and Medical Research Council Dietary Salt Study Management Committee. "Fall in Blood Pressure with Modest Reduction in Dietary Salt Intake in Mild Hypertension." *Lancet* 1989; I:399–402.

[6] Williams, Redford. *The Trusting Heart*, New York: Times Books, 1989 176–196.

[7] Moore, Thomas J. "The Cholesterol Myth." *The Atlantic* 1989; 264(3):37–70.

[8] Dolnick, Edward. "Le Paradoxe Francais." *In Health* 1990; 4(3):40–47.

[9] Brett, Allan S. "Treating Hypercholesterolemia: How Should Practicing Physicians Interpret the Published Data for Patients?" *N. Engl. J. Med.* 1989; 213:676–679.

[10] Taylor, William C., et al. "Cholesterol Reduction and Life Expectancy: A Model Incorporating Multiple Risk Factors." *Ann. Int. Med.* 1987; 106:605–614.

[11] Gordon, David J., and Rifkind, Basil, M. "High-Density Lipoprotein—The Clinical Implications of Recent Studies." *N. Engl. J. Med.* 1989; 321:1311–1316.

[12] Horwitz, Nathan. "CHD With Low-Chol Camouflage." *Medical Tribune* 1988; 29(35):1–8.

[13] Margolis, Simeon, and Dobs, Adrian S. "Nutritional Management of Plasma Lipid Disorders." *J. Am. Col. Nutr.* 1989; 8(Suppl.):34S–45S.

[14] Seed, Mary, et al. "Relation of Serum Lipoprotein(a) Concentration and Apoliprotein(a) Phenotype to Coronary Heart Disease in Patients with Familial Hypercholesterolemia." *N. Engl. J. Med.* 1990; 322:1494–1499.

[15] Pollner, Fran. "Lipid Control Gets Even Stickier as Data on 'Unloading' Accrue." *Medical World News* 1990(June 11); 12–13.

[16] Fackelmann, Kathy A. "Japanese Stroke Clues: Are There Risks to Low Cholesterol? *Science News* 1989; 135:250–253.

[17] Iso-Hiroyasu, et al. "Serum Cholesterol Levels and Six-Year Mortality from Stroke in 350,977 Men Screened for the Multiple Risk Factor Intervention Trial." *N. Engl. J. Med.* 1989; 320:904–910.

[18] Fackelmann, op. cit., p. 250.

[19] Reed, D., et al. "Lipids and Lipoproteins as Predictors of Coronary Heart Disease, Stroke and Cancer in the Honolulu Heart Program." *Am. J. Med.* 1986; 80:871–878.

[20] Forette, Bernard, et al. "Cholesterol as Risk Factor for Mortality in Elderly Women." *Lancet* 1989; 1:868–870.

[21] Isles, C.G., et al. "Plasma Cholesterol, Coronary Heart Disease, and Cancer in the Renfrew and Paisley Survey." *Br. Med. J.* 1989; 298:920–924.

[22] Editorial. "Low Cholesterol and Increased Risk." *Lancet* 1989; 1:1423–1425.

[23] Cotton, Paul. "Evidence Mounting on Both Sides of Debate over Cholesterol Levels." *Medical World News* 1989 (Oct. 23); 12–13.

[24] Brett, op. cit.

[25] Forette, op. cit., p. 870.

[26] Based on a combination of U.S. recommendations and the guidelines of the European Atherosclerosis Society (EAS). Assumes no other risk ractors such as smoking, hypertension, or genetic predisposition.

[27] Vega, Gloria Lena, and Grundy, Scott M. "Comparison of Lovastatin and Gemfibrosil in Normolipidemic Patients with Hypoalphalipoproteinemia." *JAMA* 1989; 262:3148–3153.

[28] Bogdanich, Walt. "Inaccuracy in Testing Cholesterol Hampers War on Heart Disease." *Wall Street Journal* 1987 (Feb. 3);209(23):1–24.

[29] Loupe, D.E. "Turning up the Dirt in Cholesterol Screens." *Science News* 1989; 136:359.

[30] "Rapid Cholesterol Test for Physicians' Offices." *FDA Drug Bulletin* 1988; 18(2):1.

[31] Pappas, Nancy. "Oat Bran: Still the Star?" *Hippocrates* 1989; September/October:18–20.

[32] Swain, Janis F., et al. "Comparison of the Effects of Oat Bran and Low–Fiber Wheat on Serum Lipoprotein Levels and Blood Pressure." *N. Engl. J. Med.* 1990; 322:147–152.

[33] Jenkins, David J.A., et al. "Nibbling Versus Gorging: Metabolic Advantages of Increased Meal Frequency." *N. Engl. J. Med.* 1989; 321: 929–934.

[34] Anderson, J.W., et al. "Cholesterol-Lowering Effects of Psyllium Hydrophilic Mucilloid for Hypercholesterolemic Men." *Arch. Intern. Med.* 1988; 148:292–296.

[35] Bell, Larry, P., et al. "Cholesterol-Lowering Effects of Psyllium Hydrophilic Mucilloid." *JAMA* 1989; 261:3419–3423.

[36] Burr, M.L., et al. "Effects of Changes in Fat, Fish, and Fibre Intakes on Death and Myocardial Reinfarction: Diet and Reinfarction Trial (DART)." *Lancet* 1989; II:757–761.

[37] Kromhout, D., et al. "The Inverse Relation Between Fish Consumption and 20-year Mortality from Coronary Heart Disease." *N. Engl. J. Med.* 1985; 312:1205–1209.

[38] Shekelle, R.B., et al. "Fish Consumption and Mortality from Coronary Heart Disease." *N. Engl. J. Med.* 1985; 313:820.

[39] Norell, S.E., et al. "Fish Consumption and Mortality from Coronary Heart Disease." *Br. Med. J.* 1986; 293:426.

[40] Rogers, S., et al. "Effects of a Fish Oil Supplement on Serum Lipids, Blood Pressure, Bleeding Time, Hemostatic and Rheological Variables: A Double Blind Randomised Controlled Trial in Healthy Volunteers." *Atherosclerosis* 1987; 63:137–143.

[41] McLennan, P.L., et al. "Fish and the Heart." *Lancet* 1989; II:1451.

[42] Riemersma, R.A., and Sargent, C.A. "Dietary Fish and Ischaemic Arrhythmias." *J. Intern. Med.* 1989;225(Suppl. 1):111–116.

[43] Deck, C. and Radack, K. "Effects of Modest Doses of Omega-3 Fatty Acids on Lipids and Lipoproteins in Hypertriglyceridemic Subjects." *Arch. Int. Med.* 1989; 149:1857–1862.

[44] Saynor, R., and Gillott, T. "Fish Oil Revisited." *Lancet* 1989; II:810–811.

[45] Dujovne, Carlos A., and Harris, William S. "The Role of Fish Oils in the Treatment of Hyperlipidemia." *Modern Med.* 1989; 57:69–79.

[46] Dehmer, G.J., et al. "Reduction in the Rate of Early Restenonsis after Coronary Angioplasty by a Diet Supplemented with n-3 Fatty Acids." *N. Engl. J. Med.* 1988; 319:733–740.

[47] Reis, Gregg J., et al. "Randomised Trial of Fish Oil for Prevention of Restenosis after Coronary Angioplasty." *Lancet* 1989; I:177–181.

[48] Weinter, Bonnie H., et al. "Inhibition of Atherosclerosis by Cod-Liver Oil in a Hyperlipidemic Swine Model." *N. Engl. J. Med.* 1986; 315:841–846.

[49] Knapp, Howard R., and FitzGerald, Garret A. "The Antihypertensive Effects of Fish Oil: A Controlled Study of Polyunsaturated Fatty Acid Supplements in Essential Hypertension." *N. Engl. J. Med.* 1989; 320:1037–1043.

[50] Bønaa, Kaare H., et al. "Effect of Eicosapentaenoic and Docosahexaenoic Acids on Blood Pressure in Hypertension: A Population-Based Intervention Trial from the Tromsø Study." *N. Engl. J. Med.* 1990; 322:795–801.

[51] Bittiner, S.B., et al. "A Double-Blind, Randomized, Placebo-Controlled Trial of Fish Oil in Psoriasis." *Lancet* 1988; II:378–380.

[52] Kremer, J.M., et al. "Fish-Oil Fatty Acid Supplementation in Active Rheumatoid Arthritis." *Ann. Intern. Med.* 1987; 106:497–503.

[53] Knapp, op. cit.

[54] Dujovne, op. cit.

[55] Zaidins, Mindy G. Hermann. "Is Public Interest in Fish Fading?" *Environmental Nutrition* 1989; April:3.

[56] Dupont, Jacqueline, et al. "Food Safety and Health Effects of Canola Oil." *J. Am. Col. Nutr.* 1989; 8(5):360–375.

[57] Mensink, Ronald P., and Katan, Martijn B. "Effect of a Diet Enriched with Monounsaturated or Polyunsaturated Fatty Acids on Levels of Low-Density and High-Density Lipoprotein Cholesterol in Healthy Women and Men." *N. Engl. J. Med.* 1989; 321:436–461.

[58] Grundy, Scott M. "Comparison of Monounsaturated Fatty Acids and Carbohydrates for Lowering Plasma Cholesterol." *N. Engl. J. Med.* 1986; 314:745–758.

[59] Williams, Paul T., et al. "Associations of Dietary Fat, Regional Adiposity, and Blood Pressure in Men." *JAMA* 1987; 257:3251–3256.

[60] Trevisan, Maurizio, et al. "Consumption of Olive Oil, Butter, and Vegetable Oils and Coronary Heart Disease Risk Factors." *JAMA* 1990; 263:688–692.

[61] Kleijnen, J., et al. "Garlic, Onions and Cardiovascular Risk Factors, A Review of the Evidence from Human Experiments with Emphasis on Commercially Available Preparations." *Br. J. Clin. Pharmacol.* 1989; 28:525–544.

[62] Grunwald, Jorg. "Garlic." *Lancet* 1990; 335:115.

[63] Block, Eric. Personal communication, January 25, 1990.

[64] Hurley, Jayne, and Schmidt, Stephen. "A Clove a Day?" *Nutrition Action Healthletter* 1989; December:8–9.

[65] Rendu F., et al. "Ajoene, the Antiplatelet Compound Derived from Garlic, Specifically Inhibits Platelet Release Reaction by Affecting the Plasma Membrane Internal Microviscosity." *Biochem. Pharmacol.* 1989; 38:1321–1328.

[66] Roser, David. "Garlic." *Lancet* 1990; 335:114–115.

[67] Grunwald, op. cit.

[68] Block, op. cit.

[69] Kleijnen, op. cit.

[70] Harenberg , J., et. al. "Effect of Dried Garlic on Blood Coagulation, Fibrinolysis, Platelet Aggregation and Serum Cholesterol Levels in Patients With Hyperlipoproteinemia." *Atherosclerosis* 1988; 74:247–249.

[71] Misawa, K., et al. "An Epidemiological Study on the Relationships among HDL-Cholesterol, Smoking and Obesity." *Nippon Eiseigaku Zasshi* 1989; 44:725–732.

[72] Margolis, op. cit.

[73] Frimpong, N.A., and Lapp, J.A. "Effects of Moderate Alcohol Intake in Fixed or Variable Amounts on Concentration of Serum Lipids and Liver Enzymes in Healthy Young Men." *Am. J. Clin. Nutr.* 1989; 50:987–991.

[74] Spagnolo, A., et al. "High Density Lipoprotein Cholesterol Distribution and Predictive Power in Some Italian Populations Studies." *Eur. J. Epidemiol.* 1989; 5:328–335.

[75] Fraser, G.E., and Babaali, H. "Determinants of High Density Lipoprotein Cholesterol in Middle-Aged Seventh-Day Adventist Men and Their Neighbors." *Am. J. Epidemiol.* 1989; 130:958–965.

[76] Gordon T., et al. "Diet and its Relation to Coronary Heart Disease and Death in Three Populations." *Circulation* 1981; 63:500–515.

[77] Thelle, D.S., et al. "The Tromso Heart Study. Does Coffee Raise Serum Cholesterol? *N. Engl. J. Med.* 1983; 308:1454–1457.

[78] "Coffee: Benign Beverage or Dangerous Drink?" *Environmental Nutrition* 1989; 12:1–3.

[79] Wilson, P.W., et al. "Is Coffee Consumption a Contributor to Cardiovascular Disease? Insights from the Framingham Study." *Arch. Intern. Med.* 1989; 149:1169–1172.

[80] Aro, A., et al. "Boiled Coffee Increases Serum Low Density Lipoprotein Concentration." *Metabolism* 1987; 36:1027–1030.

[81] Bonna, Kaare, et al. "Coffee and Cholesterol: Is it All in the Brewing? The Tromso Study." *Br. Med. J.* 1988; 297:1103–1104.

[82] Bak, Annette A.A., and Grobbee, Diederick E. "The Effect of Serum Cholesterol Levels of Coffee Brewed by Filtering or Boiling." *N. Engl. J. Med.* 1989; 321:1432–1437.

[83] Bishop, Jerry E. "Decaffeinated Coffee May Increase Levels of 'Bad' Form of Cholesterol." *Wall Street Journal* 1989; Nov. 14:B4.

[84] Illingworth, D. Roger. "Lipid–Lowering Drugs: An Overview of Indications and Optimum Therapeutic Use." *Drugs* 1987; 33:259–279.

[85] Conner, Paul L., et al. "Fifteen Year Mortality in Coronary Drug Project Patients: Long-Term Benefit with Niacin." *J. Am. Coll. Cardiol.* 1986; 8:1245–1255.

[86] Figge, Helen L., et. al. "Comparison of Excretion of Nicotinuric Acid After Ingestion of Two Controlled Release Nicotinic Acid Preparations in Man." *J. Clin. Pharmacol.* 1988; 28:1136–1140.

[87] Knopp, Robert H., et al. "Contrasting Effects of Unmodified and Time-Release Forms of Niacin on Lipoproteins in Hyperlipidemic Subjects: Clues to Mechanism of Action of Niacin." *Metabolism* 1985; 34:642–650.

[88] Ibid.

[89] Heart Health. "Sustained-Release Niacin Worsens Side Effects." *Medical Nutrition* 1990; Winter:6–7.

[90] Henkin, Yaakov, et al. "Rechallenge with Crystalline Niacin after Drug-Induced Hepatitis from Sustained-Release Niacin." *JAMA* 1990; 264:241–243.

[91] Hodis, Howard N. "Acute Hepatic Failure Associated with the Use of Low-Dose Sustained-Release Niacin." (letter) *JAMA* 1990; 264:181.

[92] Luria, M.H. "Effect of Low-Dose Niacin on High-Density Lipoprotein Cholesterol and Total Cholesterol/High Density Lipoprotein Cholesterol Ratio." *Arch. Intern. Med.* 1988; 11:2493–2495.

[93] Medical Meeting Digest. "Nicotinic Acid: Lower Dose Effective, Reduces Side Effects." *Modern Med.* 1988; 56(2):37.

[94] Alderman, J., et al. "Effect of a Modified, Well-Tolerated Niacin Regimen on Serum Total Cholesterol, High Density Lipoprotein Cholesterol and the Cholesterol to High Density Lipoprotein Ratio." *Am. J. Cardiol.* 1989; 64:725–729.

[95] "Low-Dose Niacin: Effect on Lipid Levels." *Physicians' Drug Alert* 1989; 10(11):81.

[96] Bertolini, S., et al. "Lipoprotein Changes Induced by Pantethine in Hyperlipoproteinemic Patients: Adults and Children." *Int. J. Clin. Pharmacol. Ther. Toxicol.* 1986; 24:630–637.

[97] Donati, C., et al. "Pantethine, Diabetes Mellitus and Atherosclerosis. Clinical Study of 1045 Patients." *Clin. Ther.* 1989; 128:411–422.

[98] Arsenio, L, et al. "Effectiveness of Long-Term Treatment with Pantethine in Patients with Dyslipidemia." *Clin. Ther.* 1986; 8:537–545.

[99] Gruberg, Edward R., and Raymond, Stephen A. *Beyond Cholesterol: Vitamin B6, Arteriosclerosis, and Your Heart,* New York: St. Martin's Press, 1981, *xv.*

[100] Kok, Frans J., et al. "Decreased Selenium Levels in Acute Myocardial Infarction." *JAMA* 1989; 261:1161–1164.

[101] Manninen, V., et al. "Lipid Alterations and Decline in the Incidence of Coronary Heart Disease in the Helsinki Heart Study." *JAMA* 1988; 260:641–651.

[102] Kostner, Gerhard M., et al. "Clinical Investigation: HMG CoA Reductase Inhibitors Lower LDL Cholesterol Without Reducing Lp(a) Levels." *Circulation* 1989; 80:1313–1319.

[103] Blum, Conrad B., and Levy, Robert I. "Current Therapy for Hypercholesterolemia." *JAMA* 1989; 261:3582–3587.

[104] Illingworth, op. cit.

[105] "Choice of Cholesterol-Lowering Drugs." *Med. Let.* 1988; 30:85–88.

[106] Gwynne, John T., and Lawrence, Mary Katherine. "Current Concepts in the Evaluation and Treatment of Hypercholesterolemia." *Mod. Med.* 1989; 57(March):126–136.

[107] Steinberg, Daniel, et al. "Beyond Cholesterol: Modifications of Low-Density Lipoprotein That Increase Its Atherogenicity." *N. Engl. J. Med.* 1989; 320:915–925.

[108] Fuster, Valentin, et al. "Aspirin in the Prevention of Coronary Disease." *N. Engl. J. Med.* 1989; 321:183–185.

[109] Steering Committee of the Physicians' Health Study Research Group. "Final Report on the Aspirin Component of the Ongoing Physicians' Health Study." *N. Engl. J. Med.* 1989; 321:129–135.

[110] Lorenz, Reinhard L., et al. "Superior Antiplatelet Action of Alternate Day Pulsed Dosing Versus Split Dose Administration of Aspirin." *Am. J. Cardiol.* 1989; 64:1185–1188.

[111] Friesinger, Gottlieb C., and Leigovits, Eric R. "Management of Stable Angina Pectoris: Evaluation and Therapy." *Mod. Med.* 1989; 57(12):40–53.

[112] Monagan, David. "Thrombosis Delivery System Occluded: Most MI Victims Are Missing Out." *Medical Trib.* 1989; 30(31):8.

[113] ISIS-2 (Second International Study Of Infarct Survival) Collaborative Group. "Randomised Trial of Intravenous Streptokinase, Oral Aspirin, Both or Neither Among 17,187 Cases of Suspected Acute Myocardial Infarction.: ISIS–2." *Lancet* 1988; 2:349–360.

[114] Ibid.

[115] Carpenter, Alan L., and Caravalho, Joseph, Jr. "Early Public Use of Aspirin in the Face of Probable Ischaemic Chest Pain." *Lancet* 1990; 335:163.

[116] Collins, P., and Fox, K.M. "Pathophysiology of Angina." *Lancet* 1990; 335:94–96.

[117] Anderson, T.W., et al. "Ischemic Heart Disease, Water Hardness and Myocardial Magnesium." *Can. Med. Assoc. J.* 1975; 113:199.

[118] Hopps, H.C., and Feder, G.L. "Chemical Qualities of Water that Contribute to Human Health in a Positive Way." *Sci. Total Environ.* 1986; 54:207–216.

[119] Seelig, M. "Cardiovascular Consequences of Magnesium Deficiency and Loss: Pathogenesis, Prevalence and Manifestations—Magnesium and Chloride Loss in Refractory Potassium Repletion." *Am. J. Cardiol.* 1989; 63:4G–21G.

[120] Gottlieb, S.S. "Importance of Magnesium in Congestive Heart Failure." *Am. J. Cardiol.* 1989; 63:39G–42G.

[121] Whelton, P.K., and Klag, M.J. "Magnesium and Blood Pressure: Review of the Epidemiologic and Clinical Trial Experience." *Am. J. Cardiol.* 1989; 63:26G–30G.

[122] Wester, P.O., and Dyckner, T. "Magnesium and Hypertension." *J. Am. Coll. Nutr.* 1987; 6:321–328.

[123] Surawicz, Borys. "Editorials: Is Hypomagnesemia or Magnesium Deficiency Arrhythmogenic?" *J. Am. Col. Cardiol.* 1989; 14:1093–1096.

[124] "Ciba-Geigy Ads Appearing on Cable Health Network's 'Physician's Journal Update.' " *F-D-C Reports* 1983; 45(28):11.

[125] Minitran ad in the *Daily News Magazine.* 1989; Oct 9.

[126] "Nitroglycerin Patches—Do They Work?" *Medical Letter* 1989; 31:65–66.

[127] Fleckenstein, A., et al. "Experimental Antiarteriosclerotic Effects of Calcium Antagonists." *J. Clin. Pharmacol.* 1990; 30:151–154.

[128] Lichtlen, Paul R., et al. "Retardation of Angiographic Progression of Coronary Artery Disease by Nifedipine: Results of the International Nifedipine Trial on Antiatherosclerotic Therapy (INTACT)." *Lancet* 1990; 335:1109–1113).

[129] Packer, Milton. "Combined Beta-Adrenergic and Calcium-Entry Blockade in Angina Pectoris." *N. Engl. J. Med.* 1989; 320:709–718.

[130] Busby, M.J., et al. "Prevalence and Long-Term Significance of Exercise-Induced Frequent or Repetitive Ventricular Ectopic Beats in Apparently Healthy Volunteers." *J. Am. Col. Cardiol.* 1989; 14:1659–1665.

[131] Kirkham, N., et al. "Diagonal Earlobe Creases and Fatal Cardiovascular Disease: A Necropsy Study." *Br. Heart J.* 1989; 61:361–364.

[132] Skluth, Hilary, et al. "Ventricular Arrhythmias." *Postgraduate Medicine.* 1989; 85:137–153.

[133] The Cardiac Arrhythmia Suppression Trial (CAST) Investigators. "Preliminary Report: Effect of Encainide and Flecainide on Mortality in a Randomized Trial of Arrhythmia Suppression After Myocardial Infarction." *N. Engl. J. Med.* 1989; 321:406–412.

[134] Ruskin, Jeremy N. "The Cardiac Arrhythmia Suppression Trial (CAST)." *N. Eng. J. Med.* 1989; 321:386–388.

[135] Hine, Louis K., et al. "Meta-Analysis of Empirical Long-Term Antiarrhythmic Therapy After Myocardial Infarction." *JAMA* 1989; 262:3037–3040.

[136] "Propafenone for Cardiac Arrhythmias." *The Medical Letter* 1990(Apr. 20); 32:37–38.

[137] Thomas, Patricia. "Heart Failure." *Medical World News* 1989; Nov. 13; 32–38.

[138] Langsjoen, P.H., et al. "Effective and Safe Therapy with Coenzyme Q_{10} for Cardiomyopathy." *Klin. Wochenschr.* 1988; 66:583–590.

[139] Greenberg, S.M., and Frishman, W. H. "Coenzyme Q_{10}: A New Drug for Myocardial Ischemia?" *Med. Clin. North Am.* 1988; 72:243–258.

[140] Mortensen, S.A., et al. "Long-Term Coenzyme Q_{10} Therapy: A Major Advance in the Management of Resistant Myocardial Failure." *Drugs Exp. Clin. Res.* 1985; 11:581–593.

[141] Topi, P.L., et al. "Efficacy of Ubidecarenone in the Treatment of Patients with Cardiac Insufficiency." *Minerva Cardioangiol.* (Italy) 1989; 37:255–258.

[142] Greenberg, Steven, and Frishman, William H. "Co-Enzyme Q_{10}: A New Drug for Cardiovascular Disease." *J. Clin. Pharmacol.* 1990; 30:596–608.

[143] Fleg, Jerome L. "Congestive Heart Failure in the Elderly." *Journal of Geriatric Drug Therapy* 1988; 3(2):5–22.

[144] Sueta, Carla A., et al. "Reassessment of Indications for Digoxin: Are Patients Being Withdrawn? *Arch. Intern Med.* 1989; 149:609–612.

[145] Keifetz, Norma. "Reassessing Use of Digoxin in Aged." *Med. Trib.* 1989; 30(17):4.

[146] Editorial. "Digoxin: New Answers; New Questions." *Lancet* 1989; I:79–80.

[147] CONSENSUS Trial Study Group. "Effects of Enalapril on Mortality in Severe Congestive Heart Failure: Results of the Cooperative North Scandinavian Enalapril Survival Study." *N. Engl. J. Med.* 1987; 316:1429–1435.

[148] Amadio, Peter, et al. "ACE Inhibitors: A Safe Option for Hypertension and Congestive Heart Failure." *Postgrad. Med.* 1990; 87(1):223–243.

[149] Thomas, Patricia, op. cit. p. 38.

[150] DiBianco, Robert, et al. "A Comparison of Oral Milrinone, Digoxin, and Their Combination in the Treatment of Patients with Chronic Heart Failure." *N. Engl. J. Med.* 1989; 320:677–683.

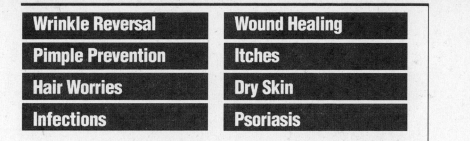

Wrinkle Reversal	Wound Healing
Pimple Prevention	Itches
Hair Worries	Dry Skin
Infections	Psoriasis

Skin Solutions

4

So much of who we are is tied up in our appearance—how others see us, how we feel about ourselves. No wonder we notice conditions that affect our skin, hair, and nails, which are so important to the face we present to the world. From the teenager with pimples to the grandmother concerned about wrinkles, self-esteem slips when something goes wrong with the skin. Fortunately, however, we now have an array of medications, some old and some new, that can help against common skin problems.

Wrinkle Reversal

RETIN-A

With the baby boomers beginning to worry about wrinkles, **Retin-A** (tretinoin) has surged in popularity. This prescription "wrinkle cream" is not a new drug, and the Food and Drug Administration has not approved it for aging skin.[1] But judging both from its popularity with patients and research reports that are starting to surface, this old anti-acne medication also works well in combating fine wrinkles and mottling of older skin. Dermatologists conducting one multicenter study issued an interim report after six months: more than two-thirds of the people using **Retin-A** (at the .05 percent concentration) had a measurable reduction in sun damage scores.[2]

According to Dr. John Voorhees, the Michigan dermatologist who captured headlines when he announced that **Retin-A** really does work to reverse sun damage, the benefits continue as long as the person keeps using the product.[3] Wrinkle reversal is not the only benefit. The tone and texture of the skin often improve and brown spots due to sun exposure fade. But Dr. Voorhees cautions against unrealistic expectations: "It is not a face lift in a bottle, it is not a miracle, and it is not a fountain of youth."[4]

Even more significant, perhaps, is **Retin-A**'s action against precancerous skin blemishes called *actinic keratoses*.[5] Although **Retin-A** is slower than **Efudex** or **Fluoroplex** (fluorouracil), the conventional treatment for actinic keratoses, it is easier to take. The usual medications tend to turn the skin into a "flaming torch," as Dr. Albert Kligman puts it. A one-two approach of one month on

How to Use Retin-A

- Apply **Retin-A** once daily on clean dry skin over the entire face. Dr. John Voorhees suggests using the highest concentration that is tolerated (the highest available is 0.1%).
- If the skin becomes uncomfortably red, flaky, and tender, a lower concentration (0.05% or 0.025%) is appropriate. Very fair skin may need a .01% strength. Stopping the medicine for a few days can also limit irritation.
- Don't apply **Retin-A** to damp skin. To avoid irritation, allow thirty minutes or so between washing your face and applying **Retin-A.**
- **Retin-A** makes the skin more sensitive to sunburn. Protect yourself from sun exposure—and further sun-induced skin aging—with a good sunscreen or a hat. Many sunscreens can inactivate **Retin-A**, so don't put them on at the same time. Using **Retin-A** in the evening and sunscreen in the morning is one solution.
- Dr. Al Kligman suggests a maintenance program of two applications a week after two or three years of daily use.

Retin-A and two to three weeks (instead of the usual four to five) of **Efudex** or **Fluoroplex** can "blast out" any incipient skin cancers, even if the actinic keratosis is exceptionally large or if there are many of them.[6]

AN OUNCE OF PREVENTION

Even though **Retin-A** can undo some of the damage wrought by the sun over years of sunbathing, prevention is still the best medicine. A little reflection on the rapid rise in skin cancer statistics (with melanoma up 93 percent in the past decade[7]) reinforces the old proverb. Fortunately, you don't need to hide in the library with your beach-reading just to protect your skin. Many effective sunblocking preparations are now available. Together with sun-smart strategies, they can minimize the damage done and even allow healing of some invisible sun-induced injuries.

The Unhealthy Tan

What's a tan all about anyway, and why do dermatologists keep harping on it? Most of us can get a tan only by taking our noses off the grindstone and going outside to play—golf, tennis, gardening, skiing, swimming, lounging, whatever. So a tan is a sort of status symbol, telling the world we don't have to work all the time. (In the middle of the winter, it may even be a little more ostentatious, showing off the bucks it takes for a vacation in a sunny spot.) But what actually happens when ultraviolet light hits the skin is that some pigment-producing cells get alarmed. They put out more pigment in a desperate attempt to shield the rest of the tissue from damage. This shield is only partially effective, but it is one of the skin's few built-in defense mechanisms. The result is what looks to all the world like a deep even tan, but is really a skin screaming for help to keep from burning.

Beyond tanning, ultraviolet rays have other effects on skin and eyes. Cataracts are associated with chronic exposure to sunlight,[8] and the ultraviolet light from indoor tanning lamps or booths can harm the cornea or the retina of the eye.[9] Light from either the sun or a tanning bed causes immunological changes in the skin that are incompletely understood but probably negative.[10,11] Add wrinkles, age spots, and a greater risk of skin cancers of all kinds to the list, and a tan starts to look a lot less attractive.

PROTECTION

Nobody wants to stay inside all the time, and hats and long sleeves, though helpful, have their limitations. (Just think about trying to waterski in a broad-brimmed hat!) The trick is to pick the appropriate sunscreen and use it every time you go out. But which one is right? If you have fair skin and light hair—and especially if you have freckles and sunburn easily—you should look for an SPF (skin protection factor) of fifteen or higher. (If you burn less easily you can afford to go lower, but sunburn is not the only story.)

Don't be stingy. It takes about an ounce of most sunscreens to provide the protection their SPF claims, and if you smear on only half as much, you may get half—or less—of the protection. And if you are sweating or in the water, reapply the sunscreen at intervals while you are out. The label on waterproof sunscreen will give you some idea how often (for example, "waterproof for at least eighty minutes").

Is there an advantage to using a "broad spectrum" sunscreen? Theoretically, there should be. Until recently, most sunscreens did a good job of blocking the burning UV-B rays, but let photodamaging UV-A rays, with their longer wave-

---

Selected High-Protection Sunscreens
(SPF 15 or higher)

Almay Fragrance Free Suncare Oil Free Spray*	Hawaiian Tropic Swim 'n'Sun
	Photoplex Broad Spectrum
Block Out by Sea & Ski	Bullfrog
Coppertone Sunblock w/ Vitamin E & Aloe	Ray Block
Hawaiian Tropic Baby Faces Sunblock	Sundown Ultra Protection
Hawaiian Tropic 15 Plus	TI-Screen*
Noskote Sunblock	Water Babies Sunblock
PreSun (by the numbers)	Super Shade
Solbar Plus 15*	Total Eclipse Sunscreen

*PABA-free

lengths, zip on through. Now manufacturers are struggling to provide formulations that can protect against the insidious chronic damage of photoaging, due mostly to UV-A, as well as against sunburn. Some products, especially those that contain oxybenzone or dioxybenzone, are better at blocking UV-A, but none of the available sunscreens get an "A" on UV-A blocking yet.

Sunscreen Sensitivity

About three people in a hundred get a nasty surprise with their sunscreen: they break out in itchy hives after they put it on, or they get an exaggerated sunburn.[12] A person who has had a reaction to sunscreens doesn't need to swear off sun protection, however. There are at least four different kinds of chemicals used in sunscreens, and very few people are sensitive to all of them. But locating the one that will be appropriate may require some sleuthing, so pull out the magnifying glass and prepare to read labels before you buy.

What was in the sunscreen you reacted to? If it was PABA, for example, look for a product that contains a different active ingredient. Then test it for a few days by putting a bit on the inside of your forearm. If you react with reddening, itching,

---

Guide to Label Language

Type of drug	Name on the label
Benzophenones	oxybenzone
	dioxybenzone
PABA	p-aminobenzoic acid
	PABA
	Padimate O
	octyl dimethyl PABA
	glyceryl PABA
Cinnamates	cinoxate
	ethylhexyl-p-methoxycinnimate
Salicylates	octyl salicylate
	homosalate
Other	methyl anthranilate
	digalloyl trioleate

Source: *Drug Facts & Comparisons*, 1990 (p. 2016).

hives, or other signs of allergy, don't use it, but hunt for something else to test. Some of the higher SPF products contain several different ingredients, so you may have to decipher a lot of labels to find a product that's free of your problem chemical.

If the problem you experienced was an unexpected sunburn rather than a rash, you had a photosensitivity reaction. (This is slightly more likely with benzophenones, but not common.) You'll still need your magnifying glass and label interpreter, but the test will be different. Instead of wearing your new, untried sunscreen on the inside of your forearm, put it on the back of your hand or on one ankle, and spend a little time out in the sun. If you normally burn easily, twenty minutes should be enough exposure to tell if the skin under the sunscreen got pinker than the unprotected skin nearby. If not, there's a good chance that sunscreen will work for you.

When you find a sunscreen your skin can tolerate, remember to use it every time you go outside, even if the day is overcast. (Be especially careful if you will be on sand, snow, or water, as ultraviolet light reflects off those surfaces. High altitudes increase UV exposure.) Smear sunscreen generously on all exposed areas of the skin, and underneath loosely woven or light clothing, such as a T-shirt or gauzy cover-up.[13] If you cannot find a sunscreen that is compatible with your skin, consider a physical blocker such as zinc oxide or titanium dioxide. Lips are susceptible to sunburn, too, so protect them—but read the label. Ultraviolet-absorbing chemicals in lipsticks are similar to those in sunscreens, so stay away from any that might provoke a bad reaction. Don't neglect your eyes, either. Some expensive sunglasses do not provide ultraviolet protection. Pick a pair that is labeled as filtering at least 96 percent of the ultraviolet light, or look for a sticker showing "UV" covered with the international "prohibited" symbol: ⊘ .

Pimple Prevention

TOPICAL TREATMENTS

Acne is not just the bane of teenagers. Many adults, especially women, suffer with zits long after adolescence. Treatments for acne depend more upon its severity than the age of the patient. For mild acne, with few if any red inflamed pimples, an over-the-counter preparation containing benzoyl peroxide is often effective. Television commercials implying that you can be rid of pimples with a single swipe are misleading, but daily use can help keep skin from breaking out. Benzoyl peroxide often causes dryness, peeling, or redness and may sting or burn when it is applied. If these problems are troublesome, it should be applied less frequently, or a lower concentration product (5 percent) should be selected. Some people are allergic ("contact dermatitis") to benzoyl peroxide, so if you break out in a rash after applying one of these products, forget over-the-counter treatment and make an appointment with a dermatologist.

Benzoyl peroxide is also available in a number of prescription products, and some dermatologists like to prescribe a combination of benzoyl peroxide with erythromycin, called **Benzamycin**, which may be more effective than either drug alone.[14] In general, however, the topical antibiotics are quite effective for mild to moderate acne on their own, and are often less expensive. Applying antibiotics like tetracycline (**Topicycline**), erythromycin (**A/T/S, Erycette, EryDerm, Erymax, T-Stat**, and others), or clindamycin (**Cleocin T**) directly to the skin instead of taking them by mouth means less worry about food-drug interactions and serious nonskin side effects. In rare instances (less than 0.1 percent of the time)[15], **Cleocin T** has provoked a severe bloody diarrhea and abdominal cramps. If anyone using **Cleocin T** starts to have diarrhea, he or she should contact the doctor immediately.

One of the most popular treatments prescribed for moderately severe acne is **Retin-A** (tretinoin). Long before it made headlines as a wrinkle-remover, it was being used successfully for pimple prevention. It takes about six weeks to get

---

Some Benzoyl Peroxide Products

Acne-Aid
Ben-Aqua
Benoxyl
Buf-Oxal 10
Clearasil
Cuticura Acne
Del Aqua
Dry and Clear
Fostex
Loroxide
Oxy 5/Oxy 10
PanOxyl 5
Xerac BP5/Xerac BP10

Cleocin T (clindamycin)

Topical antibiotic extremely effective against mild to moderate acne. Can also be used to "spot treat" individual pimples or trouble areas. Side effects: contact dermatitis, skin dryness with solution but not with lotion; stomach pain and diarrhea are rare but potentially serious.

★ ★ ★

the full benefit of **Retin-A**'s anti-acne power, and the face may break out more severely before it gets better. However, persistence pays off in most cases, and a maintenance program of **Retin-A** usually keeps acne under control. (See sidebar, "How to Use **Retin-A**," page 110.) The concentration (which ranges from 0.01 percent in a gel to 0.1 percent in a cream) may have to be adjusted to get the right balance between effectiveness and irritation: if redness and peeling become unpleasant, a lower concentration or every-other-day schedule may be appropriate.

Dermatologists will soon have another topical acne medication in their armamentarium. In testing, isotretinoin cream and gel (**Isotrex**) appear to be as effective as **Retin-A** for moderately severe acne.[16] The manufacturer anticipates FDA approval for this product sometime soon. The major side effects appear to be redness and irritation.

ANTI-PIMPLE PILLS

Acne Rosacea

The term is misleading because the red inflamed bumps that are typical of acne rosacea are a different condition from ordinary pimples. It usually begins between ages thirty and fifty with the expansion of tiny blood vessels close to the surface of the skin, giving nose, cheeks, or forehead a rosy or flushed appearance. If not treated, it may lead to skin damage and a W. C. Fields-like appearance.

W. C. Fields had no choice, but no one needs to look like that nowadays. Acne rosacea is treated with low-dose oral tetracycline or with a topical antibiotic called **Metrogel** (metronidazole).[17] **Metrogel** may irritate or dry the skin, but is unlikely to cause the serious side effects possible with oral metronidazole (**Flagyl**).

Accutane

For really severe scarring acne, creams, lotions, or gels rarely work. Bad (cystic) acne calls for major medicine: **Accutane** (isotretinoin). This drug is chemically similar to vitamin A, but has been tweaked in the test tube to make it more effective against acne. **Accutane** is wonderful in cases where nothing else has worked. In fact, for some people a four- or five-month course of this medicine is a cure for acne.

Accutane may work like a miracle, but it has some significant drawbacks. It is very expensive. It has a variety of possible side effects, some of which occur in nearly everyone who takes the medication (for example, dry and fragile skin, dry nose, dry mouth, and cracked lips). Most important, women taking **Accutane** *must not* become pregnant, as it causes tragic birth defects. As a consequence, some physicians prefer not to prescribe it for teenage girls, believing that they are irresponsible about birth control. Others urge women taking **Accutane** to use two methods of birth control—a barrier contraceptive such as condoms or a diaphragm in addition to oral contraceptives—just to be safe.[18] Despite the dangers and disadvantages, dermatologists occasionally prescribe this medicine for patients whose acne is troublesome but not disfiguring, if they are convinced that the patients will be scrupulous about birth control and able to tolerate the likely side effects in exchange for freedom from pimples.

ANDROGENIC ACNE

Some women may suffer from acne caused by a hormonal imbalance. When too much androgen circulates in the bloodstream, it can be converted to testosterone and dihydrotestosterone (DHT) in oil glands and hair follicles.[21] These male hormones can cause facial hair growth (hirsutism *à la* the bearded lady) and acne that does not respond to the usual treatments. Many of these women may be helped by an old-fashioned blood pressure drug that also blocks DHT: **Aldactone** (spironolactone). At a dose of 100–150 mg per day, **Aldactone** cleared acne in 60 percent of the women tested recently at Boston University; however, nearly half experienced menstrual problems.[22] Other side effects of spironolactone include fatigue, dizziness and mental confusion (which would make driving hazardous); nausea, diarrhea, or bleeding

Why Not Vitamin A for Acne?

With the success of the synthetic retinoids tretinoin and isotretinoin against acne, you may wonder about using the original, retinol (vitamin A).

We can't recommend that. For mild or moderate acne, **Retin-A** is effective enough and far safer. For severe acne, **Accutane**, although not safer, is more effective. At the effective doses of vitamin A (100,000 units or more for several weeks), many people experience toxic effects such as dry skin, brittle nails, hair loss, cracked lips, gum inflammation, nausea, headaches and bone or muscle pain. Liver toxicity is not unusual,[19] and pregnant women should avoid high doses of this vitamin, as it can cause birth defects.[20]

Does Makeup Cause Acne?[23,24]

Women's blemishes are often blamed on their use of cosmetics. However, it appears that while facial makeup can aggravate acne, it is rarely responsible for acne. Few cosmetic products encourage pimple formation on their own, according to Dr. Al Kligman, who first came up with the idea of acne due to cosmetics and now wishes he could take it back. In fact, says Dr. Kligman, "The more comedogenic [pimple-provoking] substances are not cosmetics, they are our own topical therapies, the things we dermatologists use every day in clinical practice," such as benzoyl peroxide or sulfur-containing drugs. Dr. Kligman does warn women not to be "cosmetics crazies" or "moisturizer nuts," especially since interactions among skin care products can turn a relatively harmless formulation into one that actively promotes blemishes.

stomach; headache; deepening of the voice; itchy rash; and breast enlargement. This medication causes cancer in rats, so questions have been raised about its safety for humans.

We can hope that future antiandrogenic medications now under development may prove helpful for this indication, but it will be some time before they can be tested. These include **Proscar** (finasteride), an oral medication that appears to prevent the conversion of testosterone to DHT, which is currently being tested for its effect on prostate enlargement; and cyoctol, a weak topical antiandrogen being tested as an acne and antibaldness medication.

Hair Worries

BALDNESS

Rogaine Topical Solution

More words may have been written about **Rogaine** (minoxidil) than about any other drug in recent years. The idea that there might really be something to reverse male pattern baldness was electrifying after all those decades of hearing that nothing would do any good at all for receding hairlines. The development of **Rogaine** has definitely changed the dermatologists' standard line on baldness. We now know that there is something that works—at least for some people, for a while.

Unfortunately, that is the catch. As an antibaldness medicine, **Rogaine** is far from perfect. Although up to two-thirds of men who apply the solution faithfully for four months have a measurable increase in hair, only 30 to 40 percent get a really satisfactory result. Moreover, even though **Rogaine** can shake those hair follicles out of their lethargy and get them growing again, it can't keep them going at high speed. A person who gives up on **Rogaine**, either because of cost or inconvenience, will lose the new hair grown under the influence of the drug. Even worse, those who continue using **Rogaine** often see hair growth rate

Male pattern baldness

drop off dramatically in less than three years.[25] It remains to be seen whether **Rogaine** will be able to help some men postpone balding by as much as five years. Those who don't get good results on this medicine may find that surgery offers a better solution.

Now that **Rogaine** has been out for some time, dermatologists have a fairly good handle on who will respond better. The younger the patients are (under forty), the more hair they have and the shorter the time they've been losing their hair, the more likely it is they will respond at least moderately to this medication.[26] Hair lost from a circle at the back of the head (the "vertex") seems to respond better than the hair creeping away from the forehead. Women with thinning hair seem to respond to **Rogaine** about as well as men do, or perhaps a bit better. Here again, those who start treatment with more hair are most likely to see the benefit.[27,28]

One promising approach to the treatment of male pattern baldness is the combination of both **Retin-A** and **Rogaine**. Dr. Nia Terezakis, a dermatologist who has done clinical research on minoxidil, sums up her experiments so far: "I think there really is a synergism between tretinoin and minoxidil for stimulating hair growth, which appears to involve the very important process of transforming vellus hairs [the fine "fuzz" that grows on the body] to terminal hairs [normal scalp hair that grows long]. Maybe we don't have the right retinoid or the right concentration yet, but I think this approach is definitely worth studying."[29]

Dr. Terezakis' subjects used a specially compounded medicine that contained both drugs. Dermatologists willing to help their patients experiment have to prescribe the available medications. Since there is a possibility that **Rogaine** might interfere with **Retin-A**'s action, just as sunscreen does (see p. 110), it would probably be best to schedule different times for the application of each product, at least an hour apart. With luck, this combination may give a lot more people a chance at keeping their hair a while longer. We don't yet know if it will boost the number of people who get a really excellent response, from less than 10 percent with **Rogaine** alone to a considerably higher

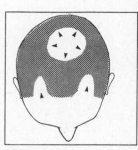

Male pattern baldness

Rogaine
(minoxidil)
Stimulates new hair growth in 40–60 percent of cases of male pattern baldness; continued application is needed for maintenance. Most likely to work in individuals with limited hair loss. Useful for brittle nails. Expensive.

★

proportion getting "dense regrowth" from the combination therapy.

Hope for the Future

Although **Rogaine** has not lived up to the high expectations people initially had for it, it has done one extremely important thing. This medicine has proven beyond a doubt that it is possible to fight baldness medically. For those who respond to **Rogaine**, it offers a holding action to keep hair loss from progressing to the point of no return, if there is such a thing, while newer and better drugs are developed. Cyoctol is being tested for its ability to hold off hair loss, and preliminary results are positive, with ten out of twelve men tested responding well.[30,31] But even if cyoctol doesn't turn out to be much better than minoxidil, researchers are now convinced that it's possible to reverse male pattern baldness, and other active compounds will undoubtedly be investigated in the future. There is currently no OTC or herbal treatment that can conquer hair loss, and effective nonprescription treatments are unlikely to surface anytime in the near future.

What's Wrong?

When hair loss isn't typical of inherited male pattern baldness, it may require some medical sleuthing to figure out what is wrong. Hair loss can signal metabolic problems, such as hypothyroidism, thyrotoxicosis, an adrenal gland problem, or a hormonal imbalance in women. Many medications are also capable of interfering with hair growth. The worst offenders are the anticancer drugs. In most cases, though, a person who needs cancer medicine is willing to trade temporary baldness for the possibility of a cure. But many other medications that can cause hair thinning are less critical. It's not something most doctors like to talk about, but if you notice more hair than usual accumulating around the drain in the tub, you might want to ask if there are alternatives that are less likely to cause the problem.

Some Drugs That Can Cause Hair Loss

Allergy Medicine
terfenadine (**Seldane**)

Antibiotics
gentamicin (**Garamycin**)
nitrofurantoin (**Furadantin,
    Macrodantin**)

Anticancer Drugs
cyclophosphamide (**Cytoxan**)
daunorubicin (**Cerubidine**)
doxorubicin (**Adriamycin**)
etoposide (**VePesid**)
interferon (**Intron A**, **Roferon**)
methotrexate (**Folex**, **Mexate**)
vinblastine (**Velban**)

Anticoagulants
4-bishydroxycoumarin (**Dicumarol**)
heparin
warfarin (**Coumadin**, etc.)

Anticonvulsants
carbamazepine (**Tegretol**)
mephenytoin (**Mesantoin**)
trimethadione (**Tridione**)
valproic acid (**Depakene**)

Antipsychotics
haloperidol (**Haldol**)

Arthritis Medicines
auranofin (**Ridaura**)*
diclofenac (**Voltaren**)*
fenoprofen (**Nalfon**)*
flurbiprofen (**Ansaid**)*
ibuprofen (**Advil**, **Motrin**, etc.)*
indomethacin (**Indocin**)*

ketoprofen (**Orudis**)*
meclofenamate (**Meclomen**)*
methotrexate (**Rheumatrex**)
naproxen (**Anaprox**, **Naprosyn**)*
piroxicam (**Feldene**)*
penicillamine (**Cuprimine,
    Depen**)*
sulindac (**Clinoril**)*

Asthma Medicines
ipratropium (**Atrovent**)*
theophylline (**Bronkodyl,
    Theobid,** etc.)
oxtriphylline (**Choleclyl**)

Beta Blockers
acebutolol (**Sectral**)
atenolol (**Tenormin**)
betaxolol (**Betoptic**)*
carteolol (**Cartrol**)
labetalol (**Normodyne**, **Trandate**)
levobunolol (**Betagan Liquifilm**)*
metoprolol (**Lopressor**)*
nadolol (**Corgard**)*
pindolol (**Visken**)
propanolol (**Inderal**, etc.)*
timolol (**Blocadren**, **Timoptic**)*

Blood Pressure Drugs
amiloride/HCTZ (**Moduretic**)
captopril (**Capoten**, **Capozide**)
clonidine (**Catapres**)
diltiazem (**Cardizem**)*
enalapril (**Vaseretic**, **Vasotec**)
guanethidine (**Esimil**, **Ismelin**)
prazosin (**Minipress**)
verapamil (**Calan**, **Isoptin**)*

continued on next page

Cholesterol-Lowering Drugs
clofibrate (**Atromid-S**)
dextrothyroxine (**Choloxin**)
gemfibrozil (**Lopid**)
lovastatin (**Mevacor**)
nicotinic acid (niacin)

Depression Drugs
amitriptyline (**Elavil**, etc.)
bupropion (**Wellbutrin**)*
desipramine (**Norpramin**,
    Pertofrane)
doxepin (**Adapin**, **Sinequan**)
fluoxetine (**Prozac**)*
imipramine (**Tofranil**, etc.)

Gastrointestinal Drugs
sulfasalazine (**Azulfidine**)

Gout Medicines
allopurinol (**Zyloprim**)*
colchicine (**ColBenemid**)
probenecid+ (**Benemid**)

Thyroid Suppressants
methimazole (**Tapazole**)
propylthiouracil
levothyroxine (**Levothroid**,

Synthroid) at suppressant
doses

Ulcer Medicines
cimetidine (**Tagamet**)*
famotidine (**Pepcid**)*
ranitidine (**Zantac**)*
mioprostol (**Cytotec**)*

Vitamin A & Derivatives
etretinate (**Tegison**)
isotretinoin (**Accutane**)

*Hair loss occurs infrequently or in less than 1 percent of patients.
Sources: *Drug Facts & Comparisons.* St. Louis: Lippincott, 1990. *Drug Interactions and Side Effects Index* and *Physicians Desk Reference.* Oradell, NJ: Medical Economics Company, 1990. Bruck, Laura B. "Consider Pharmacologic Effect in Alopecia." *Dermatology Times* 1988; 9(12):23. Fraunfelder, F.T., et al. "Alopecia Possibly Secondary to Topical Ophthalmic β-Blockers." (letter) *JAMA* 1990; 263:1493–1494. Price, Vera H., et al. "Sorting Out the Clues in Alopecia." *Patient Care* September 15, 1989;70–90. Bruinsma, W. "A Guide to Drug Eruptions." *The File of Adverse Reactions to the Skin*, 1977–1982.

Other possible causes of hair loss include a serious illness (especially if there was fever), a severe chronic condition such as tuberculosis or syphilis, major surgery, significant weight loss from a restricted diet, or the birth of a child. Even extreme mental or emotional pressure could contribute to hair loss.[32] Iron deficiency anemia may also be responsible for thinning of hair.[33] Bacterial or fungal infections of the scalp may also cause hair loss.

However, the most common cause of sudden dramatic hair loss is *alopecia areata,* an autoimmune disease in which round, bald patches appear. They may grow larger and be joined by new bald spots, but most of the time it clears up by itself within three years. Recurrence is not unusual, however, and three years is a long time to wait. Monthly steroid injections into the affected areas may help them heal within six months; some dermatologists report success with topical treatments of dinitrochlorobenzene (DNCB), anthralin, or PUVA (psoralen and ultraviolet light exposure), which irritate the scalp but may stimulate new hair growth within about three months.[34]

HAIR DYE

Watching your hair turn gray may be almost as bruising to the vanity as watching the bare spot at the back get bigger. As the baby boomers move into middle age, hair coloring manufacturers look forward to a booming market. More and more people may want to cover their gray, but is this a good idea? The questions that have been raised about the safety of hair dyes remain unanswered.

Several years ago, the FDA planned to require cosmetics manufacturers to put warnings on the labels of hair dyes containing certain coal-tar-derived chemicals. Instead, the companies removed the chemicals in question and replaced them with others that had not been thoroughly tested.[35] The agency could not have begun to test all the possible chemicals involved, and turned its attention to other matters.

> ### *Lead Acetate*
>
> Careful label readers will note that a number of products designed to cover up gray hair (especially those marketed for men) contain lead acetate. Although a small amount of lead is absorbed through the scalp, the FDA considers this exposure trivial compared to the much higher background levels of lead we all absorb from food, water, and air. The agency is confident that lead acetate hair colors pose no risk of lead poisoning as long as they are used correctly and not applied to irritated, cut, or abraded skin.[36]

Recently, however, epidemiologists have discovered some unsettling associations between hair dye use and disease. Men in Iowa and Minnesota appear to have almost double the risk of leukemia and of non-Hodgkin's lymphoma (types of cancer) if they use hair dyes.[37] Scientists investigating a reported cluster of connective tissue diseases such as lupus or scleroderma in Georgia found no geographical concentration of these conditions—but did discover an association of connective tissue disease with the use of hair dye.[38]

Too Much Hair

Excess facial hair is a problem for many women. Sometimes it is due to an overdose of androgen, (male hormone) produced either by the adrenal gland or the ovary. Most women who see a dermatologist for mustaches, beards, or extra body hair will be tested to make sure there is nothing wrong with these organs. If the ovary is not functioning well, estrogen-containing birth control pills may be prescribed. In other cases, spironolactone (**Aldactone**)may be prescribed.

Finnish doctors report beneficial results with six months of oral ketoconazole (**Nizoral**).[41] However, side effects such as nausea, vomiting, stomach pain, dizziness, and rare but serious liver damage or blood disorders may discourage the use of **Nizoral** tablets for this purpose.

Severe hirsutism has been treated experimentally with Cyproteron of Androcur (cyproterone). A small study has also shown good results with Tagamet (cimetidine) in less serious cases.[42]

Now, leukemia, lymphoma, and lupus are not especially common diseases, so few people are likely to come down with them, even at double the risk. But some folks might be smart to let vanity take a backseat. Anyone with a family history of polymyositis, sytemic sclerosis, systemic lupus erythematosus, scleroderma, or other connective tissue disorder is already at higher risk of developing one of these serious diseases. According to the researchers, "Until more is known about the association between connective tissue disease and hair dyes, it would be prudent to advise family members of patients with these disorders to refrain from using hair dyes."[39] Others who should be wary include those taking verapamil (**Calan** or **Isoptin**), as this drug appears to increase the potential danger from several chemicals, including a hair dye ingredient.[40] Common sense suggests restraint: if you do decide to use a hair dye, stretch out the time between applications as much as possible, and don't leave the chemical in contact with your scalp any longer than necessary.

DANDRUFF

Dandruff is not all alike. There is a wide spectrum, from the person who can stir up a few tiny flakes with a vigorous scalp massage to the individual whose shoulders are generously adorned with fair-sized pieces of sloughed-off skin. Fittingly, there is also a range of recommended treatments—but some common approaches help all the way along the continuum.

Mild dandruff, presumably caused by skin cells on the scalp growing and turning over slightly faster than usual, can often be controlled with nothing more elaborate than a daily shampoo. Some people claim that apple-cider vinegar in the rinse water is also a help.[43] Although this treatment hasn't been thoroughly tested for effectiveness, it's unlikely to do much harm.

Dandruff Shampoos

There is quite an array of over-the-counter dandruff shampoos on the shelf of any pharmacy. Many of them can be helpful if they are used properly, but one ingredient stands out as the first line of defense. Zinc pyrithione (ZPT), the dandruff-fighter in **Breck One**, **Danax**, **Head & Shoulders**, **Sebulon**, and **Zincon**, among others, has been proven effective in a double-blind study in which each dandruff sufferer had half a head of hair washed with a ZPT shampoo and the other half with unmedicated shampoo. After a month, flakiness was down 79 percent on the treated side, compared with only 7 percent on the side that had gotten plain shampoo.

In addition to slowing down cell growth, ZPT discourages the multiplication of a yeast called *Pityrosporum ovale*, now recognized as the culprit in the condition known as seborrheic dermatitis. Seborrheic dermatitis shows up on the scalp like super dandruff: itchy, with big scales. But it can also affect the face, causing red, itchy, scaly patches on the forehead, over the eyebrows, inside the ears, at the side of the nose, or along the crease that runs from the nose to the corner of the mouth. Dermatologists now prescribe the antifungal cream **Nizoral** (ketoconazole) for this problem.[44] Before long, they should also be able to prescribe **Nizoral** shampoo for everything from major dandruff to seborrheic dermatitis on the scalp.

This antifungal shampoo has been available in Europe, Thailand, Singapore, and South Africa for some time now, and approval for U.S. marketing is expected imminently. An inter-

How to Use Anti-Dandruff Shampoo

1. First, lather and rinse using a mild nonmedicated shampoo to remove dirt and oil.
2. Lather up with the dandruff shampoo. Leave it on the scalp for *five* minutes.
3. Rinse thoroughly, especially when using a coal tar- or selenium-sulfide-based shampoo which may stain light-colored hair.
4. Do not use a blow dryer, as it may aggravate dandruff.
5. Give your hair a break. Use dandruff shampoos as infrequently as possible to still maintain dandruff control.
6. If your dandruff shampoo stops working for you, try switching to a different type of antidandruff shampoo for a while. (If, for example, you had been using a ZPT product like **Sebulon**, you might try a coal-tar product like **Tegrin** or a salicylic acid shampoo like **Ionil**.) This may help with dandruff control and as an added benefit, your old favorite may work better when you go back to it after several weeks or months.
7. If these measures don't help, check with the dermatologist. A prescription antifungal shampoo such as **Capitrol** (chloroxine) or **Nizoral** (ketoconazole) may be just what you're itching for.

nationally known researcher, Dr. Jan Faergeman of Sweden, has demonstrated the effectiveness of **Nizoral** shampoo in controlled studies. Side effects are uncommon.[45] For best results, this prescription lather should be left on the scalp for five minutes before thorough rinsing, just as the OTC dandruff shampoos should.

Infections

ATHLETE'S FOOT AND OTHER FUNGUS

P. ovale is not the only fungus lurking on the human skin. A variety of yeastlike fungi can cause problems such as athlete's foot, jock itch, ringworm, and finger or toenail infections. In a susceptible person, or someone whose immune system isn't working well, such conditions can be very tenacious. The first step in treating athlete's foot or jock itch is often an OTC antifungal preparation such as **Lotrimin AF** (clotrimazole), **Micatin** (miconazole), or **Aftate**, **Footwork**, **Tinactin**, **Zeasorb-AF**, or other brands of tolnaftate.

However, if twice-a-day use of one of these, together with the precautions of keeping the affected area clean and dry, doesn't clear up the condition within several weeks, it's wise to see a dermatologist. He or she can determine whether the problem is plain old fungus or something more complicated. Depending on the diagnosis, the doctor may also prescribe a more potent topical medication, such as **Loprox** (ciclopirox), **Spectazole** (econazole), **Nizoral** (ketoconazole), or the new **Naftin** (naftifine), or an oral medicine like griseofulvin or **Nizoral**.

Although most of these antifungal creams are quite similar, there are some distinctions. **Loprox** is useful in treating fungal infections of the nails, which don't respond to the other creams but only to griseofulvin pills. Either way, treatment of nail fungus takes many months. **Naftin**, the newest of these medications, seems to be a little bit faster and possibly more effective in treating a variety of skin fungi, but it probably won't do much for nail or scalp problems.[46] In fact, about all any of the creams can be expected to do for ringworm of the scalp is cut down on the chances of spreading it to other people. To really clear it up, griseofulvin has to be taken orally for a month or so.

BACTERIAL INFECTIONS

We are constantly barraged by bacteria, but normally the skin does an excellent job of keeping them out where they belong. When the skin is broken with a cut, scrape, or burn, though, the bacteria may sometimes get a foothold. The result can be a nasty infection that calls for an antibiotic.

Impetigo

Kids are the usual victims of this skin infection. They are often quite generous with it, too, passing it around a day-care center or kindergarten. Used to be, the way to deal with this was a full ten-day course of erythromycin, and an oral antibiotic is probably still appropriate if there is a very large area involved or if the infection gets complicated.[50] But doctors now have the option of prescribing a antibiotic ointment called **Bactroban** (mupirocin). **Bactroban** has tested out at least as effective as oral erythromycin against children's impetigo infections, and the studies hint that it may even act more quickly in some cases.[51,52] Unlike oral antibiotics, which may give children diarrhea or other side effects, the only reactions reported from **Bactroban** are irritation or rash where it is applied. In addition, it doesn't seem to interact with food or oral medications. (Oral erythromycin interacts with food and some asthma medicines.)[53] One drawback: it is fairly expensive.

Treating Nail Fungus

Doctors hate to treat fungus infections of the toenails and fingernails. When fungus moves in, the nails look disgusting and it takes a long time to clear them up. Six months is the usual minimum treatment time for fingernails with griseofulvin pills, and for toenails treatment may take more than a year. Then the infections often come back. *Frustration!* Now you understand why many physicians would just as soon leave fungus-ridden toenails alone unless the patient has diabetes or severe circulation problems.

Future developments may change that, by offering antifungal medications that are more effective, if not faster. Oral itraconazole appears more effective for nail fungus than griseofulvin, though Janssen, the manufacturer developing the drug, has no plans to seek approval for that use.[47] **Lamisil** (terbinafine) appears to be much more effective against nail fungus than existing drugs, and much less likely to allow relapse.[48] Perhaps the best news is a new topical antifungal called amorolfine, which has been tested as a cream and as a nail polish. Six months of twice weekly applications of the polish led to 70 percent recovery from toenail and 80 percent from fingernail fungus.[49]

Cuts and Burns

Bactroban is also gaining favor with physicians for infected cuts, scrapes, and burns, displacing the old standby—a combination of polymyxin B, bacitracin, and neomycin.[54] In some cases, **Bactroban** is even being used preventively, before wounds become infected. It probably should be a staple in most families' first aid kits, as putting it on cuts and scrapes might help most of them heal without complications. If you are uneasy about spending a fair bit on a prescription product for such a homely use, though, the previous favorite is still available over the counter under a wide variety of names and prices. In most cases, it will work nearly as well as **Bactroban** at helping minor cuts and scratches clear without infection.

For stubborn skin infections, some dermatologists are trying the topical antibiotic **Metrogel** (metronidazole). Besides controlling acne rosacea, it does a very credible job of wiping out a broad range of bacteria that can cause trouble on the skin. In addition, the oral version of **Cleocin** (clindamycin) can be helpful in persistent, hard-to-treat infections.[55] This can be tricky, however, as **Cleocin** has the potential to cause some serious side effects, especially a dangerous form of diarrhea. Although only a low dose of clindamycin capsules should be prescribed for chronic skin infections, patients still need to be prepared to alert their doctors if they develop rash or any sign of diarrhea.

VIRAL INFECTIONS

Viruses may be smaller than bacteria or fungi, but they can still cause trouble for the skin. Leaving aside full-fledged diseases (measles, chicken pox, or the like), the most common viruses that tangle with skin are probably those that cause warts and those that cause herpes lesions.

Warts

Warts are fascinating. Garden-variety warts often go away in response to nearly any kind of healing ritual that's convincing to the sufferer; they will usually disappear within a year or so even without any treatment. They can also be removed surgically, and they will respond to treatment with salicylic acid, in drops or in a plaster. This is available both with prescription (**Occlusal-HP**, **Salacid**, **Trans-Ver-Sal**) and without (**Compound W**, **Freezone**, **Mediplast**, **Off•Easy**, **Wart-Off**). But warts on the soles of the feet or the palms of the hands as well as those on the genitals are extremely difficult to treat and tend to come back. The dermatologist may remove genital warts with a caustic chemical—**Podofin** (podophyllum)[57] or trichloroacetic acid. (See p. 348.) Another treatment involves surgery, using electricity, laser, or liquid nitrogen. Genital warts should *not* be subjected to home treatment with salicylic acid. In addition, because the human papilloma virus that causes genital warts is transmitted through sexual contact, all partners should also see a dermatologist. Although other warts need to be treated only if they are bothersome, it is important to treat genital warts even if they're not causing any symptoms, as some strains increase the risk of cervical cancer.

Plantar warts may also be surgically removed, but only with great care, as scars on the bottom of the foot can sometimes be as painful as the original wart. Injecting **Blenoxane** (bleomycin) into the wart at three-week intervals is a different treatment strategy that often works. Oral supplements of vitamin A or dessicated liver, although untested, are reported to be helpful, but they shouldn't be substituted for appropriate plantar wart treatment. Remember, too much vitamin A can be toxic!

Herpes Infections

The herpes family of viruses causes a variety of problems, including common cold sores, genital herpes lesions in both men and women, and herpes zoster, or shingles. All of these viruses can "hide" in the body for years. In fact, shingles is a memento of childhood chicken pox that may not flare up until many decades after the first illness. When a cold sore or genital

---

Chicken Pox

By now, most parents are aware that aspirin is a no-no for children suffering from chicken pox. It may increase their risk of a rare but dangerous condition known as Reye's syndrome. So what about acetaminophen (**Anacin-3**, **Panadol**, **Liquiprin**, **Tylenol**, **Tempra**)?

A recent study[56] suggests that acetaminophen does not help substantially, and may increase the itching and slow healing of the rash. Perhaps a low-tech solution of a tepid bath with baking soda added is the way to go, both for lowering fever and reducing itch for a little while.

Zovirax
(acyclovir)
Effective treatment
and prevention of
cold sores and
genital herpes
lesions.
High dose useful
against shingles.
Topical form is less
effective and can't
be used for
prevention.
Side effects:
Headache, nausea,
dizziness, joint pain.

★ ★ ★ ★

lesion appears (often after a stress to the immune system, as for example by sunburn), the best treatment is **Zovirax** (acyclovir) pills. This medicine does not cure herpes, but a person who starts early on—and some people can feel when they've got a sore coming, even before it's visible—and takes **Zovirax** for five days will often be successful. The sore will be less severe and not last as long, or in some cases, it may be aborted completely.

For prevention, some people swear by the supplement l-lysine. In one study, large amounts of this amino acid (1,248 mg daily) reduced the number of attacks of herpes, in comparison with placebo. Once an attack began, however, l-lysine did nothing to curtail it.[58] There is little danger for adults taking this supplement, but it is not recommended for children.

For people who suffer frequent, severe recurrences of herpes lesions, **Zovirax** offers protection. Taken every day, it prevents most outbreaks, and seems to stay effective and safe for years.[59] However, some patients report a "rebound" of more frequent lesions when they stop long-term **Zovirax** therapy. It is not clear whether preventing lesions reduces the risk of transmitting herpes virus to a partner. Researchers have found that women not on medication can shed viruses from the genital tract even when they have no sign of lesions.[60] There's no information on how or whether **Zovirax** would affect this, but these data suggest it might be prudent to use a condom whenever either partner has a history of genital herpes.

Shingles can't be prevented, for there's no telling when this painful rash may appear. Generally it strikes middle-aged and older people (only those who had chicken pox as children, which is most everybody). Not only is the rash itself extremely tender, but it can leave its victim with horrible pain that can linger for years after the rash recedes. This is a case where the old "wait and see" philosophy doesn't hold up. If a person starts soon enough, within three days of the first appearance of the rash, and takes high doses of **Zovirax** (800 mg five times a day for a week to ten days), the attack itself can be lightened and shortened considerably, and there's likely to be less risk of lasting postherpetic pain.[61] Side effects, including nausea, mental confusion, diarrhea, and headache, are more likely for an individual downing 4 grams of this medicine daily, instead of the much smaller doses used to treat genital herpes, but there isn't a more effective treatment for shingles. Unfortunately, this medication is not cheap: a seven-day course of therapy runs about $150.[62]

After the fact, **Zovirax** is not helpful for postherpetic pain, but a nonprescription ointment may be. The active ingredient in **Zostrix** is capsaicin, the chemical that gives hot peppers their kick. If you've ever cooked with chile peppers, you'll understand why it's crucial to keep **Zostrix** out of eyes and away from any cuts or skin irritation. It may sting or burn when it is first applied, but the trick in using this medicine is repetition.[63] It depletes substance P from nerve endings near the skin, and if it is used often enough, the body does not have a chance to replenish the supply. Since substance P, whatever it is, seems to be essential in transmitting messages of pain back to the brain, smearing on **Zostrix** four to six times a day for several weeks can mute the pain message.

People who don't respond to **Zostrix** may want to try electrical stimulation. A transcutaneous electrical nerve stimulation unit, or TENS, provides high- or low-frequency electric current. The electrodes are placed on the painful area or near the appropriate nerve. A doctor must prescribe use of a TENS rig; some doctors or hospitals make them available to patients for a rental fee, but for long-term use, it is possible to purchase one.

Although postherpetic pain can't be chalked up to psychological problems, dermatologists report that they sometimes have success easing this condition when they prescribe an antidepressant, **Elavil** (amitriptyline) for example, together with a major tranquilizer like **Mellaril** (thioridazine), **Prolixin** (fluphenazine), or **Taractan** (chlorprothixene).[64] Side effects of these medications, including dizziness upon rising ("orthostatic hypotension"), dry mouth, nausea, confusion, blurred vision, and incoordination, among others, may be especially troublesome for older people, making it unsafe to drive a car and increasing the risk of a fall. But as a desperate measure, it may provide some relief.

> *Zostrix*
> *(capsaicin)*
> *ointment*
> Reduces sensation of postherpetic pain.
> Available without prescription.
> For best results, apply repeatedly.
> Do not apply to broken skin. Wash hands after applying.
>
> ★ ★ ★

Healing Wounds

Whether it's a cut, a burn, or a surgical incision, a wound should heal rapidly and completely. It might be smart to keep your medicine chest stocked so that you can treat everyday scrapes the same way plastic surgeons treat lacerations, for speedy effective healing. What will you need? First, you'll need a supply of adhesive bandages or nonstick pads and tape so you can cover cuts and scratches well. Although Mother may have advised you to let a skinned knee get plenty of air so it could dry out and scab over, clinical experience shows that a scrape, blister, cut, or burn actually heals better if it is kept covered and moist. A product like **2nd Skin**, a see-through synthetic dressing that covers a wound tightly, can help keep air out if applied under the tape. (This kind of product is often sold with hiking boots or running shoes for treating blisters.) According to Dr. George W. Cherry, a moist bandage that lets no air in allows skin cells to migrate more quickly across the surface of the wound and makes for more rapid healing.[65]

> ### *Splinter Removal the Easy Way*[66]
>
> If you've ever tried to pull a tiny splinter out for a squirming, screaming child, you'll appreciate the innovation Dr. Russell Copelan tested and found effective. Rather than poke around with a needle or a pair of sharp tweezers trying to tease out a splinter you may need bifocals to see, apply a tiny piece of salicylic acid plaster under an adhesive strip. Take it off twelve hours later. By that time the splinter shouldn't hurt anymore. Most splinters (roughly three-fourths) work their way out after two or three days. Time enough to reach for the tweezers if this simple no-ouch method doesn't work. Salicylic acid plaster is available as (**Mediplast**) or by prescription as **Trans-Ver-Sal**.

To keep the wound moisturized and discourage infection, you should have an antibiotic ointment on hand, to be applied underneath the airtight bandage. You could use **Bactroban**, but a nonprescription antibiotic ointment like **Polysporin** will probably work almost as well. It should be reapplied when the dressing is changed.

Severe wounds require special treatment. Dr. Richard Knutson is an orthepedic surgeon in Greenville, Mississippi. He has been treating serious skin injuries, puncture wounds and bed sores, with a sugar and iodine mixture. He started using plain sugar at the suggestion of a retired nurse who remembered the old-fashioned remedy from the preantibotic era. At first the surgeon was skeptical. "When we started I thought it was absolutely nuts. Sugar! The first thing you think about is the old jar of marmalade in the fridge growing all that junk. You think you'll create a perfect medium for bacterial growth. That turned out not to be the case."[67]

Dr. Knutson's technique is not yet popular in this contry but European surgeons have found that it works. After five thousand patients and over fifteen years' experience, Dr. Knutson shared his recipe with us and convinced us that his sugar cure is worth a try.

HERBAL REMEDY

Some people swear by aloe vera gel for scrapes and burns, either squeezed straight from a fresh-cut leaf or from a tube. Aloe has a venerable history, reaching back to well before the time of Christ. The Egyptian *Book of Remedies* cites aloe for curing infections and treating the skin, as well as preparing laxatives. Its popularity lasted through the centuries and spread far, to Greece and beyond; when the Spanish conquistadors came to the New World, they brought aloe with them.[68]

Does aloe deserve all this respect? Scientists are undecided. Although aloe gel contains several compounds that could, in theory, relieve pain, reduce inflammation, kill bacteria, and prevent the release of itch-provoking histamine, studies of its impact on wounds haven't provided a clear answer.[69] Many of these contradictory clinical studies were done decades ago, but one recent study used experimental burns in guinea pigs to test its efficacy. The creatures treated with aloe vera gel healed in thirty days and the control animals treated with simple bandaging or other creams needed fifty days to heal.[70]

Keeping an aloe vera plant on the kitchen or bathroom windowsill may be a smart move. In any event, even if aloe leaves turn out not to be extra helpful in speeding wound healing, daubing the gel on small burns and other wounds

---

Dr. Knutson's Sugar Dressing

Warm one pound of povidone iodine ointment (**Betadine**) in the top of a double boiler. As it melts, add six and a half ounces of **Betadine** solution, and then stir in four pounds of granulated table sugar. The mixture will have the consistency of natural-style chunky peanut butter.

The wound should be cleaned with soap, water, and hydrogen peroxide and allowed to dry before the dressing is applied (to a depth of about one-fourth inch). It must not be used on a wound that is still bleeding. The wound or bed sore should be covered with a clean gauze pad and the dressing changed at least once a day.

This is not a do-it-yourself project. Severe wounds require medical treatment. Physicians can contact Dr. Knutson for details at the Delta Medical Center, 130 North Shelby Street, Greenville, Mississippi 38701.

Aloe vera

Gel from the center of the leaf may provide temporary pain relief and aid healing.
Research results are equivocal.
Do not take internally (sap is a strong laxative).

★ ★ ★

As burns heal, they are often painful. Yet smearing anything on the affected area can make things worse. Our consultants suggest taking **Vitamin B₆**, twice a day, may help in controlling postburn pain.

doesn't seem to do much harm. It is not *first* aid for burns, though. If a burn occurs, *immediately* immerse the burned area in cold water to limit tissue damage and relieve pain. Only after that is it appropriate to apply aloe vera gel to minor burns. Serious burns or other wounds should get medical attention promptly.

FUTURE DRUGS

Given the uncertainties about aloe's efficacy, it's not surprising that researchers are working on a salve that would speed wound healing more dramatically. One of the most exciting new developments in the treatment of severe burns comes from China. A still-secret herbal concoction has produced dramatic results in Chinese burn patients according to its developer, Dr. Xu Rongxiang. People with disfiguring third-degree burns have recovered virtually unscarred.

Canker sores are a problem for many people. Doctors think that they usually result from trauma, such as biting the cheek, rather than from infection. There's no good explanation why some people get them so frequently, but there is a treatment. A little dab of **Temovate** (clobetasol), a very potent steroid ointment, usually clears up canker sores quickly. This prescription medication should not be overused, however. An over-the-counter product such as **Orabase** or the newer **Zilactin** may provide some relief if you can't get a prescription steroid cream.

Dr. Anthony Barbara of the Hackensack Medical Center Burn Unit and Harry Gaynor, president of the National Burn Victim Foundation in Orange, New Jersey, traveled to China to see first-hand the results of Dr. Xu's herbal remedy. When they met patients who had been treated and saw five more patients receiving the ointment, their initial skepticism turned to enthusiasm.[71] Dr. Barbara is planning scientific studies to determine if the ointment is as good as it appears to be.

Research is also proceeding on a variety of preparations of natural body chemicals that may promote healing. Some results have been positive, demonstrating 10 to 15 percent faster healing when epidermal growth factor is used.[72] There is much still to be learned about epidermal growth factor and related compounds, however. There seem to be several sorts of growth factor that may each have slightly different actions, and it appears that epidermal or other growth factors produced by the body's own tissues are involved in some skin diseases.[73] Until the scientists get this story completely sorted out, epidermal growth factor is not a practical solution. A plastic surgeon who has experimented with epidermal growth factor feels that lanolin may work better as a healing agent for many patients.[74]

Another medication under development that shows promise for wound healing is the serotonin blocker, ketanserin. Although it was originally developed to treat high blood pressure in pill form under the name **Sufrexal**, a preliminary study showed that ketanserin significantly hastened healing when it was applied to skin sores as an ointment. It may work by improving circulation to the wound.[75]

Itches and Ouches

INSECTS

No question about it, insect bites account for a lot of scratching. Mosquitoes are most notorious, but chiggers, fleas, and flies do their share of damage as well.

Prevention

Without a doubt the best way to deal with bug bites is to avoid getting bitten, but this is more easily said than done. Most of the popular insect repellents on the market contain a very effective chemical called "deet." Deet discourages mosquitoes, fleas, flies, ticks, and chiggers from biting.[76] Generally speaking, the more deet there is in a repellent, the more effective it is against bugs. Operating on that principle, a number of brands containing almost nothing but deet have appeared on the market in recent years. The only trouble with deet is its side effects: it can cause contact dermatitis, with the skin breaking out in a most dramatic fashion. Some people develop an allergy to it, and life-threatening allergic

Skin-So-Soft

Many people insist that Avon's Skin-So-Soft bath oil makes a dandy insect repellent. What do the experts say? They admit that Skin-So-Soft contains an ingredient that could repel mosquitoes, and one study showed that it works—but it may not retain its effectiveness against biting insects for long periods of time. No one knows how safe it is to smear this bath oil directly on the skin instead of using it in bathwater.

reactions have occurred. In addition, it is absorbed into the body and has caused convulsions in some people. Young children are especially vulnerable to this problem, so it is probably best to avoid using insect repellents on babies and use lower-concentration products, if needed, on kids under age five.

With Lyme disease on the loose, there is plenty of interest in a new product that can repel ticks from clothing. **Permanone Tick Repellent**, sold in garden stores and mountaineering supply shops, contains permethrin. If you have a hard time locating **Permanone**, you can contact the manufacturer: Coulston International (P.O. Box 30, Easton PA 18044). Customer service information is available at (215) 253-0167.

This insecticide is similar to those derived from chrysanthemum flowers, and when it is sprayed on long pants or long-sleeved shirts it can keep mosquitoes as well as ticks from burying their mouth parts in your skin.

The army operates in a lot of mosquito-infested places, so it has a strong interest in mosquitoes. It tested and discovered the most effective way to avoid mosquito bites. A combination of the standard military-issue deet repellent on exposed skin together with the **Permanone** spray on uniforms offered 99 percent protection in a part of Alaska buzzing with mosquitoes. The soldier guinea-pigs using this protection got only about four mosquito bites per person per hour—compared with 1,188 bites per person per hour for unprotected soldiers.[77] Ouch!

Relieving the Itch

Nothing but time will cure an itchy bite, but some remedies can relieve that maddening feeling for a while. Plantain, which grows as a backyard weed nearly everywhere, is reputed to soothe itchy bites if the leaves are crushed and applied as a poultice.[78]

OTC ointments can also help itches from bites. Our standby is

Plantain

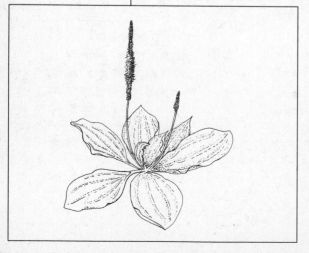

Tronolane, because it contains an anesthetic that can make a bite feel better long enough for a child to stop scratching and go to sleep. The same anesthetic, pramoxine, is also found in the nonprescription products **Tronothane**, **PrameGel**, and **Prax**.

For really major itches, though, we often turn to a stronger corticosteroid ointment. Check with your doctor about a small sample tube of a medication like **Kenalog** (triamcinolone), **Lidex** (fluocinonide), or **Synalar** (fluocinolone). It usually takes only a tiny dab of one of these potent medicines to quiet the most insistent itch for several hours. A person who used large quantities of these or similar steroid creams for many days might absorb enough to cause dangerous reactions throughout the body, not just on the skin, but a small amount used from time to time is rarely a problem. One caveat: babies have thinner skin and absorb drugs through their skins much more readily than adults. Don't use any topical corticosteroid on an infant or young child unless it was prescribed especially for them, with clear instructions on dosing.

Stings

A sting is worse than a bite. For one thing, it is a bit harder to avoid stings, since no insect repellents work on bees, wasps, and the like. For another, a sting doesn't just itch, it hurts, at least for a time. Then it may start to itch! But the real reason a bee sting may be more serious than a mosquito bite is the possibility of an allergic reaction. Many people are allergic to bees, yellow jackets, hornets, wasps, or fire ants and the reaction can be life-threatening. Emergency action is essential, because without prompt treatment the person may die.

Herbal Remedies

A sting that doesn't trigger an allergic reaction isn't dangerous, but it still hurts. Hopping up and down while clutching the toe that got stung is dramatic, but doesn't help much. One of our newspaper column readers suggested the onion cure for stings:

> When I get stung by a bee or yellow jacket, the area swells up and turns red, and you wouldn't believe the pain. Unfor-

---

EpiPen Auto-Injector

Epinephrine self-injector for reversing anaphylactic (allergic shock) reaction. Further emergency treatment may be needed.
Check expiration date periodically and store away from heat (*not* in the car glove compartment).

★ ★ ★

tunately my backyard swimming pool attracts hundreds of yellow jackets, and I frequently risk getting stung.

A friend told me to cut an onion in half and press the cut side to the sting, holding it there at least ten minutes. I tried it the last time I got stung, and miracle of miracles, it really helped: no pain, no swelling, no problems. Don't ask me how it works, but it does!

International onion expert, Dr. Eric Block, chairman of chemistry at the State University of New York at Albany explains why: onions contain an enzyme that breaks down the prostaglandins that form in response to a sting. Since this prostaglandin reaction is largely responsible for the feeling, the onion reduces the pain.

If you're all out of onions, reach for the meat tenderizer. Entomologists who spend their professional careers studying bees keep a supply on hand, and if they get stung, they mix it into a paste or goo with water and smear it on the sting.[79] The meat tenderizer is an enzyme that breaks down proteins, and stops the pain and swelling if applied quickly enough.

Lice

Lice are not a significant source of disease at this point in history, but they are both common and annoying. Head lice crop up in mini-epidemics at schools around the country every year, because children unwittingly pass them from one to another. Treating them is tedious, especially if you have to go through the drill more than once in a school year, but it's not especially difficult.

Nonprescription lice shampoos contain pyrethrins, chemicals derived from the chrysanthemum. They are at least as effective as **Kwell**, the prescription lice shampoo that contains the insecticide lindane, and appear to be less toxic. To prevent reinfestation after using any of these louse-killing products, it is necessary to remove the nits, or louse eggs, that are stuck on the hair close to the scalp. A fine-tooth comb is supplied with these preparations but hand removal of nits offers a whole new perspective on certain turns of phrase. A rinse called **Step2** weakens the cement that glues nits to hair, and can make the process somewhat easier, but combing out nits is still not likely to rank high on anyone's list of favorite things to do on a Sunday afternoon. A second treatment seven to ten days after the first is often recommended to take care of any nits that might have escaped notice and hatched out lice.

Besides removing the nits, bedding and clothing need to be washed and dried at hot temperatures. Combs and brushes must be treated. Hats, scarves, or coats that can't be washed need to be dry-cleaned. Many children have a menagerie of stuffed animals that "belong" in or on the bed, and often these creatures don't take kindly either to machine washing or to dry-cleaning. They'll need to be quarantined in a sealed plastic bag for two weeks in the closet—or for a week in the freezer. Upholstered furniture that the infested person has used needs to be vacuumed; and if the child likes to lie on the floor to read (ours do), the carpet should be vacuumed as well. These measures keep the infestation from spreading to other people as well as the original patient.

Such precautions to prevent the spread of lice are also necessary when the after-shampoo lice treatment **Nix** is used. **Nix** contains permethrin, a synthetic pyrethrinlike compound that is highly effective. Because it comes in the form of a creme rinse rather than a shampoo, the compound stays on the hair long after treatment and is supposed to protect against hatchling lice and "intruders" up to two weeks. (Some schools require nit removal before the child can return to class regardless of what treatment is used.)

POISON IVY AND COUSINS

Poison ivy, poison oak, and poison sumac all produce a resin (called urushiol) that is highly irritating to most people. After touching the leaves, stems, roots, or berries of these plants, the skin begins to itch, turn red, and blister. The offending chemical doesn't evaporate quickly, so it is possible to run into trouble just patting the fur of a dog or cat that has brushed up against a poison ivy plant in its rambles. Firewood that may have been

Nix
creme rinse
Prescription after shampoo lice treatment
Because this after-shampoo lice treatment remains on the hair shaft up to two weeks and kills any lice that hatch from nits, nit removal is necessary only if the school requires it.

★ ★

dragged through the brush can also be a source of the resin. So can tools and clothing. One person described a very uncomfortable rash she developed when, knowing she had brushed up against poison ivy leaves, she stripped off all her clothing before entering her house—then sat on the pile to remove her boots!

If she had only gotten straight into the shower after dropping her clothes in the washing machine, she could have saved herself a lot of grief. Prevention of poison ivy or poison oak rashes is much better than treatment. The primary rules are to stay away from the plants (or possible sources of contamination) if possible; and if you can't avoid contact, wash as soon as possible with plenty of water. People out hiking far from running water might want to carry disposable wipers with alcohol, and use them immediately after any contact. To be effective, washing with water (no harsh soap) should be done within five minutes of exposure.[80]

Poison ivy grows everywhere in the United States but is especially common on the east coast and the midwest. Like poison oak, which is especially abundant along the west coast, it bears its leaves in clusters of three and develops white berries by late summer. Poison sumac, found mostly in wet parts of the southeast, also has white berries. Recognizing the plants and giving them a wide berth is the best approach; but lumberjacks, telephone line workers, hunters, birdwatchers, and others who must spend a lot of time outdoors don't always have that option.

Poison Ivy

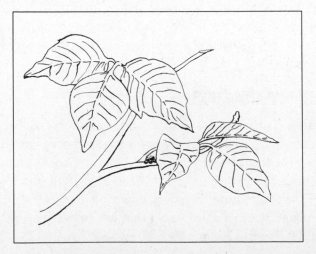

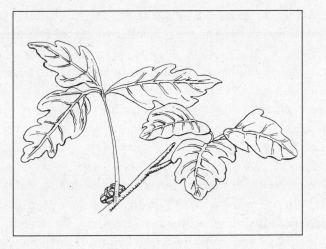

Poison Oak

A barrier skin cream that partially protects the skin from contact with urushiol may be helpful for such people. The product is called **Ivy Shield** and is supplied through outdoor equipment stores. (Manufacturer is Interpro, Inc., located in Haverhill, MA.) Even for those using **Ivy Shield**, it's important to remember that tools and clothing (don't forget gloves, hats, or shoes) that are contaminated with urushiol need to be thoroughly cleaned, or later contact with them could provoke a rash.

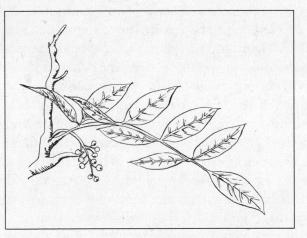

Poison Sumac

If you come down with the rash, what can be done for the itch? For a rash that's not too troublesome, a cool compress or tepid bath may be soothing. One reader recommends baking soda and witch hazel:

You should know about a remedy I have often used for poison ivy. It is soothing and helps get rid of the poison ivy blisters.

Make a thick paste of bicarbonate of soda with enough witch hazel to give it the consistency of cold cream, or at least cream cheese, and spread it over the blisters. While it dries and cakes, it will cool the irritation and then it will dry out the blisters.

We can't vouch for the effectiveness of this remedy, but it might help and probably won't do any damage for a mild case of poison oak or ivy. A very intense rash or one that covers a lot of territory, however, calls for a prescription corticosteroid. A strong ointment like **Temovate** (clobetasol), **Diprosone** or **Maxivate** (betamethasone), or **Aristocort** or **Kenalog** (triamcinolone) should do the trick. It is applied two or three times daily to the rash. Even though the rash should feel much better within two days, the treatment needs to be continued for a week, gradually changing to once daily application. If the ointment is discontinued too early, a rebound rash, at least as bad as the original, may appear.[81]

In very severe cases, there are two options. If only a small area is affected, one of these same strong steroid ointments may be applied. Then a piece of plastic wrap is cut to cover the area and fastened down with adhesive tape. This kind of airtight bandaging seems to force the skin to absorb more of the medication. If a bad rash covers a large area, the best treatment is an oral corticosteroid such as prednisone. This treatment isn't appropriate for pregnant women or people with other medical conditions, such as ulcers, diabetes, or high blood pressure, but for those who can take it, prednisone offers very dramatic relief.[82] It's extremely important to follow the prescribed dosing instructions, even though they will be complicated: the dose starts out very high, to provide prompt action, then gradually tapers down. Although relatively safe, this treatment isn't totally innocuous. Nearly one-fifth of the people on this short-term steroid therapy experience side effects, including digestive tract upset, insomnia, nervousness, or even weight gain.

Dry Skin

In arid climates, or in the winter when the furnace goes on and the humidity drops, dry skin bothers many folks. When there's little moisture in the air, water tends to evaporate from the skin, leaving it parched and often scratchy. This problem is especially common as we age, for the outer layer of the skin gets coarser, less compact, and isn't as good a barrier against moisture loss. With less active sweat glands, the moisture that migrates to the surface isn't replaced as quickly. Oil-producing glands also slow down, so there is less "grease" on top of the skin to trap water inside. No wonder older people often suffer with cracked, scaling skin along their shins, forearms, and the backs of their hands.

> Dry skin usually comes on gradually, or in response to environmental conditions. If it develops suddenly, for no apparent reason, check in with a dermatologist or your primary doctor. Dry skin may be a symptom of low thyroid gland activity or other problem.

Although dry skin is especially troublesome for older people, it can strike at any age. It doesn't matter how many candles are on your birthday cake if your hands are in soapy water several times a day, or if you're out in cold dry winds for several hours at a time. Spending a lot of time in the low humidity of airplanes can also be an invitation to dry skin.

NONPRESCRIPTION REMEDIES

Getting rid of dry skin is an ongoing process for as long as the air is dry. Detergents, soaps, and solvents can strip away the skin's natural oils, so dive into waterproof gloves before sticking your hands in the dishpan, and cut back on bathing to no more than every two or three days. Wash water should not be too hot, and the soap should be mild—**Dove** rates very favorably. After bathing, the skin should be patted dry, not rubbed, and a heavy-duty moisturizer should be slathered on immediately. How heavy-duty? Well, petroleum jelly like **Vaseline** has always been high on the dermatologists' hit parade, although some people object to the

Instead of Soap

It's possible to get clean without soap. Except when you can actually see the dirt, it may be possible to get by using soap only on the hands, armpits, and genital areas when you bathe. Plain old water will take off most of the dirt you can't see. Or use a soap alternative. A soap-free cleanser like **Cetaphil** or **Keri Facial Cleanser** is often recommended for washing off the dirt without stripping the skin of oils and leaving it uncomfortably dry.

slippery-slimy feeling. The idea is to trap all that moisture in the skin, and **Vaseline** is great at that. So are **Eucerin**, **Lubriderm**, and **Nivea**.

Don't save the moisturizing lotion just for when you climb out of the tub. Daily use may help keep dry skin under control. If you can't learn to love **Vaseline** or **Nivea**, you may want to check out **Aquaphor**, **Complex 15**, **Curel**, or **Moisturel**. *Consumer Reports* testers ranked **Sea Breeze Moisture Lotion** as tops. Like **Moisturel** or **Complex 15**, **Sea Breeze** is light enough to use on the face. Dermatologists also recommend creams containing urea, such as **Aqua Care**, **Carmol,** or **Nutraplus**.

Fish Oil Against Dry Skin

Some of our readers have a different favorite: **Preparation H**.

Some time ago I read your column about using Preparation H for dry skin. I had a cracked, bleeding dry spot on my index finger, and had tried everything to no avail. After I put Preparation H on my finger, it cleared up like magic.

We don't know quite why **Preparation H** should be so great for dry skin, but it does rank high on the greasiness scale. Its other ingredients, shark liver oil and live yeast cell derivative, may also have some beneficial impact. It is certainly readily available and many enthusiastic users will vouch for it.

Bovine Beauty Aids

If **Preparation H** isn't to your taste, you might want to consider shopping for skin cream at your local farm supply store. When we printed a letter from a farmer's wife suggesting **Bag Balm** for cracked, dry skin, we thought our readers would be amused by the idea of bovine beauty aids. Thousands of letters poured in from people wanting to know where to find this ointment. Many others wrote to testify to its effectiveness. Both **Bag Balm** and **Bova Cream** are udder ointments, designed to protect cows' teats from chapping. They contain such basic moisturizing ingredients as petroleum jelly, lano-

---

Preparation H

Contains live yeast cell derivative, shark liver oil, and phenylmercuric nitrate.

Live yeast cell derivative seems to accelerate wound healing.

Testimonials suggest the ointment may be effective in treating dry skin.

★ ★ ★

lin, and the related allantoin, so it's little wonder so many people find them effective for dry skin.

While a few upscale city stores have started to carry these products, farm co-op stores may still be the most reliable source. They may also be ordered directly from the manufacturers. **Udder Cream**, (a.k.a. **Bova Cream**) has a sweet fragrance like hand cream rather than a barnyard product. It may be ordered by calling 1-800-345-7339, or by writing Redex Industries, Inc., PO Box 939, Salem, OH 44460. To order **Bag Balm** from its maker, the Dairy Association Company, write to them in Lyndonville, VT 05851. It is also carried by the Vermont Country Store Mail Order Office (PO Box 3000, Manchester Center, VT 05255-3000). The phone number is (802) 362-2400.

Other sources for lanolin include such moisturizing creams as **cutemol** [Summers Laboratories, Inc., PO Box 162, Fort Washington, PA 19034, (800) 533-SKIN], **A and D** ointment, **Keri**, **Lanolor**, **Lanoline**, **Ultra Derm**, or **Wondra**. Any of these should be available without a prescription at your local pharmacy.

PRESCRIPTION DRUGS

Those who react badly to lanolin or don't get relief from **Bag Balm** may want to see a dermatologist for a prescription treatment called **Lac-Hydrin**. It's strong medicine for painfully dry, cracking skin. The active ingredient, buffered lactic acid (also known as alpha-hydroxy acid), improves the outer layer of the skin so it is less likely to lose moisture. (It may even be slightly helpful against fine wrinkles on the face, but that's another story.) **Lac-Hydrin** is supposed to be used twice daily for the first month, then once a day thereafter, and it does make a major difference when dry skin has reached the critical level.

There are a few nonprescription skin creams that provide alpha-hydroxy acid, although in much lower concentrations than the 12 percent present in **Lac-Hydrin**. For similar but less dramatic benefits, look for **Aqua Glycolic Lotion**, **Lac-Hydrin Five**, or **LactiCare**. Unless dry skin is severe, these lotions should be able to help put moisture back into the skin and relieve the itch that sometimes accompanies dryness.

> *Lac-Hydrin*
> *(ammonium lactate)*
> Simply the best thing there is for dry skin. Too bad it's available only by prescription. May sting or burn when first applied to irritated skin. Keep away from eyes, nose, or mouth.
>
> ★ ★ ★ ★

Psoriasis

Psoriasis could give a person some understanding of the trials and tribulations of Job. Reddish or salmon-colored patches of psoriasis covered with silvery scales may detract from a person's appearance, and the irrational fear of friends and acquaintances that it could be contagious (it isn't) may be socially and emotionally devastating. But what is most likely to try the sufferer's patience is that psoriasis can't be cured. It can, however, be controlled. Good control requires close teamwork between doctor and patient, so the first job is to find a knowledgable and empathetic dermatologist who really cares about psoriasis. This doctor will be able to help a patient figure out what is making the psoriasis flare up and how to avoid making it worse, as well as work out therapeutic strategies.

Skin cells normally take a month or more to develop, migrate to the surface of the skin, and be sloughed off. In psoriasis, they go through that entire trip, start to finish, in a matter of days. There is wide variation in how much of the skin is covered with these psoriatic patches, and this influences the type of treatment that is appropriate. If there are lots of little patches scattered widely over the body, the entire body may need to be exposed to ultraviolet-B (UVB) radiation, for example,

---

Spotting Flare-Up Triggers

People with psoriasis need to treat their skin gently, for flare-ups commonly occur a few weeks after any sort of trauma to the skin.

- Scratching at patches often aggravates the situation. Psoriasis doesn't always itch, but may when the skin is too dry. Using a mild soap and a good moisturizer can help.
- Sunshine may help, but sunburn will aggravate the problem. Keep an eye on the clock.
- Emotional upset can make psoriasis worse, so stress management becomes a priority.
- Infections can trigger a psoriasis flare. Strep infections are notorious, but the flu or other infectious illnesses can also cause trouble.
- Many medications make psoriasis worse. Tell your dermatologist about any drugs prescribed by your other physicians, so that if necessary, a different type of medication can be substituted. Beta-blockers, lithium, and antimalarial drugs such as **Plaquenil** are notorious.

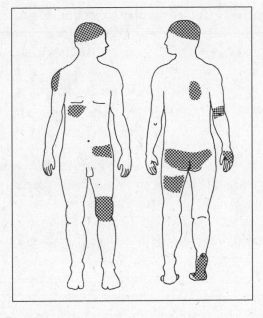

*Psoriasis
Hot Spots*

or to anthralin. When only small, scattered areas are involved, covering no more than about three percent of the body, spot treatment with cortisone creams usually works well. A more severe case, involving up to 20 percent of the body, often requires more aggressive treatment.

SKIN THERAPIES

Sunshine

The simplest and most "natural" topical therapy is often very effective, especially when scaling is not too severe. Although we have all been hearing about the dangers of sun exposure for normal skin, sunlight can work wonders for psoriasis. Care must be taken to avoid sunburn. A weekend at the beach might seem like a strange prescription, but often it does a lot of good, presumably because of the exposure to both A and B wavelengths of ultraviolet rays.

Topical Corticosteroids

There are a number of topical cortisone-like medications used for psoriasis, all available only by prescription. Over two-

---

Sun

A glorious tan could just be one of the cheapest and most pleasant home remedies for psoriasis.
It is often very effective. Take precautions not to burn, as this could aggravate the condition.

★ ★ ★ ★

thirds of patients using **Diprolene** (betamethasone) ointment twice daily can clear about 85 percent of their psoriasis patches in about three weeks. After that, the patches are kept clear by using the ointment only on weekends (Saturday morning and night, and Sunday morning). Weekend-only dosing is necessary because this steroid ointment is so strong that it poses a serious risk of absorbing too much cortisone into the system or of damaging the skin.

Temovate (clobetasol) is also highly effective, with 80 percent of patients clearing most psoriasis patches after two weeks of twice-a-day use. After the first two-week course, it is necessary to take a week off before treating again for another two weeks. Clearing can be maintained with a twice-a-week application—one Monday, one Friday, just before and after the weekend. **Temovate**, like **Diprolene,** is a super-potent corticosteroid cream, and should not be used on the face or in skin folds such as under the arms or the breasts, where it could cause excessive thinning and permanent stretch marks.[83] Using **Temovate** more often than prescribed can be very dangerous, with such potential side effects as ulcers, fluid retention, high blood pressure, glaucoma, cataracts, muscle weakness, and osteoporosis.

More familiar steroid creams, like **Synalar** (fluocinolone) or **Lidex** (fluocinonide), may also work, especially if the treated patch is covered with plastic wrap or an airtight dressing in the evening after the medication is applied. Injecting a corticosteroid into a localized patch of psoriasis is another treatment that is often effective for small areas.

Anthralin

Anthralin is an old-fashioned prescription drug that's proven very helpful with a new way of using it, the anthralin "minutes" therapy. Instead of smearing it on affected patches at bedtime and waking in the morning to find bedclothes stained purple, then having to scrub the goo off with mineral oil, psoriasis patients now can apply fresh-mixed anthralin over the entire body, affected and unaffected skin both, leave it on for ten minutes, and wash it off in the shower. No purple pajamas, only itching or pink skin as possible side effects. This therapy must be carefully supervised by a dermatologist, since periodic checks of liver and kidney function are advisable.

Coal Tar with Ultraviolet

Coal tar preparations applied to the skin before exposure to ultraviolet-B radiation (UVB), the "Goeckerman therapy," is another skin-deep treatment for psoriasis that is frequently helpful. However, this procedure is somewhat messy and requires a strictly controlled source of ultraviolet. Unlike anthralin, which can be used at home, Goeckerman therapy generally calls for a patient to go to the hospital or a special psoriasis day-care center where a tar can be applied afternoon, evening, and morning and ultraviolet exposure can be monitored. Proper eye protection is crucial.

ORAL TREATMENTS

Fish Oil

One oral medicine for psoriasis is not a treatment in itself, but seems to make other treatments work better. Dermatologists studying fish oil have found that patients given fish oil capsules (twenty per day) and exposed to UVB did no better than those taking an equal amount of olive oil in capsules; once the ultraviolet therapy stopped, however, the patients taking fish oil continued to do well, while those on olive oil relapsed rather quickly. According to Dr. John J. Voorhees, who supervised the study, "it [fish oil] may be a minimal, but useful and important, adjunctive therapy."[84]

The active ingredient in fish oil is presumably eicosapentaenoic acid, or EPA for short. Prefer to get it from food rather than capsules? Strap on the hip waders: it takes about two pounds of fish to provide 2.8 grams of EPA, which is what dermatology researcher Vincent A. Ziboh considers "a reasonable amount" against psoriasis.[85]

> **MaxEPA**
> *(fish oil)*
> Not very effective against psoriasis on its own.
> Other treatments may work better or last longer for a person taking fish oil.
> Side effects: fish breath, increased tendency to bleed
> ★

**Foods to
Avoid during
PUVA
Treatment**

Certain foods
contain natural
psoralens that
could possibly
make PUVA therapy
more dangerous:

  carrots
  celery
  figs
  limes
  mustard
  parsley
  parsnips

PUVA

Perhaps the most commonly used oral medicine for psoriasis is a psoralen, taken before exposure to ultraviolet-A radiation to make the skin more responsive to the UVA. (Parsley, celery, figs, and certain other foods contain natural psoralens, but are not used for treatment because of the difficulties of getting the right dose.) The pill, **Oxsoralen** (methoxsalen), is taken two hours before the UVA exposure, but the body remains sensitive to UV radiation for the full twenty-four hours afterward. It is important to protect the skin and the eyes from sunlight during that time, even from sunshine indoors coming through a window. UVA-absorbing wraparound sunglasses are needed, because the medication in the lens of the eye could hasten cataract formation if touched by ultraviolet rays. After a day, most of the drug has been eliminated from the eye and other parts of the body so sunshine no longer poses an extra hazard, but sunbathing should be avoided for forty-eight hours after taking the medication.[86] Of course, during the UVA therapeutic exposure, proper eye protection is crucial.

PUVA treatment is effective in 85–90 percent of patients.[87] However, it is not innocuous. Unintentional exposure to sunlight or ultraviolet can cause severe burns. This therapy also increases a person's lifetime risk of skin cancer, and the risk rises with exposure to PUVA.[88]

Methoxsalen can also cause nausea, insomnia, nervousness, depression, headaches, or edema. Taking the medication with a small amount of food may help counteract the nausea, which is not uncommon. It's important for the doctor supervising PUVA therapy to know about all other drugs that you are taking, as any other medicine that can cause photosensitivity could increase the risk and interfere with the therapy.[89]

Methotrexate

Another oral medication sometimes used for severe psoriasis is methotrexate. This drug, originally used against cancer, is usually reserved for cases that haven't responded to other therapies, and for those whose psoriasis has affected the joints (psoriatic arthritis). It may be given as tablets or an injection, with the dose adjusted for the individual patient. Dr. Gerald D. Weinstein, chairman of dermatology at the University of California, Irvine, suggests to his colleagues that they use the lowest dosages and the longest rest periods that can still provide adequate (not complete) control of the condition. In addition, he recommends that some patients will do well off methotrexate during the summer and shouldn't take it then.[90]

Why the caution? Methotrexate can have nasty side effects. Perhaps the most common is liver damage. About one-fourth of the patients in one Scandinavian study had cirrhosis or fibrosis of the liver after a cumulative dose of about four grams—the amount a person might get in about three years at maximum dose with short rest periods.[91] Patients using methotrexate regularly need periodic liver biopsies and must avoid other drugs that could harm the liver, especially alcohol. Other potential side effects include blood abnormalities, diarrhea, and mouth ulcers. But for some people, the benefits of using methotrexate—cautiously—outweigh the risk.

Tegison

Tegison (etretinate) is a synthetic derivative of vitamin A. This makes it a kissing cousin of **Accutane** as well, but **Tegison** is much more effective for psoriasis. This oral medicine is usually reserved for the more severe cases as an "end of the line" kind of option. It is one of the few treatments that may be effective for pustular psoriasis, although it can be a real benefit for some other psoriasis sufferers as well, working for 80 percent of the patients who try it. **Tegison**'s no cure, but can lead to a remission lasting anywhere from a few weeks to several months, almost a year. For best absorption, **Tegison** should be taken with milk.

Although **Tegison** works well, it should not be used by women who are planning to have children in the future. This drug causes serious birth defects, and lingers in the body for years. There are a variety of other potential side effects, too, including liver problems (which may be very serious), elevated blood cholesterol and other fats, and calcium buildup in tendons or ligaments, leading to bone spurs. Most of the moist areas of the body dry out: chapped lips, dry eyes, sore mouth, and nosebleed from a dry nose are common, and may be noticed before any improvement in the psoriasis. Persistence is rewarded, but the doctor should be notified right away in the event of headaches, blurred or disturbed vision, nausea, yellowish skin or eyes, flulike symptoms, dark urine, or unusual aches in the joints. These symptoms might be the warning flag of a serious problem.

If **Tegison** is used for a short period of time before PUVA treatment is started, it may enhance significantly the effectiveness of the PUVA. Dermatologists call this combo approach RePUVA. (The "Re" stands for retinoid.) RePUVA can speed the clearing of psoriasis patches and dramatically reduce the amount of ultraviolet radiation needed.

FUTURE POSSIBILITIES

Topical Vitamin D

A new topical treatment being developed for psoriasis utilizes activated vitamin D_3. In one double-blind study of this experimental medication, 57 patients had the vitamin in a petroleum jelly base applied to a psoriasis plaque on one side of their body; a similar plaque on the other side of the body, plain petroleum jelly was applied. After a month and a half, nearly all the areas treated with vitamin D_3 were noticeably better, and there wasn't any visible improvement on the patches that had gotten plain petroleum jelly.[92]

At the University of Aarhus, Denmark, Dr. Knud Kragballe has studied the effectiveness of a synthetic vitamin D-like compound called calcipotriol. (The active form of oral vitamin D_3 is calcitriol.) Dr. Kragballe reports "marked improvement" in most patients using calcipotriol, and in another European study, calcipotriol with betamethasone was significantly more effective than the betamethasone ointment alone.[93] One significant advantage of using vitamin D compounds on the skin, rather than taking the vitamin orally, is that there is little risk of side effects. Taken as a vitamin or oral medication, vitamin D or D_3 can alter calcium metabolism in the body, with potentially serious consequences. According to Dr. Kragballe, calcipotriol is a hundred times less active in its impact on calcium than oral vitamin D_3. However, calcipotriol is not yet available in this country.

Soriatane

Soriatane (acitretin) is a "second-generation" retinoid that has much in common with **Tegison**. It seems to be about as effective for severe psoriasis, with 74 percent of the patients in one small study getting a good or excellent result.[94] Very likely **Soriatane** will be as beneficial as **Tegison** in RePUVA therapy, and more patients may be able to use it. **Soriatane** is cleared from the body in a far shorter time than **Tegison**. It has a half-life of two days, compared with several months for **Tegison**, and the drug can't be measured in the blood after about three weeks of stopping. Consequently, women will not automatically be excluded from the benefits of this medication just because they are still capable of childbearing. Of course, like any retinoid, **Soriatane** should not be taken shortly before or during pregnancy because of the risk of birth defects.

Adverse effects are quite similar to those that **Tegison** causes: chapped lips are almost univeral, hair loss is common, and nearly three-quarters experience fingertip peeling. Joint pain may be more common with **Soriatane**—perhaps as high as two-thirds to three-quarters. Other side effects of concern include possible liver damage, elevated cholesterol, and calcium deposits in ligaments or tendons. Headaches, fatigue, and digestive tract upset are also possible.[95]

Piritrexim

Another medication under development is piritrexim, a compound that is related to methotrexate. Like methotrexate, piritrexim seems to slow the turnover of psoriasis-affected cells without noticeably affecting normal skin cells. Researchers hope that piritrexim will prove less likely than methotrexate to accumulate in the liver and cause harm, but clinical studies are in an early stage.[96] If piritrexim actually lives up to the hope that it will be as effective as methotrexate for severe or resistant psoriasis without being as toxic, it will be a great advantage for those patients who don't respond to other therapies.

Sulfasalazine

This is an experimental new use of an old drug generally used for inflammatory bowel disease. Dr. John Voorhees of the University of Michigan reports that an eight-week, double-blind, placebo-controlled study was somewhat promising. Those patients who were able to tolerate the medication (starting at a low dose and gradually increasing to 1 gram four times a day) had a 50 percent improvement in the percentage of the body surface involved with psoriasis. Patients on placebo did not have a similar improvement. The difficulty was that many people couldn't handle the drug: it often causes nausea, vomiting, loss of appetite, and other digestive tract disturbances. Sulfasalazine is not approved by the FDA for the treatment of psoriasis, and more research on this use of the drug is needed.

Cyclosporine

Another medication that is available but used for problems other than psoriasis is cyclosporine. This immunosuppressant is usually prescribed to prevent rejection of transplanted kidneys, livers, hearts, or other organs. Scientists are investigating its use as a last resort for people suffering from "severe recalcitrant psoriasis." In a study at the University of Michigan, the overwhelming majority of the patients showed at least some clearing of their psoriasis, with about one-fifth getting great results.[97] Unfortunately, most of these patients experienced a relapse almost as soon as they stopped the medication. Although in this study no patients experienced a rebound effect, one French patient nearly died after stopping cyclosporine suddenly.[98]

The use of cyclosporine is limited both by its exorbitant cost and by its potentially serious side effects. Although patients using this medication are regularly monitored for kidney function, research suggests that the usual kidney function tests (serum creatinine or creatinine clearance) are not reliable indicators of the level of kidney damage the drug may have done.[99] Other side effects of concern include increased blood pressure, hair overgrowth, tremor, headaches, and gum overgrowth.

Researchers in Great Britain have attempted to get around the problem of side effects by prescribing very low doses of cyclosporine for long periods of time. Dr. Christopher E. M. Griffiths reports positive results, with the average patient getting nearly 80 percent relief from psoriasis that had responded to no other treatment. However, more than half of these patients experienced side effects of the treatment.[100] At this time, cyclosporine should be considered an experimental, last-ditch psoriasis treatment, with considerable potential to do harm.

The future for skin treatments is rosy indeed. Effective new treatments are being developed for a range of problems from acne and hair loss to burns and psoriasis. With preventive care, especially sun protection, there is no reason most people won't be able to look good as they get older.

Quick Takes

- **Retin-A** does work for wrinkles. Don't expect miracles, but regular use can undo some of the damage brought on by years of sun exposure.

- Pimples can be prevented with **Retin-A**, or a topical antibiotic such as **Cleocin T**, **Erymax**, or **Topicycline**. When **Isotrex** (the topical version of **Accutane**) becomes available, we will have another important tool in the fight against blemishes.

- **Rogaine Topical Solution** can help stop hair loss for some people. The sooner after thinning begins the drug is started, the better it works, but don't count on long-term improvement. When the **Rogaine** is discontinued, hair loss returns.

- Some drugs cause hair loss .If you think your medicine may be making you bald, check with your physician. There may be an alternative medication that would not have this effect.

- Dandruff is easily controlled these days by rotating medicated shampoos. For a bad case of dandruff or seborrheic dermatitis, check with your doctor about a new prescription shampoo containing the antifungal drug **Nizoral**.

- There are now so many effective antifungal agents on pharmacy shelves that no one need suffer from athlete's foot any more. Patience and persistence are the keys to success. Prescription products, such as **Nizoral** cream, **Loprox**, **Naftin**, or **Spectazole** can help clear up any serious infection.

- **Bactroban** is the most exciting new topical antibiotic to come along in over twenty years. This prescription cream works against a wide range of skin infections, especially staph bugs responsible for impetigo.

- Herpes is still incurable, but it can be controlled by **Zovirax**. It works well against both genital sores and fever blisters. This extraordinary antiviral medicine has recently been shown to speed healing of shingles as well as chicken pox. When the pain of shingles lingers, **Zostrix** (made from hot peppers) can help provide some relief.

- For speedy healing of wounds, keep them clean, moist and covered. Any topical antibiotic ointment can help under a dressing. **2nd Skin** offers protection of burns, blisters and abrasions.

- Sugar is an old-fashioned remedy for wounds that is gaining respect and new converts. It helps them heal more rapidly, especially hard-to-treat bed sores or deep puncture wounds. See Dr. Richard Knutson's formula on page 153.

- Effective anti-itch products are best obtained from your doctor. Small sample tubes of steroid creams such as **Lidex**, **Kenalog**, or **Synalar** can work wonders against insect bites. Don't go hog wild, however, since such strong prescription medications should be treated with respect.

- Bovine beauty aids are the latest rage against dry skin. **Bag Balm** and **Udder Cream** are excellent moisturizers. The magic ingredients are lanolin and pretroleum jelly. **Preparation H** also has many enthusiastic supporters for everything from wound healing to wrinkle treatment and dry skin. Some surgical patients swear that it is the best remedy they have found to relieve the itching of surgical scars.

- Psoriasis responds to sunshine as long as you don't get burned. If you can afford a trip to the Dead Sea for a soak in the briny water and a relaxing sun bath, you might be amazed by the results. Strong topical steroids such as **Diprolene** and **Temovate** also work extremely well when used cautiously under a doctor's supervision.

References

[1] "Ortho *Retin-A* 'Efficacy with Accuracy' Ads Introduce *Delcap*." *FDC Reports (The Rose Sheet)* 1990 (Feb. 12); 11(7):6.

[2] "*Retin-A* Reduced Photodamage in 68% of Subjects Using .05% Concentration." *FDC Reports (The Rose Sheet)* 1990 (Jan. 8); 11(2):1–2.

[3] Henahan, John F. "Preliminary Drug Effects Show Continued Success in Photoaging." *Dermatology Times* 1989 (Oct.); 10(10):2, 4.

[4] Conference Proceedings: 48th Annual Meeting of the American Academy of Dermatology (San Francisco, December 2–7, 1989), January 1990; 4.

[5] Wright, Martha. "Tretinoin Appears to Be Hopeful in Reducing Actinic Keratoses." *Dermatology Times* 1988 (July); 9(7):4.

[6] "Tretinoin Q & A." *Dermatology Times* 1989 (Mar.); 10(3):22.

[7] Sweet, Cheryl A. " 'Healthy Tan'—A Fast-Fading Myth." *FDA Consumer* 1989; 23(5): 11–13.

[8] Council on Scientific Affairs. "Harmful Effects of Ultraviolet Radiation." *JAMA* 1989; 262:382.

[9] "Injuries Associated with Ultraviolet Tanning Devices—Wisconsin." *MMWR* 1989 (May 19); 38:333–335.

[10] Council on Scientific Affairs, op. cit. p. 383.

[11] Rivers, J.K., et al. "UVA Sunbeds: Tanning, Photoprotection, Acute Adverse Effects and Immunological Changes." *Brit. J. Dermatology* 1989; 120: 767–777.

[12] "Allergic Reaction to One Sunscreen Held No Reason to Avoid All." *Skin & Allergy News* 1989; 20(3):3, 35.

[13] Schoen, Linda Allen, and Lazar, Paul. *The Look You Like*. New York: Marcel Dekker, Inc., 1990.

[14] Henahan, John F. "Antibiotic Varieties Available for Acne Treatment Are Increasing." *Dermatology Times* 1988 (July); 9(7):23.

[15] Facklam, David P., et el. "An Epidemiologic Postmarketing Surveillance Study of Prescription Acne Medications." *Am. J. Public Health* 1990; 80:50–53.

[16] Elbaum, David J. "Comparison of the Stability of Topical Isotretinoin and Topical Tretinoin and their Efficacy in Acne." *J. Am. Acad. Dermatology* 1988; 19:486–491.

[17] Henahan, John F. "Metronidazole Found Extremely Effective Against Acne Rosacea." *Dermatology Times* 1988 (July); 9(7):11.

[18] "OC Plus Barrier Contraceptive Advised for Women on Accutane." *Skin & Allergy News* 1990; 21(2): 3, 27.

[19] "Effects of Hypervitaminosis A May Be Misdiagnosed as Cirrhosis." *Skin & Allergy News* 1989; 20(4):35.

[20] Hendler , Sheldon Saul. *The Doctors' Vitamin and Mineral Encyclopedia*. New York: Simon and Schuster, 1990.

[21] Wright, Martha. "Determine the Source of Excess Androgen Before Treating Acne." *Dermatology Times* 1989 (Sept.): 17–18.

[22] Prescott, Lawrence M. "Antiandrogen Can Help in Acne." *Med. World News* 1990 (Jan. 2); 31(2):39.

[23] " 'Acne Cosmetica' Called Fallacy by MD who Originated Concept." *Skin & Allergy News* 1988; 19(12):2, 35.

[24] Ball, Chris. "Cosmetics Only a Contributing Factor in Adult-Onset Female Acne." *Dermatology Times* 1989; 10(6):1, 29.

[25] Koperski, J.A., et al. "Topical Minoxidil Therapy for Androgenetic Alopecia." *Arch. Dermatol.* 1987; 123:1483–1487.

[26] Price, Vera H., et al. "Sorting Out the Clues in Alopecia." *Patient Care* 1989 (Sept. 15); 72.

[27] "Minoxidil's Effectiveness Seems to Extend to Women." *Med. World News* 1989 (June 26); 23.

[28] "Results with Minoxidil Perhaps as Good in Women as in Men." *Skin & Allergy News* 1989; 20(4):3, 22.

[29] Henahan, Sean. "Better Hair Growth Seen With Retinoid, Minoxidil Combination." *Dermatology Times* 1989; 10(10):17.

[30] "Phase II Results with Cyoctol." *Scrip* 1989 (Dec. 15); 1473:28.

[31] Prescott, Lawrence M. "Hair Loss Halted by Topical Antiandrogen." *Med. World News* 1990 (Jan. 22); 31(2):39.

[32] Price, et al., op. cit. p. 81.

[33] Burke, Karen E. "Hair Loss." *Postgraduate Medicine* 1989; 85(6):52–77.

[34] Ibid. p. 57.

[35] "The Risks of Dyeing." *University of California, Berkeley Wellness Letter* 1986; 2(11):2.

[36] Bailey, John E. Personal communication, March 6, 1990.

[37] Cantor, Kenneth P., et al. "Hair Dye Use and Risk of Leukemia and Lymphoma." *Am. J. Public Health* 1988; 78:570–571.

[38] Freni-Titulaer, Lambertina W.J., et al. "Connective Tissue Disease in Southeastern Georgia: A Case-Control Study of Etiologic Factors." *Am. J. Epidemiology* 1989; 130:404–409.

[39] Ibid. p. 408.

[40] Ferguson, Lynnette R., and Baguley, Bruce C. "Verapamil as a Co-Mutagen in the Salmonella/Mammalian Microsome Mutagenicity Test." *Mutation Research* 1988; 209:57–62.

[41] "Ketoconazole 'Significantly Decreases Hirsutism' After 6 Months." *Skin & Allergy News* 1988; 19(11):13.

[42] Stulberg, Daniel L., and Caruthers, Barbara S. "Hirsutism: A Practical Approach to Improving Physical and Mental Well-Being." *Postgraduate Medicine* 1990; 87(8):199–205.

[43] Bricklin, Mark. *The Practical Encyclopedia of Natural Healing.* Emmaus, PA: Rodale Press, 1983,. p. 141.

[44] Guttman, Cheryl. "Ketoconazole Found Effective for Seborrhea." *Dermatology Times* 1989; 10(6):1, 28.

[45] "Antifungal Shampoo Effective against Dermatitis of Scalp." *Med. World News* 1989 (April 10); 60.

[46] "Naftifine for Fungal Skin Infections." *Medical Letter* 1988; 30: 98–99.

[47] "Onychomycosis." *Itraconazole: A New Era in Oral Antifungal Therapy.* Proceedings of a Round Table Meeting held at the occasion of the British Association of Dermatologists' Annual Meeting, London, 8 July 1988, pp. 55–57.

[48] "Onychomycosis and Terbinafine." *Lancet* 1990; 335:636.

[49] "Roche's Amorolfine Nears Filings." *Scrip* 1990 (Mar. 21); 1498:25.

[50] Odom, Richard. "Effective Drug Therapy in Streptococcal Skin Infections." *Modern Medicine* 1989; 57(5):130–139.

[51] "Mupirocin: Safe and Effective for Impetigo." *Dermatology Times* 1989 (June); 10(6):36.

[52] "Mupirocin vs Erythromycin for Impetigo." *Physicians' Drug Alert* 1989;84.

[53] Henahan, Sean. "New Treatments Improve Odds in Fighting Problem Skin Infections." *Dermatology Times* 1989; 10(10):13.

[54] Ibid.

[55] Ibid.

[56] Doran, T.F., et al. "Acetaminophen: More Harm than Good for Chickenpox." *J. Pediatr*. 1989; 114:1045–1048.

[57] Peterson, Ila M., and Rao, Robert. "Genital Warts." *Postgraduate Medicine* 1989; 86: 197–204.

[58] Hendler, op. cit. p. 225.

[59] "Daily Acyclovir for Genital Herpes 'Appears Effective and Safe Beyond 6 Months.' " *Skin & Allergy News* 1989; 20(4):1, 20.

[60] Brock, Brigit V., et al. "Frequency of Asymptomatic Shedding of Herpes Simplex Virus in Women with Genital Herpes." *JAMA* 1990; 263:418–420.

[61] "Acyclovir May Benefit Healthy Zoster Patient Over Age 60." *Skin & Allergy News* 1989; 20(3):1, 20.

[62] McNulty, Karen. "New Shingles Rx Priced through the Roof." *Med. Tribune* 1989 (Aug. 17); 4.

[63] Guttman, Cheryl. "Repetitive Use of Capsaicin Works Best." *Dermatology Times* 1989; 10(6):1, 28.

[64] Murphy, Terence M. "Postherpetic Neuralgia." *JAMA* 1989; 262: 3478.

[65] "Study: Moist Bandages Hasten Wound Healing." *Modern Med.* 1987; 55:15.

[66] Copelan, R. "Chemical Removal of Splinters without Epidermal Toxic Effects." *J. Am. Acad. Dermatol*. 1989; 20:697–698.

[67] Rosenthal, Elisabeth. "Healing Treatment, 4,000 Years Old, Is Revived." *New York Times* April 5, 1990.

[68] "Aloe." *The Lawrence Review of Natural Products*. St. Louis: Facts & Comparisons, J. B. Lippincott, 1988.

[69] Ibid.

[70] Rodriguez-Bigas, Miguel, et al. "Comparative Evaluation of Aloe Vera in the Management of Burn Wounds in Guinea Pigs." *Plastic and Reconstructive Surgery* 1988; 81:386–389.

[71] Cowley, Geoffrey, with Elliott, Dorinda. "A Simpler Way to Save Lives." *Newsweek* May 7, 1990; 68–69.

[72] Brown, G., et al. "Enhancement of Wound Healing by Topical Treatment with Epidermal Growth Factor." *N. Engl. J. Med.* 1989; 321:76–79.

[73] Wright, Martha. "Growth Factor Interactions May Affect Skin Disease." *Dermatology Times* 1989; 10(10):13.

[74] Stets, Joan. Personal communication, March 24, 1990.

[75] Janssen, P.A.J., et al. "Use of Topical Ketanserin in the Treatment of Skin Ulcers: A Double-Blind Study." *J. Am. Acad. Dermatol.* 1989; 21:85–90.

[76] "Insect Repellents." *The Medical Letter on Drugs and Therapeutics* 1989; 31:45–47.

[77] Ibid.

[78] Bricklin, op. cit. p. 306.

[79] vanArsdall, Robert B. Personal communication. March 10, 1990.

[80] Guin, Jere D., et al. "Treating Poison Ivy, Oak, and Sumac." *Patient Care* 1989 (June 15); 227–237, 285–286.

[81] Ibid. p. 231.

[82] Ibid. pp. 230–232.

[83] Gilgor, Robert S. and Levy, Stanley B. "Super Potent Topical Steroids for Psoriasis." Unpublished patient handout, 1987 (Dec.).

[84] "Fish Oil 'Minimal but Useful' Adjunct in Psoriasis." *Skin & Allergy News* 1988; 19(12):30.

[85] "Prefers Retinoids to Methotrexate for Severe Psoriasis." *Skin & Allergy News* 1988; 19(12): 4A.

[86] "Psoralens." *Drug Facts & Comparisons*. St. Louis: J.B. Lippincott, 1990; p. 2391.

[87] "Treatment of Psoriasis: An Update." Portland, Ore.: National Psoriasis Foundation, 1987, 12.

[88] "PUVA's Link with Squamous Cell Cancer Seems Dose-Dependent." *Skin & Allergy News* 1988; 19(11):27.

[89] Edwards, Lynn R. "PUVA Treatments Continue to be Effective for Psoriasis Cases." *Dermatology Times* 1989; 10(2):17.

[90] Prescott, Lawrence M., "Methotrexate Toxicity Is Major Concern in Severe Psoriasis Tx." *Dermatology Times* 1989; 10(2):47, 49.

[91] Ibid. p. 47.

[92] "Oral, Topical Vitamin D Preparations Found Effective in Psoriasis." *Skin & Allergy News* 1989; 20(7):35.

[93] "Calcipotriol Effective as Psoriasis Therapy." *Dermatology Times* 1990; 11(2):1, 34.

[94] Wright, Martha. "Etretinate Metabolite Produces Similar Effect in Tx of Psoriasis." *Dermatology Times* 1989;1,18.

[95] Ibid. p. 18.

[96] Wright, Martha. "Drug Abates Liver Toxicity in Psoriasis Tx." *Dermatology Times* 1989; 10(3):1, 26.

[97] Clark, Timothy. "Cyclosporine Added to Treatment Options for Recalcitrant Psoriasis." *Dermatology Times* 1989; 19(3):20, 39.

[98] "Severe Reaction Reported after Sudden Withdrawal of Cyclosporine." *Skin & Allergy News* 1988; 19(12):11.

[99] Gilbert, S.C., et al. "Cyclosporine Therapy for Psoriasis: Serum Creatinine Measurements Are an Unreliable Predictor of Decreased Renal Function." *J. Am. Acad. Dermatol.* 1989; 21(3, part 1): 470–474.

[100] Wright, Martha. "Long-term, Low-dose Cyclosporine Helps Severe Psoriasis." *Dermatology Times* 1989; 10(2):1, 26.

High Anxiety

5

In the beginning, doctors couldn't offer patients suffering from anxiety and insomnia much more than a sympathetic ear or an herbal remedy. By contrast, today's modern medicine men write so many prescriptions for powerful mood-altering drugs that they often fail to take the time to listen and provide support.

When "minor" tranquilizers like **Miltown** (meprobamate), **Librium** (chlordiazepoxide), and **Valium** (diazepam) first became available, physicians must have felt a little like fairy godmothers. With the wave of a magic pen they could write a prescription that promised to make cares and worries seem to disappear.

Grieving widows and harried housewives helped turn **Valium** into the number-one prescription best seller in the 1970s. It has only been in the last few years that we have learned there is a price to be paid for unlimited access to sleeping pills and antianxiety agents. Besides the very real risk of dependency, there is an increased danger of automobile accidents and falls leading to fractures.[1]

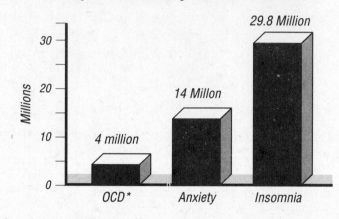

People with Anxiety-Related Disorders

*obsessive-compulsive disorder

Simply put, traditional medicines prescribed for anxiety and insomnia may help alleviate symptoms, but they fall far short of a cure and produce side effects that are in some cases worse than the condition being treated. Once upon a time people trusted their physicians when they were promised risk-free stress reduction in a bottle. Today they are wary. They are less willing to trade drug dependency for a chemical calm. Fortunately, pharmaceutical manufacturers have made some important discoveries in brain chemistry and newer compounds are emerging that may very well provide safer, more effective relief from some of mankind's most common and distressing mental disorders.

Anxiety

Stress, nerves, jitters, heebie-jeebies—whatever you call it, anxiety is part of our modern way of life. It is estimated that over fourteen million people (8.3 percent of American adults) will suffer from excessive worry at some time in their lives.[2] Sometimes anxiety can be both appropriate and sudden, like when you get a flat tire on a lonely road late at night and you don't have a jack. Deadlines and speeches are good at turning otherwise normal people into uptight nervous Nellies. Financial woes can worry just about anyone. And a marital relationship that goes bad can be at least as stressful as the loss of a loved one.

How people deal with day-to-day, garden-variety stress depends a lot on their personalities, upbringing, and coping skills. Those with a strong support network may find that talking out troubles is a tremendous relief—the old "shoulder-to-cry-on" technique. Others may discover that exercise is a great tension reducer—the chopping-wood routine.

Alcohol has unfortunately been the antianxiety agent of choice for millions. And in the last several decades benzos (benzodiazepine drugs like **Valium** and **Xanax**) have come increasingly to represent the medical solution. It is estimated that somewhere between sixty and eighty million prescriptions are written for benzodiazepines each year.[3] Assuming roughly fifty pills per prescription (a conservative number), you end up with approximately 250 pills annually for every one of the fourteen million anxious adults in the country.

NONDRUG REMEDIES

Before following the yellow brick benzo road, it pays to examine alternative antianxiety options. First, accept the fact that we all have worries at some time in our lives. Whether it's paying the bills, coping with an illness, or dealing with grief, stress is part of life. How we persevere is the key. We can all benefit from an action plan of specific things we can do that will allow us to focus our energy on overcoming obstacles. It is amazing how anxiety diminishes or disappears completely when the underlying problem is eliminated.

For suggestions on how to develop a concrete action plan, we recommend a wonderful book, *Kicking Your Stress Habits*, by Donald A. Tubesing. If you follow his realistic guidelines, we promise that you will have taken a very important first step toward overcoming anxiety.

Learning how to relax is not easy. But one of the best ways we know is to listen to soothing music and a calming voice. You can have both rolled up into one by ordering Dr. Emmett Miller's relaxation tapes. This physician has one of the world's great voices. He will lead you into an almost trancelike state of deep relaxation. No matter how uptight we get, all we have to do is spend a few minutes listening to Emmett Miller and his ocean waves and the tension just begins to melt away.

Another important nondrug measure for reducing anxiety is to cut caffeine consumption. Caffeine is so much a part of our daily lives, in coffee, colas, tea, and a number of over-the-counter pain killers that we may forget it is a stimulant drug. Some people are more susceptible to this compound, but almost anyone will experience jitters from a high dose of caffeine. Cutting out coffee, tea, cola, and other sources of caffeine may need to be done gradually, as withdrawal symptoms, particularly headache, are not uncommon. However, this is a sensible first step.

Herbal Answers

Mother Nature offers us a number of herbal products for mild anxiety. Valerian's reputation as a calmative stretches back almost a thousand years.[4] It has also been used for insomnia and nervous stomach. Scientific studies have produced mixed results; some have shown measurable tranquilizing effects, whereas others have been negative.[5] Perhaps that is because some of the active ingredients in valerian root are unstable and may break down over time. It is unclear whether the valerian root commercially available in health food stores either as a tea or in capsules contains enough active ingredient to be truly effective.

The most effective way to use this herb would be to make a tea from fresh valerian root (*Valeriana officinalis*). Be sure to add a little honey or sugar. Dr. Judith Wurtman, a leading researcher on foods and brain biochemistry at MIT, claims that sugar and other simple carbohydrates can have a calming effect on the nervous system. According to Dr. Wurtman, a dose of sugar (two -and-one-half tablespoons) can facilitate the passage of the amino acid tryptophan into the brain where it can be converted into serotonin, a natural brain calmer.[6,7] Our preferred drug—several sweet cookies that are low in fat.

Another herbal remedy for nervousness is hops (*Humulus lupulus*). When most people hear hops, they think of beer (this herb provides a distinctive beer flavor and is a natural preservative). European herbalists praise hops for its calmative action. Like valerian, however, the active ingredients are unstable and there is some doubt that commercial dried hops can actually provide a sedative effect.

Perhaps just the act of drinking a nice warm cup of tea, whether it be made from valerian root, hops, or chamomile, will have a calming effect. If you have a couple of sugar cookies to increase serotonin in the brain and spend a few minutes relaxing while you take some deep belly breaths, you can't go too far wrong. And if you have time to listen to an Emmett Miller tape, we think you will have done yourself a big favor.

DRUG TREATMENTS

What do you do when herbal teas, audio tapes, support networks, and antistress workbooks don't do the job? If you are still feeling overwhelmed and anxious, you are probably past due for professional help. Psychological counseling can make a big difference. And to get over the hump, a prescription may also be useful.

Valerian Root

Used for centuries as an herbal sedative. One or two cups of tea (with sugar, honey, or a sweet cookie). Alternative: two capsules (do not exceed 1000 mg in twenty-four hours). Avoid if liver or kidney problems exist.
Do not undertake activities that require mental alertness.

★ ★ ★

Benzodiazepines

There is nothing wrong with taking a benzodiazepine for a few days or weeks. There has been so much bad press directed at these drugs over the years that a lot of people have been led to believe they are morally weak—or worse, risking drug addiction—if they take an occasional **Valium**. But just as you wouldn't hesitate to use a cane after a bad sprain, there is no reason to shun a chemical crutch that can provide a little temporary relief from excessive anxiety that has not responded to other treatments. Such medications work. They help people calm down and feel less apprehensive. Problems that seemed insurmountable lose some of their threat.

Longer-term use is even possible with careful medical supervision, especially if the drug is used intermittently. We know one newspaper editor who functioned extremely well on occasional **Librium** for three years. After triple bypass surgery following a heart attack, his cardiologist prescribed **Librium** as a way to combat the extreme stress of deadlines and disasters. This is not the kind of guy who goes in for counseling, deep breathing, relaxation tapes, or touchy-feely enounter groups. He wasn't about to find another job because he loved the newspaper business, high pressure and all. He probably averaged less than ten **Librium**s a month, but he found the medicine a life-saver when the pressures became unbearable, like when the computers went down or a reporter blew a story and was threatened with a libel suit. We can't prove it, but we suspect the **Librium** may have helped stave off another heart attack during those critical years.

Selecting the "best" benzo is impossible. No one drug stands out as better than the others, though fashions in prescribing come and go. In the early days, **Librium** was king. It was replaced by its kissing cousin, **Valium**, which peaked in popularity in 1975 when roughly sixty million prescrip-

Benzodiazepines

Brand	Generic
Ativan	lorazepam
Centrax	prazepam
Dalmane	flurazepam
Halcion	triazolam
Klonopin	clonazepam
Librium	chlordiazepoxide
Paxipam	halazepam
Restoril	temazepam
Serax	oxazepam
Tranxene	chlorazepate
Valium	diazepam
Xanax	alprazolam

tions were filled in that year alone. In 1987, **Xanax** took over as the hottest tranquilizer.

The major difference between all these products is their duration of action. Some start working quickly and leave the system quickly as well (**Ativan**, **Halcion**, **Paxipam**, **Serax**, **Xanax**). Others linger longer in the body (**Centrax**, **Dalmane**, **Librium**, **Tranxene**, **Valium**). The shorter-acting drugs have been in ascendency of late because doctors apparently assumed that they were somehow safer. This may be partially true for older people who are vulnerable to falls, since there are some data to suggest that the longer-acting drugs are associated with an increased risk of hip fractures.[8] Such people might do better on medications like **Serax** or **Ativan**.[9]

But the shorter-acting compounds may be a little harder to stop taking after several months of use.[10] They may also be more likely to cause problems with memory, especially delayed recall for new information.[11,12] What this means is that someone who takes **Halcion** at bedtime to get a good night's sleep may wake up the next morning feeling refreshed and alert. The person may appear completely normal and respond appropriately to questions from friends or relatives. But events that occur in the morning may, in some cases, be completely erased from the memory banks as if they had never occurred. For example, the person may not remember a phone conversation or a visit from the mailman. Drugs that may be less likely to affect memory appear to be the longer-acting agents like **Tranxene** or **Restoril**.

The real problem with all these medications occurs when they are taken for granted. Benzos are not "mother's little helpers" to be used daily, month-in and month-out, year after year. For one thing, there is a very real risk of dependence. After about six months on such medications something seems to change in the brain. Many people find that if they then stop taking their pills they may experience withdrawal symptoms, including nervousness, insomnia, headache, nerve jerking, concentration problems, depersonalization, and fatigue.[13, 14]

Such testimonials are enough to scare anyone out of taking a benzodiazepine. Fortunately, not everyone experiences this kind of nightmare. Successful benzo use seems to depend on due diligence. If a particularly dificult period looms, a few days or weeks of **Xanax**, **Valium,** or **Tranxene** are unlikely to "hook" anyone. Why some are affected more than others is a mystery. Although four to eight months of continuous daily dosing seems necessary to allow this process to occur, we suspect that some folks may get into

---

Xanax Letter from A.C.

I began taking **Xanax** in the summer of 1988 due to difficulty in eating and keeping food in my system. It was prescribed by my family physician who told me this drug was potentially addicting. A year later I realized I had become physically addicted and I could not function without this drug. When I tried to decrease the dose I had trouble talking, my stomach was in knots and my body shook terribly. These withdrawal symptoms were so intense I found it impossible to decrease the dosage at all. Since that time my life has been a nightmare.

I informed my physician of my condition and he consulted several chemical dependency programs to find a safe way to get this drug out of my system. We were told I would have to enter an "in-house program" for detoxification because of physical problems that can occur—seizures, elevated blood pressure, etc. With my full time job, this was not an option. Eventually an outpatient clinic was willing to detoxify me if I would participate in an intense group therapy program. I entered the program, stopped taking **Xanax** and was given phenobarbital to prevent seizures. I cannot express in words how awful the following three days were, not only physically but emotionally as well.

As of today, I have not taken a **Xanax** in ten weeks. Unfortunately, I have experienced physical symptoms (stomach discomfort, heart palpitations, shakiness, etc.) since discontinuing the drug and can't find anyone knowledgeable enough to treat the after-effects. The most informative person, a pharmacist for a chemical dependency program, says pharmacists are finding out new information about **Xanax**—for example, it may take some people months to recover completely.

I have talked to chemical dependency clinicians at dozens of treatment centers. They all seem to agree that this drug is incredibly difficult to stop taking because it is so addicting. I fear that physicians are prescribing **Xanax** without knowing how harmful it truly is. I am concerned for myself and others who may be in my situation and feel it is extremely important to speak up and share my experience.

Virginia, September 1, 1989

trouble after only a few months of regular dosing, whereas others may be able to go more than a year without developing dependence. But what do you do when you discover that your body has become dependent on one of these drugs?

Getting Off Benzos

First and foremost, do *not* stop taking any benzodiazepine suddenly! For some, withdrawal can be unpleasant at best and downright dangerous at worst. There are reports of seizures when people stopped drugs like **Xanax** cold turkey. Any decision to cut back on benzos requires medical supervision. *This is not a do-it-yourself project.*

The only problem is that most doctors are not trained in appropriate tapering techniques. For one thing, many physicians have a hard time coming to terms with the reality that

> ### *Benzo Withdrawal Symptoms*
> - Anxiety, irritability, restlessness, jitteriness.
> - Sensations of panic, agitation.
> - Insomnia, tremor, dry mouth, fatigue, nausea, GI upset, headache, sweating.
> - Difficulty concentrating, impaired memory, depression.
> - Extreme sensitivity to sound, light, touch, etc. Sense of depersonalization.
> - In extreme cases, seizures, paranoia, hallucinations.

their prescriptions may have led to addiction and would prefer to deny that a problem exists. For another, the experts do not always agree on the best program for phase out. And some people seem more susceptible to symptoms than others.

We have received letters from people who barely even noticed a difference when they were tapered off a sedative or sleeping pill. Others have complained of a "living hell" that lasts for months. Finally, the kind of drug people have been taking may influence symptoms. Although there is relatively little data comparing the dependency potential of various benzos, it is our impression that short-acting drugs like **Ativan** and **Xanax** may be more likely to precipitate immediate problems after withdrawal than longer-acting agents like **Valium**, **Librium,** and **Klonopin**.

No matter which drug someone is dependent on, most of the experts seem to agree on one thing—gradual tapering is essential.[15] As one physician put it, "It may seem to take forever to wean a patient off benzodiazepines without causing withdrawal symptoms, but the process must be approached slowly and carefully."[16]

Dr. Otis L. Baughman, III, Director of Medical Education, Self Memorial Hospital, Greenwood, South Carolina, has worked with patients who have become dependent on these drugs and has developed what we believe to be a sensibly slow tapering program.

Some physicians may say that such a slow process isn't worth the effort. Fine. If someone can taper off tranquilizers in six to eight weeks, that's great. But if withdrawal begins to turn into a nightmare, we like Dr. Baughman's slow and steady approach. By switching people from short-acting drugs like **Ativan** and **Xanax** to longer-acting compounds like **Klonopin** (especially helpful against panic attacks), he has had excellent success in avoiding unpleasant symptoms. **Klonopin** can cause drowsiness, unsteadiness, dizziness, slurred speech, and other psychological effects, so it too must be used with caution under careful supervision.

Other doctors may respond that the "benzo brouhaha" is a tempest in a teapot. They don't worry about the addictive liability of these agents and believe they can be prescribed safely for years or even a lifetime. We disagree. Although certain people may need lifetime treatment (some individuals with epilepsy, uncontrollable muscular contractions, or those with overwhelming, uncontrollable chronic anxiety), there's always a risk.

For one thing, there is growing evidence that benzos and other sedatives make people hazardous on the highways. Anyone who takes one of these drugs and gets behind the wheel may be as dangerous as if he were driving drunk, even though he might feel sober as a judge. Second, there is a very real risk of falls and hip fractures associated with benzos, especially the longer-acting brands.[18,19] These drugs interact dangerously with alcohol and other medications that affect the brain, including over-the-counter allergy and cold remedies. Tranquilizers can lower libido and create other sexual impairments. Finally, there have been reports of forgetfulness, especially with the short-acting agents like **Ativan**, **Halcion**, and **Xanax**.

In our opinion, people who need a chemical crutch would be best served by a physician who takes a conservative approach. Benzos are a little like bandages that can allow a psychic wound time to heal while you seek support, counseling, and realistic ways to solve underlying problems. They are not cures, but for some they may allow a little time for the body to heal itself. These drugs are relatively safe when carefully monitored and used for short periods of time (several weeks to several months). People should not drive or operate machinery while on these medications, and older people must be extremely careful to avoid falls.

BuSpar (buspirone)

When **BuSpar** was launched in 1986, it was touted as an ideal answer to anxiety. Here was a completely different kind of compound that did not cause addiction, did not cause sedation or euphoria, did not interact dangerously with alcohol or other tranquilizers, did not interfere with driving ability or coordination, did not cause mental cloudiness and forgetfulness, did not cause sexual side effects, and did not produce withdrawal symptoms when stopped.

Wow! Sounds perfect, almost too good to be true. Bingo! **BuSpar** has not taken the market by storm. It is not easy to get a clear answer as to why **BuSpar** did not immediately become the number-one antianxiety agent on the market. Some say it's because the drug does not produce a "buzz," which is why people like the benzos so much, since they help people relax and feel a pleasant sense of well being. Others say it's because the drug has its own set of side effects, especially nausea, dizziness, headache, and nervousness. The last thing someone with anxiety needs is to take a drug that makes him feel nervous.

People who have been on **Valium** or **Xanax** tell us that **BuSpar** just does not cut the mustard. It doesn't relieve their anxiety the way the old standbys do. You can't switch from a benzo right to **BuSpar**. If that is tried, the withdrawal

BuSpar side effects:

diarrhea
dizziness
excitement
GI upset
headache
insomnia
light-headedness
nausea
nervousness

symptoms will be as bad as usual. It may also take **BuSpar** up to three weeks to establish an antianxiety effect, so patience is necessary.

BuSpar may not be the perfect solution to stress. It does, however, represent an alternative to benzos. Some people, especially those who are older or must drive or maintain a clear head, may benefit the most from this medication. And people who are benzo virgins (never exposed to **Xanax** and company) may find this new approach to anxiety quite helpful. [20]

FUTURE DRUGS

A key brain chemical called serotonin is involved in a wide range of mood disorders, from anxiety, aggression, and depression, to insomnia and impulsivity. New serotonin-modifying drugs like **BuSpar** are generating considerable interest within the pharmaceutical industry. Bristol-Myers has a second-generation drug in the pipeline called gepirone, which may have good antidepressant action as well as antianxiety effect.[21] Ipsapirone and tandospirone are other experimental drugs that look promising against anxiety.

A completely new class of compounds has been discovered: the beta-carbolines. Schering has one of the first in testing (ZK-112,119). It is expected to be as effective as a benzo but less likely to cause sedation or incoordination. Hoffmann-La Roche, maker of **Valium** and **Librium**, has a new medicine called bretazenil, which it hopes will prove especially effective for both anxiety and panic attacks. But no matter what the alchemists dream up, we still believe no chemical will ever substitute for good old-fashioned common sense, action-oriented problem-solving, and practical stress management.

Stage Fright

Performance anxiety is something most of us have to face at some point in our lives. It may be brought on by a presentation to a business group, a speech to the Kiwanis Club, or a solo at a musical recital. For some people getting up in front of a group can be a horrifying experience. Their stomachs get tied up in knots, their hearts begin to pound, their hands begin to shake and turn cold and clammy, and their mouths go dry.

Athletes, actors, and musicians are just some of the people who can suffer such an attack. But you would be surprised how many others can be overcome by an adrenaline rush. A municipal judge in San Diego won a lifetime disability pension (at age forty-four) because of uncontrollable "stage fright" on the bench. Some test-takers get so scared that they freeze up and cannot perform up to their ability.

What can be done when this happens? Behavioral therapy is our first recommendation. There are psychologists who specialize in desensitizing people to scary situations like speeches or airplane rides. But when counseling is not available or is insufficient, a prescription may help.

Benzos are generally not recommended because they can interfere with performance. The last thing a violin player needs during a recital is to lose her touch or nod off because of a dose of **Valium**. Enter stage left the beta-blockers. These drugs, which are normally prescribed for high blood pressure and heart problems, are superb at blocking adrenaline, the chemical behind the pounding heart and shaky hands.

There are now quite a few studies documenting the benefits of beta blockers for string players, singers, and even test takers.[22–24] The only problem is that the manufacturers of beta-blockers have not bothered to do the research and jump through the bureaucratic hoops necessary to get their drugs approved by the FDA for this novel use. That means that although the drugs are available for angina, high blood pressure, and other heart problems, most physicians are unaware of this other special application.

Even when a doctor has heard it through the grapevine, he may not realize that lower doses are necessary for stage fright. If standard beta-blocker doses are prescribed, a patient may risk impaired performance and ability to concentrate.[25] For example, a 20 mg dose of **Corgard** (nadolol) enhanced singing performance, whereas 80 mg impaired performance.[26] **Inderal** (propranolol), at doses of 40 mg and up, can reduce the ability to concentrate, even though this is a standard blood pressure dose. Most physicians may not realize that a much smaller amount (10 mg) is recommended for stage fright, just as 25 mg (half of a 50 mg tablet) is suggested for **Tenormin** (atenolol).[27]

Before anyone begs for a beta-blocker to get through a final exam, a solo recital, or a big speech, we suggest that it might be worthwhile to go through a trial run. You wouldn't want to stand up in front of a crowd for the biggest performance of your life only to discover that the medicine ruined your presentation or made you sick. Sensitive people can develop terrible asthma on beta-blockers.

These drugs are not a panacea for performance anxiety any more than benzos are a cure for stress. Behavioral therapy is always our first choice. But for someone who can barely bring himself to stand in front of an audience with a pounding heart and shaky hands, a beta blocker just may help him over the hump.

PANIC ATTACKS

No one knows why some people develop gut-wrenching fears when they leave the security of their homes. The attacks can come on suddenly in the middle of an elevator or supermarket. Feelings of disorientation and confusion may be followed by dizziness and faintness. A dry mouth, sweating, rapid breathing, and butterflies in the stomach are not uncommon symptoms. The room may start to swim, and the person may actually believe he is dying. Eventually such attacks may turn victims into recluses, afraid to socialize or carry out even the most basic tasks outside the home.

Physicians have tried all sorts of medications to combat panic attacks. Benzodiazepines like **Ativan** (lorazepam), **Valium** (diazepam), and **Xanax** (alprazolam) work up to a degree. **Klonopin** (clonazepam) has also become popular with some physicians because it is longer acting than **Ativan** or **Xanax.** But when such medications are discontinued, rebound anxiety and panic may return with a vengeance.

Tricyclic antidepressants such as **Aventyl** (nortriptyline),

Elavil (amitriptyline), **Norpramin** (desipramine), **Pamelor** (nortriptyline), **Pertofrane** (desipramine), **Sinequan** (doxepin), and **Tofranil** (imipramine) have been tried with success ranging from 70-90 percent. The monoamine oxidase inhibitor (MAOI) antidepressant **Nardil** (phenelzine) has proven quite effective too. An experimental drug in this class, **Aurorix** (moclobemide) from Hoffmann-La Roche, may prove to be safer and equally effective. Two other possibilites include the new drugs **Prozac** (fluoxetine) and **Anafranil** (clomipramine). Such medications are unlikely to precipitate rebound anxiety or panic; however long-term benefits and risks are still uncertain. When the medications are discontinued, there is always the possibility that anxiety and panic may return.

Behavioral therapy is an important component in dealing with this problem, whether drugs are used or not. We highly recommend a book by Dr. R. Reid Wilson called *Don't Panic: Taking Control of Anxiety Attacks*. It is published by Harper & Row. Most important of all, though, is finding the right therapist. The goal is to find someone who understands both the biological and psychological issues and can provide both support and guidance.

Obsessive-Compulsive Disorder

OCD sounds so ominous—obsessive-compulsive disorder, like some really bizarre psychiatric illness. And yet many children go through a phase when they won't step on a crack (for fear of breaking their mother's back). Some like to have their stuffed animals placed on the bed in a special position. And what child hasn't worried about monsters? Some repeatedly check the closet or under the bed just to make sure there are no creatures hiding out. One might even think of thumb-sucking and nail-biting as compulsions.

These little habits and rituals are considered harmless and they usually disappear as we grow up. But most of us can probably recall leaving the house and then worrying that we had forgotten to lock the door or turn off the oven. If our fear

What is OCD?

- **Obsessions** = persistent, disturbing, unwanted thoughts, images, or impulses.
  Examples: Preoccupation with dirt, germs, or contamination.

- **Compulsions** = repetitive, stereotypic, unwanted actions.
  Examples: Repeated hair-pulling, excessive hand-washing, cleaning, counting, arranging, or checking.

becomes great enough, or if we are "compulsive" enough, we may return home to check, even though the chances are slim that we slipped up. When prudent caution turns into ritualistic behavior that begins to interfere with our lives, the head-doctors call it OCD.

One woman feared that every time she drove her car and hit a bump or a pothole she had actually hit a person. She would circle around and around searching for the body, and even when she didn't find one she would still doubt her eyes. Doubt plays a big role in OCD. Even though victims know that they locked the door, or turned off the iron, they may feel so anxious that they are compelled to return home time after time to double-check. Other people wash their hands repeatedly or pull hairs out one by one. Neatness freaks can become so compulsive about "a place for everything and everthing in its place," that they make life miserable for themselves and everyone around them. There are compulsive gamblers, compulsive eaters, "sex addicts," and laxative abusers.

No one really knows how many people suffer from OCD. Until Dr. Judith Rapoport's famous book, *The Boy Who Couldn't Stop Washing,* this was pretty much a closet disease—often a secret kept from spouse and physician. It is now suspected that anywhere from four to seven million people are victims of persistent, intrusive thoughts or unwanted actions.[28,29] The numbers may actually be much higher.

Researchers believe that OCD is not some sort of strange psychological shortcoming. Although it is easy to blame the victim for his excessive hand-washing, hair-pulling, or irrational fear, it is now assumed that obsessions and compulsions are caused by a special kind of faulty brain wiring or neurochemical imbalance. It's as if the person has his needle stuck in a groove or developed an endless tape loop in the brain that keeps playing over and over.

Psychotherapy and psychonalysis are rarely effective for OCD, though behavioral therapy can produce dramatic results.[30] Clinicians gradually expose their patients to the triggering situations and then attempt to desensitize them. For example, a person who is afraid of dirt and washes his hands dozens of times a day may be encouraged to touch the floor until it is no longer threatening. Skilled behavioral therapists claim a good success rate against compulsions, although obsessions are tougher to deal with.[31]

> ### *Anafranil* (clomipramine)
> First approved treatment for OCD. Benefits may take two to eight weeks to become apparent. Up to 66 percent of patients respond, though some OCD symptoms may remain.
>
> **Side Effects** (similar to other tricyclic antidepressants): Dry mouth, drowsiness, constipation, nausea, indigestion, blurred vision, weight gain, dizziness on standing, tremor, impaired memory, difficult urination, and sexual problems (impotence, ejaculation failure). Seizures are a rare but troubling adverse reaction (0.7%).

DRUG TREATMENTS

Traditional antidepressants, antianxiety agents, and antipsychotic drugs have been disappointing against OCD. But a new generation of medications that modulate the brain chemical serotonin have produced impressive results.

Anafranil (clomipramine)

Although **Anafranil** has been available in other countries for over ten years, it is a relative newcomer to the United States. This medication is considered a tricyclic antidepressant, but it has the special ability to allow serotonin to accumulate at nerve endings. This action is apparently responsible for its anti-OCD effect. **Anafranil** has demonstrated effectiveness against excessive hair-pulling (trichotillomania) and various other obsessive-compulsive behaviors.[32–34]

The woman who was compelled to circle the block looking for a dead body every time she hit a bump or a pothole was put on **Anafranil**. Five weeks later the compulsions had virtually disappeared. She reported that "after having them my whole life, it was amazing." Instead of driving back to check, she could re-create in her mind the pothole that had triggered the fear that she had hit someone. For the first time she was free of the anxiety. Her relief was expressed this way: "It's like you don't doubt anymore."[35]

As effective as **Anafranil** may be against OCD, the drug clearly has its downside. The incidence of side effects is not trivial. In one premarketing study, 20 percent of the patients on **Anafranil** quit the program because of adverse reactions.

The good news is that there are other medications that enhance serotonin transmission and may also work against OCD. The antidepressant **Prozac** (fluoxetine) has fewer side effects (see page 212) than **Anafranil** and has been shown to help relieve symptoms of obsessive-compulsive disorder.[36,37] Another antidepressant, **Desyrel** (trazodone), may also be partially effective. Unfortunately, none of these drugs is 100 percent effective. Even when they do work, people often admit that they still have some unwanted thoughts; they just aren't as bothersome or intrusive and the patients aren't driven to perform unwanted behaviors.

On the horizon is a third drug called fluvoxamine, sold in Europe under the brand name **Faverin.** This medicine is available in Austria, Britain, France, Germany, and Switzerland. The Reid-Rowell company has submitted it to the FDA for treatment of depression. Preliminary studies suggest that fluvoxamine is well-tolerated and may be very effective against OCD.[38–40] It may ultimately become the drug of choice for this strange but common affliction.

Insomnia

We have all had trouble sleeping at some time in our lives. But for 20–40 percent of adults, insomnia can be more than a minor annoyance. As many as ten million suffer severe sleep disturbances.[41] That means night after night these folks toss and turn. It takes them more than an hour to fall asleep. Even when they finally fall into slumberland, it may not be restful or refreshing. They may wake two or three times during the course of the night or stay awake after only three or four hours of sleep. These people often have to drag themselves out of bed in the morning, beat before the day even begins.

An occasional sleepless night does not demand much, if any,

treatment. Sure it's a drag to lie awake watching the clock, but chances are good that the body will pay back its sleep debt the next night. Anxiety, obsessive-compulsive disorder, excitement, caffeine, pain, or medication can all cause insomnia. A surprisingly large number of drugs can make sleeping difficult for some people.

If you suspect that your high-blood-pressure pill or asthma medicine is causing your sleepless nights, you might want to ask your physician if there is an alternative that is less likely to produce insomnia.

Ironically, the class of medicines that can cause some of the worst sleeping problems are sleeping pills and sedatives. For one thing, the sleep-inducing benefits of these drugs can wear off over time. A severe insomniac may be tempted to raise the dose and that can lead to disaster. Even when drugs like **Ativan**, **Dalmane**, **Halcion**, **Restoril**, **Serax**, **Tranxene**, **Valium**, or **Xanax** are taken in normal doses, they can produce terrible rebound insomnia when they are discontinued.

In recent years doctors have turned from longer-acting sleeping pills like **Dalmane** to shorter-acting compounds such as **Ativan**, **Halcion**, and **Serax**. The reasoning was that a fast-on-and-fast-off drug would be desirable, so that you could fall asleep quickly and wake up refreshed with no morning hangover.

Drug-Induced Insomnia

(There are over three hundred medications that may cause sleeping problems. Here are just a few examples.)

Asendin (amoxapine)	**Ritalin** (methylphenidate)
BuSpar (buspirone)	**Slo-bid** (theophylline)
Cylert (pemoline)	**Slo-Phyllin** (theophylline)
Elixophyllin (theophylline)	**Somophyllin** (aminophylline)
Fastin (phentermine)	**Suprol** (suprofen)
Inderal (propranolol)	**Tenex** (guanfacine)
Lopressor (metoprolol)	**Tenuate** (diethylpropion)
Orudis (ketoprofen)	**Theo-24** (theophylline)
Preludin (phenmetrazine)	**Theobid** (theophylline)
Proventil (albuterol)	**Theo-Dur** (theophylline)
Provera (medroxyprogesterone)	**Ventolin** (albuterol)
Reglan (metoclopramide)	

Halcion
(triazolam)

According to Dr. Bruce H. Dobkin, associate clinical professor of neurology, UCLA, "Even on the lowest dose of Halcion, 0.125 mg, taken at night, for 1 to 15 days, up to 10 percent of users in clinical studies experienced daytime drowsiness, nervousness, light-headedness, nausea, incoordination, and memory problems."[48]

So much for theory. The reality has turned out to be a bit of a nightmare. Some studies report that because medications like **Halcion** are so short-acting, they may occasionally produce a rebound insomnia the same night—waking up the person in the early morning hours.[42-44] In addition, they may cause a daytime rebound anxiety leading to panic attacks, depression, feelings of unreality, confusion, amnesia, and sometimes even paranoia.[45-47] Sudden discontinuation of **Halcion** or **Ativan** can also bring on rebound tension.

TACTICS

There are lots of little tricks when it comes to getting a good night's sleep. Some things require planning ahead, like avoiding caffeinated beverages and medicines (**Anacin**, **Cope**, **Excedrin**, **Midol**, **Synalgos**, **Vanquish**, etc.). Get as much exercise as possible during the day. We're sure lumberjacks and farmers suffer insomnia once in awhile, but it's hard to stay awake tossing and turning if you have put in a vigorous day. Don't watch late-night television. A stimulating movie or interview show can keep you wired for hours. Same goes for talk radio. Go to bed and get up at the same time every day. Don't sleep in to try and catch up. And avoid naps. They can perpetuate a vicious cycle of night-time sleeplessness.

Snacking to Sleep

Perhaps the easiest and safest approach for falling asleep is food. Selecting the right bedtime snack can do wonders for mild insomnia. According to Dr. Judith Wurtman, an MIT research scientist, pure carbohydrates are the key. Her research has led her to conclude that carbos help increase the amount of the amino acid tryptophan that can be transported into the brain. As tryptophan levels increase they allow for greater production of serotonin, the brain's calming and sleep chemical. Dr. Wurtman maintains that the right foods will help people feel less anxious and more relaxed and they will transition naturally from drowsiness into sleep.[49]

Carbohydrates are sugars and starches. Foods that will trigger tryptophan transmission into the brain include bagels, bread, cake, candy, cereal, cookies, corn syrup, crackers, honey, jelly, muffins, oatmeal, pasta, sugar, and rolls. It is important, however, to keep protein to a minimum since it will reduce tryptophan. That means that you won't want to smother your cereal in milk or spread your bagel with cream cheese.

You will want to experiment to find the combination of foods that works best for you. Remember to eliminate protein from your bedtime snack and cut down on daytime calories to allow for this little sleepy-time indulgence.

> ### Dos and Don'ts for Insomniacs
> - No caffeine or other stimulants.
> - Exercise during the day (not in the evening).
> - No napping during the day.
> - Don't sleep in. Get into a regular pattern for going to bed and getting up.
> - No TV or radio in the bedroom.
> - Relax several hours before bedtime—a warm bath may help.
> - No chocolate or nightcaps. Alcohol is counterproductive.
> - If you can't fall asleep, listen to Emmett Miller's audio tape "Easing into Sleep." (see page 168.)
> - If that doesn't work, move to a different bed or read for half an hour and try again.

L-Tryptophan

For several decades l-tryptophan has been marketed as a natural sleeping pill because it serves as a building block for serotonin in the brain. This natural amino acid was a big seller for other purposes as well, including depression, premenstrual syndrome (PMS), anxiety, weight loss, jet lag, panic attacks, and pain relief. Despite Dr. Judith Wurtman's admonition to avoid amino acid supplements and stick to natural foods, we have to admit that when occasional sleeplessness hits, we have resorted to 500 mg of tryptophan with excellent results, especially if we added a few crackers or cookies to enhance brain absorption. L-tryptophan seemed particularly beneficial when sleeping problems were caused by jet lag.[50]

But in October 1989, people started reporting strange symptoms to physicians—severe muscle pain, high fever, weakness, joint pain, rash, swelling of arms and legs, and shortness of breath. Even more worrisome was an extremely high number of white blood cells called eosinophils. Once the word got out, hundreds of other cases were quickly diagnosed, with some patients showing up with the highest eosinophil counts ever seen in some labs. This strange medical malady was quickly dubbed EMS (eosinophilia-myalgia syndrome). And what all the patients had in common was l-tryptophan. Some had taken it for insomnia, while others were using it for PMS, overweight, or pain. L-tryptophan was quickly removed from the market.

At the time of this writing no one knows exactly why l-tryptophan started causing this dangerous reaction. After all, millions of people used l-tryptophan for decades with no apparent harm. Experts speculated that a major supplier from Japan had somehow contaminated a large batch of raw material. This is currently the most likely explanation.

Others believed the strange EMS reactions showed up because people had recently started using extra large doses (from one to fifteen grams a day) to treat depression, obsessive-compulsive disorder, and PMS. An alternative explanation was offered by physicians at Georgetown University Medical Center and the Washington, D.C. Medical Center. They "believe that this disorder may be caused by an abnormal accumulation of metabolites of tryptophan."[51] They found patients with EMS who had other symptoms of connective tissue diseases such as scleroderma. They speculate that these people have some sort of built-in error in tryptophan metabolism. When they eat food containing this amino acid they can handle it, but the large doses found in supplements may overwhelm their system and lead to this potentially life-threatening syndrome. Until the controversy is resolved, stay away from tryptophan.

Herbal Remedies

In lieu of l-tryptophan you might want to consider a cup of good old chamomile tea. It has been used for centuries as a sleeping aid. (People with hay fever or other allergies may also be sensitive to chamomile.) Other herbal helpers for insomnia include sage (*Salvia officinalis*), catnip (*Nepeta cataria*), and

Saint-John's-wort (*Hypericum perforatum*). Prolonged use or large doses of sage may be toxic, so moderation is appropriate. Saint-John's-wort may cause a photosensitivity reaction. Anyone trying it should stay out of the sun.

DRUG TREATMENTS

What can you do when everything you try still does not help you get a good night's sleep? If you are still functioning well during the day, you may not need to do anything. Some people find that as they age they just need less sleep. You might consider this a blessing in disguise. Other people overestimate the actual time they toss and turn. In reality you may be losing less sleep than you think. But if you've given Emmett Miller's tape "Easing into Sleep" a shot and it still leaves you wired, if you've snacked yourself into overweight, if you're fed up with herbal teas, and you still feel wiped out and sleep deprived, perhaps it is time to consider a medication.

Antihistamines

Over-the-counter sleeping pills contain either diphenhydramine or doxylamine (**Doxysom, Ultra Sleep, Unisom**). These remedies may be mildly effective for occasional insomnia, but they should not be swallowed by anyone with asthma, glaucoma, an enlarged prostate gland or difficulty urinating, emphysema or any other chronic lung condition. Never increase the dose if you don't achieve the desired results, as an overdose may lead to delirium or even psychosis. Some people report a morning hangover or sluggish feeling on arising.

Benzodiazepines

When all else fails, the court of last resort is a benzo. There is little doubt that these prescription sleeping pills do the job when used infrequently. People who rely on any sedative or hypnotic every night "just in case" (because they fear they may not fall asleep) are asking for trouble. Not only does the benefit wear off after several weeks, but addiction is a very real possibility.

Which benzo is best for insomnia? Ask a dozen docs that

> ### Drugs with *Diphenhydramine*
> **Benadryl**
> **Compoz**
> **Nervine**
> **Nytol**
> **Sleep-Eze 3**
> **Sleepinal**
> **Sominex**
> **Sominex 2**
> **Twilite**

question and you might receive twelve different answers (there are, after all, a dozen benzos on the market). Some physicians prefer a long-acting sleeping pill (like **Dalmane**) so there is less likely to be early-morning wakefulness, rebound daytime anxiety, or memory loss. Others fear morning hangover, incoordination, and driving difficulties, which may accompany the longer-acting agents, and so they prescribe the current short-acting favorite, **Halcion**.

We try to avoid either extreme. **Ativan** (lorazepam), **Restoril** (temazepam), and **Serax** (oxazepam) are intermediate in action. That means they last a little longer in the body than **Halcion** and therefore are less likely to cause rebound insomnia during the early-morning hours. But they are not so long-lasting as to accumulate during the day. Consequently, they may be somewhat less likely to increase the risk of falls or make driving hazardous. **Serax** and **Restoril** are a little slow up front because of gradual absorption. They should probably be taken roughly thirty to sixty minutes before bedtime.[52]

How is performance during the day after such sleeping pills? We can't speak for all these drugs, but there is one interesting anecdote worth mentioning. It has been reported that "temazepam **[Restoril]** helped pilots during the war in the Falkland Islands to sleep during brief rest periods and to sustain high levels of performance."[53, 54] Most of us won't be required to fly airplanes under wartime conditions, so the track record of **Restoril** is somewhat reassuring. Nevertheless, all benzos have the potential to produce "hangover effects, impaired memory and performance, and difficulty driving."[55]

No matter which benzo is ultimately selected, such medicine should be used cautiously, and should rarely, if ever, be relied on for long-term insomnia. There is a distinct possibility that prolonged sleep disturbances are symptoms of some more fundamental mental problem. As many as two-thirds of people with severe, chronic insomnia may suffer some other psychiatric illness such as depression. If this is the case, then an antidepressant is a far more effective form of treatment, especially since benzos may actually make depression worse.

FUTURE DRUGS

Given all the risks associated with currently available sleeping pills, it should come as no surprise to learn that drug companies are trying to come up with a better mousetrap. Zolpidem (marketed under the brand name **Stilnox**) just might fit the bill. It was developed in Europe by a company called Synthélabo. It is not a benzodiazepine, but it is as effective as benzos at putting people to sleep. In fact it works so well you wouldn't want to take it more than a few minutes before you are ready to hit the sack.

The American sleep researcher who knows more about the compound than any other scientist in the world, Dr. Martin Scharf, is excited about zolpidem. Normally cautious about sleeping pills, he calls **Stilnox** "very effective—it really looks like a good compound."[56] Most of the sleeping pills on the market (including OTC remedies) interfere with the normal architecture of sleep. They may suppress dreaming (REM sleep) or deep sleep. According to Dr. Scharf, zolpidem "produces pretty normal sleep" and does not cause rebound insomnia like **Halcion**.

Zolpidem does not shortchange insomniacs on deep (slow-wave) sleep, which should mean they will awake refreshed. Preliminary data suggest that zolpidem does not lose its effect over time (no tolerance) and has a low potential for dependence or abuse.[57, 58] This sleeping pill has been marketed in France along with an antianxiety agent that is chemically similar called alpidem (**Ananxyl**). A subsidiary of the G. D. Searle pharmaceutical company (Lorex) in Skokie, Illinois is developing **Stilnox** (zolpidem) in this country and has submitted it to the U.S. Food and Drug Administration for approval.

As good as zolpidem seems, we will hold back our hurrahs until it has stood the test of time. One other new European sleeping pill, zopiclone, was also promoted as being a nonbenzo

---

Where to Turn When You're Desperate

Dr. Marty Scharf is the smartest sleep researcher we have ever met. This man is at the cutting edge of research on narcolepsy, insomnia, bed wetting, and so on. In our opinion, anyone who has a serious sleep disorder should have his physician contact Dr. Scharf for a referral and access to the most effective treatment options for insomnia and narcolepsy.

Dr. Martin B. Scharf
Center for Research in Sleep Disorders
Mercy Hospital
1275 E. Kemper Road
Cincinnati, OH 45246

Another alternative for referral is:
The American Sleep Disorders Association
604 2nd St. S.W.
Rochester, MN 55902

with little potential to produce tolerance, withdrawal symptoms, morning hangover, or memory disturbances. An editorial in the British journal *Lancet* punctured the balloon, however, taking the manufacturer to task for "irresponsible and inaccurate" claims, since the drug apparently *can* cause rebound insomnia.[59] This proves that when it comes to antianxiety agents and sleeping pills, you can never be too cautious.

Narcolepsy

Serendipity

Accidental discoveries sometimes lead to important new treatments. The observation that the heart- and high-blood-pressure medicine **Inderal** (propranolol) helped control sleep attacks led Dr. Martin Scharf to try it in a number of patients. To his surprise they did improve.[60] **Inderal** has its own set of side effects, however, including asthma, fatigue, depression, forgetfulness, insomnia, hair loss, and impotence.

Codeine may also help people who don't respond to stimulant drugs. [61]

In a cruel kind of way narcolepsy represents the flip side of insomnia. People are plagued with irresistible attacks of sleepiness, sometimes at the most inopportune moments—while driving, eating, or during business meetings. These sudden sleep attacks are almost impossible to resist and usually last from five to ten minutes. They can be accompanied by cataplexy, a condition whereby the person becomes weak and loses muscular control, often after an emotional trigger such as fear or laughter. Imagine walking across a busy street and falling over asleep.

Then there are the hypnagogic hallucinations—dreams that break through into wakefulness. A person may actually think they see a face or feel another person's presence even though they are fully awake. It is possible that such a narcoleptic might be considered borderline schizophrenic, although he is perfectly sane. Finally, there is sleep paralysis—a situation where someone almost wakes up, is aware of the surroundings in the room, but is unable to move, cry out, or open his eyes. All these unpredictable, uncontrollable narcoleptic attacks can turn normal life into a kind of waking nightmare.

TRADITIONAL TREATMENTS

Physicians assumed that the best way to prevent people

from having sleep attacks during the day was to give them stimulants—drugs like amphetamine, **Ritalin** (methylphenidate), or **Cylert** (pemoline) that would keep them wired. The only trouble is that the benefits tend to wear off over time and there is a risk that people may increase the dose. Such drugs also produce a kind of "high" that can be disconcerting if not addicting. They may also cause insomnia, palpitations, and increase the risk of high blood pressure, especially when combined with antidepressant medications.

Antidepressants such as **Anafranil** (clomipramine), **Tofranil** (imipramine) and **Vivactil** (protriptyline) are also prescribed, but Dr. Martin Scharf claims that they may make narcolepsy worse because they suppress REM or dreaming sleep. The narcoleptic can suffer breakthrough attacks of cataplexy during the day because of the body's demand for REM sleep. And when such drugs are discontinued the rebound effect becomes much worse. The narcoleptic may well find himself collapsing far more frequently than before he started treatment.

NATURAL TREATMENTS

In 1988 an article appeared in the journal *Lancet* that suggested the amino acid l-tyrosine might be effective against narcolepsy and depression.[62] Since this compound is made in the body and is an essential building block for the neurochemicals dopamine, epinephrine, and norepinephrine, it is considered quite safe, even in large doses. (There is concern that some people may develop headaches on l-tyrosine. It should never be combined with MAO-inhibitor antidepressants. And people with melanoma should avoid all l-tyrosine.[63]) Unfortunately, a follow-up study employing a total daily dose of nine grams of l-tyrosine (in three equally divided doses of three grams each) did not confirm any benefit.[64] We hope there will be additional research to resolve this controversy.

Gamma-Hydroxybutyrate (GHB)

The most exciting treatment of narcolepsy originated in Canada over ten years ago. GHB (gamma-hydroxybutyrate) is a natural substance found in cells throughout the body. It is especially high in the brains of newborns and may help protect against sudden infant death syndrome. Dr. Martin Scharf has had more experience with this substance than any other sleep researcher, and he believes it may protect the brain against oxygen deprivation (he calls it the "hibernation chemical"). His research also shows that GHB is an excellent treatment against narcolepsy.[65]

Dr. Scharf has over three hundred patient-years of experience with this natural chemical. Given at bedtime, GHB reduces the number of daytime sleep attacks and also improves cataplexy, hypnogogic hallucinations, and sleep paralysis.[66] The patients also seem to be able to get by with a lower dose of stimulant medication to stay alert during the day. Dr. Scharf also found the sleep of these narcoleptic patients improved while they were taking GHB. Apparently the only side effect of this substance is quite rare—sleepwalking—which, although disturbing, is probably safer than cataplexy.

At the time of this writing, GHB is not yet approved for sale. Dr. Scharf does make it available to patients under a special investigational drug status through FDA. It is supplied by Biocraft Labs of Elmwood Park, N.J. We hope this exciting experimental substance will be approved by the FDA in short order. Another future option may be **Catatrol** (viloxazine), being developed by ICI.

Life is fraught with stress. We know firsthand what it is like to deal with deadlines, health problems, economic uncertainty, and many of the other problems people encounter. There is no magic pill or potion that can make real-life troubles disappear. Anxiety and sleeplessness are sometimes the price we pay for living. But new medicines are making treatment of severe anxiety-related conditions safer and more effective.

Quick Takes

- Develop an action plan against anxiety. For specific advice, read Donald Tubesing's wonderful book, *Kicking Your Stress Habits*.

- Herbal remedies, relaxation tapes, and social support are the first line against tension. Never forget, "Eat dessert first; life is uncertain!"

- Don't walk the tranquilizer tightrope for too long. When you start relying on **Xanax**, **Tranxene**, **Valium**, or **Ativan** for more than a few weeks in a row, you could be in for a rough time. If you have trouble letting go, you and your physician might find that Dr. Otis Baughman's guidelines for getting off benzos provide a reassuring safety net.

- **BuSpar** *is* different, but is it better? **Valium** virgins may do great on this new-generation antianxiety agent. But be patient; it may take several weeks to see any benefit. Never stop taking a benzo cold turkey and think **BuSpar** will rescue you.

- Performance anxiety, test-taking jitters, stage fright—whatever you call it, shaky hands, butterflies in your stomach, and pounding in your chest can interfere with your personal best. Beta-blockers may help—check with your doctor about low-dose therapy. Stay away if you have asthma or some other serious health condition.

- You can break the obsessive-compulsive cycle with exciting new medications. **Anafranil**, **Prozac**, and **Faverin** offer relief from self-destructive thoughts and behaviors.

- Don't let your medicine keep you awake at night. If you think your insomnia is caused by your blood-pressure or asthma medicine, check with your doctor for an alternative drug.

- **Halcion** can put you to sleep, but it just might wake you up in the early-morning hours. If you find that you are awake before dawn, tossing and turning, ask your doctor about a longer-acting sleeping pill, such as **Restoril**.

- A good night snack can go a long way toward putting you into slumberland. Our favorites are a big bowl of Cheerios with honey on top. Other options include graham crackers, bagels, or English muffins with jam. Keep the milk to a minimum and sip a cup of chamomile tea as a nightcap.

- Keep your ear to the pillow for a new sleeping pill called **Stilnox** (zolpidem). It may become the safest and most effective hypnotic on the market when the FDA gives it the green light.

- GHB (gamma-hydroxybutyrate) may be the "hibernation chemical." For people with daytime sleep attacks (narcolepsy), GHB could be a godsend. Have your doctor check with Dr. Martin Scharf for access.

References

[1] Ray, Wayne A., et al. "Benzodiazepines of Long and Short Elimination Half-life and the Risk of Hip Fracture." *JAMA* 1989; 262:3303–3307.

[2] Upjohn Science Information. "Factsheet: Anxiety." April 1989.

[3] Data offered by Mead Johnson Pharmaceuticals and The Upjohn Company, 1987–1989.

[4] Tyler, Varro E. *Hoosier Home Remedies*, West Lafayette, Indiana: Purdue University Press, 1985, 115–116.

[5] Tyler, Varro E. *The Honest Herbal: A Sensible Guide to the Use of Herbs and Related Remedies*, Philadelphia: George F. Stickley Co., 224–225.

[6] Wurtman, J.J. "Ways that Foods Can Affect the Brain." *Nutr. Rev.* 1986; 44(Suppl.):2–6.

[7] Wurtman, Judith J. *Managing Your Mind and Mood Through Food*, New York: Perennial Library, 1988.

[8] Ray, op. cit.

[9] Bond, William S. "Anxiety Disorders and Their Treatment." *Facts and Comparisons Drug Newsletter* 1989; 8:25–27.

[10] Dubovsky, Steven L., et al. "Anxiolytics: When? Why? Which One? *Patient Care* 1987; Oct. 30:60–81.

[11] Scharf, Martin B., et al. "Differential Amnestic Properties of Short- and Long-acting Benzodiazepines." *J. Clin. Psychiatry* 1984: 45:51–53.

[12] Scharf, Martin B., et al. "Comparative Amnestic Effects of Benzodiazepine Hypnotic Agents." *J. Clin. Psychiatry* 1988; 49:134–137.

[13] Busto, Usoa, et al. "Withdrawal Reaction After Long-term Therapeutic Use of Benzodiazepines." *N. Engl. J. Med.* 1986; 315:854–859.

[14] Lader, M.H. "The Patient and Dependence." *Internal Medicine for the Specialist* 1985; 35(Special Issue).

[15] Marks, J. "Techniques of Benzodiazepine Withdrawal in Clinical Practice: A Consensus Workshop Report." *Medical Toxicology* 1988; 3:324–333.

[16] Talley, Joseph H. "But What if a Patient Gets Hooked?" *Postgraduate Medicine* 1990; 87:187–204.

[17] Baughman, Otis L., III. "Anxiolytic Perspectives for Primary Care Physicians." *Family Practice Recertification* 1989; 11(No. 9, Suppl.):117–125.

[18] Ray, Wayne A., et al. "Psychotropic Drug Use and the Risk of Hip Fracture." *N. Engl. J. Med.* 1987; 316:363–369.

[19] Ray, op. cit., 1989.

[20] Feighner, J.P., and Boyer, W.F. "Serotonin-1A Anxiolytics: An Overview." *Psychopathology* 1989; 22(Suppl. 1):21–26.

[21] Robinson, D.S., et al. "Serotonergic Anxiolytics and Treatment of Depression." *Psychopathology* 1989; 22(Suppl. 1):27–36.

[22] Drew, P.J., et al. "The Effect of Acute Beta-adrenoceptor Blockage on Examination Performance." *Br. J. Clin. Pharmacol.* 1985; 19:783–786.

[23] Lader, M. "Beta-adrenoreceptor Antagonists in Neuropyschiatry: An Update." *J. Clin. Psychiatry* 1988; 49:213–223.

[24] James, I., and Savage, I. "Beneficial Effect of Nadolol on Anxiety-induced Disturbances of Performance in Musicians: A Comparison with Diazepam and Placebo." *Am. Heart J.* 1984; 108:1150–1155.

[25] Currie, D., et al. "Central Effects of Beta-adrenoceptor Antagonists. I—Performance and Subjective Assessments of Mood." *Br. J. Clin. Pharmacol.* 1988; 26:121–128.

[26] Gates, G.A., et al. "Effect of Beta Blockade on Singing Performance." *Ann. Otol. Rhinol. Laryngol.* 1985; 94:570–574.

[27] Dubovsky, op. cit.

[28] Jenike, Michael A. "Obsessive-compulsive and Related Disorders: A Hidden Epidemic." *N. Engl. J. Med.* 1989; 321:539–541.

[29] Gelman, David. "Haunted by Their Habits." *Newsweek* 1989(Mar.); 71–75.

[30] Jenike, Michael A., op. cit.

[31] Rifkin, Arthur. "Obsessive-compulsive Disorder." *Postgraduate Medicine* 1989; 86:157–168.

[32] Swedo, W.E., et al. "A Double-blind Comparison of Clomipramine and Desipramine in the Treatment of Trichotillomania (Hair Pulling)." *N. Engl. J. Med.* 1989; 321:497–501.

[33] Jenike, Michael, A., et al. "Obsessive-Compulsive Disorder: A Double-Blind, Placebo Controlled Trial of Clomipramine in 27 Patients." *Am. J. Psychiatry* 1989; 146:1328–1330.

[34] "Clomipramine for Obsessive Compulsive Disorder." *Med. Let.* 1988; 30:102–104.

[35] Gelman, David, op. cit.

[36] Jenike, Michael A., et al. "Open Trial of Fluoxetine in Obsessive-Compulsive Disorder." *Am. J. Psychiatry* 1989; 146:909–911.

[37] Turner, Samuel M., et al. "Fluoxetine Treatment of Obsessive-compulsive Disorder." *J. Clin. Psychopharmacol.* 1985; 5:207–212.

[38] Perse, Teri L., et al. "Fluvoxamine Treatment of Obsessive-compulsive Disorder." *Am. J. Psychiatry* 1987; 144:1543–1548.

[39] Price, L.H., et al. "Treatment of Severe Obsessive-compulsive Disorder with Fluvoxamine." *Am. J. Psychiatry* 1987; 144:1059–1061.

[40] Goodman, Wayne K., et al. "Efficacy of Fluvoxamine in Obsessive-Compulsive Disorder." *Arch. Gen. Psychiatry* 1989; 46:36–44.

[41] Gillin, J. Christian, and Byerley, William F. "The Diagnosis and Management of Insomnia." *N. Engl. J. Med.* 1990; 322:239–248.

[42] Kales, A., and Kales, J.D. "Sleep Laboratory Studies of Hypnotic Drugs: Efficacy and Withdrawal Effects." *J. Clin. Psychopharmacol.* 1983; 3:140–150.

[43] Kales, A., et al. "Rebound Insomnia and Rebound Anxiety: A Review." *Pharmacology* 1983; 26:121–137.

[44] "Oral Hypnotic Drugs." *Medical Letter* 1989; 31:23–24.

[45] Adams, K., and Oswald, I. "Can a Rapidly-eliminated Hypnotic Cause Daytime Anxiety?" *Pharmacopsychiatry* 1989; 22:115–119.

[46] Kales, A., et al. "Comparison of Short and Long Half-life Benzodiazepine Hypnotics: Triazolam and Quazepam." *Clin. Pharmacol. Ther.* 1986; 40:378–386.

[47] Kales, A., et al. "Lorazepam: Effects on Sleep and Withdrawal Phenomena." *Pharmacology* 1986; 32:121–130.

[48] Dobkin, Bruce H. "Sleeping Pills." *New York Times Magazine* 1989 (Feb. 5); 39–40.

[49] Wurtman, op. cit., 1988: 90–92.

[50] Spinweber, C.L., et al. "Jet Lag in Military Operations: Field Trial of L-tryptophan in Reducing Sleep-Loss Effects." Report no. 86–15. San Diego: Naval Health Research Center, 1986.

[51] Clauw, Daniel J., et al. "Tryptophan-Associated Eosinophilic Connective-Tissue Disease." *JAMA* 1990; 1502–1506.

[52] Gillin and Byerley, op. cit.

[53] Ibid.

[54] Nicholson, A.N. "Long-range Air Capability and the South Atlantic Campaign." *Aviat. Space Environ. Med.* 1985; 55:269–270.

[55] Gillin and Byerley, op. cit.

[56] Scharf, Martin. Personal communication, March 15, 1990.

[57] Prous, J.R. "The Year's New Drugs." *Drug News and Perspectives* 1989; 2(1):31.

[58] "Zolpidem: Synthélabo's New Non-benzodiazepine Hypnotic." *Scrip* 1989; 1424:21.

[59] Editorial. "Zopiclone; Another Carriage on the Tranquilliser Train." *Lancet* 1990; 335:507–508.

[60] Scharf, Martin B., et al. "Current Pharmacologic Management of Narcolepsy." *American Family Physician* 1988; July: 143–148.

[61] Fry, J.M., et al. "Treatment of Narcolepsy with Codeine." *Sleep* 1986; 9(1pt):269–274.

[62] Mouret, J., et al. "Treatment of Narcolepsy with L-Tyrosine." *Lancet* 1988; 2:1458–1459.

[63] Nash, Margo. "Low-Amino-Diet Immune Boost." *Medical Tribune* 1990; 31(3):1–12.

[64] Elwes, R.D., et al. "Treatment of Narcolepsy with L-Tyrosine: Double-Blind Placebo-Controlled Trial." *Lancet* 1989; 2:1067–1069.

[65] Scharf, Martin B., and Fletcher, Kathleen A. "GHB—New Hope for Narcoleptics." *Biol. Psychiatry* 1989; 26:329–330.

[66] Scharf, Martin B., et al. "The Effects and Effectiveness of g-Hydroxybutyrate in Patients with Narcolepsy." *J. Clin. Psychiatry* 1985; 46:222–225.

Mind Matters

6

When doctors get together and talk about mental illness, what they usually mean is serious depression and schizophrenia. Once upon a time it was believed that these were "psychological" problems. It was common to blame parents if a child ended up suicidal or schizophrenic. If you just underwent analysis and talked out your convoluted family relationships, you could be healed of hallucinations and thoughts of suicide.

Unfortunately, it has rarely been so easy. Many patients spent thousands of dollars only to find themselves as confused and depressed after years of therapy as when they started. Today we realize that it's a lot more complicated. Much of mental illness is thought to be biochemically and genetically regulated.

When antipsychotics and antidepressants were introduced in the 1950s, they were quickly embraced as the answers to mental illness. For decades health professionals overlooked the darker side of these medications because they represented such an advance. Compared to frontal lobotomies, wet sheets, straight jackets, or other crude techniques that were used to treat severe mental and emotional disturbances, antipsychotics such as **Thorazine** (chlorpromazine), **Haldol** (haloperidol), **Mellaril** (thioridazine), and **Stelazine** (trifluoperazine) must have seemed like miracles.

But now we know that such "neuroleptics" may cause a kind of irreversible brain damage called tardive dyskinesia (TD), manifested by uncontrollable twitching and muscle spasms. A host of other unpleasant effects have also tarnished the initial enthusiasm for such drugs. Schizophrenics have been caught between a devil of delusions and a sea of side effects.

Depressed patients have not escaped a similar double bind. On one hand they find themselves in a seemingly bottomless pit where life offers little pleasure. But the antidepressant medications like **Elavil** (amitriptyline), **Sinequan** (doxepin), and **Tofranil** (imipramine), which have been prescribed to lift them out of the darkness, can cause confusion, dry mouth, constipation, weight gain, dizziness, urinary problems, and sexual dysfunction.

Thirty years ago people were willing to put up with a lot to buy a little relief from psychic pain. Now they are less willing to trade hallucinations for brain damage or put up with substantial weight gain as the price for an improved mood. That is why pharmaceutical manufacturers are scrambling to produce better and safer medicines for mental illness. For the first time in decades we are actually optimistic that there will soon be better mousetraps for the mind.

DRUG-INDUCED MENTAL ILLNESS

Is your medicine making you crazy? We can't imagine anything much scarier than the feeling that you may be losing your mind. Panic attacks, hallucinations, paranoid fears, sui-

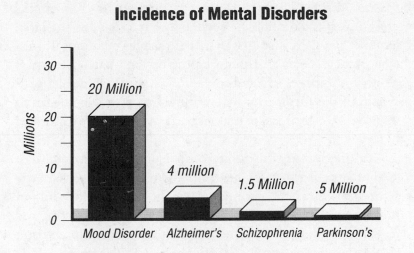

Incidence of Mental Disorders

cidal compulsions, manic attacks, horrible nightmares, memory loss, confusion, and delirium are all considered heavy-duty symptoms of mental illness. Yet they could all be side effects of commonly prescribed medications.

A reader of our syndicated newspaper column wrote about her experiences with two stomach drugs:

> My doctor prescribed **Reglan** (metoclopramide) and **Pepcid** (famotidine) for severe heartburn. After several days on these drugs I suffered a severe muscle spasm in my neck and shoulder. Within three weeks I was suffering from uncontrollable muscle twitching, hallucinations, severe insomnia, and suicidal thoughts. I thought I was going crazy.
>
> The first psychiatrist I saw prescribed **Valium**, but that didn't help at all. The next doctor tried, in order, **Ativan** (lorazepam), **Desyrel** (trazodone), **Halcion** (triazolam), and a combination of lithium and **Elavil** (amitriptyline). Nothing helped. I even checked myself into the psychiatric ward of a hospital for three days. It was the most horrible experience of my life.

Fortunately, this woman finally read about the side effects of **Reglan**, the stomach medication that started this whole mess. They include uncontrollable muscle twitching and neck spasms, depression, restlessness, fatigue, anxiety, insomnia, drowsiness, and dizziness. **Pepcid** may have added to the problem as it can also cause "psychic disturbances including depression, anxiety, decreased libido, hallucinations; paresthesia [tingling or numbness in hands or feet], insomnia; somnolence."[1] When all the medications were finally stopped, she began to improve, though occasional attacks of depression have continued to plague her.

It is hardly surprising that this person did not suspect that medicine prescribed for heartburn would cause psychiatric symptoms. But it was criminal that the psychiatrists did not immediately ask about all the medications she was taking and realize the muscle twitching, insomnia, depression, and suicidal thoughts were probably drug-induced side effects.

A surprising number of prescription and over-the-counter medications can throw a monkey wrench into the mental machinery.

The best way to avoid ending up with a drug-induced depression or other psychiatric problem is to remain, as the military would say, "armed and ready." Armed with information about psychological side effects, and ready to report anything unusual to a well-informed, sensitive health provider. We

---

Drug-Induced Psychiatric Symptoms:[2,3]

(There are over 150 medications that may cause psychiatric problems. Here are just a few examples.)

Adapin (doxepin)
Memory impairment, mania or hypomania, agitation

Afrin (oxymetazoline)
Anxiety, insomnia, hallucinations (with high doses)

Capoten (captopril)
Anxiety, insomnia, hallucinations

Elixophyllin (theophylline)
Anxiety, insomnia, restlessness, mania, hyperactivity

Elavil (amitriptyline)
Memory impairment, mania or hypomania, agitation

Halcion (triazolam)
Memory impairment, anxiety, rebound insomnia, confusion, agitation, depression, hallucinations

Inderal (propranolol)

Depression, paranoia, nightmares, forgetfulness, hallucinations

Lopressor (metoprolol)

Depression, paranoia, nightmares, forgetfulness, hallucinations

prednisone

Depression, delusions, mania, hallucinations

Prozac (fluoxetine)

Anxiety, restlessness, insomnia, violent suicidal thoughts

Proventil (albuterol)

Anxiety, tremor, edginess, hallucinations, paranoia

Reglan (metoclopramide)

Depression, confusion, mania, muscle twitching, restlessness, anxiety, uncontrollable crying, insomnia

Seldane (terfenadine)

Anxiety, insomnia, restlessness, euphoria

Sinequan (doxepin)

Memory impairment, mania or hypomania, agitation

Slo-Bid (theophylline)

Anxiety, insomnia, restlessness, mania, hyperactivity

Slo-Phyllin (theophylline)

Anxiety, insomnia, restlessness, mania, hyperactivity

Somophyllin (aminophylline)

Anxiety, insomnia, restlessness, mania, hyperactivity

Symmetrel (amantadine)

Hallucinations, paranoia, nightmares

Tagamet (cimetidine)

Depression, confusion, hallucinations, mania, disorientation, delirium (elderly more vulnerable)

Theo-24 (theophylline)

Anxiety, insomnia, restlessness, mania, hyperactivity

Theo-Dur (theophylline)

Anxiety, insomnia, restlessness, mania, hyperactivity

Theobid (theophylline)

Anxiety, insomnia, restlessness, mania, hyperactivity

Ventolin (albuterol)

Anxiety, tremor, edginess, hallucinations, paranoia

Wellbutrin (bupropion)

Nervousness, insomnia, paranoia, hallucinations

have seen too many people develop depression because of a blood pressure medicine and then receive an antidepressant to counteract that side effect. Don't let the vicious-cycle syndrome put you in the hospital.

Depression

The numbers are staggering. One out of every twelve people will suffer a mood disorder. That means that twenty million Americans will be depressed or manic at some time during their life.[4] Even more shocking is the changing pattern of depression. We used to think this was a disorder of middle-aged or older people. But nowadays childhood depression is an increasing issue, especially as adolescent suicide-attempts zoom.[5]

Perhaps the most disturbing aspect of this common mental health problem is that doctors often fail to recognize and treat depression appropriately. Half of the depressed patients in one study were not diagnosed correctly by their family physicians.[6] What that means is an awful lot of people are psychologically in the dumper, don't realize it, and are not getting adequate help.

Everyone feels blue sometime. Perhaps that is why it is so hard for an individual to distinguish between a garden-variety slump and a true melancholia. A bad day at the office, a fight with a spouse, or just a normal down cycle can make anyone feel depressed. Most people bounce back within a few days or weeks with no special treatment. When the depression lasts and intensifies and you begin to feel like you've forgotten what it's like to be happy, you need professional help.

Signs of Depression:

(If some of the following signs or symptoms seem familiar, get in touch with a mental health professional immediately!)

- If you have difficulty with sleep (trouble falling asleep or awakening in the early morning hours).
- If you feel gloomy, down in the dumps, and sad longer than several weeks.
- If food has lost its appeal and you eat because you should rather than because you're hungry or the food tastes good.
- If you find that sex is no longer a big deal and you can't remember the last time you felt sexy.
- If your energy level is at an all-time low or you feel like you are in slow motion.
- If you feel restless and agitated and find yourself pacing the floor.
- If you find it hard to mobilize yourself to visit friends or participate in social events.
- If you doubt your abilities and feel pessimistic a lot of the time.
- If you have a hard time concentrating or remembering simple things.
- If thoughts of suicide start running through your mind.

NONDRUG REMEDIES

Forty years ago talking therapy was the primary approach to severe depression. When antidepressant medications became widely available, many doctors adopted the theory that depression was due to an imbalance of chemicals in the brain. They hopped on the drug bandwagon and conveniently overlooked common adverse reactions or reassured patients that these were "minor" side effects that could be tolerated easily. Lots of people put up with dry mouth, constipation, sexual dysfunction, and weight gain, but they often complained bitterly of these persistent annoyances. Many reported that they felt less depressed, but they didn't feel really great either.

Now the pendulum has swung again, and talking therapy is back. A sympathetic ear, social support, and a little guidance may work as well as drug treatment for mild to moderate depression. Dr. Irene Elkin, a psychologist at the Mood, Anxiety, and Personality Disorders branch of the National Institute of Mental Health, conducted the largest study to date comparing different forms of treatment. She found that when a therapist just listened to the patient's problems, even for only twenty minutes a week, the patient was likely to do about as well as with drug therapy, psychotherapy, or cognitive behavioral therapy, which is designed to change a negative personal and world view.[7]

This does not mean that medications are unnecessary. But it demonstrates that psychological support is a valuable tool against depression, either on its own or in combination with an antidepressant drug. Every patient should be encouraged to participate in selecting his or her therapy, for this depends on personal considerations. Some may choose to delay a drug because of sensitivity to side effects, whereas others may need immediate medication. A family physician who can spend twenty minutes a week listening and guiding may be as helpful for some patients as a psychiatrist. Others may find a minister, friend, relative, or support group works best for mild to moderate depression.

Exercise

As effective as talking therapy may be, there are also other things people can do to combat depression. Exercise just might be powerful medicine for some folks. We're not suggesting that a walk around the block will instantly cure the blues, but research has shown that a moderate aerobic training program can help improve general mood and outlook.[8–10] Dr. Russ Jaffe, Director of the Princeton Brain Bio Center, maintains that "recent onset depression is hard to sustain with low impact aerobic exercise."[11] He recommends swimming, bicycling, cross country skiing, and even brisk walking followed by a warm shower, then followed by a cold shower.

Vigorous regular exercise can also help relieve insomnia, irritability, poor appetite, and anxiety. Although the research is still preliminary, there have been suggestions that brain biochemistry may actually change after a good workout. No one should start such a physical fitness plan from scratch, however. Medical supervision is essential to make sure there are no underlying complications and to assist in developing a realistic program.

NUTRIENTS

In her wonderful book, *Managing Your Mind and Mood Through Food*, MIT researcher Dr. Judith Wurtman points out that our diet can have a profound effect on brain biochemistry. The building blocks of neurotransmitters like dopamine and norepinephrine come from amino acids in food, and these chemicals are keys to mental health. Dr. Wurtman has discovered that if you are feeling sluggish, a protein snack, alone or with carbos as a chaser will have an alerting or energizing effect on mood because the amino acid tyrosine becomes more available in the brain.

L-Tyrosine

Although Dr. Wurtman is opposed to taking amino acid supplements, there are preliminary data to suggest that l-tyrosine may offer some antidepressant action. A decade ago several researchers reported anecdotal findings that l-tyrosine might help relieve depression.[12,13] More recently a French researcher, Dr. Jacques Mouret, has reported that certain depressed patients responded to l-tyrosine supplementation.[14,15]

Better double-blind studies are necessary, however, before depressed patients start dosing themselves on megamilligrams of this amino acid, especially since there are several potential dangers associated with tyrosine. It should never be combined with antidepressant medications. Drugs like **Nardil**, **Marplan,** and **Parnate** could interact with tyrosine to drive blood pressure sky high. Anyone taking l-tyrosine (even by itself) should monitor blood pressure frequently. There is also concern that susceptible individuals may develop migraines after l-tyrosine. Anyone with melanoma should also steer clear of tyrosine, as recent research on animals suggests that elimination of this amino acid may have a protective effect against this dangerous kind of skin cancer.[16]

L-Phenylalanine

L-phenylalanine is another amino acid that is crucial for brain biochemistry. A pilot study published some years ago demonstrated impressive results against depression when the Parkinson's drug **Eldepryl** (deprenyl, selegiline) (5–10 mg daily) was combined with 250 mg of l-phenylalanine.[17] This work unfortunately has not been confirmed, and as tantalizing as it may be, the combo can't be recommended at this time. There may a be a risk of hypertension with l-phenylalanine, so this amino acid should not be taken unless under a physician's supervision. The same questions about malignant melanoma that have been raised with l-tyrosine apply also to l-phenylalanine.

Vitamins and Minerals

When it comes to depression, there is not much good research on the role of vitamins, minerals, and other nutrients. Dr. Carl Pfeiffer was one of the country's leaders in orthomolecular medicine (use of selective nutrients). He recommended vitamin C (2 grams a day in divided doses), vitamin B_6

(at bedtime in levels adequate to produce dream recall), and zinc (30 mg) at bedtime. As long as doses of vitamin B$_6$ are kept under 100 mg a day, we don't see much danger in this regimen and it might help some people.

There is one report in the medical literature that links high levels of the mineral vanadium to depression (unipolar depression) and manic depression (bipolar depression).[18] A number of medications prescribed for mental illness help detoxify vanadium. Apparently, so does vitamin C, which may explain its potential benefits.

SAD

They call it seasonal affective disorder, or SAD for short. It comes on cat's paws, sneaking up on the unwary when they are least able to defend themselves. We are talking about people who get the blues when the season changes. These folks find themselves down in a very deep pit when the days are short and the sun doesn't shine. People with SAD often find that they have no energy when they are caught up in this web.

Investigators aren't sure why low levels of sunshine seem to trigger SAD. It may be that the internal clock and hormonal rhythms are thrown out of whack during winter.

Light Box

If money is no object, hop a plane to the islands and spend the winter relaxing on the beach soaking up lots of glorious rays. (Don't forget the sunscreen.) A more realistic alternative for most of us would be to spend more time outdoors in the winter, especially when the sun is shining. Make sure the window shades are pulled back and as much light can get into the house as possible. Another alternative might be a light box. These babies aren't cheap (they run around $350–$400), but preliminary research suggests that as many as 85 percent of those with SAD may get benefit from phototherapy.[19] And if your doctor invests in a light box, you may be able to use his.

These light boxes are not to be confused with tanning booths. Sunscreen is apparently unnecessary, since people are not exposed to enough ultraviolet radiation to even cause a tan.

They use a full-spectrum light bulb that more nearly resembles natural sunlight than fluorescent or regular bulbs do. People look into the box for about ten to fifteen seconds each minute for up to an hour. Investigators believe the retina is involved in this strange disorder by modulating the body's manufacture of melatonin, a brain hormone. If someone is going to respond favorably, she should do so within a few days of starting phototherapy. That is why it would be best to find a physician to supervise therapy initially so you don't have to shell out a huge amount of money for a light box, only to discover it doesn't help.

> ### Brad's SAD Attack:
> Brad explained his winter doldrums to us this way: "I could barely drag my body out of bed in the morning during January and February. I gained weight [carbohydrate craving is common], slept much more than usual, had almost no interest in sex, and didn't want to do anything or see anybody. **Wellbutrin** (bupropion) turned my life around."

DRUG TREATMENTS

There is a time to every season, and that includes depression. There is a time to try exercise, and talking therapy, and perhaps even nutrients or a light box. And there is a time to reach for a medicine. These drugs save lives and make life worth living. Anyone who begins to think about suicide or feels helpless and hopeless needs to seek immediate assistance from a health professional. Chances are good a prescription is in order.

Brain chemistry seems to be altered during depression. And no matter how hard you may try to "snap out of it," the neurons may not cooperate. People should stop beating themselves up for feeling depressed. It is not anyone's fault and it is virtually impossible to pull yourself out of one of these funks with willpower alone. Friends and relatives must *never* lay blame.

In the old days we had two basic classes of antidepressants to choose from: MAO (monoamine oxidase) inhibitors and tricyclics. They worked . . . sort of. Many people reported that after about two or three weeks they no longer felt lower than a snake's belly. But they also had to pay a price for this relief.

Tricyclic antidepressants (TCAs) can produce a range of side effects including dry mouth, constipation, weight gain, blurred vision, glaucoma, urinary difficulties, dizziness, mental confu-

Tricyclic-type Antidepressants

Adapin	**Norpramin**
(doxepin)	(desipramine)
Amitril	**Pamelor**
(amitriptyline)	(nortriptyline)
Asendin	**Pertofrane**
(amoxapine)	(desipramine)
Aventyl	**Sinequan**
(nortriptyline)	(doxepin)
Elavil	**Surmontil**
(amitriptyline)	(trimipramine)
Endep	**Tofranil**
(amitriptyline)	(imipramine)
Janimine	**Vivactil**
(imipramine)	(protriptyline)

Triazolopyridine Antidepressant

Desyrel
   (trazodone)

Possible MAO Inhibitor Side Effects:

- Dizziness on standing, muscle twitches.
- Headache, jitteriness, mania, insomnia.
- Impaired memory, anxiety, fatigue, drowsiness.
- Constipation, diarrhea, nausea, stomach-ache.
- Dry mouth, blurred vision, sweating, weight loss.
- Impotence, loss of orgasm, skin rash.

sion, disturbed concentration, impaired memory, sexual dysfunction, impotence, drowsiness, incoordination, dental problems, periodontal disease, and fatigue. These drugs can also interact dangerously with a wide variety of other medications.

Despite such complications, the tricyclic antidepressants can be a godsend for many people—the difference between barely existing and enjoying life. They may be especially effective for those who have trouble sleeping, lose their appetite, and become apathetic. But for others, the weight gain, mental cloudiness, and sexual dysfunction are almost as depressing as the illness they suffered. **Norpramin** and **Pertofrane** (both desipramine) and **Desyrel** (tradozone) seem less likely to cause forgetfulness, dry mouth, and constipation than many other TCAs, although **Desyrel** should probably be taken at night since it does produce considerable drowsiness (a possible plus for depressed insomniacs).

MAO inhibitors like **Marplan** (isocarboxazid), **Nardil** (phenelzine), and **Parnate** (tranylcypromine) may offer special benefit for people who find their depression is associated with snacking and overeating or who find they are sleeping more rather than less.

MAO inhibitors have their own set of side effects, though. For one thing, there are some very strict dietary restrictions. People cannot eat foods high in tyramine, which include most cheeses (from cheddar and Brie to Parmesan and Stilton), certain kinds of fish and meat (from chicken liver and herring to salami and pepperoni), alcoholic beverages (from red wine and sherry to imported beer and ale) and even certain fruits and vegetables (from bananas and avocados to raisins and canned figs). Such foods could precipitate a hypertensive crisis.

There are also drug interactions to be wary of. People taking **Nardil**, **Marplan,** or **Parnate** must avoid all over-the-counter cold and allergy medicines that may contain decongestants, as this combination could raise blood pressure to stratospheric levels. Caffeine can also pose problems. So we are talking about some substantial lifestyle changes for anyone on MAO inhibitors. There are also enough side effects to make people feel uncomfortable.

A NEW GENERATION

Prozac

When **Prozac** (fluoxetine) was introduced in 1987, it barely made a splash. The Eli Lilly Company had been badly battered by the **Oraflex** scandal of the early 1980s. This prescription arthritis drug had been aggressively promoted with a full-court publicity blitz, but was later found to cause potentially life-threatening kidney and liver damage. The drug was eventually outlawed, but only after thousands of adverse reactions and over one hundred deaths worldwide. It was one of the darkest moments in Lilly history, especially since there had been charges of a cover-up.

Perhaps because of the **Oraflex** debacle Lilly planned the **Prozac** promotion carefully. Instead of launching the drug with great fanfare, the company initially introduced this entirely new antidepressant only to psychiatrists. There were no glitzy press kits and no dog and pony shows. But the drug took off like a shooting star!

In 1988 **Prozac** chalked up sales of $125 million, a very respectable number in the pharmaceutical industry for a new drug. The next year sales had leaped to over $350 million.[20] In less than two years, the American public spent more on **Prozac** than it had previously spent on all of the other twenty antidepressants combined. The drug was projected to top $1 billion by 1995, if not sooner. (Only six other medications have reached such rarified atmosphere, and few so fast.) At the time of this writing, 650,000 prescriptions are being filled each month and that number is quickly expected to reach one million a month. This is even more amazing given the steep price of **Prozac**—about $1.50 a capsule. The monthly tab can range anywhere from $50 to $200 depending on the dosage, versus only $7 for generic amitriptyline, a commonly prescribed tricyclic.

The American public is clearly voting with its pocketbook. **Prozac** is a major hit. It even made the cover of *New York* magazine and *Newsweek*. So what's the big deal? Why has this antidepressant become so popular so fast, even though it is no more effective (and perhaps even a little less effective) than traditional antidepressants?

Perhaps the biggest reason is that **Prozac** is so much better tolerated by the body. People may have been less depressed after taking drugs like **Elavil** or **Pamelor**, but they didn't like feeling sluggish, dizzy, or constipated. The dry mouth and weight gain were also a major obstacle to acceptance. Along came **Prozac** with a lot fewer side effects and some extraordinary new uses. For one thing, **Prozac** causes weight loss instead of weight gain. People who get on the scale after six months on **Sinequan** and see twenty additional pounds are delighted to learn that there is an alternative medicine that will maintain their improved mood while simultaneously helping them shed the extra weight.

Another advantage for some people is **Prozac**'s mild stimulant action. Instead of walking around feeling like a space cadet, this drug may make some folks feel slightly energized, almost wired. Better yet are all the other potential uses for **Prozac**. The Eli Lilly company has applied for permission to market the drug in the treatment of obesity (at 60 mg a day instead of 20 mg, the drug may help overweight people lose about one pound a week).[21] The drug also appears to work quite well against obsessive-compulsive disorder, perhaps almost as well as **Anafranil** (see page 181). Then there are all **Prozac**'s other treatment possibilities—bulimia, nicotine withdrawal, drug addiction, diabetes control, alcoholism, and PMS.

Lest the initial enthusiasm surrounding **Prozac** turn into a love fest, it is crucial to remember that there is a downside to this antidepressant. For some people, side effects can be significant. In the premarketing test period, 15 percent of the subjects quit taking **Prozac** because of adverse reactions. Quite a few complained that the drug made them feel worse rather than better—nervous, anxious, sleepless, and nauseous. Some develop what is being called the caffeine syndrome. They become restless, experience tremors, start sweating, feel dizzy and light-headed.

Several years ago we received a troubling letter from a physician who told a tragic story about the death of his forty-year-old daughter:

> During the time when she found she was going through a difficult emotional period, her counsellor recommended that she see a physician who, because Jeanne was not eating properly, started her in a program for eating disorders.

> He prescribed the medication **Prozac**. One month later, after taking this medication, she committed suicide by hanging herself. What was so strange about this unsuspected action was that she was not behaving like a person who was depressed or suicidal.

At first we discounted the significance of this story. Unfortunately, emotionally disturbed people sometimes commit suicide whether they are taking an antidepressant or not. But in February 1990 an article appeared in the *American Journal of Psychiatry* that shed a new light on this case history. Physicians associated with the Department of Psychiatry at Harvard Medical School reported on six patients who suddenly developed an "intense violent suicidal preoccupation after 2–7 weeks of fluoxetine [**Prozac**] treatment."[22]

It would be disastrous if an antidepressant medication actually produced "obsessive, recurrent, persistent, and intrusive" thoughts of suicide. This may be a rare occurrence, but the Harvard psychiatrists warn that people who feel fatigued and restless or sleep much more than usual may be at higher risk.

Prozac Side Effects

- Headache, anxiety, agitation, nervousness, insomnia.
- Drowsiness, tremor, fatigue, light-headedness, dizziness, depersonalization.
- Nausea, diarrhea, upset stomach, loss of appetite, dry mouth, constipation, abdominal pain.
- Lowered libido, loss or delay of orgasm, abnormal ejaculation.
- Impaired concentration and memory, strange dreams.
- Sweating, rash, itching, dry skin, hair loss.
- Flulike symptoms, sore throat, stuffy nose, back pain.
- A rare but worrisome side effect is seizure.

Anyone who starts to feel in the least suicidal on this medicine should contact a psychiatrist immediately! The company believes that **Prozac** is no more likely to cause this type of problem than any other form of therapy, but for the moment this is a small cloud on **Prozac**'s otherwise bright horizon.

Wellbutrin

A unique new antidepressant has been overlooked amidst the **Prozac** hoopla. **Wellbutrin** (bupropion) was actually approved by the FDA late in 1985, almost two years before **Prozac** got its green light. The Burroughs Wellcome company had already started shipping **Wellbutrin** to pharmacies around the country when disaster struck. A small study of fifty bulimic women uncovered an alarming statistic. Four out of the fifty (8 percent) had suffered a seizure, making for an unacceptably high risk. The drug was pulled off shelves and returned to the company. The FDA demanded additional tests, but the company resisted, claiming that this was an atypical situation and that the actual seizure incidence was comparable to traditional antidepressants.

For over a year it was a standoff, with neither side willing to give in. Executives at the company even considered giving up on the drug completely. Burroughs Wellcome eventually threw in the towel and undertook a large follow-up study of over three thousand patients. Sure enough, the seizure incidence turned out to be only 0.4 percent, in line with other antidepressants and way below the strange 8 percent seen in the bulimia study. Finally, in August 1989 **Wellbutrin** reached the marketplace. It may be tolerated as well as **Prozac**, if not better.

Wellbutrin works differently from any other antidepressant on the market. Like **Prozac** it does not cause weight gain, and may even help people lose pounds. Unlike tricyclics **Wellbutrin** doesn't produce drowsiness, blurred vision, mental confusion, cardiovascular problems, or impaired memory. And best of all, unlike virtually all previous antidepressants, including **Prozac**, **Wellbutrin** does not muck up your sex life. If anything, it may be more likely to stimulate sexuality.

You would think that a medicine that could relieve depression, help you lose weight, *and* make you sexy would be an instant bestseller. Although **Wellbutrin** has done reasonably well, it has not turned into the overnight success that **Prozac** has. For one thing, the company has kept a low profile, promoting **Wellbutrin** primarily to psychiatrists. For another, the long three-and-a-half-year lag in marketing the drug slowed it down substantially. Finally, the memory of a seizure controversy has probably scared some physicians.

It would be a shame if **Wellbutrin** didn't get a fair shake. Physicians who have had experience with this drug are enthusiastic. **Wellbutrin** sometimes works when other antidepressants have failed. It may also help selected patients with bipolar depression (manic depression).[24] Many psychiatrists we have talked to say that it is so well-tolerated that a substantial number of their patients don't even feel like they are taking a medication.

This does not mean **Wellbutrin** can't cause side effects. It does have some stimulant action, so sensitive people report agitation, insomnia, and tremor. Headache, dry mouth, sweating, skin rash, nausea, and constipation are other potential adverse reactions. To minimize seizure risk, the dose should be started low and increased gradually. For example, a standard formula would be to start with 100 mg taken twice daily. Depending on the response, this can be increased after three days to 100 mg taken three times a day (one pill in the morning, midday, and evening). It may take up to four weeks before an antidepressant effect is established. The total daily dose should not exceed 450 mg (150 mg taken three times daily, with each single dose not to exceed 150 mg). Medications that may affect the seizure threshold, especially when they are discontinued (antianxiety agents or sleeping pills such as **Xanax**, **Halcion,** or **Ativan**), should probably be used cautiously, if at all, with **Wellbutrin**.

Overall, the first of the new generation antidepressants,

> ### *Wellbutrin* *(bupropion)*
> A unique new antidepressant with fewer side effects than traditional antidepressants. Can have the added bonus of helping people lose weight and may also stimulate sexuality. People tend to feel energized rather than sluggish.
> Side effects: agitation, insomnia, tremor, headache, and dry mouth. Seizures are a rare but worrisome possibility.
>
> ★ ★ ★

Prozac and **Wellbutrin**, represent an extraordinary advance in the therapy of mood disorders. For the first time depressed people can take a medicine and start to feel good again without ruining the quality of their lives. Instead of feeling sluggish and worrying about driving under the influence of a tricyclic, most people will be able to embrace life with gusto. Of course some patients will not be able to tolerate these new medications, but the exciting news is that we are just at the beginning of a new age of antidepressant drug development.

FUTURE DRUGS

Pharmaceutical manufacturers have watched the extraordinary success of **Prozac** (fluoxetine) with a certain degree of amazement. The antidepressant market had remained more or less static for over a decade and then out of the blue a star was born. Many companies are now looking eagerly for new antidepressants. One of the likeliest contenders is a **Prozac** look-alike called **Faverin** (fluvoxamine). It too modulates serotonin within the brain and appears to be very promising in the treatment of both depression and obsessive-compulsive disorder. It may be more selective and even better tolerated than **Prozac**. **Faverin** is already available in Europe and is being developed for the American market by Reid-Rowell.

There are a number of other serotonin modulators also in the pipeline. Pfizer has a promising new compound called sertraline. It was submitted to the FDA in April 1988 and should become available soon. SmithKline Beecham has a drug called **Aropax** (paroxetine). And Bristol-Myers Squibb is looking at its already-available antianxiety agent **BuSpar** (buspirone) [see page 175] for a new use against depression. The company also has a new chemical cousin, gepirone, that may prove to be especially helpful for people who suffer anxiety and depression simultaneously.[25]

A fascinating compound from Janssen Pharmaceutica (a subsidiary of Johnson and Johnson) called ritanserin also appears to work very well against depressed mood and anxiety (80 percent success rate). In preliminary studies, patients described themselves as calmer, more relaxed, less fatigued, and more energetic. An added bonus of ritanserin may be its ability to control tremors of Parkinson's disease and involuntary muscle twitching induced by major tranquilizers. The drug may also be helpful for insomnia, especially when induced by jet lag. Initial reports suggest that the side-effect profile of ritanserin is excellent—dizziness and light-headedness are uncommon reactions that often disappear over time. Some people reported constipation.

Glaxo has a new drug under investigation called fluparoxan that is described as "a novel antidepressant with the potential for a faster onset of action and a more favorable side-effect profile than current therapy."[26] For major depression, another novel drug called reboxetine (Erbamont of Europe) has potent action with fewer side effects. If just a few of these promising new agents pan out, the future will be bright indeed for millions of depressed patients.

Schizophrenia

The eyes give them away almost every time. Sometimes it's the intensity of the stare. Other times there is a vacant, faraway look as if they're in a different place or time. We call them schizophrenic, but that's just a label that allows us to ignore their individuality.

In our neighborhood there is a woman the kids call "the crazy lady." She's probably close to fifty and clearly different. In the summer she wears miniskirts, high socks, and a big floppy hat and strides up and down the streets at a furious pace. In the winter she is covered up with multiple layers. If you come across her in the park or see her at the bus stop, she is often holding an animated conversation with an invisible friend.

Dr. Adria Burrows describes a similar woman from her days as a medical student:

> We used to call her "the Duck Lady."
> The Duck Lady always sat on a stone ledge in front of our

inner-city hospital with a shopping bag nearby, quacking like a duck. She was a short woman with no teeth and a dirty scarf wrapped around her head. She always wore a tattered raincoat and her feet were bare, although they were so filthy it looked almost as if she had shoes on. I wondered how she ate and if she lived anywhere . . .

My classmates made fun of her at some of our teaching sessions, imitating her choppy gait and making duck sounds. One even used a drawing of her in a slide presentation, as a joke.[27]

Schizophrenias

Variable psychiatric disorders of misperception, thought disorders, abnormal fears, hallucinations, paranoia, obsessions, compulsions, blank mind, and confusion.

Society laughs at the "duck ladies" of this world partly because they make us feel so uncomfortable. They do not play by our rules or participate in our reality. We avert our eyes and turn away as quickly as possible and pretend they aren't really there. But hard as we try to ignore them, they will not disappear. They have no place to go, no possibility of holding down a normal job, and often even no warm bed. Others lead quiet lives, almost unnoticed, but still feared. They may hold down jobs and try to cope with a confusing world. But they get very little help except from family and friends. Our society has let the mentally ill down.

In one of the great deceptions of all time, deinstitutionalization, in full swing in the 1970s, was supposed to get schizophrenic patients out of mental institutions and somehow rehabilitate them back into society. The theory was that local communities would pick up the slack and provide shelter, support, and therapy in the form of halfway houses. It sounded like a far more humane and effective system than warehousing them in the back wards of big, impersonal asylums. They would be close to family and friends and have an opportunity to reenter a wider world.

DRUG TREATMENT

This move couldn't have been considered without the magic of medicine. Antipsychotic agents (also known as major tranquilizers or neuroleptics) that were developed in the 1950s were supposed to calm the internal volcanoes, silence the voices, and dim the visions that no one else could hear or see. The pharmaceutical revolution promised to reorient patients and provide a path to help them reenter society.

The reality is a travesty. Lost souls have been abandoned—thrown out in the cold like so much litter on our nation's streets. The money that was necessary to provide support for community mental health centers never came close to meeting the need. The halfway houses and support networks rarely materialized. Families were left to cope on their own. But no matter how hard they tried, it was an impossible task—a Sisyphean struggle that left parents, spouses, and siblings frustrated, exhausted, guilty, and furious.

The medicines did not cure schizophrenia. The policy makers and politicians who passed the legislation mandating deinstitutionalization didn't understand pharmacology. The magic bullets that were supposed to return mentally ill patients to mainstream society frequently caused serious side effects. Just trying to read words on a printed page could become an exercise in futility because of blurred vision. Even a short exposure to the sun can produce visual problems and a severe skin reaction, making patients spend most time indoors. A terrible internal restlessness can become overwhelming, forcing patients to pace the floor endlessly with no relief. This condition, called akathisia, appears to be far more common than most mental health professionals realized. Mental confusion can be incredibly frustrating, especially for a creative person.

One of the worst side effects is tardive dyskinesia (TD), an often irreversible brain damage brought on by these drugs. After several months or years of continuous therapy, it can start with a numbness of the tongue that slowly turns into mouth twitching, lip smacking, chewing motions, facial contortions, and neck twisting. Involuntary muscle spams can affect arms, legs, and body. Even when antipsychotics are discontinued, TD may never disappear. Although the incidence of this adverse reaction has been hotly debated within psychiatric circles, estimates

Antipsychotic Medications

Compazine
(prochlorperazine)

Haldol
(haloperidol)

Loxitane
(loxapine)

Mellaril
(thioridazine)

Moban
(molindone)

Navane
(thiothixene)

Permitil
(fluphenazine)

Prolixin
(fluphenazine)

Serentil
(mesoridazine)

Sparine
(promazine)

Stelazine
(trifluoperazine)

Taractan
(chlorprothixene)

Thorazine
(chlorpromazine)

Tindal
(acetophenazine)

Trilafon
(perphenazine)

Vesprin
(triflupromazine)

Side Effects of Antipsychotic Drugs

- Mental confusion, apathy, emotional flattening, depression, despondency.
- Parkinsonlike symptoms: slow shuffling walk, "mask face," tremors.
- Drowsiness, dizziness, fainting, headache, weakness, incoordination, slurred speech.
- Agitation, restlessness, hyperactivity, pacing (higher doses can make this condition [akathisia] worse, not better!).
- Neck twitching, uncontrollable lip chewing, tongue biting, uncontrollable muscle spasms.
- Rash, dry skin, itching, sun sensitivity, hair loss.
- Nasal congestion, dry mouth, asthma, sweating, constipation, urinary difficulties, weight gain.
- Breast engorgement, menstrual irregularities, sexual dysfunction, impotence.
- Glaucoma, blurred vision, eye changes (retinitis pigmentosa).

range that from 24 to more than 60 percent of patients will experience some degree of impairment.[28, 29]

It should come as no surprise that some mentally ill patients consider antipsychotic medications as being worse than their hallucinations. When given their freedom, many schizophrenics have chosen not to take chemical straitjackets that often make them feel like zombies. But then the demons return and reality as we know it begins to fade. They often end up wandering the streets, moving from rooming houses to cheap hotels to alleys.

These people deserve something better than a choice between toxic drugs or the streets. Families cannot be expected to do it all. Local, state, and federal governments must provide adequate services. Researchers have to unlock the secrets of schizophrenia and discover better treatments. Fortunately, there is new hope and some real advances may lie ahead.

NONDRUG REMEDIES

Not very long ago many psychiatrists placed a huge burden of guilt on families by blaming the "schizophrenogenic" mother for producing a schizophrenic child. According to this theory, mom messed up the child in part through a process of faulty upbringing. To put it in computer lingo, the software was programmed incorrectly. Today we know that parents are not to blame and that it is more likely that the hardware (the human computer) has been miswired. It is as if somehow a monkey wrench was placed inside the human brain, and this biological blooper has led to faulty processing and outputting of data.

A study of twins published in the *New England Journal of Medicine* recently proved that there are clear-cut structural abnormalities within the brains of schizophrenic patients.[30]

Researchers do not know what causes these anatomical aberrations (such as enlarged cerebral ventricles). Some of the proposed biological culprits at the root of schizophrenia include genes, viruses, environmental toxins, or a hyperactive immune system.[31]

Dr. Carl Pfeiffer and his colleagues at the Princeton Brain Bio Center devoted much of their careers in the field of orthomolecular medicine trying to understand the biochemical constitution of such patients and determine various triggers for different categories of schizophrenias. (Joe Graedon spent two years working under Dr. Pfeiffer in the neuropharmacology laboratory of the New Jersey Neuropsychiatric Institute.) Dr. Pfeiffer identified a number of foods and other environmental factors that he believed could precipitate "cerebral allergy." By eliminating a variety of foods (such as wheat gluten, pasta, cake, cookies, crackers, pastry, oats, rye, barley, milk, dairy products, beer, gin, and whiskey) and providing special nutrients, Dr. Pfeiffer believed he could help schizophrenic and depressed patients.

Traditional psychiatry has for the most part rejected the cerebral allergy theory and made fun of vitamin, mineral, and amino acid supplementation. Orthomolecular medicine has evolved as a controversial and somewhat illegimate stepchild to

> ### *Orthomolecular Medicine*
>
> The Princeton Brain Bio Center offers a treatment program for schizophrenia and depression that includes special diagnostic testing, immune system modulation, avoidance of allergic substances in the diet and environment, and nutritional supplementation. They also refer patients to over three thousand orthomolecular physicians around the country.
>
> Princeton Brain Bio Center
> 862 Route 518
> Skillman, NJ 08558
> (609) 924–8607

conventional psychiatry. But compared to the toxicity of antipsychotic medications, we feel that these low-risk approaches are worth considering as a first-line adjunctive treatment.

Dr. Russ Jaffe has continued Dr. Pfeiffer's tradition at the Princeton Brain Bio Center and has refined testing techniques in the diagnosis of various schizophrenias. Besides eliminating certain foods, they tailor nutritional supplements like vitamin C, riboflavin, pyridoxidine, niacin, and essential amino acids to individual needs. In addition, Dr. Jaffe recommends vegetable juice and broth to supply other minerals and vitamins along with three to five servings of fresh fish per week. Considering the side effects of antipsychotic drugs (tardive dyskinesia, drowsiness, mental confusion, and restlessness), these nutritional suggestions seem reasonable.

NEW HOPE FOR MEDICINE

Although there has been a twenty-year dry spell in the development of safer and more effective antipsychotic medications, pharmaceutical companies appear on the verge of taking an important step forward. Of the two million schizophrenic patients in the United States, it is estimated that up to 20 percent do not respond to standard medications.[32] And many others cannot tolerate symptoms of tardive dyskinesia. In the past we abandoned these patients. Now there is hope that some may be helped for the first time.

Clozaril (clozapine)

Although this antipsychotic drug has been prescribed in Europe for almost two decades, it has only recently made it to the United States. What makes **Clozaril** unique is the fact that it doesn't appear to cause TD. Patients do not develop irreversible, uncontrollable muscle spasms. In fact, the drug may even reverse some of the symptoms of tardive dyskinesia.[33] **Clozaril** can also help patients who have not responded to traditional medications like **Compazine** and **Haldol**. It is estimated that 30–50 percent of patients who have been resistant may respond favorably to this new compound, especially if they have paranoid tendencies or are emotionally withdrawn.[34]

Unfortunately, **Clozaril** has one very serious complication. It can cause a potentially fatal blood disease called agranulocytosis in 1 or 2 percent of patients. If the medicine is stopped at the very first sign of trouble, people recover. But this requires frequent blood tests. The Sandoz company came up with a unique way to prevent problems. "All patients who receive **Clozaril** are required to undergo white blood cell (WBC) counts every week for as long as they receive the medication and for four weeks after discontinuation of therapy. No additional medication is dispensed until the weekly blood test is performed."[35] Physicians can facilitate this testing service for their patients by calling toll-free: (800) 237–CPMS.

Such precautions seem prudent. The only trouble is that patients have to pay, and it is estimated that between the medicine and the weekly blood tests the annual bill will exceed $9,000. Now add additional services and doctor's bills and you can see why families might look upon **Clozaril** as a mixed blessing. It may salvage a desperate child or spouse, but it could cause the family to go broke in the process.

Another serious complication of **Clozaril** is seizures. At low doses (less than 300 mg/day) the incidence is 1–2 percent. But at a dose of 600–900 mg the seizure rate jumps to 5 percent. What all this means is that once again the mentally ill are faced with terrible trade-offs. They can reduce their risk of neck twitching, lip chewing, and tremor while increasing the risk of blood disease, seizures, and unpleasant salivation. **Clozaril** may represent an advance but we desperately need even better compounds.

FUTURE DRUGS

Excitement is running high that pharmaceutical manufacturers are on the verge of developing some breakthrough medications in the treatment of schizophrenia. Glaxo has developed a unique drug for severe nausea and vomiting brought on by cancer chemotherapy. **Zofran** (ondansetron) has been shown to be extremely effective and is very well tolerated (constipation and headache appear to be relatively minor side effects).[36, 37] The company is also investigating **Zofran**'s potential for the treatment of schizophrenia, anxiety, drug abuse, memory loss, and perhaps even Alzheimer's disease.[38, 39] It has already been approved for sale in Britain and in France (under the name **Zophren**) for nausea and is expected to receive a fast green light from the U.S. Food and Drug Administration.

Another very promising drug is risperidone from Janssen Pharmaceutica (a subsidiary of Johnson and Johnson). Because of its ability to affect the brain chemicals serotonin and dopamine, this drug is expected to enhance the quality of

*Clozaril
Side Effects*

sedation
(39 percent)
excess salivation
(31 percent)
rapid heart rate
(25 percent)
constipation
(14 percent)
low blood pressure
(9 percent)
seizures
(up to 5
percent—at high
doses)
hypertension
(4 percent)
weight gain
(4 percent)
agranulocytosis
(1–2 percent)
Other: Dizziness,
sweating,
fever,
headache,
tremor,
nausea, and
vomiting.

sleep, control delusions and hallucinations, and reduce the emotional withdrawal, bizarre behavior, and apathy of schizophrenia. Preliminary studies on schizophrenic patients suggest that risperidone improves disorientation, depressed mood, hostility, anxiety, and confused thoughts. Side effects are less severe than with traditional antipsychotics. They include dizziness, fatigue, blurred vision, headache, and drowsiness.

Other companies that are actively developing new medications for schizophrenia include Astra (their Swedish medicine is known as **Roxiam** [remoxipride]), Bristol-Myers Squibb, ICI, Mitsui (they are working on **Barnetil** [sultopride]), Rhone-Poulenc, Hoffmann-La Roche, SmithKline Beecham, and Warner-Lambert (their drug is known as CI-943).

No matter which exciting new treatments finally pan out, we must all do a better job caring for the mentally ill people of our society. We must not turn our heads away when we see a strange look in the eyes of a disturbed person. We must work to eliminate the fear, distrust, scorn, and abuse that is still far too common in our society. These people deserve our empathy and help. Treatment must be humane, fair, safe, and effective.

Alzheimer's Disease and Memory Loss

Few conditions are more frightening than Alzheimer's disease. As terrible as cancer and heart disease may be, it is worse to fear that you may be losing your mind or to stand by helplessly and watch while a loved one sinks slowly into oblivion.

A few years ago the "experts" told us that approximately two million people in the United States had Alzheimer's disease—roughly 12 percent of the population between seventy-five and eighty-five years of age and 20 percent of those over eighty-five.[40] We suspected they were way off with those stats because almost every family we met had a war story to tell of an older relative or friend who had some kind

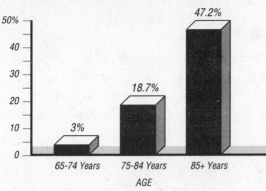

Incidence of People with Alzheimer's Disease

of memory disorder. Thousands of letters have poured in from people coping with "dementia" in their families.

It came as no surprise to us to learn that the experts have recently revised their numbers dramatically upward. A study from Boston's Brigham and Women's Hospital reveals that over 10 percent of those over sixty-five suffer Alzheimer's disease and almost half (47.2 percent) of people over eighty-five are afflicted.[41] The National Institute on Aging (NIA) now estimates that four million people have this disease and by the year 2050 there will be fourteen million walking wounded. In our opinion, Alzheimer's disease and other related memory disorders represent the most serious health threat of the twenty-first century.

No one yet understands what causes Alzheimer's and other so-called senile dementias. There are lots of theories: genetics, immune system changes brought on by some mysterious infectious agents, head trauma, environmental toxins (see aluminum discussion page 20), hormonal imbalance causing metabolic strain, or some combination of elements. Although researchers have made greater strides in the last few years than in all the previous decades combined, we still seem very far from unlocking the secrets of Alzheimer's. That doesn't mean we must give up hope. There is an amazing number of new medicines under development and some look quite promising in the fight against the mind slayers.

NEW DRUG TREATMENTS

THA (Cognex, tacrine)

One medication that has captured headlines is THA, otherwise known as tetrahydroaminoacridine. It is also known generically as tacrine and the Warner-Lambert company that is developing the drug, has given it the brand name **Cognex**. We will refer to it merely as THA.

In 1986 Dr. William Summers reported in the *New England Journal of Medicine* that this old drug produced dramatic improvement in some patients with Alzheimer's disease.[42] There was shock and disbelief within the small, inbred scientific community doing research on this disease. Dr. Summers was an outsider and somehow he had scooped the experts. At first a lot of energy went into criticizing Dr. Summers' research, but eventually a multicenter study was organized to confirm or reject his results.

At the time of this writing the final THA data have not yet been analyzed, but preliminary review suggests some benefit in roughly 25–40 percent of the patients who have been selected for study.[44, 45] That may not be great, but it is the best we have from any drug so far. One extraordinary outcome of the THA trials is the occasional anecdote of dramatic improvement. Talk informally to investigators at some of the ninety centers around the world testing the drug and you get whispers of true success stories.[46] We received just such an anecdote from a woman in Houston, Texas:

> After reading about THA and contacting *X* I decided to try THA. Of course I had to get it "black market," but I was willing to do anything—and, as I told the doctor, elevated liver enzymes were the least of our worries.
>
> My dad lives with me. He is a retired school teacher and Baptist deacon. He has Alzheimer's, and he had reached the point where he was disoriented most of the time, especially

---

THA (Cognex)

Researchers aren't sure how THA works. They suspect it raises levels of the brain chemical acetylcholine. The drug may also affect other important neurochemicals. Preliminary research suggests it can "augment histamine neurotransmission in the brain."[43]

at night. He had begun to wander off, and some mornings we'd find him walking miles from home. He could not find the bathroom and talked nonsense most of the time.

Since starting on THA, he has improved so much that his friends and family are in shock! He is never disoriented, never "lost," and his sense of humor and joy in family and life is back. It is truly an amazing difference.

Papa's doctor is monitoring him (checking carefully on liver enzymes), and he is fully enthusiastic about his taking THA.

I am angry, of course, that this medication is being withheld from so many who need it desperately, and I'm angry that it is costing so much (6 pills a day at $2 a pill takes a big chunk out of Papa's retirement check!).

Nevertheless, I'm grateful that we can get THA, whatever the cost, and I'm grateful to you for your interest. Had I not read your column on the subject, I'd not have been able to track it down!

Houston, Texas, August 17, 1989.

Such reports are extremely rare, but they do happen. At a recent Alzheimer's conference, the Lee family of Wildwood, Florida, related their experience with THA. Before the medicine Mr. Lee had become confused, did not know his daughter, and rejected his grandchildren. One daughter heard about a clinical trial being conducted at Duke University Medical Center. She called and the operator put her in touch with Dr. Albert Heyman. He listened with a sympathetic ear and encouraged her to bring her father to Duke for evaluation. Eventually he was included in the study. After taking THA he was happier, regained his sense of humor, laughed at jokes, gave the grandchildren hugs and kisses, and knew his daughter again. The family moved from a state of depression to hope and optimism.[47]

THA is not without risks. Elevation in liver enzymes is the

THA and Other Drug Research (Official)

Ask for information on test sites and list of drug companies conducting research:
Alzheimer's Association
70 East Lake Street, Suite 600
Chicago, IL 60601
(800) 621–0379; in Illinois (800) 572–6037

biggest concern. Frequent blood tests can catch this problem, however, and once the dose is lowered or the drug discontinued enzyme levels should return to normal. Other less serious side effects include nausea, belching, skin rash, and urinary difficulties.

Most Alzheimer's patients will not notice dramatic results with THA. It is certainly no cure. But many will show some benefit and others may not deteriorate as fast as they normally would. Even when there is success, it may not last indefinitely. In his original report, Dr. Summers acknowledged that the effects may eventually begin to wear off. But most families would be delighted with any small improvements that would make day-to-day life easier. At this writing FDA approval for **Cognex** (THA or tacrine) is expected shortly.

PREVENTING ALZHEIMER'S

One of the most fascinating new theories of Alzheimer's disease involves mitochondria—the cells' energy factories. Although the research is preliminary at best, scientists are collecting some tantalizing data that suggests mitochondrial metabolism may be mucked up in Alzheimer's patients. Dr. W. Davis Parker, Jr., is a mitochondria expert at the University of Colorado Health Sciences Center in Denver. He has suggested that "if Alzheimer's results from mitochondrial malfeasance, researchers might possibly treat or prevent it with drugs such as Co-enzyme Q and deprenyl **[Eldepryl]**, which can suppress oxidative damage."[48] What's neat about this theory is that if it holds up, the compounds that have been suggested are already available on the market and are very safe.

Coenzyme Q_{10}
(CoQ or ubiquinone)
This vitaminlike nutrient is crucial for mitochondria to function correctly. It may also help in the treatment of congestive heart failure (see page 89) as well as enhance the immune system, prevent gum disease, and serve as a general antioxidant.
CoQ is available from most health-food stores and mail-order vitamin suppliers.
For more information we suggest you read *The Miracle Nutrient Coenzyme Q_{10}* by Dr. Emile G. Bliznakov and Gerald L. Hunt (published by Bantam Books).

Eldepryl (deprenyl or selegilene)

A revolutionary prescription medicine against Parkinson's disease was approved for sale in the United States in 1989. Although **Eldepryl** (known generically as either selegilene or deprenyl) has been available in Europe since the early 1980s, its exciting potential is only now being realized in the United States. Levodopa (**Dopar**, **Larodopa**) is the usual drug for Parkinson's disease, as it serves as a building block for the neurochemical dopamine. But eventually levodopa's effectiveness begins to wear off. **Eldepryl** has been shown to reestablish benefit in 50–70 percent of patients with advanced Parkinson's disease.[49,50]

Neurologists are just as enthusiastic about using **Eldepryl** at the earliest stages of Parkinson's disease. New research shows that the drug's antioxidant action appears to protect brain cells from slow deterioration and can significantly delay onset of Parkinson's symptoms.[51,52]

Eldepryl may shine for other conditions as well. For one thing, it may have some antidepressant action.[53] But it is the drug's antioxidant action that has scientists really excited. This mechanism may protect the brain cell's mitochondria and make the drug effective against Alzheimer's disease and perhaps even aging itself.[54] Dr. Joseph Knoll, one of the original Hungarian developers of **Eldepryl**, reported on the fascinating results of a rat study. To take one measure of brain function, he and his colleagues tested the male rats' sexual activity once a week, starting from the time they were two years of age. At this ripe old age, none of the rats was completely capable of sexual function. Half the animals were injected with **Eldepryl**, the other half with saline three times a week. By the thirty-third month, the rats treated with saline couldn't get excited about sex at all, but almost all of those receiving **Eldepryl** were as randy as young rats. These effects on sexual activity paralleled the impact the drug had on the rats' longevity:

> The longest living rat in the saline-treated group lived 164 weeks. The average lifespan of the group was 147 weeks. The shortest living animal in the deprenyl-treated group lived 171

*Eldepryl
(deprenyl,
selegiline)*

New treatment for Parkinson's disease.

When given early in the disease, delays onset of symptoms. When given late, improves "on-off" effect of levodopa. (Dose of levodopa can often be reduced.) May also help against depression and Alzheimer's.

Rat data suggest Eldepryl may improve sexuality and longevity. Superb safety profile. Few side effects (rarely: nausea, dizziness, insomnia).

★ ★ ★ ★

Parkinson's Disease and Eldepryl

Aaron had become an invalid because of advanced Parkinson's disease. Levodopa had worn off and Aaron could barely shuffle across the room with the aid of a walker. His hands shook so badly he could not write and he could no longer speak. Within several months of starting on **Eldepryl,** Aaron was able to walk normally. His hands had stopped shaking and he could communicate again almost as well as before the disease started.

When patients are as bad as Aaron was, they usually do not react so spectacularly, but **Eldepryl** has been a breakthrough for many people with this disease.

weeks and the longest living rat died during the 226 week of its life. The average lifespan was 198 weeks, i.e. higher than the estimated maximum age of death in the rat (182 weeks.) This is the first instance that by the aid of a well-aimed medication members of a species lived beyond the known lifespan maximum.[55]

No other drug, food supplement, vitamin, mineral, or magic wand has ever accomplished such startling results. We don't know if these results can be extrapolated to people, but if this drug could prolong life in the same way for men as for rats, the maximum human lifespan could reach nearly 150 years, with an average **Eldepryl**-treated lifespan of perhaps one hundred. Dr. Knoll has stirred up controversy by announcing that he is taking **Eldepryl** himself and believes it will allow people to live longer and remain sexually active later in life.[56]

There is preliminary evidence that **Eldepryl** may be able to decrease depression, anxiety, tension, and excitement and improve recognition, learning, self-care, alertness, short-term memory, and social interaction in Alzheimer's disease patients.[57–61] There is yet much work to be done before **Eldepryl** can be proven unequivocally effective against Alzheimer's. And yet the initial reports are exciting. What makes **Eldepryl** especially high on our list is its remarkable safety record.

Aspirin for Alzheimer's?

It is hard to imagine that aspirin could help against Alzheimer's disease. And yet recent discoveries have proven aspirin can help prevent heart attacks, strokes, and migraines.[62,63] Aspirin has even been shown to be effective against a kind of senility called multi-infarct dementia (MID) which is caused by small blood clots forming in the brain. MID is thought to be the second most common senile dementia, representing about 20 percent of all cases. In a pilot study patients who received one aspirin tablet daily for three years showed improved thinking and reasoning ability, while the patients who did not get aspirin declined. The patients on aspirin were less dependent and better able to cope with daily living.[64]

At a recent gathering of leading Alzheimer's researchers at the National Institute of Aging, the question of aspirin and Alzheimer's disease came up. "Discussions of early cell membrane disruption and immune-inflammatory mechanisms in Alzheimer's were punctuated by the suggestion that 'an aspirin a day might keep the gerontologists away.' "[65] Dr. Patrick McGeer, a professor of psychiatry at the University of Columbia in Vancouver, Canada, suggested that aspirin might help in preventing the inflammatory response that may underlie Alzheimer's. He added, "I've never seen a rheumatoid arthritis patient with signs of Alzheimer's on autopsy."[66, 67]

It is far too soon to recommend aspirin as a prophylactic against Alzheimer's disease, but if the trend continues, low-dose aspirin may turn out to be good for almost everything that ails us.

Alcar (acetyl-l-carnitine)

Like Coenzyme Q_{10}, acetyl-l-carnitine is a natural substance found in the body. A synthetic version, **Alcar**, is one of the more promising new drugs being tested against Alzheimer's. It too can act as an antioxidant in the brain and protect the cell's energy factories, the mitochondria. Research with rats suggests this drug may be able to slow memory impairment seen with old age. **Alcar** is already a hot number in Italy and parts of Europe where it has been available since 1985. Unpublished data show that this drug slowed the progression of Alzheimer's disease, though it may take up to six months to start to work.[68]

FUTURE DRUG TREATMENTS

Pharmaceutical manufacturers are hot on the trail of "cognitive activators," "memory pills," or "antidementia drugs." The handwriting is on the wall. Americans are getting older and as the baby boomers start sprouting gray hairs, they will become more and more concerned about so-

Alcar Test Sites

University of California-San Diego, Dr. Leon Thal
University of Texas Southwestern, Dr. Myron Weiner
Johns Hopkins, Dr. Marshall Folstein
Duke, Dr. Allen Roses
New York University, Dr. Steven Ferris, Dr. Barry Reisberg
University of Washington, Seattle, and Veterans Administration, Dr. Murray
   Raskind, Dr. Elaine Peskind
Cornell, Dr. John Blass, Dr. Ronald Black, Dr. Karen Nolan
Rush Alzheimer Disease Center, Chicago, Dr. Jacob Fox
Columbia-Presbyterian Medical Center, New York City, Dr. Richard Mayeux

Experimental Treatments for Alzheimer's and Other Brain Insufficiencies

Medicine	Manufacturer
Alcar (acetyl-L-carnitine)	Sigma-Tau (Gaithersburg, MD)
Avan (idebenone)	TAP Pharmeceuticals (Chicago, IL)
BMY 21502	Bristol-Myers Squibb (New York, NY)
Capoten (captopril)	Bristol-Myers Squibb (New York, NY)
Cognex (tacrine, THA)	Warner-Lambert/Parke-Davis (Morris Plains, NJ/Ann Arbor, MI)
Denbufylline	SmithKline Beecham (Philadelphia)
DuP 996	Du Pont (Wilmington, DE)
Emopamil	Knoll (Whippany, NJ)
HOE 427	Hoechst-Roussel (Somerville, NJ)
HP 128	Hoechst-Roussel (Somerville, NJ)
Milacemide	G. D. Searle (Chicago, IL)
NGF (nerve growth factor)	Upjohn (Kalamazoo, MI)
Nimotop (nimodipine)	Miles, Inc. (Elkhart, IN)
Oxiracetam	SmithKline Beecham (Philadelphia)
Posatirelin	Richter/Alza (Palo Alto, CA)
Sabeluzole (R 58,735)	Janssen Pharmaceutical (Piscataway, NJ)
SQ 29852	Bristol-Myers Squibb (New York, NY)
Sygen (GM1 ganglioside)	Fidia (Washington, DC)
Tenex (guanfacine)	A. H. Robins (Richmond, VA)
Zacopride	A. H. Robins (Richmond, VA)
Zofran (ondansetron)	Glaxo (Research Triangle Park, NC)

called age-associated memory impairment. Alzheimer's disease aside, some people do lose a little of their alertness, attention span, and motivation as they get older. Why some people seem more impaired than others is still a mystery. It may be genes, toxins in the environment, lifestyle, or some mystery element like electromagnetic radiation.

There is an impressive number of compounds undergoing tests for an ability to improve memory and learning. Some are old drugs being reviewed for novel uses. Others are brand new and may turn out to be the breakthrough we've all been waiting for. Researchers are also looking at the possibility of transplanting fetal nerve cells to compensate for the neuronal degeneration of Alzheimer's and Parkinson's.

One of the more promising compounds under investigation is **Sygen** (GM1 ganglioside). It is one of the hottest drugs in Italy for Alzheimer's disease and other memory disorders. The company that developed and markets **Sygen** in Italy is Fidia. Major studies are under way in the United States to see if **Sygen** is effective for stroke and Alzheimer's patients.

Another interesting drug is sabeluzole from Janssen Pharmaceutica (a subsidiary of Johnson and Johnson). Pilot studies show that sabeluzole, although no cure for Alzheimer's disease, may help "hold the line." It may also end up improving learning and memory for normal folks who are just "poor performers."

With all the new compounds under investigation, we suspect that something exciting is bound to emerge. Although it is unlikely that a drug like **Eldepryl** will prove to cure Parkinson's disease, senility, or depression, *and* improve sexuality and longevity, some of these compounds are bound to help delay the ravages of the mind slayers. Whether it be schizophrenia, depression, or memory loss, we are about to arrive at the next frontier.

Quick Takes

- Make sure your medicine isn't making you a mental case. Short-acting sleeping pills like **Halcion** can bring on daytime anxiety or panic attacks. The heartburn remedy **Reglan** can make you depressed, sleepless, and restless. Always check with your doctor and pharmacist if you suspect psychological side effects.

- Don't try to tough out depression. If you have trouble sleeping, lose your appetite, can't muster any energy, have no interest in sex, feel sad and pessimistic, or think about suicide, see a professional immediately!

- Talking with someone who can lend a sympathetic ear may be almost as effective as medicine. Other nondrug approaches that can help fight depression include exercise, amino acids (l-tyrosine), vitamins, and minerals. If you get SAD during the winter, special full-spectrum lights can lift your spirits.

- Most traditional antidepressants helped relieve the blues, but they didn't make people feel great. Side effects included fatigue, blurred vision, constipation, disturbed concentration, dizziness, drowsiness, dry mouth, impotence, mental confusion, and weight gain.

- **Prozac** represents the first of the new generation antidepressants. Its extraordinary success is due to more tolerable side effects. The energizing effect is often welcome. Other benefits may include treatment of obsessive-compulsive disorder, PMS, obesity, bulimia, diabetes control, and substance abuse. Adverse reactions to **Prozac** include insomnia, headache, nervousness, nausea, and tremors. If thoughts of suicide enter your mind, seek professional help immediately!

- **Wellbutrin** is an exciting alternative to **Prozac**. It too is very well-tolerated and does not inhibit sexuality. Weight loss instead of weight gain is an additional bonus. Side effects include agitation, insomnia, tremor, dry mouth, nausea, and headache.

- Antipsychotic medications like **Compazine**, **Haldol**, **Mellaril**, **Navane**, **Stelazine**, and **Thorazine** may help dampen delusions and hallucinations, but they can make people feel terrible. Adverse reactions include agitation, apathy, depression, despondency, dizziness, drowsiness, emotional flattening, fainting, headache, hyperactivity, incoordination, "mask face," mental confusion, neck twitching, pacing, Parkinsonlike symptoms (slow shuffling walk), restlessness, slurred speech, tongue biting, uncontrollable lip chewing, uncontrollable muscle spasms, and weakness.

- Compared to the toxicity of antipsychotic medications, we feel that orthomolecular medicine represents a reasonable option. Nutritional therapies are relatively low-risk approaches that may help some people.

- **Clozaril** is a new antipsychotic medication that does not cause tardive dyskinesia. This is an important advance, but the danger of a fatal blood disease, agranulocytosis, requires constant blood tests that can be terribly expensive. Annual costs of treatment may reach almost $10,000. Side effects of **Clozaril** include constipation, excess salivation, rapid heart rate, sedation, and seizures.

- **Zofran** is an exciting new antinausea medicine that may turn out to have additional benefits against schizophrenia and Alzheimer's disease. **Eldepryl** may also turn out to have multiple uses. Besides being an impressive treatment for Parkinson's disease, this new drug offers potential against Alzheimer's disease and aging.

- THA (**Cognex**, tacrine) has received all the limelight in the battle against Alzheimer's disease. Although there have been a few spectacular successes, this medicine is no cure. There are a surprising number of exciting compounds in the pipeline. Only time will tell which drugs will truly make a difference.

References

[1] *Physicians' Desk Reference*. Oradell, N.J.: Medical Economics Co., 1990, p. 1429.

[2] "Drugs that Cause Psychiatric Symptoms." *Medical Letter* 1989; 31:113–118.

[3] Rush, David R., and Stimmel, Glen. "When Drugs Cause Psychiatric Symptoms." *Patient Care* 1989; 23(16):57–75.

[4] Goode, Erica E., et al. "Beating Depression." *U.S. News & World Report* 1990; 108(9):48–56.

[5] Klerman, Gerald L., and Weissman, Myrna M. "Increasing Rates of Depression." *JAMA* 1989; 261:2229–2235.

[6] Wells, K.B., et al. "Detection of Depressive Disorder for Patients Receiving Prepaid or Fee-for-service Care. Results from the Medical Outcomes Study." *JAMA* 1989; 262:3298–3302.

[7] Elkin, I., et al. "National Institute of Mental Health Treatment of Depression Collaborative Research Program. General Effectiveness of Treatments." *Arch. Gen. Psychiatry* 1989; 46:971–982.

[8] Sexton, H., et al. "Exercise Intensity and Reduction in Neurotic Symptoms. A Controlled Follow-up Study." *Acta Psychiatr. Scand.* 1989; 80:231–235.

[9] Steptoe, A., et al. "The Effects of Exercise Training on Mood and Perceived Coping Ability in Anxious Adults from the General Population." *J. Psychosom. Res.* 1989; 33:537–547.

[10] Labbe, E.E., et al. "Effects of Consistent Aerobic Exercise on the Psychological Functioning of Women." *Percept. Mot. Skills* 1988; 67:919–925.

[11] Jaffe, Russ. Personal communication, March 23, 1990.

[12] Gelenberg, A.J., et al. "Tyrosine for the Treatment of Depression." *Am. J. Psychiatry* 1980; 137:622–623.

[13] Gelenberg. A.J., et al. " Neurotransmitter Precursors for the Treatment of Depression." *Psychopharmacol. Bull.* 1982; 18(1):7–18.

[14] Mouret, Jacques, et al. "Treatment of Narcolepsy with L-Tyrosine." *Lancet* 1988; 2:1458–1459.

[15] Mouret, Jacques, et al. "L-Tyrosine Cures, Immediate and Long Term, Dopamine-dependent Depressions. Clinical and Polygraphic Studies." *C.R. Acad. Sci [III]* 1988; 306:93–98.

[16] Nash, Margo. "Low-Amino-Diet Immune Boost." *Medical Tribune* 1990; 31(3):1–12.

[17] Birkmayer, W., et al. "L-Deprenyl Plus L-Phenylalanine in the Treatment of Depression." *J. Neural. Transm.* 1984; 59:81–87.

[18] Naylor, G. J. "Vanadium and Manic Depressive Psychosis." *Nutr. Health* 1984; 3 (1–2):79–85.

[19] Practical Briefings. "The SAD Story." *Patient Care* 1989 (Nov. 15); 16–20.

[20] Cowley, Geoffrey, et al. "The Promise of Prozac." *Newsweek* 1990 (Mar. 15); 38–41.

[21] Eli Lilly Company. Personal communication, March 21, 1990.

[22] Teicher, Martin H., et al. "Emergence of Intense Suicidal Preoccupation During Fluoxetine Treatment." *Am. J. Psychiatry* 1990; 147:207–210.

[23] Carey, Benedict. "The Sex Pill." *Hippocrates* 1988 (July/Aug.); 24–25.

[24] Currents interview. "Bupropion (Wellbutrin) in Clinical Practice. An Interview with Jonathan R.T. Davidson." *Currents* 1989; 8(10):5–13.

[25] Products. "Buspirone & Gepirone—an Expanding Role in Psychiatry?" *Scrip* 1990; 1482:24.

[26] Lomax, Percy. "Glaxo Holdings Company Report." *Prudential-Bache International Research* 1989 (Aug. 7); 24.

[27] Burrows, Adria. "The Duck Lady." *JAMA* 1989; 262:2842.

[28] Tepper, S.J., and Haas, J.F. "Prevalence of Tardive Dyskinesia." *J. Clin. Psychiatry* 1979; 40:508–516.

[29] Simpson, G.M., et al. "Tardive Dyskinesia and Psychotropic Drug

History." *Psychopharmacology* 1978; 58:117–124.

[30] Suddath, Richard L., et al. "Anatomical Abnormalities in the Brains of Monozygotic Twins Discordant for Schizophrenia." *N. Engl. J. Med.* 1990; 322:789–794.

[31] Mesulam, M.-Marsel. "Schizophrenia and the Brain." *N. Engl. J. Med.* 1990; 322:842–844.

[32] Kane, John, et al. "Clozapine for Treatment-Resistant Schizophrenic." *Arch. Gen. Psychiatry* 1988; 45:789–796.

[33] Casey, D.E. "Clozapine: Neuroleptic-Induced EPS and Tardive Dyskinesia." *Psychopharmacology* 1989; 99:S47–53.

[34] Editorial: "Clozapine." *Lancet* 1989; 2:1430–1432.

[35] Question and Answers. "The Clorazil Patient Management System (CPMS)." Press materials, Sandoz Pharmaceuticals, October 1990.

[36] Cubeddu, Luigi X., et al. "Efficacy of Ondansetron (GR 38032F) and the Role of Serotonin in Cisplatin-Induced Nausea and Vomiting." *N. Engl. J. Med.* 1990; 322:810–816.

[37] Marty, Michel, et al. "Comparison of the 5-Hydroxytryptamine$_3$ (Serotonin) Antagonist Ondansetron (GR 38032F) with High-Dose Metoclopramide in the Control of Cisplatin-Induced Emesis." *N. Engl. J. Med.* 1990; 322:816–821.

[38] Editorial. "Drugs Acting on 5-Hydroxytryptamine Receptors." *Lancet* 1989; 2:717–719.

[39] Chustecka, Zofia. "Glaxo's Ondansetron—The First of a New Class of Drugs?" *Drug News and Perspectives* 1989; 2(6):347–349.

[40] Larson, Eric B. "Alzheimer's Disease in the Community." *JAMA* 1989; 262:2591–2592.

[41] Evans, Denis A., et al. "Prevalence of Alzheimer's Disease in a Community Population of Older Persons." *JAMA* 1989; 262:2551–2556.

[42] Summers, William Koopmans, et al. "Oral Tetrahydroaminoacridine in Long-term Treatment of Senile Dementia, Alzheimer Type." *N. Engl. J. Med.* 1986; 315:1241–1245.

[43] Cumming, P., et al. "Inhibition of Histamine Metabolism by THA (9-amino-1,2,3,4-Tetrahydroacridine)." *Society for Neurosciences Abstracts* 1989; 15:1111.

[44] Parke-Davis, a Division of Warner Lambert. Personal communication.

[45] Kidder, Peabody Equity Research. "Warner-Lambert: Tacrine at the Neuroscience Meetings; Trick or Treat?" October 31, 1989.

[46] Gracon, Steve, Associate Director, Clinical Development: Cognition; Parke-Davis Company. Personal communication, February 22, 1990.

[47] The Fourth Annual Joseph and Kathleen Bryan Alzheimer's Disease Research Center Conference "The '90s: Decade of Promise for Alzheimer's Research: Family Perspectives on Participation in Alzheimer's Research." Duke University Medical Center, February 22, 1990.

[48] Weiss, Rick. "Toward a Future with Memory." *Science News* 1990; 137:120–123.

[49] Golbe, Lawrence I., et al. "Deprenyl in the Treatment of Symptom Fluctuations in Advanced Parkinson's Disease." *Clinical Neuropharmacology* 1988; 11:45–55.

[50] "Pergolide and Selegilene for Parkinson's Disease." *Medical Letter* 1989; 31:81–83.

[51] Tetrud, James W., and Langston, William J. "The Effect of Deprenyl (Selegiline) on the Natural History of Parkinson's Disease." *Science* 1989; 245:519–522.

[52] The Parkinson Study Group. "Effect of Deprenyl on the Progression of Disability in Early Parkinson's Disease." *N. Engl. J. Med.* 1989; 321:1364–1371.

[53] Quitkin, F.M., et al. "Monoamine Oxidase Inhibitors in Bipolar Endogenous Depressives." *J. Clin. Psychopharmacol.* 1981; 1:70–74.

[54] Tariot, P.N., et al. "L-Deprenyl in Alzheimer's Disease. Preliminary Evidence for Behavioral Changes with Monoamine Oxidase B Inhibition." *Arch. Gen. Psychiatry* 1987; 44:427–433.

[55] Knoll, Joseph. "The Striatal Dopamine Dependency of Life Span in

Male Rats. Longevity Study with (-)Deprenyl." *Mech. Aging Develop.* 1988; 46:237–262.

[56] Thomas, Patricia. "Anti-Aging Ploy Evokes Doubts." *Medical World News* 1990(June 11); 16.

[57] Tariot, P.N., et al. "Tranylcypromine with L-deprenyl in Alzheimer's Disease." *J. Clin. Psychopharmacol.* 1988; 8:23–27.

[58] Martini, E., et. al. "Brief Information on an Early Phase-II Study with Deprenyl in Demented Patients." *Pharmacopsychiatry* 1987; 20:256–257.

[59] Tariot, P.N., et al. "Cognitive Effects of L-deprenyl in Alzheimer's Disease." *Psychopharmacology* (Berlin) 1987; 91:489–495.

[60] Tariot, P.N., et al. "L-deprenyl in Alzheimer's Disease. Preliminary Evidence for Behavioral Change with Monoamine Oxidase B Inhibition." *Arch. Gen. Psychiatry* 1987; 44:427–433.

[61] Schneider, L.S., et al. "L-Deprenyl in Alzheimer's Disease." University of Southern California School of Medicine, Los Angeles, Abstract, 1988.

[62] Fackelmann, K.A. "Low Dose of Aspirin Keeps Migraine Away." S*cience News* 1990 (Feb. 17); 103.

[63] Stroke Prevention in Atrial Fibrillation Study Group Investigators. "Preliminary Report of the Stroke Prevention in Atrial Fibrillation Study." *N. Engl. J. Med.* 1990; 322:863–868.

[64] Meyer, J.S., et al. "Randomized Clinical Trial of Daily Aspirin Therapy in Multi-infarct Dementia. A pilot study." *J. Am. Geriatr. Soc.* 1989; 37:549–555.

[65] Pollner, Fran. "Alzheimer's Disease: Experts Pursue Plethora of Drugs." *Medical World News* 1990 (Feb. 12); 16–17.

[66] Ibid.

[67] McGeer, Patrick L., et al. "Anti-Inflammatory Drugs and Alzheimer Disease." (letter) *Lancet* 1990; 335:1037.

[68] "Sigma-Tau Acetyl-L-Carnitine Alzheimer's Multicenter Trials." *F-D-C Reports* 1990; 52(12):T&G–12.

Pain Relief

7

Pain is marvelously adaptive. If you feel pain, you know something's wrong. And you take action to do something about it. The cause may be obvious: if you put your hand on a hot stove and it hurts, you probably can figure out why. But when the source of pain is puzzling—if your hip hurts when you walk, or your head is throbbing—that is another story. Pain is the ultimate biofeedback mechanism, an internal device that has protected people throughout evolution, telling them what activities to avoid or when to give a broken limb a rest. If we only had such an internal biofeedback setup for some things that now we monitor with machines (blood pressure and blood sugar come to mind), we might be able to stay a lot healthier.

Of course, we have to live with the consequences of this elegant biofeedback system, and that's not always easy. It is nice to know when your hand's on a hot stove, but after you've snatched it away, it still hurts like blazes. Once your doctor has confirmed that, yes, you have arthritis in your elbow, then how do you deal with it? What can you do to make the hurting go away?

After all, pain can't be ignored easily. If you have a headache, no matter whether it's from overindulging at that really great cocktail party last night or from your recurring sinusitis, it's there, and you can't get away from it. Some pain is only slightly annoying and short-lived, while other pain is overwhelming and makes it impossible to think about anything else while you are suffering. There isn't any good way to measure the level of pain a person is experiencing, though. According to one group of clinicians, "Pain is a complex phenomenon that involves not only the immediate sensation and stimulus of hurt, but also the individual responses of the person experiencing it. These responses are influenced by the physiological, psychological, cultural, and spiritual makeup of the person in pain."[1]

Because pain is so intensely personal, it's up to you to do something about it. Now, that doesn't mean you can waltz up to your pharmacist and request a prescription for codeine. But it does mean that pain management will work better when you are actively involved. There are a lot of things you can do for pain, with the options ranging from massage to pills and from herbs to electrical stimulation. Nothing works all the time, but most of the time it's possible to get some respite. The goal is to get the most relief for the least danger, and that may require patience. It also makes sense to start with the safest alternatives reasonable for managing your pain, and work up from there if necessary. If aspirin does the trick, then morphine is definitely not the ticket. The rule here is "start low; start slow." Many of the nondrug alternatives are most likely to be utilized by people with recurrent or chronic pain, because of the problems of side effects or dependence that crop up with long-term use of pain medications.

Nondrug Pain Relievers

TEMPERATURE TREATMENTS

It's no accident that the usual recommendation for a sprain or strain is ICE (ice, compression, elevation). Cold is a simple, easy, and often surprisingly effective treatment for a lot of different kinds of short-term pain. For minor burns in the kitchen, for bumps or bruises, even sometimes for a bee sting, ice water works great (see p. 134). It eases the pain right away, and may even diminish the pain felt later. A cold compress is soothing for some sorts of headaches. And there are arthritis sufferers who swear by an ice pack for an inflamed aching joint. It is sensible, however, not to use ice directly on the skin for more than a few minutes to avoid cold damage. A commercial ice pack has enough insulation to be safe, but dropping your crushed ice into a plastic bag and wrapping that in a dishtowel can be equally effective.

Many people with arthritis also rely on heat for the relief of day-to-day stiffness and pain. Whether it's a hot shower to help them get going in the morning, or a melted paraffin treatment for aching hands and fingers, the warmth seems to help sore joints feel better. A relaxing soak in a hot tub may also sometimes alleviate a tension headache or tender, abused muscles. A heating pad or hot compress for up to twenty minutes at a time may be helpful on a strained muscle in the back.[3]

RELAXATION

Pain is uncomfortable. Discomfort makes us tense and amplifies pain. This vicious cycle is the bane of anyone with chronic pain. The way to break the cycle is by relaxation.

A month in the Caribbean with no cares and no responsibilities sounds great but isn't practical for most of us. Luckily, it's possible to let go and unwind without going too far away from home. (No hassles, no packing, no stopping the mail and the paper, no last-minute arrangements for the neighbor to feed the plants and water the cats—going on vacation can be stressful!)

Getting relaxed can be simple (take a couple of minutes a

Muscle Spasm

When a muscle contracts painfully and won't let go, so that whenever it's moved it hurts, the best treatment is often ice and gentle movement, so far as the pain will allow. The doctor may also be able to help with a cooling spray of ethyl chloride on the muscle.[2]

couple of times a day to close your eyes and just dream of the Caribbean beach) or complex (take a formal relaxation course, where you're taught a variety of techniques for inducing a relaxed state). One method may work better for you than any others. When you find the one or two you like best, they can be a big help in managing recurrent or chronic pain. Learning about what ails you may help relieve the stress and tension that can make pain worse, and may assist you in visualization exercises, if they are helpful for you. For an audio guide to relaxation, we like to stretch out and listen to a tape.

BIOFEEDBACK

Another approach to relaxation that has had some success is biofeedback. It is not for everyone, but certain people who are willing to practice regularly can benefit. During   biofeedback training they learn to control blood flow or relax a particular muscle by seeing a light or hearing a bell when they achieve the goal. The beneficial effects of biofeedback are limited, but it may be useful for some people, especially those with muscle spasms and similar sorts of pain.

Biofeedback has shown some efficacy in controlling muscle temperature, muscle tension, and heart rate. To be helpful, the electrodes measuring muscle tension need to go right on the muscle in spasm. For migraine headaches or Raynaud's phenomenon, temperature may be measured on the hand or finger.[4]

Unfortunately, there has been a lot of bio-B.S. connected with biofeedback. It seemed for a while that anyone who could hook up some bells and whistles could be in business as a biofeedback therapist; people in chronic pain would be wise to utilize biofeedback training offered through a pain clinic that can give assistance with an integrated pain management program. Four to six sessions are generally enough for learning the technique; "refresher" sessions may be helpful, and home practice is a must. One major advantage of biofeedback is that it is totally harmless, unless you delay seeking other medical advice while waiting for biofeedback to cure your problem— another good reason for going through a pain clinic with appropriate medical supervision.

MANIPULATION

Acupuncture/Acupressure

The Chinese practice of sticking extremely fine needles into very specific points on the body and rotating the needles has a two thousand-year history of success. For too long, perhaps, Americans have believed that if we couldn't explain it according to standard science, it must be strange and somehow suspect. (This logical approach overlooks the fact that we don't have a good understanding of precisely how a lot of unquestionably effective drugs work.) Nowadays, though, many people with chronic or recurrent pain are turning to acupuncture.

Even though medical science can't explain how acupuncture works, many people treated by a trained acupuncturist experience some relief of their pain. Usually this is temporary, lasting for several hours or days, and some sorts of pain—not to mention some individuals—seem more amenable to this kind of treatment than others.[5] Check that the acupuncturist sterilizes all the equipment thoroughly or uses disposable needles, to minimize the risk of infection.

Acupressure involves some of the same specific points on the body, but instead of needles, pressure is applied. It can work surprisingly well, and a needle-shy person may prefer it. In addition, people who learn their own acupressure points have a pain control or management technique right at their fingertips. As with acupuncture or aspirin, don't expect any cures or miraculous long-term respite, but temporary relief is certainly possible for many people.

Trigger Points

Trigger points are literally sore spots. They're really areas of degenerated muscle tissue, normally at the place where a muscle either enters or exits an attachment point.[6] Unfortunately, the term *trigger point* is used a bit loosely by many alternative healers, who sometimes use it to mean "the place from which I've decided your pain is probably coming." The doctor or physical therapist (or chiropractor or acupuncturist)

Recurrent muscle tension headaches may be treated with trigger-point injection. For such headaches, trigger-point treatment may offer temporary respite of several weeks' duration rather than long-term relief.[7]

finds these trigger points by feel. They are exquisitely tender to the touch, and there's little doubt when one is nudged.

What's done with trigger points depends on the kind of therapist. MDs often prefer to inject trigger points with lidocaine, saline, or just a dry needle. This procedure is usually uncomfortable in its own right, and will lead to a couple of days of soreness. Some cure! But when the pain abates, the trigger spot should stop hurting unless it's injured again.

Other therapists aren't licensed to shoot, so instead they poke, probe, twiddle, and fiddle. Any or all of these ministrations may have a beneficial effect on true trigger points. If your pain problem consists of a specific spot, especially if the pain occurs in response to a particular movement, then prodding for one or more trigger points might prove valuable.

Massage

Taut muscles loosen with a good massage. And what could be more relaxing than getting a back rub? For both acute and chronic pain, massage can offer useful assistance toward relaxation, a more positive frame of mind, and a more comfortable state of body. A good neck massage might help ward off a muscle tension headache, and a strained back muscle may feel better with massage. Although massage offers only temporary relief, it may have a place in a pain management program for chronic muscle problems. Remember, a massage should feel good.

Massage at Home

For concise, step-by-step instructions on giving back rubs, including a pressure point massage for sore backs, we highly recommend this guide:
Anne Kent Rush, *The Back Rub Book* (New York: Vintage, 1989)

Chiropractic

Chiropractors may use a variety of treatment methods, but they specialize in manipulation of and around the spine. Perhaps for this reason, back-pain sufferers are especially likely to visit a chiropractor at some point in their quest for relief. For some people, a chiropractic "correction" or manipulation can be remarkably successful. (If pain is due to a chronic condition such as arthritis or a degenerating disk in the back, manipulation can provide no more than temporary comfort, if it doesn't aggravate the situation.[8]) Be wary if you decide to try this route, though, because results vary from one patient to the next as well as from one practitioner to another. In one survey of people with arthritis, 12 percent of those who had consulted a chiropractor or osteopath for manipulation ended up feeling worse instead of better after treatment.[9]

TENS

Pain messages travel nerve pathways in an electrochemical code, so it should come as no surprise that electricity may have an impact on pain perception. Many years ago, physicians discovered that patients with certain types of pain could find relief in having a slight electrical current applied through the skin to the affected nerve endings.

> ### What Kind of Pain Does Best with TENS?
>
> TENS can help ease acute pain on a short-term basis. Doctors report that chronic pain traced to multiple injuries to peripheral nerves, for example after the rash of a shingles outbreak disappears, often responds to TENS. So does some pain due to constant muscle tension.[10]

Thus came TENS — transcutaneous electrical nerve stimulation. It consists of having electrodes placed on the skin, not right where it hurts, but generally between there and the spinal cord. A gentle electrical current is then applied. Although the tools we now have for administering it are new, the technique dates back centuries to a time when the electrical source was electric eels.[11]

What does it do? There are lots of guesses and no good answers. Although a recent study showed conclusively that TENS does not provide significant relief for people suffering with chronic low back pain,[12] TENS may offer pain relief to a significant number of people with other sorts of nerve and muscle pain. In some cases it has provided dramatic relief to people who had literally tried everything else.

There are a couple of advantages to TENS. First, it is portable. The unit usually consists of a small, battery-powered electrical source and a couple of electrodes. That means you can keep one in your home and use it when you need to, on your own schedule. It's relatively inexpensive. And it won't interact with drugs you might also be taking, so you don't have to stop taking a pain reliever in order to try TENS also. You may have to experiment a good bit to find a current frequency and strength that is effective for your condition, but persistence could pay off.

EXERCISE

Maintaining Motion

When some part of the body hurts, we tend to favor it and avoid moving it too much. This is a sensible response to the short-term pain that follows an injury, so that the damage can be repaired. But not moving a joint that's ridden with chronic pain can lead to a vicious circle, with muscles and ligaments tightening and making it more difficult to use. A sensible exercise program that can maintain range of motion can make a tremendous difference in the ability to function in day-to-day situations. Needless to say, overdoing is a bad idea—anyone who's in pain shouldn't "exercise till it hurts."

Some disorders—back problems, joint problems, headaches—call for special exercises. For help in learning the appropriate exercises and tailoring them to your condition and your lifestyle, it may be appropriate to see a physical therapist. A person suffering with chronic pain can often benefit greatly from this kind of professional help, but it's best to have specific goals in mind—being able to get into and out of the car, for example.[13] Picking a meaningful and achievable goal may be nearly as important as doing the exercises regularly. The physical therapist may also help with relaxation and posture.

Posture

Poor posture habits may be a culprit in recurrent cases of headache.[14,15] Some cases of back pain due to muscular strain may also benefit from an improvement in posture. Physical therapists can help people correct their posture so that it puts the least strain on sore muscles. They can often teach a person body mechanics as well, so that lifting or other necessary tasks are accomplished efficiently and with minimal risk. There are a number of alternative therapists who deal with posture. It's not clear if one is better than another, but we have heard some glowing testimonials from their clients. If you can, try to talk to several different people who have been through any therapy that you are considering, to understand what you are getting into and whether it will be right for you.

Herbal and Nutritional Remedies

Pain is as old as humanity, so herbal approaches to pain reduction have a long history. Some popular plant-based remedies eventually led to the development of drugs. Aspirin (acetylsalicylic acid), for example, has a heritage going back to ancient Egyptian, Greek, and Assyrian manuscripts. The American Indians used to chew white willow bark to alleviate pain and bring fever down. The bark contains an analgesic component called salicin, which was isolated by European chemists in the 1820s. (Seventy years later, they developed the salicin derivative, acetylsalicylic acid.)[16] With this history in mind, researchers are taking a closer look at some herbs, plants, and oils to discover whether their medicinal properties are indeed valid.

HERBS

Feverfew

For centuries, feverfew (*Chrysanthemum parthenium*) has been used as a remedy for headaches and joint pain. Research is now showing that this common flowering plant may be quite effective in treatment and prevention of migraines and may be helpful in alleviating some arthritic pain.

A number of studies have been done on feverfew's effect on migraine. One placebo-controlled study, in which a daily supplement of ground-up leaves, about 80 mg, was administered, resulted in a 24 percent reduction of the number of migraines, and those that did occur were milder with less vomit-

---

How does feverfew work?

Feverfew contains chemicals that inhibit secretions of blood platelets and white blood cells.

The platelets secrete serotonin, which constricts blood vessels and therefore contributes to migraine headache.

Some secretions from white blood cells (prostaglandins) are believed to lead to the kind of inflammation seen in arthritis.

ing.[17] Some people who had been on feverfew but were switched to placebo experienced incapacitating headaches. Anxiety, poor sleep, and joint stiffness were also reported by people who suddenly stopped taking this herb.

In a larger group of feverfew users, about 18 percent reported unpleasant side effects, especially mouth ulcers.[18] An increased heart rate has also been reported. Anyone on medication to prevent clotting should be aware there is a theoretical possibility that feverfew could interact adversely with their drug, although no cases have been reported.[19] As with many herbs, the potency of feverfew varies from one preparation to another.

Capsaicin

If your doctor told you to rub red chile powder on your skin to get rid of your pain, you'd be surprised. But if you were suffering from the awful pain following a shingles outbreak, you might well use **Zostrix** , a cream containing capsaicin, when your doctor recommended it.

Capsaicin is what makes hot peppers hot, and when it's put on the skin, it stings or burns. In response to the capsaicin, nerves release their substance P, a compound needed for pain transmission. Regular use of capsaicin several times a day uses up all the substance P and blocks pain perception. That is why people who suffer from postherpetic pain finally have some relief for their ordeal, although they may have to put up with additional pain from the burning of the **Zostrix** for three or four days . (This also explains why a couple of drops of capsaicin, spread around the gums, was an old home remedy for a toothache.) There is some evidence that pain lingering after a mastectomy or amputation may be lessened with the use of capsaicin-containing cream.[20] Two over-the-counter products that contain capsaicin are "rubs": **Heet** lotion and **Sloan's** liniment. We don't know if they contain enough of this ingredient to deplete substance P and reduce pain transmission.

**Zostrix
(capsaicin)
ointment**

Reduces sensation of pain after shingles (sometimes useful for other neuralgias).
Available without prescription.
For best results, apply several times daily.
Keep out of eyes, nose, and mouth.
Do not apply to broken skin.

★ ★ ★

Zostrix for Arthritis?

Some OTC rubs used for arthritis, bursitis, sore muscles, and the like contain small quantities of capsaicin. No one has yet looked at whether a more concentrated formulation like **Zostrix** would be helpful for sore joints and muscles.

Clove

Another time-honored toothache remedy is oil of clove (*Eugenia caryophyllata*). The most active ingredient in clove oil is eugenol, a chemical that is very closely related to capsaicin. Like capsaicin, oil of clove has been used as a counterirritant, or "rub." Clove-containing cigarettes apparently anesthetize the throat and lead to lung damage. They should be avoided.[21]

Devil's-Claw

In Africa, devil's -claw (*Harpagophytum procumbens*) is a folk remedy for rheumatism, fever, malaria, and headache. European herbalists recommend a tea made from the roots for arthritis, senility, and allergies, among other things. Although one German study indicated that this tea may have potent anti-inflammatory activity, other animal and human tests do not confirm it. It does not appear to have any adverse effects, but there is doubt as to whether it is beneficial for arthritis or other pain.[22]

Echinacea

One all-American herbal remedy that is generating some excitement in research laboratories is Echinacea (*Echinacea angustifolia*). This plant, native to Nebraska, Kansas, and Missouri, was used more than a hundred years ago by the Plains Indians for treating pain and snakebite. Midwestern folk medicine picked it up, but not until very recently has research begun to show the potential of this plant. It has strong activity against inflammation, both when injected and when applied to the skin.[23,24] Scientists are probably most intrigued about animal research that indicates Echinacea extract has significant immune-stimulating effects.[25] One preliminary study suggests, however, that while a single dose may stimulate the immune system in humans, repeated daily doses may depress it.[26] Although this plant, which is also known as purple coneflower, snakeroot, and several other vernacular names, does not have a reputation for toxicity, it hasn't been well-studied. (A word of caution to amateur herbalists: a different plant known as white snakeroot, with the Latin names of *Eupatorium rugosum* or

> *Echinacea*
> *(extract)*
> Taken internally, or applied to the skin. Topical anti-inflammatory power nearly as strong as topical indomethacin. Stimulates immune activity in animals. For short-term use, appears reasonably safe. No information on long-term safety.
>
> ★ ★

Ageratina altissima, is quite toxic and should not be taken internally.[27])

Myrrh

Who hasn't heard of myrrh? With its aroma, it was often used to make perfume and incense. It too contains eugenol and has been used dissolved in alcohol as a mouthwash or a gargle for mouth ulcers and sore throat.[28]

OILS

Evening Primrose

Oil of evening primrose is a rich source of gamma-linolenic acid (GLA), which the body manufactures from essential omega-6 fatty acids. The GLA in the body then turns around and contributes to the manufacture and regulation of the prostaglandins that have anti-inflammatory action, leading researchers to believe that GLA might be of some considerable use in the treatment of arthritis.

A double-blind, placebo-controlled study in 1988 revealed that those patients who got 540 mg of GLA a day, in the form of oil of evening primrose, significantly improved during the course of a year's treatment and needed other anti-inflammatory drugs (NSAIDs—see p. 263) less frequently. Those getting the placebo felt no better and used as many doses of NSAIDs as before. The clincher? Those who received the GLA and then were switched to the placebo relapsed.[29]

Further studies are warranted, and because the findings to date are limited, evening primrose oil should be used only under a doctor's supervision for symptomatic relief from rheumatoid arthritis.

Evening primrose oil has also been suggested for the relief of discomfort with premenstrual syndrome (PMS). Double-blind placebo controlled studies have demonstrated greater relief from premenstrual breast tenderness and irritability with GLA than with placebo.[30] However, some doctors who have tried GLA for their patients with PMS have been disappointed at the response.[31]

Evening primrose oil appears to be fairly safe except for people with epilepsy and manic depression. It may be worth a try, but because study results have been contradictory, its effectiveness isn't yet established.

Fish Oil

There's nothing fishy about the research being done on fish oils these days. We all know that people who eat lots of seafood, like the Japanese and the Eskimos, are at lower risk of heart and circulatory disorders than the rest of us. Now scientists are checking the possibility that the omega-3 fatty acids contained in fish oils—eicosapentaenoic acid (EPA) and docosahexaenoic acid (DHA)—may be helpful in treating arthritis and other inflammation.

Fish oils have reduced inflammation in both animal and human experiments. Progression of rheumatoid arthritis was seemingly stopped in one study of people given daily fish-oil supplements (in a dose equal to 1.8 grams of EPA daily), whereas those given placebos continued to worsen. Minimal side effects such as stomach upset, were experienced. As with GLA, anyone planning to try fish oil for rheumatoid arthritis would be wise to discuss it with the doctor first. This will make it possible to make any adjustments needed in the plan of care, and it may also be helpful to have an objective bystander helping to monitor the effectiveness of the treatment. Even though EPA and DHA seem to reduce the symptoms of rheumatoid arthritis, possibly even slowing its progression, it's not a cure.

Fishy breath is a potential social liability, and there is a possibility of dangerous bleeding. Diabetics should definitely avoid fish oil supplementation. For most people, though, increasing the amount of fish in the diet is safe and tasty. The fattier fish, such as salmon, herring, and trout, provide significant amounts of fish oil.

> **MaxEPA**
> *(fish oil)*
> The optimum dose is not established. Studies have used doses of 1.8–2.7 grams of EPA daily.
> Side effects: fish burp; bruising and bleeding.
> Avoid if pregnant, child, diabetic, on other blood thinners, or if at increased risk of hemorrhage.
>
> ★

ALTERNATIVE REMEDIES

D-Phenylalanine

A nonnutrient amino acid, d-phenylalanine, has been shown to inhibit an enzyme that breaks down enkephalins, which serve as natural pain relievers in the brain. D-phenylalanine's blocking action leads researchers to believe that this amino acid may be helpful in alleviating pain. It has been tested successfully with acute back pain and dental pain, but its usefulness for chronic pain needs more study.[32] D-phenylalanine is available in health-food stores in combination with an essential amino acid, l-phenylalanine, which has no analgesic action. If you are taking a monoamine oxidase inhibitor (**Marplan** [isocarboxazid], **Nardil** [phenelzine], or **Parnate** [tranylcypromine]) for high blood pressure or depression, stay away from these supplements. (People with PKU or melanoma must also shun them.)

A Pain-Relief Diet?

A diet formulated to have an effect on pain relief would be remarkably similar to one designed to control cholesterol: limited amount of eggs; vegetable oils in place of saturated fats; green, leafy vegetables; lean meats. Add to this three servings a week of fatty fish, such as salmon or tuna. Seasoning liberally with rosemary leaf, which has a traditional reputation as an analgesic, can't hurt.

Of course, migraine sufferers should be aware that certain foods like chocolate and red wine, can aggravate the problem.

DMSO

In the 1940s DMSO (dimethyl sulfoxide) was introduced as an industrial solvent. During the 1960s it began to be used as a topical treatment for arthritis, bruises, sprains, and strains. The FDA once banned research on DMSO, but later rescinded that order and approved its use for treatment of symptoms of interstitial cystitis, a bladder condition. Studies are going on for a number of other uses, but to date there has been no further FDA approval. However, some states have approved the use of DMSO for various ailments, and low doses of this drug have not been reported to cause serious problems.[33] DMSO should be used only under the supervision of a physician, however, and it is important only to use prescription-grade DMSO despite its significantly greater cost. The DMSO sold over the counter, or "under the table," as the case may be, may contain impurities that could be unsafe.

Over-the-Counter Medicines

Don't expect any exciting new over-the-counter pain-killers in the near future. Although some of the arthritis medications may follow ibuprofen from prescription to over-the-counter status, drug manufacturers are becoming increasingly more reluctant to pour money into developing products that probably won't be much better than what's already on the shelves.[34] But that doesn't mean the existing products can't be effective against pain or inflammation. On the contrary.

ASPIRIN: THE WONDER DRUG

There may be some truth to the old saying, "familiarity breeds contempt." Aspirin has been around for almost a century, since 1899, and if you are like most people, you probably have some on hand. But you may not appreciate the true power of this humble and inexpensive drug.

Pain or Inflammation?

Aspirin works well against both these symptoms of disease or injury, but at different doses. The usual pain-relieving dose of aspirin is two tablets every four to six hours. Anti-inflammatory action requires a much higher dose—up to fourteen or twenty aspirin tablets a day in some cases. At these levels, it's not unusual for people to experience side effects. If your condition—arthritis, bursitis, or whatever—involves inflammation, have your doctor supervise aspirin use.

Pain and Inflammation Treatment

By the turn of the century, aspirin (originally a brand name the Bayer Company picked out for its new product, acetylsalicylic acid) was being used to bring fevers down, chase headaches away, and reduce inflammation. It was, in fact, the prototypical NSAID (nonsteroidal anti-inflammatory drug).[35] And it is still the gold standard for this kind of medication. The others, and there are many (see list, p. 27), may offer certain advantages—less stomach irritation at anti-inflammatory doses, perhaps, or once-a-day schedules—but none offers better pain and inflammation control than aspirin. No wonder Americans swallow twenty billion tablets a year!

Migraine Headache Prevention

Scientists impressed with the potential for aspirin to

prevent heart attacks designed the Physicians' Health Study to investigate this possibility. (See p. 78 for a discussion.) Later analysis of that research also showed that the doctors taking aspirin (one every other day) suffered 20 percent fewer migraines than those given a placebo. This result was astonishing, as such a small amount of aspirin can have no effect once the migraine headache begins.[36] This confirms a similar finding in an earlier but much smaller British study

---

Treating Migraine Headaches

Migraine headaches, also called vascular headaches because they seem to be related to constriction and dilation in the blood vessels to the brain, are complicated to treat. Several drugs are currently used to halt a migraine in progress, but all have drawbacks:

- Ergotamine must be taken early in an attack, or it will be ineffective; may produce nausea and vomiting; do not take more than three pills per day or 10 mg. per week; not for prolonged use; not for people with circulatory problems, heart conditions, kidney or liver trouble.
- Naproxen must be taken early in an attack; less effective than ergotamine; may cause stomach upset.
- Narcotics may work in severe migraine, but can cause nausea and vomiting or sedation and are not appropriate for recurrent attacks

Future treatments should be far more satisfactory:

- Butorphanol (**Stadol**) is currently available but not often used. Administered nasally, this new narcotic works as well as methadone and does not cause sedation.
- Sumatriptan offers the greatest promise for migraine. In clinical trials, it has been effective in two-thirds to three-fourths of patients, depending on dose. Side effects are feelings of warmth, heaviness, and pressure about the chest. For more details on this experimental medication, see p. 272.

Sources: Diamond, Seymour, et al. "Therapy for Migraine Headache." *Modern Medicine* 1987; 55:48–62. Edmeads, John. "Four Steps in Managing Migraine." *Postgraduate Medicine* 1989; 85:121–134. Peroutka, Stephen J., and Von Miller, Kurt. "Emergency Care: Evaluation of Headache and Exclusion of Serious Etiologies." *Modern Medicine* 1990; 58:67–75. "Migraine Treatments: Butorphanol Transnasally Administered." *F-D-C Reports* (The Pink Sheet) May 15,1989: T&G-2. "Glaxo's Sumatriptan Highlighted at Headache Congress." *Scrip* 1989; 1462: 26.

that reported a 29 percent reduction in migraine risk for those taking aspirin.[37]

A plus in the use of aspirin to prevent migraines is that even though aspirin does have side effects, people who have to take it regularly have fewer adverse reactions than they would from other migraine-prevention drugs.[38] Presumably aspirin works partly by preventing platelets in blood from clumping together. These bunches of blood platelets can form a clot, which might bring on a heart attack; they also release serotonin, a nerve messenger that may be responsible for the blood vessel changes that trigger a migraine.

Other Benefits of Aspirin

A recent study shows that doctors' assumptions about aspirin's stroke-preventing power hold up: in certain heart patients at high risk of stroke, aspirin lowers the odds dramatically, by nearly half.[39] Since nearly a million Americans are at risk because of this condition, the possibility exists for one lowly aspirin daily to have a serious impact on public health.[40] Other studies indicate that the risk of bleeding into the brain increases with aspirin use, however, so people planning to take this superdrug should check with their doctors.

If that's not enough to convince you that aspirin, which is less expensive than any other NSAID,[41] is a powerhouse that scientists are just beginning to understand, just think about the fact that it has recently proved useful in preventing problems with high blood pressure during pregnancy, and shows some promise for slowing the deterioration of blood vessels leading to the retina, which occurs in diabetics, thus delaying the development of blindness, one of the devastating consequences of diabetes. In addition, some researchers speculate that aspirin may help to hold off the development of Alzheimer's disease (see p. 230).

Side Effects

Nothing is perfect, of course, not even aspirin. Since the 1940s physicians have been very aware that aspirin can cause damage to the stomach. There is demonstrable injury to the

Dr. Richard Peto, a British researcher, offers this advice: "A migraine patient should consider taking a baby aspirin a day."

Aspirin
(acetylsalicylic acid)
Two 325 mg tablets every four to six hours for pain and fever reduction.
Fourteen to twenty tablets daily for reducing inflammation.
One baby tablet (80 mg) daily to cut risk of migraine headache by 20 percent.
Side effects: stomach irritation, ringing in the ears (high doses).
Interacts with many other drugs.
Daily use calls for a physician's supervision.
★ ★ ★ ★ ★

stomach lining in almost everyone who takes as little as two tablets of aspirin.[42] Although with just one dose this injury is slight and usually heals quickly, with repeated doses it builds up. Some people who repeatedly take high doses of aspirin go on to develop stomach ulcers, while others seem to suffer few ill effects. What's happening?

It appears there are aspirin-sensitive and aspirin-insensitive people. In aspirin-sensitive folks, the initial damage to the stomach lining evolves, upon further exposure to aspirin, into a larger and larger crater that is eventually recognized as a stomach ulcer. In nonreactors, the stomach lining adapts. Instead of going from bad to worse, the damage actually lessens. The body seems to figure out how to deal with the irritant, and even hastens the repair process. Eventually, a delicate kind of equilibrium is established.

For the person who takes an occasional pair of aspirin to numb the pain of a headache or muscles made sore by too much weekend basketball, stomach injury isn't much of an issue. If that's your situation, you can just ignore the ads for competing painkillers that suggest aspirin causes a major problem with stomach irritation. People who must take large doses of aspirin for long periods—primarily arthritis sufferers, who need the drug's anti-inflammatory punch as well as its painkilling capability—do need to be concerned about ulcers. (See p. 28 for a discussion of ulcer prevention with aspirin and other NSAIDs.) Buffered aspirin, unfortunately, isn't much help in this regard. But there's a good chance that either enteric-coated aspirin or slow-release aspirin may lower the risk of aspirin-related tummy trouble.

Although aspirin is about as safe and effective as a drug can get, there are people who shouldn't take it. Anyone who's ever had an allergic reaction to aspirin (hives, wheezing, or swelling) needs to steer absolutely clear of it to avoid a potentially life-threatening reaction. Someone on anticoagulant or gout medicine should pass up aspirin, too. It's not for people with ulcers. People with reduced kidney function should be monitored by their doctors if they're taking aspirin on a regular basis.

Children should not be given aspirin if they have chicken pox or the flu—in practice, since it may be hard for a parent to tell if a kid is coming down with chicken pox or flu, children should only be given aspirin on the pediatrician's say-so. (Aspirin together with these viral illnesses has been associated with a rare but sometimes life-threatening condition in children called Reye's syndrome. Reye is, of course, the doctor who described it first; his name is pronounced "rye.") Pregnant women, too, should avoid aspirin unless the obstetrician is administering it for a specific condition, as it could lead to excess bleeding during or after delivery.

Ringing in the ears, headache or dizziness, sleepiness, and shortness of breath are all possible indicators that blood levels of aspirin are too high. Back off a bit on the dose and check in with the doctor.

> ### *Sustained Release*
>
> Slow-release (SR) formulations may also reduce irritation a little, but they primarily make it easier to keep blood levels of aspirin high enough to reduce inflammation without swallowing a fistful of pills every few hours. The slow-release formulation, available in **8-Hour Bayer Timed-Release**, **Measurin**, and **ZORprin**, as well as house brands, allows for a much more even and much more sustained level of the drug.[43] The SR version is as effective as regular and enteric-coated aspirin in dealing with rheumatoid arthritis. It is also likely to be equally hard on the GI tract.

IBUPROFEN: THE OTHER OTC NSAID

Although aspirin was the first nonsteroidal anti-inflammatory drug, the chemists have come up with plenty of others. None can beat aspirin on efficacy or price, but several are more convenient to take because one or a few pills reduce inflammation as much as a dozen or more aspirin tablets. And one of these NSAIDs, ibuprofen, is widely available over the counter. Doctors tend to think first of prescription drugs to get rid of pain, but research has shown that **Advil, Ibuprin, Medipren, Motrin IB, Nuprin,** or any other brand of nonprescription ibuprofen can be just as effective, in certain cases, as a combination of acetaminophen and codeine.

In one study, dental patients who had impacted wisdom teeth removed got more relief from 400 mg of ibuprofen than from 600 mg of acetaminophen combined with 60 mg of codeine.[44] Ibuprofen also outperformed acetaminophen, both in OTC doses, in alleviating the pain after an episiotomy. The women in this study had had normal, uncomplicated deliveries, but complained of moderate to severe pain.[45]

For painful menstrual cramps (dysmenorrhea), nothing (including aspirin) beats the NSAIDs. Some doctors go, with full confidence, for the cheapest product available. Dr. William F. O'Brien, an OB/GYN in Tampa, Florida, says that ibuprofen is his drug of first-choice for dysmenorrhea because "it's OTC and dirt-cheap." If that doesn't work, he tries a prescription NSAID.[46]

Although ibuprofen works about as well as aspirin for a sprained muscle or temporarily inflamed joint—tennis elbow, say—and the leaflet in the box recommends it for "the minor pain of arthritis," people who find themselves taking some ibuprofen every day need to be careful. The medicine is somewhat less likely than aspirin to irritate the digestive tract, but daily use can lead to heartburn, indigestion, or ulcers. Even more ominous is its potential to damage the kidney. Two recent studies confirm this danger, especially for older people with high blood pressure.[47] Early kidney failure often does not pro-

---

Risks of Combination Painkillers

In 1984, the National Institutes of Health invited a prominent panel of experts to consider the problem of kidney disease and analgesic use, focusing particularly on the question, "Can analgesics, alone or in combination, cause kidney disease and chronic renal failure?"[50]

After due deliberation, the experts decided, "The weight of evidence supports the view that combinations of antipyretic analgesics taken in large doses over long periods can cause kidney disease and chronic renal failure."[51]

The FDA decided not to act on the panel's recommendation that "Serious consideration should be given to limiting over-the-counter products to those containing a single antipyretic-analgesic agent."[52]

Although combination painkillers are still available without prescription, we cannot recommend their use. The following contain more than one analgesic ingredient: **Duradyne Tablets, Excedrin Caplets** and **Tablets, Gemnisyn Tablets, Goody's Headache Powders, Presalin Tablets, Saleto Tablets, Salocol Tablets, Tenol-Plus Tablets, Trigesic Tablets, Tri-Pain Tablets, Vanquish Caplets**.

duce symptoms, and by the time people experience nausea, vomiting, lethargy, and weakness, serious damage may have been done.

ACETAMINOPHEN

The only other significant nonprescription pain reliever is a drug called acetaminophen. Never heard of it, you say? Of course you have—**Tylenol**, **Datril**, **Panadol**, and **Anacin-3** are all acetaminophen.

When acetaminophen first came on the market, it got sort of a ho-hum reaction from the aspirin makers. It didn't seem much of a threat, particularly since acetaminophen doesn't reduce inflammation, while aspirin excels in that regard. As a result, **Tylenol** is not the drug of choice for those with arthritis, which is a major chunk of the pain reliever market. Strong advertising, however, can overcome many other obstacles, and

> Dr. William L. Henrich, kidney specialist at the University of Texas Southwestern Medical School, says this about the recent findings on ibuprofen: "Our concern is that if patients take this stuff for great lengths of time and not just in short bursts of therapy that they could wind up with kidney damage." [48]
> Be smart. If you take ibuprofen every day, get a doctor to supervise.

Using OTC Pain Relievers Safely

As long as they pay attention to the label, most people can use over-the-counter analgesics safely. Overdoses of aspirin can cause stomach irritation or ringing in the ears. Acetaminophen in high doses can be toxic to the liver. Here are some common-sense rules to follow:

- Read the label and follow the instructions and warnings.
- Do not exceed the maximum dosage.
- Adults shouldn't take pain relievers for more than ten days, except under doctor's care (for fever, three days tops).
- Teenagers and younger kids should limit use to five days (three days for fever).
- Children and young adults (ages two to twenty) should not take aspirin for chicken pox or flu because of the danger of Reye's syndrome.
- If you are allergic to aspirin, don't take any medicine that contains aspirinlike ingredients, like carbaspirin calcium, magnesium salicylate and sodium salicylate. (Read the labels for ingredients.)
- If pregnant, avoid aspirin during the last three months of pregnancy unless advised by a doctor. [53]
- Don't mix pain relievers. Taking more than one kind at a time can increase the risk of kidney damage without offering any greater relief.

acetaminophen is just about as good as aspirin for fever and the kind of occasional short-term pain, the sore throat or sprained ankle, that people often encounter.

To compete against the more established drug, many brands of acetaminophen were advertised as being aspirin's equal in banishing pain with none of the stomach problems. That's certainly true as far as it goes, but acetaminophen carries dangers of its own.

Just as with aspirin or ibuprofen, the occasional user who pops a couple of tablets or capsules to quell a headache is in no imminent danger. The regular user, however, may be risking either liver or kidney damage. A study published in mid-1989 reported that "the long-term daily use of acetaminophen, the major metabolite of phenacetin, is associated independently with an increased risk of chronic renal [kidney] disease."[49] Add the well-documented risk of liver damage, particularly in combination with alcohol, and acetaminophen doesn't look very friendly for the regular user.

Does this mean you should rush to your medicine cabinet and throw out the **Tylenol** or **Anacin-3**? Certainly not. Acetaminophen has its place. A significant number of people are allergic to aspirin, and many of them are likely to experience allergic symptoms with ibuprofen (or any other NSAID) as well. Acetaminophen offers them the next best bet for treating that occasional ache or pain. It is not any better than aspirin as a painkiller, but in the majority of studies that have been conducted, it does as well as aspirin for most folks.

But acetaminophen, like the other nonprescription pain relievers, is not meant for day-in and day-out use with no doctor's input. It cannot control the inflammation of arthritis even though it may dull the discomfort, so it shouldn't be a mainstay of arthritis treatment. A person who is taking **Tylenol** or some other OTC analgesic every day for a headache may be caught in a vicious cycle and needs professional help for the headaches, not more pain reliever. And the chronic back pain sufferer may get more relief from a multifaceted program of treatment and, if called for, rehabilitation than from a daily diet of acetaminophen.

Prescription Painkillers

NONSTEROIDAL ANTI-INFLAMMATORY DRUGS: NSAIDS

When pain is due to arthritis or a pulled muscle, many doctors whip out the prescription pad and scribble the name of their favorite NSAID. These drugs are effective pain killers—though not better than aspirin—and they can minimize inflammation far more conveniently than aspirin, with fewer pills.

At one time, the only really strong weapons doctors had against inflammation were the steroid drugs, primarily prednisone. The problem with prednisone is that it is *really* strong, and long-term use almost always upsets the equilibrium

---

NSAIDs

These nonsteroidal anti-inflammatory drugs are currently available in the United States. The generic name is in plain type; the brand name is in bold-face. In some cases, patents have expired and the drug is available by its generic name, as well as by one of several trade names.

- **Anaprox, Naprosyn** (naproxen). 250–500 mg twice a day.
- **Ansaid** (flurbiprofen). 100mg two or three times a day.
- **Clinoril** (sulindac). 150–200 twice a day.
- **Feldene** (piroxicam). 20mg a day.
- **Indameth, Indocin,** and others (indomethacin). 25–50 mg three times a day.
- **Meclofen, Meclomen** (meclofenamate sodium). 200–400 mg three or four times a day.
- **Motrin**, **Rufen**, and several others (ibuprofen). 600–800 mg a day.
- **Nalfon** (fenoprofen). 300–600 mg a day.
- **Orudis** (ketoprofen). 50–75 mg a day.
- **Tolectin** (tolmetin). 200–400 mg a day.
- **Voltaren** (diclofenac). 50 mg a day.

Phenylbutazone (**Butazolidin**) and oxyphenbutazone are rarely prescribed because of a higher risk of serious side effects, including blood disorders.

of many physiological systems. The adrenal gland, for instance, where the body normally produces its own supply of steroids, tends to shut down production altogether, and sometimes it doesn't bounce back even when the external supply is withdrawn. Lots of times, particularly when swelling was really severe, there were no other choices, but prednisone always represented a significant trade-off.

That explains the warm welcome that the nonsteroidal anti-inflammatory drugs got when they were developed. The first was **Indocin** (indomethacin), which came along in 1965. **Motrin** (ibuprofen) came along nine years later, and since then there have been many, many more. They are all quite similar in their action and effectiveness, but they differ in convenience, in cost, and to a certain extent in side effects. For short-term pain relief, they're all pretty similar.

But for chronic pain, like arthritis, the differences begin to come into focus. Each individual responds a little differently, and when you're going to be taking a drug for a long time, it makes sense to use the one that gives you the best relief. "It is virtually impossible," writes one observer, "to predict which patients will respond favorably to NSAIDs, or which NSAID they will respond to."[54] And that's the truth, frustrating though it may be. With so many choices, finding the right NSAID can be a little like shopping for a new suit. You may need to try one on to see how it fits. A generally accepted rule of thumb is that a patient should take an NSAID for two to three weeks or a few months before concluding that it isn't working.

Aspirin and other salicylate-containing drugs, including the prescription-only **Dolobid** (diflunisal) are also nonsteroidal anti-inflammatory drugs, but when doctors say NSAIDs, they are usually referring to the drugs listed on page 263. These NSAIDs are unquestionably effective pain relievers, at

Timing the Treatment

In a study conducted in England, researchers tried varying the schedule on which they gave sixty patients with long-term low back pain their daily dose of ibuprofen.

One batch of people got 1200 mg in the morning, and 600 mg noon and night. The other half got 600 mg in the morning and at noon with a 1200 mg jolt in the evening.

They all got the same amount of drug over the course of the day. But they didn't all get the same relief.

Pain and spinal flexibility improved considerably more for those who got the high dose in the morning. These people also tended to sleep better at night.

Future research should allow doctors to prescribe medication according to the body's daily cycles of chemical and physical variables.

least in part, presumably, because of their ability to interfere with prostaglandin production. It is clear, though, that this type of medication doesn't lead to tolerance (a need to take more and more of a drug to get the same pain relief) and people don't develop physical dependence on them. This lack of addiction potential makes them especially useful for the treatment of long-term pain.

With daily use for months or years, NSAIDs can have toxic effects. All cause digestive tract problems, at least in some people. (See p. 28 for ways to counteract this.) Although these compounds vary with respect to their effect on the kidneys, nearly all can cause serious damage. Liver enzymes may be affected, and hearing or vision is occasionally harmed by one of these drugs. Older people are more susceptible to all of these difficulties, although they may be less capable of detecting them. The doctor who prescribes one of these compounds for long-term use needs to monitor patients to catch any serious reactions before they get out of hand.

Cost

If aspirin at a few cents a tablet doesn't do the trick and the painkiller of choice turns out to be an NSAID, taking your medicine can get expensive. The price on the sticker seems to depend partly on whether it's still on patent or available generically, and partly on the pricing whims of the manufacturer.

One survey found that NSAID prices ranged from as low as $3.69 for a thirty-day supply of indomethacin ordered generically to as high as $49.16 for a month's supply of **Meclomen** (meclofenamate sodium). Those were the wholesale prices to the pharmacist. You will pay more (perhaps much more) at the checkout counter.

If the doctor prescribes **Motrin** (ibuprofen), it's $22.10 for a thirty-day supply, wholesale. The same drug under the name **Ibumed** is $9. Now you know what's in a name. A similar study, conducted at the University of California School of Medicine, found that a month of ibuprofen was $22.95, a month of indomethacin was $17.61, and a month of double-strength tolmetin was a rather staggering $75.41.[55]

It is convenient to be able to buy ibuprofen (and soon, perhaps others) over-the-counter, but it is not necessarily cheaper. Someone has to pay for all the advertising to convince you to use it. Ibuprofen purchased at the store as **Advil** averaged out at $19.12 for a thirty-day supply, and Bristol-Myers' competing version, **Nuprin**, weighed in at $18.01 for the same supply. Looking for a house brand could offer significant savings.

NARCOTICS

Although the NSAIDs have some advantages over aspirin in terms of convenience and side effects, to get noticeably better pain relief, you have to turn to the narcotics. Humans have used one form or another of narcotic drug for a long time. As far as we can tell, opium was in use by around 1500 B.C.[56] Codeine, morphine, and other derivatives of opium, as well as several synthetic drugs, make up this arsenal.

Addiction Fears

In today's society, people worry a lot about drug addiction. As a result, there's a lot of irrational behavior surrounding these potent pain relievers. Unfortunately, patients sometimes suffer unbearable pain because their doctors don't prescribe the appropriate drug, or prescribe the proper drug but in doses that are too low to be really effective.[57, 58] Children are often treated even more cautiously, with the result that they're expected to tolerate more pain.[59-61]

The idea that people taking narcotics for relief of intense short-term pain will become addicted isn't supported by the medical literature. Study after study says that addiction is rarely an outcome of pain relief with narcotic drugs. One careful and extensive study put the risk of addiction in hospital patients at about one in one thousand,[62] and a burn-ward nurse whose patients all get large quantities of narcotics says that in ten years of experience she has never seen a person walk out the door addicted.[63] Another study of twelve thousand patients who had received narcotic drugs found a grand total of four cases of dependence.[64] Addiction, says one medical expert, is "a facet of opioid pharmacology which is rarely a clinical problem."[65]

Timing Considerations

One of the consequences of this timid approach to narcotics is the attempt to go halfway, either in the dose prescribed or in the timing. The patient who has just gone through surgery may be required to wait a full four hours between pain medication, even though the effect of the medication starts to wear off after about two and a half hours. As a result, the pain will be severe before the next dose is administered and more narcotic will be needed to give the same level of pain relief. This common mistake breaks the doctor's cardinal rule of pain management: "Stay ahead of your patient's pain."[66]   Experienced doctors insist that "patients in acute pain who receive adequate pain control medication in the first few days generally need fewer repeat doses and shorter courses of medication than patients whose early acute pain is poorly controlled."[67]

Drawbacks

It would be a mistake to think that narcotic drugs are a cure-all. Some types of pain are not narcotic-sensitive. For example, when nerve compression or nerve destruction is the cause of pain, the narcotic drugs do not give good relief. And some people cannot tolerate narcotics. Nausea is a common and troublesome side effect. If you can, ward it off by taking the pill along with a meal. Most of the narcotic medications can also cause drowsiness, disorientation, or other changes in mental status, so you should definitely not drive or operate any dangerous equipment while taking one of these medications.

Combinations

Although narcotics have no scarcity of side effects, they do not seem as liable as the other medications discussed so far to cause kidney damage. The Consensus Conference on Analgesic-Associated Kidney Disease did not warn against combinations of a narcotic and a less potent analgesic. Some drug combinations do seem more effective than either one would be

---

How Much is Enough?

According to one study, hospitalized patients don't fare well when the doctor has to switch them from one narcotic regimen to another. When eighty-eight medical students and house officers were asked to convert from one narcotic to a dose of a second that would provide equal analgesia, only 8 percent managed to get it right — and "right" was defined as being within 20 percent of the correct answer.

By the way, it was an open-book test![68]

Commonly Prescribed Narcotic Drugs

codeine
Demerol
  (meperidine)
Dilaudid
  (hydromorphone)
Dolophine
  (methadone)
Percodan
  (oxycodone and aspirin)
Talwin-Nx
  (pentazocine and naloxone)

Codeine

Available alone or
in such combina-
tions as acetamino-
phen (**Empracet**,
Phenaphen, or
Tylenol) with
codeine.
Adult dose for
acute mild to
moderate pain: 15–
60 mg every four to
six hours.
Also effective
cough suppressant.
Side effects:
nausea, constipa-
tion, drowsiness.
Prolonged use may
lead to withdrawal
symptoms on
stopping.

★ ★ ★

alone. For example, **Soma** (carisoprodol) may be successfully combined with **Naprosyn** (naproxen) to relieve muscle tension pain. Codeine and acetaminophen are a classic combo that has stood the test of time and relieved a lot of pain along the way. NSAIDs may also be given in combination with narcotic drugs. Because they relieve pain via different mechanisms, they can work together to produce good sustained analgesia. And tricyclic antidepressants, anticonvulsants, and amphetamines have all been shown to increase the effectiveness of narcotic drugs in certain circumstances.

Taking It Home

Most of these narcotic medications are used in the hospital. People well enough to be at home or at work, regardless of their level of pain, are rarely turned loose with anything stronger than codeine or oxycodone, considered excellent for mild to moderate pain. Addiction becomes a genuine concern if an acute-pain-control situation begins to stretch out into months or years. Sufferers may find that they no longer experience adequate pain relief at the prescribed safe dose, and if they suddenly stop taking the medicine, they may experience unpleasant withdrawal symptoms. Chronic pain deserves a thoughtful, effective control program that may integrate several approaches rather than relying on a single narcotic analgesic.

Coping with Chronic Pain

Our bodies may not distinguish between pain that started two hours ago and that which began two years ago: they both hurt. But there is a tremendous difference in the impact on our lives and our ability to cope. Chronic (long-term) pain is a whole different kettle of fish from postsurgical pain or the pain of a broken bone. It calls for a different approach, although some of the treatments already discussed can occasionally help with chronic pain as well. Although there is no absolute and generally agreed-upon length of time that moves pain from the acute to the chronic category, most practitioners would certainly agree that anyone whose pain has been with them for six months or more has a chronic pain problem.

Chronic pain is one of the most debilitating, demoralizing tests a person can face. People with intractable pain often spend years and untold thousands of dollars going from doctor to doctor in constant pursuit of relief. The pain becomes an ever-present, all-consuming force in their life, with them from the time they awaken until the time they go to sleep—if the pain lets them sleep.

While some types of chronic pain, such as arthritis, have an obvious physical cause, a substantial number of those with chronic pain have either no obvious physical problem, or a problem without a definable cure. Lower back pain is the best example of this. A small percentage of those with chronic lower back pain eventually are found to have some clearly discernible problem, such as a herniated disk. The remainder definitely hurt, but the reason why remains obscure.

Chronic pain is almost always some mixture of physical and psychological pain. One melds rather smoothly into the other, particularly when the pain continues for a long time. Although the original pain may indeed have been entirely organic, after a period of several months there is almost inevitably a psychological component, if for no other reason than because the sufferer begins to see himself or herself as a victim, and perhaps as someone for whom there is no help.

ANTIDEPRESSANTS AGAINST PAIN

One of the major discoveries in pain treatment of the last few years is the effectiveness of antidepressant drugs. Unques-

Chronic Pain Syndrome

Pain that lasts for more than six months and is not part of ongoing tissue breakdown or degeneration is called chronic benign pain. Someone who is suffering day-in and day-out with chronic pain, someone whose life is forced to revolve around the pain, may end up developing chronic pain syndrome, characterized by

- Change of behavior along with depression or anxiety.
- Restriction of activities.
- Excessive use of medication.
- No clear organic reason for the pain.
- A history of unproductive tests and treatments.[69]

What do you do when medicine won't stop the pain?[82]

If you have tried everything your doctor has prescribed and you still have chronic pain, then other options need to be explored:

- acupressure or acupuncture
- biofeedback
- operant conditioning (stimulus-response training)
- pain clinics
- relaxation
- surgery
- transcutaneous electrical nerve stimulation (TENS)
- trigger point injections

tionably, being in pain constantly can be depressing, and depression tends to make the pain experience more unbearable.[70] Antidepressants obviously work to relieve depression, and that in itself may help make people feel better. But that doesn't appear to be the whole story, since antidepressants have been shown to relieve pain in some situations where they didn't reduce depression.[71] More and more research is pointing to the fact that antidepressants have analgesic properties of their own.[72,73]

Among the drugs shown to be effective in pain relief are amitriptyline (**Elavil** and others), which has helped with chronic low back pain,[74] chronic pain of no specific origin,[75] postherpetic neuralgia,[76] and diabetic neuropathy;[77] imipramine (**Tofranil** and others), which has proved its mettle in chronic low back pain,[78] diabetic neuropathy,[79] and fibrositis;[80] and doxepin (**Adapin**, **Sinequan**), which has also proved effective in relieving chronic low back pain.[81] These drugs don't work for everyone, but they are welcome options for the person in chronic pain.

PAIN CLINICS

For the patient who continues to suffer despite the doctor's best efforts, it may be time to visit a pain clinic. There are perhaps a dozen top-flight clinics around the country, bringing together specialists from a number of realms. The patient is examined and tested from head to toe, and then treatment is prescribed and supervised by pain specialists.

The advantage of a pain clinic is that it's one-stop shopping. You could perhaps duplicate the same thing by making the rounds of a half dozen specialists, but none of them would have a comprehensive overview of the entire situation. Another advantage to be found in pain clinics is the availability of absolutely up-to-the-minute knowledge

Pain Clinics, U.S.A.

There are a number of specialized pain-treatment centers throughout the country. Most are multidisciplinary, and all have achieved relief for a substantial portion of the people who have attended. Among the clinics are

University of California San Francisco
Medical College of Wisconsin
Human Resources Association (Michigan)
Montefiore Hospital (New York)
All of these have outpatient programs.

Hospitals with inpatient programs include
Mayo Clinic (Rochester, Minnesota)
Northwest Pain Clinic (Oregon)
Scripps Clinic (La Jolla, California)
Mensana Clinic (Maryland)

For a more complete list of clinics treating chronic pain, contact the National Chronic Pain Outreach Association, Inc., (301) 652–4948.

about the latest in pain-relief techniques, both drug and nondrug, and the ability to tailor a pain management program to the individual patient.

SURGERY

There comes a point for many sufferers of chronic pain where they will do almost anything to get the monkey off their back. Having tried a variety of drugs and other treatments without success, they sometimes jump at the chance when a surgeon suggests that he can solve their problem with a few deft scalpel movements.

Although surgery is the logical choice for recurrent gallbladder pain, a damaged knee, or certain sinus conditions, surgical relief of pain generally means cutting nerves to the affected area. If that sounds like an extreme response to the problem, you're quite correct. And it's often not as completely effective as it seems it should be.[83] "Clearly," says one pain authority, "the syndrome of chronic benign pain is largely due to factors unresponsive to surgery. Corrective surgery should be contingent on the presence of a correctable lesion that is likely to impair function, and not on the basis of patient demands."[84] In other words, if there isn't something specifically wrong that can be removed or repaired, surgery is not the right option. It shouldn't even be considered until all other avenues of relief have been thoroughly explored and unless another doctor, independent of the operating surgeon, believes it offers a reasonable degree of assurance that the surgery will in fact eliminate the pain.

Future Drugs

Research on new compounds is moving ahead on several fronts, and there are innovations being made on a drug-by-drug, disease-by-disease basis. For example, researchers recently discovered a protein the body uses to shut down the immune response after it has done the work it is supposed to do.[85] When the body senses an infection or a foreign object, it rallies a substance called interleukin-1 (IL-1) to eliminate the invader. In diseases like arthritis, the body's usually-helpful immune response runs amok, destroying bone and tissue. The protein that signals the interleukin-1 to retreat fails, for unknown reasons, to do its job. In preliminary laboratory tests the newly discovered protein, called IL-1ra (interleukin-1 receptor antagonist), seems to be very effective at reducing swelling and bone destruction. Synthetic versions of this natural substance may be effective at particular sites, so that damage could be controlled without interrupting the body's overall defenses. This research is still very early, with no clinical trials yet, but the manufacturer Synergen, in cooperation with Hoffmann-La Roche, will undoubtedly be looking at its usefulness for arthritis and other chronic conditions.

Sumatriptan

Sumatriptan
Up to 80 percent effectiveness for treatment of migraine headaches.
Available as coated tablet or self-administered injection.
Not indicated for people with heart disease.
Expected availability: early 1990s.
The brand name in the United States is still under review.
Side effects: feeling of warmth, heaviness, pressure.

★ ★ ★

Another exciting discovery is the drug sumatriptan for migraine headaches. This drug is now in clinical testing, but preliminary reports have hailed its effectiveness.[86, 87] In one study, three times more patients receiving the drug than receiving placebo reported their migraine was either gone or very mild after two hours. An international multicenter trial of the drug yields an overall effectiveness rating of 80 percent.[88] The manufacturer, Glaxo, will be submitting it for approval both in an oral tablet and a self-injectable form.

Sumatriptan binds to a specific receptor for the naturally produced chemical serotonin, which is thought to play an important role in the transmission of the pain message from blood vessels in the brain. Trying to determine exactly how it works is teaching researchers a lot about the causes and biochemical nature of migraine pain. Several other companies are also actively investigating serotonin antagonists for migraine treatment, so the future for this condition may be significantly brighter.[89]

Other medications under development for migraine headaches include alpiropride (made by Delagrange), emopamil (made by Knoll), flunarizine (made by Janssen), gepefrine (made by Helopharm/Merrell Dow), and metergoline (made by Erbamont).

Ritanserin

The burst of interest in serotonin receptors and antagonists may yield a new category of painkillers. The Janssen pharmaceutical company, in investigating ritanserin, an experimental drug for psychological disorders, found that five days of treatment made people significantly more capable of tolerating pain, while placebo had no impact on pain perception. This effect on pain is working through a different pathway than narcotics do, because it can't be reversed with the opiate antagonist naloxone. Researchers believe ritanserin exerts its effects through serotonin-related receptors.[90]

PATIENT CONTROL OF ANALGESIA

The other future development uses technology that is already available. The only change required is one of attitude, and that has already begun, at least in hospital settings, via a technique called patient-controlled analgesia—PCA, for short.

When it comes to pain control, particularly in the administration of narcotic drugs, "Many of the problems with current practice may stem not from the inadequacies of the drugs themselves but from inadequate drug administration techniques."[91] With PCA, the patient is rigged to an intravenous device that has a pump and a button. This eliminates the necessity of having to wait for the nurse to show up so you can ask for pain medication. Push the button and you get a dose of medication. The doctor gets to set the minimum period that must elapse before pushing the button again will inject more drug, as well as the amount dispensed with each push of the button.

"The major concern with allowing patients to self-administer narcotics has been that they may overmedicate themselves," notes one observer. "Interestingly, the experience has been just the opposite."[92] Left to their own devices, patients achieve better pain control with less medication than when on a fixed-dosage schedule.

The implantable drug pump works on a similar principle. Developed for administering cancer chemotherapy, this device is a small pump that is implanted in the abdomen, from which it dispenses the drug directly into the bloodstream. Although it is currently approved for the delivery of only a limited number of drugs, the list will probably expand as fast as manufacturers can document the safety and effectiveness of their painkillers when delivered via internal pump. By placing the drug directly into the bloodstream or, in the case of morphine, directly into the spinal fluid, drug doses can be drastically reduced while also making the analgesia very specific. These devices will likely become smaller and more capable in the next few years, until they are tiny, computer-controlled buttons that will be placed under the skin using only a local anesthetic.

The prospect of scientific research developing new, more effective nonnarcotic pain medicines is very promising. So too is the growing recognition that since pain is such a personal experience, the best person to treat it is not the doctor, but the patient. This isn't to say that we don't need doctors. They can best determine the options that are appropriate for relieving a patient's pain. We foresee a day, however, when pain relief is a joint venture between physician and patient, with the doctor being able to offer a wide range of both drug and nondrug alternatives, and patients being able to exercise a great deal of control so that they can achieve the centuries-old goal of pain relief.

Quick Takes

- A cold compress or a hot shower can often make an arthritic joint feel better. The best, and most difficult, nondrug pain control method is relaxation: Emmett Miller comes to the rescue with "Changing the Channel on Pain." For people who have a hard time letting go, biofeedback may help with learning how to relax. Don't get taken in by unrealistic claims, though.

- Massage, acupuncture, and trigger point treatment can all be helpful for some kinds of pain. Find out what makes you feel better. For chronic neuralgia, a TENS unit may be the ticket.

- Herbal remedies offer some people impressive pain relief. **Zostrix**, a cream made from red peppers (capsaicin), is often effective for the pain that may follow shingles. Feverfew has been shown to prevent some migraine headaches, and might even be useful for some people with arthritis. A little-known herb, Echinacea, has potent anti-inflammatory properties.

- Evening primrose oil has been controversial, but some studies suggest it may be helpful in treating arthritis. In one study, people taking this drug reduced their use of arthritis drugs, while those on placebo did not.

- Fish oil (EPA) may also offer anti-inflammatory relief. The downside is fishy breath and a tendency to bleed. To get your fish oil the tasty way, eat plenty of salmon and trout.

- The amino acid d-phenylalanine may provide "natural" pain relief, especially for short-term situations like a strained back or dental pain. Avoid it if you have high blood pressure, PKU, or melanoma.

- Aspirin is a wonder drug—★★★★★! One regular-strength tablet every other day can cut migraine attacks by 20 percent. Perhaps as little as one baby aspirin daily will work as well.

- Migraine sufferers can get good relief if they act fast. Ergotamine or naproxen (**Anaprox**) can be surprisingly effective if used early. The breakthrough everyone is waiting for is sumatriptan from Glaxo. If it lives up to its promise, get ready to celebrate!

- Don't overdose on OTC pain relievers—they can do nasty things to your kidneys. Prolonged use of **Tylenol** (acetaminophen) or **Advil** (ibuprofen) without a doctor's supervision is dangerous. Combination products should be avoided.

- With a smorgasbord of nonsteroidal anti-inflammatory drugs (NSAIDs) available, there's no way for your doctor to tell ahead of time which will work best for you. The rule is trial and error—make the trial at least three weeks long, to be fair. NSAIDs are effective for many kinds of pain, not just arthritis, but long-term use can also cause trouble: stomach upset or ulcers, kidney or liver damage, changes in hearing or vision.

- Addiction is not usually a problem when people in pain use narcotic analgesics. When these potent pain medications are given at a short enough interval with high enough doses to keep patients comfortable, the total daily dose needed is much lower.

- Chronic pain deserves a creative strategy. A variety of approaches will work better than relying on one heavy-duty drug. Antidepressants can be surprisingly effective for some kinds of long-term pain. For an integrated approach to pain management, a pain clinic may be the best resource.

References

[1] Beebe, Alexandra, et al. "Pain: Its Assessment and Treatment. *J. Practical Nursing* 1989; 6:17–27.

[2] Sobel, Dava, and Klein, Arthur C. *Arthritis: What Works.* New York: St. Martin's Press, 1989, p. 333.

[3] Empting-Koschorke, L.D., et al. "Nondrug Management of Chronic Pain." *Patient Care* 1990; 24(1):165–185.

[4] Bassam, Bassam A. "Low Back Syndromes." *Postgraduate Medicine* 1990; 87(4):209–218.

[5] Empting-Koschorke et al. op. cit., p. 168.

[6] Covington, Edward C. "Management of the Patient with Chronic Benign Pain: Treatment." *Modern Medicine* 1989; 57(10):82–100.

[7] Sobel and Klein, op. cit. pp. 170–174.

[8] Empting-Koschorke, L.D., et al. "When Pain is Intractable." *Patient Care* 1989; 23:107–125

[9] Kunkel, Robert S. "Tension-Type (Muscle Contraction) Headache: Evaluation and Treatment." *Modern Medicine* 1989; 57(8): 60–68.

[10] Piller, Charles. "Who Cares about your Back?" *InHealth* 1990; 4(2):43.

[11] Sobel and Klein, op. cit. p. 169.

[12] Empting-Koschorke et al., 1990, op. cit. p. 167.

[13] Sheon, Robert P. "Transcutaneous Electrical Nerve Stimulation: From Electric Eels to Electrodes." *Postgraduate Medicine* 1984; 75(5):71–74.

[14] Deyo, R.A., et al. "A Controlled Trial of Transcutaneous Electrical Nerve Stimulation (TENS) and Exercise for Chronic Low Back Pain." *N. Engl. J. Med.* 1990; 322(23): 1627–1634.

[15] Covington, op. cit. p. 86.

[16] Kunkel, op. cit. p. 68.

[17] Fishman, Ricky. "Headache Cures." *Medical SelfCare* 1989(Nov/Dec): 24–29.

[18] Mowrey, Daniel B. *The Scientific Validation of Herbal Medicine.* Cormorant Books, 1986, p. 224.

[19] Murphy, J.J., et al. "Randomised Double-Blind, Placebo-Controlled Trial of Feverfew in Migraine Prevention." *Lancet* 1988; 11:189–192.

[20] "Feverfew." *The Lawrence Review of Natural Products.* St. Louis: Facts & Comparisons, 1986.

[21] Der Marderosian, Ara, and Liberti, Lawrence. *Natural Product Medicine.* Philadelphia: George F. Stickley Co., 1988, p. 299.

[22] "Capsicum Peppers." *The Lawrence Review of Natural Products.* St. Louis: Facts & Comparisons, 1989.

[23] "Clove." *The Lawrence Review of Natural Products.* St. Louis: Facts & Comparisons, 1987.

[24] Der Marderosian and Liberti, op. cit. pp. 284–285.

[25] "Echinacea." *The Lawrence Review of Natural Products.* St. Louis: Facts & Comparisons, 1990.

26 Mowrey, op. cit. pp. 118–119.

27 Hendler, Sheldon Saul. *The Doctors' Vitamin and Mineral Encyclopedia*. New York: Simon and Schuster, 1990.

28 Coeugniet, E.G., and Elek, E. *Onkologie* 1987; 10(Suppl. 3):27.

29 Duffy, David Cameron. "Land of Milk and Poison." *Natural History* 1990(July); 4–8.

30 Mowrey, op. cit. p. 119.

31 Belch, J.J.F., et al. "Effects of Altering Dietary Essential Fatty Acids on Requirements for Non-Steroidal Anti-Inflammatory Drugs in Patients with Rheumatoid Arthritis: A Double-Blind Placebo Controlled Study." *Ann. Rheumatic Diseases* 1988; 47:96–104.

32 "Oil of Evening Primrose." *The Lawrence Review of Natural Products*. St. Louis: Facts & Comparisons, 1989.

33 Hendler, op. cit.

34 Ibid.

35 Ibid.

36 Bankhead, Charles D. "A Push for Familiar OTC Products Is Indicated." *Med. World News* 1989(May 8); 25.

37 Lipman, Arthur G. "Comparing the NSAIDs." *Modern Medicine* 1989; 57:146.

38 Dosa, Laszlo. "An Aspirin Frequently May Keep Migraines Away." *Washington Post Health* 1990(Feb. 27); 5.

39 Fackelmann, K.A. "Low Dose of Aspirin Keeps Migraine Away." *Science News* 1990; 137(7):103.

40 Ibid.

41 Stroke Prevention in Atrial Fibrillation Study Group Investigators. "Preliminary Report of the Stroke Prevention in Atrial Fibrillation Study." *N. Engl. J. Med.* 1990; 322:863–868.

[42] Fackelmann, K.A. "Blood Thinners Lower Stroke Risk for Some." *Science News* 1990; 137:180.

[43] Lipman, op. cit.

[44] Graham, David Y., and Smith, J. Lacey. "Aspirin and the Stomach." *Ann. Int. Med.* 1986; 104:390–398.

[45] Lobeck, Frank, and Spigiel, Robert W. "Bioavailability of Sustained-Release Aspirin Preparations." *Clin. Pharm.* 1986; 5:236–238.

[46] Bankhead, op. cit.

[47] Schachtel, Bernard P., et al. "Ibuprofen and Acetaminophen in the Relief of Postpartum Episiotomy Pain." *J. Clin. Pharmacol.* 1989; 29:550.

[48] Griffiths, Joel. "Something to Those Anecdotes." *Medical Tribune* 1989(Jan. 26); 20.

[49] Squires, Sally. "Painkiller Safety Questioned." *Washington Post Health,* February 6, 1990.

[50] Ibid.

[51] Sandler, D.P., et al. "Analgesic Use and Chronic Renal Disease." *N. Engl. J. Med.* 1989; 320:1238–1243.

[52] Consensus Conference. "Analgesic-Associated Kidney Disease." *JAMA* 1984; 251:3123–3125.

[53] Ibid.

[54] Ibid.

[55] Weck, Egon. "What Can Be Done When the Pain Won't Go Away." *FDA Consumer* 1989(July/Aug.); 31.

[56] McCaffery, Margo. "Newer Uses of NSAIDs." *Am. J. Nursing,* 1985; 87(7):781–782.

[57] Sack, Kenneth E. "Update on NSAIDs in the Elderly." *Geriatrics* 1989; 44(5):71–90.

[58] Szelenyi, Istvan. "Analgesic Drugs Acting via Descending Pain-Modulating Pathways: Real Perspectives in Future Pain Treatment?" *Drug News & Perspectives* 1989; 2(1):45–49.

[59] Hill, C. Stratton. "Painful Prescriptions." *JAMA* 1987; 257:2081.

[60] Schuchman, Miriam, and Wilkes, Michael S. "Suffering in Silence." *New York Times Magazine* 1989(July 23); 36–37.

[61] Choonara, I.A. "Pain Relief." *Arch. Disease in Childhood* 1989; 64:1101–1102.

[62] Mather, L., and Mackie, J. "The Incidence of Postoperative Pain in Children." *Pain* 1983; 15:271–282.

[63] Schuchman and Wilkes, op. cit.

[64] Miller, R.R., and Jick, H. "Clinical Effects of Meperidine in Hospitalized Medical Patients." *J Clin. Pharm.* 1978; 18:180.

[65] Kibbee, Ellen. "On Pain Relief." *Emergency Med.* 1983; 15(5):141–164.

[66] Porter, J., and Jick, H. "Addiction Rate in Patients Treated with Narcotics." *N. Eng. J. Med.* 1980; 302:123.

[67] McQuary, H.J. "Opioids in Chronic Pain." *Brit. J. Anaesth.* 1989; 63:213–226.

[68] Empting-Koschorke, L.D., et al. "Chronic Pain: Using Medication Wisely." *Patient Care* 1989(Dec. 15); 16–26.

[69] Ibid. p. 17.

[70] Grossman, Stuart A., and Sheidler, Vivian R. "Skills of Medical Students and House Officers in Prescribing Narcotic Medications." *J. Med. Ed.* 1985; 60:552–557.

[71] Covington, Edward C., MD. "Management of the Patient with Chronic Benign Pain: Diagnosis." *Modern Medicine* 1989; 57:75.

[72] Hendler, N. "Depression Caused by Chronic Pain. *J. Clin. Psychiatry* 1984; 45(3 Pt. 2):30–38.

[73] Lance, J.W., and Curran, D.A. "Treatment of Chronic Tension Headache." *Lancet* 1964; 1(7345):1236–1239.

[74] Krishnan, K., and France, Randal D. "Antidepressants in Chronic Pain Syndromes." *Am. Fam. Phys.* 1989; 39(4):233–237.

[75] Lipman, Arthur, and Nielsen, James. "Antidepressants as Analgesics." *Modern Med.* 1988; 56:180–181.

[76] Pheasant, H., et al. "Amitriptyline and Chronic Low Back Pain." *Spine* 1983; 5:552–557.

[77] Pilowsky, I., et al. "A Controlled Study of Amitriptyline in the Treatment of Chronic Pain." *Pain* 1982; 14:169–179.

[78] Watson, C.P., et al. "Amitriptyline Versus Placebo in Postherpetic Neuralgia." *Neurology* 1982; 32:671–673.

[79] Turkington, R.W. "Depression Masquerading as Diabetic Neuropathy." *JAMA* 1980; 243:1147–1150.

[80] Alcoff, J., et al. "Controlled Trial of Imipramine for Chronic Low Back Pain." *J. Fam. Pract.* 1982; 14:841–846.

[81] Kvinesdal, B., et al. "Imipramine Treatment of Painful Diabetic Neuropathy." *JAMA* 1984; 251:1727–1730.

[82] Wysenbeck, A.J., et al. "Imipramine for Treatment of Fibrositis: A Therapeutic Trial." *Ann. Rheum. Dis.* 1985; 44:752–753.

[83] Hameroff, S.R., et al. "Doxepin's Effects on Chronic Pain and Depression." *Clin. Psychiatry* 1984; 45:47–52.

[84] Empting-Koschorke, L.D., et al. "Nondrug Management of Chronic Pain." *Patient Care* 1990(Jan. 15); 24:166–168, 173, 176.

[85] Wepsic, James G. "Neurosurgical Treatment of Chronic Pain." *Int. Anes. Clinics* 1983; 21(4):153–163.

[86] Covington, Edward C. "Management of the Patient with Chronic Benign Pain: Treatment." *Mod. Med.* 1989; 57:82–100.

[87] Waldholz, Michael. "An Arthritis Breakthrough Is Claimed in Finding of Anti-Inflammation Protein." *The Wall Street Journal*, January 25, 1990; B1, B4.

[88] Paulus, Walter, et al. "Specificity of Sumatriptan for Abortion of Migraine Attacks." *N. Engl. J. Med.* 1990; 335:51.

[89] Zoler, Mitchel L. " 'Milestone' Migraine Drug Hailed." *Med. World News* 1989(Dec. 11); 43.

[90] "Glaxo's sumatriptan . . ." op. cit.

[91] "Short-Circuiting Migraine Pain." *Med. World News* 1985(Sept. 9); 36.

[92] Gelders, Yves, ed. "Ritanserin: An Original Thymosthenic (R 55 667)." Investigational New Drug Brochure, Janssen Research Foundation, Belgium, 1989; 46–47.

[93] Warfield, Carol A. "Patient-Controlled Analgesia." *Hosp. Practice* 20(7):32L–32P.

[94] Ibid.

Metabolic Mysteries

8

It isn't easy to fool Mother Nature, so they say. Treatments for the most common metabolic diseases try to do just that—fool the body by replacing missing or defective hormones with synthetic ones. Yet despite years of use and research on hormones such as thyroxine, estrogen, or insulin, there is still a great deal scientists are only now discovering about how these chemicals work in the body. Doctors once believed, for instance, that thyroid hormone given to supplement a sluggish gland's inadequate output had virtually no side effects. Researchers now suspect, however, that extra thyroid hormone speeds bone loss in postmenopausal women. Any woman taking thyroid hormone should probably insist on the lowest effective dose to try to maintain maximum bone density.

Preventing osteoporosis has become nearly an obsession that has resulted in millions of women taking another prescribed hormone. Estrogen (**Premarin**), once hailed as a "feminine fountain of youth" for reversing the effects of menopause, palled when women and their doctors found it increased the risk of endometrial carcinoma, cancer of the lining of the womb. Within the past few years, though, estrogen replacement therapy (ERT) has regained or perhaps surpassed its former popularity because it helps prevent bone loss. In addition, estrogen is prescribed to relieve discomfort from vaginal dryness or hot flashes associated with menopause. Female physicians we have consulted insist that it can promote a general sense of well being in their older patients and may even improve skin tone. It is especially helpful for women who have had to undergo hysterectomies before natural menopause and may reduce their risk of cardiovascular disease.

Nowadays another female hormone, progestin (**Provera**), is given to reduce the risk of uterine cancer, but there are still any number of unanswered questions about the impact of these agents on other body systems. Taking a hormone to prevent one problem, then needing another to prevent its side effects and wondering about the potential side effects of the second hormone reminds us a little of a dog going in circles trying to catch his tail. But from a public health perspective, the benefits of estrogen in forestalling fractured hips are persuasive.

Osteoporosis and Estrogen

As you might expect in a disease where estrogen is an issue, osteoporosis is more common in women, especially as they grow older. In fact, about a third of white women over eighty-five years old eventually suffer a hip fracture that can be traced to the gradual bone loss of osteoporosis.[1] (Black women are far less vulnerable to this condition.)

It would be a mistake to think that men are immune, though. About one out of every six men is likely to break a hip after retirement age.[2] For men as well as women, a broken hip is a serious setback that increases the chance of dying in the year after the accident and often means a loss of independence or a lengthy convalescence. Fortunately, most older people don't end up breaking their hips, but almost everyone who lives long enough will wind up with less bone than they had as young adults. For women, the risk of hip fracture after age sixty-five doubles every ten years.[3]

> ### Risk Factors for Osteoporosis
> - increased age
> - white or Asian
> - little or no exercise
> - high-protein, low-calcium diet
> - irregular menstrual periods
> - high levels of thyroxine (thyrotoxicosis or supplementation)
> - female
> - short and thin
> - smoker
> - family history
> - early menopause

Some people are at high risk of serious bone loss. Just as those who start with a small savings account run out of money sooner than those with more of a nest egg, people who have less bone at their peak, between the ages of thirty and thirty-five, run into trouble more quickly. This may help explain why women, who tend to be smaller and therefore have smaller bones than men, seem more susceptible to the ravages of osteoporosis.

The sex difference may also reflect differences in exercise patterns. Many older women, especially up until the past few decades, grew up in a time when the bone-jarring sports boys favor (football, basketball, even baseball) weren't considered ladylike. A girl who played actively was apt to be considered a tomboy and expected to "settle down" as she grew up. Since scientists now believe bones get stronger in response to weight-bearing exercise, a lifelong lack of vigorous exertion could result in less dense bones.

Bone density—the amount of mineralized bone in a standard measure of space, say a cubic centimeter—also seems to be partly determined by genetics. One study found that the adult daughters of women with postmenopausal osteoporosis had less dense bones than women whose mothers did not have osteoporosis.[4] The effect was stronger for the bones of the spine than for those that make up the hip. A family history is not a sentence to broken bones, though. Each daughter has only half of her mother's genes, and early attention to diet and exercise might help to counteract the legacy. Researchers don't yet

Preventing Osteoporosis

Though none of these is foolproof, the following measures to prevent osteoporosis seem prudent even before menopause:

- Eat calcium-rich foods or take a supplement (1,000–1,200 mg/day).
- Get adequate exercise.
- Maintain normal weight—not too thin.
- Quit smoking or don't start.
- Avoid cortisonelike drugs if possible.
- If blood pressure medicine is needed, ask about a thiazide diuretic.

know how much of a difference this could make.

As important as exercise and calcium may be, a commonly prescribed diuretic may be one of the most effective defenses against bone degeneration and hip fractures. Epidemiologists interested in bone have recently published studies done in the United States[5] and in Canada.[6] They concluded that older people taking thiazide diuretics were over 30 percent less likely to break a hip. The longer they took this blood pressure medication, the lower their risk of fracture. Such results are nothing less than spectacular, especially when you consider how cheap and well-tolerated these drugs are.

Doctors are not prescribing thiazide diuretics as osteoporosis preventers—at least not yet. For one thing, we don't yet know the lowest effective dose of this drug for preserving bone. But it certainly makes sense for anyone whose bones may be growing weaker to consider a thiazide first if they need to take medicine for lowering blood pressure.

Like most other medications, the thiazides have drawbacks as well as advantages. Because they deplete the body of important minerals, blood levels of potassium, at the very least, must be monitored regularly. Additional potassium in the diet from foods or a potassium chloride salt substitute like **NoSalt** or **Nu-Salt** may be a good idea. Thiazides can also raise blood lipid levels while lowering beneficial HDL levels in some people, so periodic cholesterol checks are also a good idea. These drugs can also cause trouble for some individuals with diabetes or gout. The pluses? Generic hydrochlorothiazide is a very widely prescribed drug, so doctors and pharmacists have plenty of experience with it; it is also quite inexpensive; and

Thiazide Diuretics

Anhydron	hydrochlorothiazide
Aquatensen	(generic)
chlorothiazide	**Hygroton**
(generic)	**Hydromox**
chlorthalidone	**Microx**
(generic)	**Metahydrin**
Diucardin	**Naturetin**
Diulo	**Naqua**
Diuril	**Oretic**
Enduron	**Renese**
Esidrix	**Saluron**
Exna	**Thalitone**
Fluidil	**Uridon**
Hydrex	**Zaroxolyn**
HydroDIURIL	

now, the fact that it helps conserve bone and prevent fractures weighs heavily in its favor.

ESTROGEN

Unquestionably, the drug doctors are most likely to prescribe for osteoporosis prevention is estrogen. Natural levels of estrogen circulating in the body affect bone density. Although doctors have often explained bone loss after menopause as due to the lack of estrogen once produced by the ovaries, estrogen levels may fluctuate throughout a woman's life. A history of irregular periods is a good tip-off that estrogen levels may not be normal and bone density may be low.[7] Exercise benefits the skeleton and leads to denser bone, up to a point. But when rigorous exercise and weight loss combine to interfere with normal menstruation, a woman who wants to minimize her risk of developing osteoporosis later needs to back off a bit, ease up on her training regimen or gain a little weight until she is regular once more.

It seems logical, if estrogen protects bone, to have a woman take estrogen after menopause. This is precisely what most experts recommend.[9–13] It is clear by now that a woman taking estrogen from menopause onward doesn't lose bone—or cer-

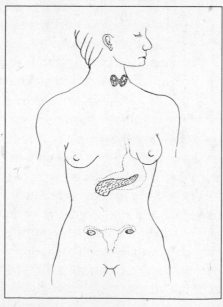

Thiazide diuretics

Blood pressure pills that protect bone; inexpensive. Side effects: Deplete potassium, magnesium, zinc; Raise cholesterol, glucose, and uric acid in blood.

★ ★ ★ ★

tainly doesn't lose it as quickly as she would otherwise. This results in denser bone and fewer hip fractures.[14] Sounds wonderful, doesn't it? If it were just that simple, every woman past menopause should take estrogen. Unfortunately, the estrogen issue is anything but simple. As with almost every therapy for osteoporosis, the experts are duking it out and haven't come up with a consensus. Questions have been raised about the safety of estrogen replacement therapy, and the answers just aren't conclusive.

Here's what we know about estrogen:

- It can prevent bone loss, but it can't build back bone that is already gone.
- Estrogen alone raises high-density lipoprotein ("good" HDL cholesterol) and reduces the risk of heart attack.[15]
- Estrogen alone increases the risk of cancer of the womb.
- Estrogen more than doubles the risk of gallbladder disease.
- Other possible side effects include nausea, breast tenderness, excess facial hair, vaginal yeast infections, headache, dizziness, depression, thinning of scalp hair, and loss of blood sugar control.

Questions about Cancer

What we don't know about estrogen covers at least as much territory. Exactly how dangerous is "unopposed estrogen" (estrogen all by itself) when it comes to cancer of the uterine lining? A woman who has not had a hysterectomy may see her risk of this cancer increase as little as 1.8 times or as much as twenty times over what it would be if she took no estrogen.[16] Estimates vary over such a wide range because the studies don't all agree. Doctors currently try to counteract the risk—however large or small—by prescribing progestin for approximately two weeks out of every month. This appears to cut the chance of endometrial cancer very significantly, but it introduces questions and side effects of its own.

Progestin (**Provera**, **Aygestin**, **Norlutate**, and others) makes some women uncomfortable with breast tenderness, psychological depression, acne, bloating, and symptoms of premenstrual tension.[17] Increased sensitivity to sunburn, rash, insomnia, excess facial hair, and loss of scalp hair are other potential side effects. In addition, some women who thought they'd finally seen the last of pads and tampons at menopause are discouraged to learn that the estrogen-progestin regimen usually triggers monthly bleeding. In addition, progestin has a negative impact on blood lipids, especially HDL cholesterol, and may interfere with the heart attack protection estrogen seems to provide.[18] There is not even complete agreement about the appropriate dose and timing of progestin, with some physicians advocating ten days or more each month of 10 mg **Provera**, for example, while others suggest a longer period, perhaps even every day of the month, at a far lower dose.

The Breast Cancer Brouhaha

The big question mark hovering over both combination estrogen-progestin therapy and estrogen alone is the issue of breast cancer. A number of studies have turned up conflicting or equivocal results. The medical establishment was shaken not long ago by a Swedish study that indicated an increased risk of breast cancer with long-term use of certain postmenopausal estrogens.[19] The researchers speculated that the risk might even increase with the addition of progestin, although they had relatively few cases. That really stirred up the hornets. A swarm of critical letters[20] and a respected gynecologist's analysis[21] pointed out the weaknesses of the study and the fact that other studies on this issue have been equivocal.

There are, no doubt, important differences between Swedish and American prescribing patterns and drugs, and it is usually possible to examine a study carefully and think of some way to do the statistics better. But do we detect a hint of defensiveness behind some of the criticisms? After all,

---

Premarin, Estrace, Feminone, Estinyl, etc.
(estrogen)

Effectively prevents bone loss.

Helps relieve hot flashes and vaginal dryness due to menopause.

May reduce the risk of cardiovascular disease, especially for women who have undergone hysterectomies.

Side effects include increased risk of gallbladder disease, elevated blood pressure, fluid retention, breast tenderness, nausea, vaginal yeast infections, headache, depression, and hair loss. Questions remain about risk.

★ ★

doctors are trying to do the best they can for their patients. Learning that a drug you had prescribed enthusiastically to many patients might raise their risk of suffering from a common cancer would be hard to take indeed. It's too bad that both women and their doctors have been left high and dry, so to speak, because none of the studies done so far has settled this issue definitively. It doesn't help that the same question about a possible increased risk of breast cancer has been raised with respect to oral contraceptives, and the data are no more conclusive in that case.

The Bottom Line

On balance, many responsible doctors feel that a woman at risk of osteoporosis is more likely to suffer pain, life disruption, or even death from a fracture than from breast cancer. After all, one in three white women breaks her hip if she lives long enough; one woman in eleven develops breast cancer at some point in her life. When the doctor recommends estrogen, he is "playing the numbers," but few of us like to feel as though we are gambling with our lives. One of our readers feels betrayed by this approach:

> I had a mastectomy 8 months ago for breast cancer. Prior to that I was on Hormone Replacement Therapy (estrogen patch and progesterone). I feel that the estrogen is what caused my breast cancer. I am 50 years old. My gyn told me it was *perfectly safe* to take and would, in fact, protect me from cancer. I want to trust in my doctors, but I don't have much confidence left. There is no history of breast disease in my family, and I blame the HRT.

Obviously, whether or not to use estrogen replacement therapy after menopause is a decision that requires careful consideration. A woman and her doctor need to discuss her risk factors carefully. Body weight (heavy women are less susceptible to osteoporosis), exercise habits, menstrual history, other conditions and other medications can all enter into the equation, which tends to be more impressionistic than mathematical.

ZOOMING IN ON BONE

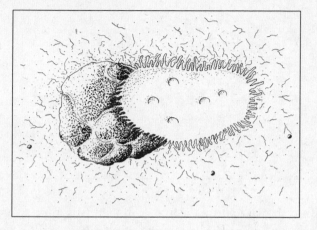

Osteoclast

Other promising treatments for osteoporosis affect bone turnover. It may seem hard and stable, but unlike rock, bone is a dynamic living tissue that is constantly being "remodeled." Cells called osteoblasts build up the framework of tissue strengthened with calcium, magnesium, manganese, boron, and other minerals, while other cells, osteoclasts, help by tearing old bone matrix down (a process called *resorption*). Gregory Mundy, a bone researcher at the University of Texas Health Science Center, imagines the scene from the bone's perspective:

> If you were sitting in an area of bone that is about to be resorbed you would see a giant multinucleated osteoclast settling down like a spaceship. It would send out processes that look like seaweed and then pump acid across this border, leaching the minerals out of the adjacent bone. And in that acid environment, the osteoclast would degrade the remaining protein matrix, leaving a crater just like a crater on the moon.[22]

As sinister as it sounds, this destruction is a necessary part of bone remodeling. Ideally, turnover is balanced, with new tissue formed as old tissue is resorbed, but the emphasis can be shifted one direction or the other by a number of hormones,

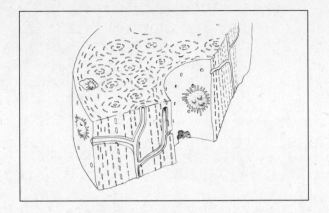

*Close-up of
Bone Tissue*

including thyroid and parathyroid hormones, human growth hormone, calcitonin, glucocorticoids (cortisonelike "stress" hormones), estrogen, progesterone, and vitamin D_3.[23] (In this activated form, "the sunshine vitamin" is indeed a hormone.)

Scientists believe that as we age, turnover becomes unbalanced, with the bone-breakdown crew of osteoclasts working faster than the osteoblasts can build up bone tissue. The solution to this problem seems simple: either boost the builders' activity or find a way to keep a lid on the osteoclasts. Estrogen seems to put the osteoclasts on hold, at least to some extent; thyroid and glucocorticoid drugs like prednisone or dexamethasone appear to put them in high gear. With this close-up view of bone dynamics in mind, researchers are working to develop new treatments in the hopes of reversing tissue loss and rebuilding bone.

OSTEOPOROSIS REVERSAL

Calcitonin

In 1985, the Food and Drug Adminstration approved calcitonin for use in osteoporosis. This medication has been shown to increase the amount of bone in the hip area and to reduce bone resorption.[24] It appears to work by interfering with osteoclast activity, giving osteoblasts the upper hand. In effectiveness, calcitonin seems to be similar to estrogen.[25]

Why isn't calcitonin used more widely? At the present, the only forms of calcitonin available in this country (**Calcimar**, **Miacalcin**, **Cibacalcin**) are given by injection. The injection technique is similar to that used by diabetics for insulin, and was readily mastered by the postmenopausal women in the studies. However, it takes a motivated patient to undertake a daily injection with the prospect of keeping it up for years; consequently, calcitonin has been reserved for women who cannot take estrogen or those whose osteoporosis is already advanced.

A nasal spray form of calcitonin (**Carbicalcin**) was introduced in Italy in 1989, at a recommended dose of two squirts every other day.[26] When editors of *The Lancet*, a British medical journal, look into their crystal ball, they see "the day may not be far off when the handbags of many healthy middle-aged women will contain a nasal spray of calcitonin as well as a lipstick."[27]

Calcitonin is given with calcium and vitamin D supplements: 1200 mg calcium and 400 IU vitamin D each day. Between one-tenth and one-fifth of those using calcitonin will feel nauseous at first, although this reaction usually goes away after a while. Allergic reactions may occur, and while they would normally show up as rashes, anaphylactic shock is a possibility, so the first several doses should be given by health-care providers equipped with epinephrine for rescue. Other possible side effects of calcitonin include frequent urination, flushing, chest pressure, shortness of breath, headaches, dizziness, and itchy ear lobes.

Etidronate—Coherence Therapy

Other medications are also being tested for osteoporosis. One of these, **Didronel** (etidronate), slows osteoclasts down to a crawl, giving bone repair a chance to catch up. It is usually given in spurts or cycles of about two weeks, followed by about three months in which only calcium supplements are taken. During this "off" time, according to theory, bone rebuilding can take place. A recent Danish study demonstrated that women on cyclic etidronate indeed increased their bone mass over a three-year treatment period, and experienced fewer fractures of the spine than the women on placebo.[28]

> ***Calcimar, Cibacalcin, Miacalcin***
> *(calcitonin)*
> Effectively prevents postmenopausal bone loss and may allow bone rebuilding. Must be given by injection. Allergic reaction possible.
>
> ★ ★ ★

In most of the **Didronel** studies conducted in Canada and the United States, there has been an extra step. A different drug—a phosphate—is given first to synchronize cell action. This coherence therapy appears to be associated with fewer spine fractures and increased bone mineral density (approximately 5–10 percent) in a majority of postmenopausal women.[29–31]

The first large-scale American study of **Didronel** against osteoporosis showed that the initial phosphate step is unnecessary and does not increase the effectiveness of the treatment. During the two years of the study, the women on cyclical etidronate had half as many new fractures of the spine as those given placebo. In addition, the medication was associated with a significant increase in the bone mineral density of the vertebrae.[32] There were very few side effects reported by either Danish or American patients. However, etidronate must be given on an empty stomach (one hour before eating or at least two hours afterward), as food interferes with its absorption.[33]

Calcitriol

Because vitamin D is crucial to bone health, both for the formation of the bone tissue and for absorption of calcium from the digestive tract, researchers have looked at vitamin D for clues to osteoporosis treatment. But plain vitamin D, in addition to being toxic, seems to have little effect on osteoporosis. Perhaps this is because the body has difficulty converting it to the active form.

People who get enough sunshine actually manufacture their own vitamin D in their skin, while others require some kind of vitamin D in their diet. (Fish oil and fish are rich in this vitamin; milk is enriched with it.) This vitamin D_3 from food or sun-exposed skin has to go through a two-step change (first in the liver, then in the kidney) before it becomes 1,25-dihydroxy-vitamin D_3, or calcitriol.[34] It is possible that as the kidneys age and function less efficiently, they are less able to produce calcitriol from ordinary vitamin D.

Both calcium alone and vitamin D supplements with calcium have been disappointing as treatments for postmenopausal osteoporosis, perhaps because of this apparent bottleneck in the kidney. In middle-aged men too, daily calcium (1000 mg) and vitamin D (1000 IU) supplements were no better than placebo at slowing bone loss of approximately 2 percent of spinal bone a year.[35]

Is the activated form, calcitriol, more effective? **Rocaltrol** (Nippon Roche's brand of calcitriol) has been approved against osteoporosis in Japan, and calcitriol is also used to treat osteoporosis in New Zealand, Australia and Europe.[36] In the United States, however, tests of calcitriol's ability to increase bone mass and prevent fractures have produced conflicting results.[37,38]

Too much vitamin D in any form can be dangerous, and calcitriol is no exception. It can lead to elevated levels of calcium in the bloodstream, and that might cause difficulty for the kidneys and calcified deposits in soft tissues. Other side effects include nausea, vomiting, constipation, headache, weakness, muscle or bone pain, sleepiness or irritability, liver enzyme changes, lack of appetite and weight loss, high blood pressure, high cholesterol, and heart rate disturbances.

FUTURE PROSPECTS

Apparently, troublesome side effects from calcitriol are more common among people of European extraction than in Japanese patients, so internationally renowned vitamin D expert Dr. Hector DeLuca has come up with a different compound, activated vitamin D_2 (ercalcitriol). He hopes it will prove easier for many Americans to tolerate.[39] Until this compound is thoroughly tested, however, there is no way to tell whether it is either safe or effective.

Researchers are still working on other drugs for osteoporosis as well. Two of **Didronel**'s chemical cousins, pamidronate and tiludronate, are being tested for effectiveness against postmenopausal bone loss.[40, 41] Scientists are also following more distant leads, looking at the calcitonin family of bone-regulating chemicals in the body.[42] Someday one of the prohormones may prove useful for promoting growth and preventing loss of bone tissue. But much more research will be needed before such a drug can be developed.

Calcitriol (Activated vitamin D_3)
Approved against osteoporosis in several foreign countries.
Probably works best together with calcium supplements.
Ability to forestall fractures unproven.
Available by prescription as **Rocaltrol** (oral) and **Calcijex** (injection).

★

Thyroid Therapy

From its unassuming place at the base of the throat, the thyroid gland puts out a couple of powerful proteins. Thyroxine, or T_4, (so called because the molecule contains four atoms of iodine) and its more active sidekick T_3 (with only three iodine atoms) determine how fast the body burns energy. But that sweeping role is just the beginning: thyroid hormone is necessary for cells to respond to growth hormone; it is important in regulating the body's use of calcium; it interacts significantly with estrogen and other female hormones; and it has an impact on emotional well-being. When the thyroid gland goes awry, the symptoms can be wide-ranging and devastating, but hard to pin down.

*Location of
Thyroid Gland*

TOO LITTLE THYROXINE

About one in a hundred Americans ends up with a thyroid gland that has quit functioning properly.[43] Without treatment, they often feel "under the weather," but symptoms like fatigue, constipation, dry skin, or a bit of weight gain are not very specific and may easily be chalked up to a change in lifestyle or the inevitable consequences of growing older. These people may chill easily or bruise readily; women may notice changes in their menstrual pattern.

When Janet was a graduate student working on her dissertation, lots of little things began to bother her. Her apartment always felt cold, so she would wear two or three sweaters and drink innumerable cups of tea to try to stay warm enough. Her husband teased her about having put on a few pounds, and she was annoyed enough to keep track of every calorie for a while. When she discovered that at 800 calories a day, she lost no weight at all, she was more than annoyed—but still not alarmed.

Janet figured that she was having psychological difficulties dealing with her dissertation, and that explained why it was so hard to drag herself out of bed in the morning and why she had so little energy overall. She told herself her dry cracked fingertips were the result of hours pounding typewriter keys—and also washing dishes. (No dishwashers on graduate-student stipends!) She more or less ignored her intermittent constipation, but when her periods became very irregular and unusually heavy, she went to see the doctor.

Doctors say it's a rare patient with all the classic symptoms of hypothyroid. But Janet had enough symptoms to make him suspicious. He ordered a blood test that confirmed Janet's thyroid gland wasn't making enough hormone.

Thyroid Function Tests

Diagnosing a thyroid condition is not a do-it-yourself project. Your doctor will need to take a careful history, asking about symptoms. But pinning down the diagnosis requires blood tests.

Signs of Low Thyroid Activity

fatigue	dry or coarse hair
drowsiness	cold intolerance
weakness	hair loss
constipation	bruising
decreased sweating	puffiness around eyes
slow heartbeat	change in weight (often
shortness of breath while exercising	weight gain)
heavy or long menstrual periods	anemia
swollen tongue	thick, brittle fingernails
loss of outer third of eyebrows	impaired attention,
dry skin	memory, or speech

Most of the thyroid circulating through the body is tightly attached to proteins in the bloodstream. Only a tiny fraction of T_3 and T_4 are independent—"free" or "unbound"—and this is what does the actual work. However, it is difficult to measure these directly. The brain responds to the levels of free thyroid hormone and tells the gland to "make more" or "ease up" with its messenger, thyroid-stimulating hormone (TSH).

Modern technology (an immunoradiometric assay, or IRMA) has brought a new TSH test that makes it easy to measure TSH levels very accurately. This appears to be a more sensitive indicator of thyroid function than the older tests that measure the amount of T_3 or T_4 in the blood.[44] TSH is high if there is not enough thyroid hormone circulating in the body.

There are a number of medications that can interfere with thyroid function tests, so be sure your doctor knows if you are

---

Normal Thyroid Test Values[45]

Total Serum T_4	5–12 mg/dL
Total Serum T_3	80–180 mg/dL
T_3 Uptake	25–35 percent
FT_4I (Free thyroxine index)	4.5–11 mg/dL
Free T_4	1–3 mg/dL
TSH by immunoradiometric assay (IRMA)	0.5–5 mg/dL

Drugs That Alter TSH Tests[47, 48]

Raise Values:	Lower Values:
Antipsychotics	Cortisonelike drugs
Haldol	**prednisone**
Thorazine	Parkinson's disease drugs
Lithium	**Sinemet**
Eskalith	**Parlodel**
Lithane	**Symmetrel**
Lithobid	
Metoclopramide	
Reglan	
Phenylbutazone	
Azolid	
Butazolidin	

taking any of them. Some medications, like the estrogen in birth control pills and postmenopausal replacement therapy, affect only test readings without having any impact on thyroid function. But other medicines, especially lithium, used to treat manic-depressive affective disorder, and the heart drug **Cordarone** (amiodarone) can sometimes suppress the thyroid and cause symptoms of thyroid deficiency.[46]

Pregnancy may also affect thyroid tests, so a doctor needs to take special care in diagnosing a thyroid condition in a pregnant woman. People who are very sick with any serious condition, from pneumonia to liver failure, may show very abnormal results on thyroid tests even though their thyroids are all right. This may be due in part to the stress hormones (glucocorticoids) the body puts out in almost any severe illness,[49] and does not call for treatment.

Treating the Underactive Thyroid

Underactive thyroid glands don't make as much active

Thyroid Therapy for Older People

The risk of thyroid inadequacy increases as people age, but unfortunately, so do the risks of inappropriate therapy. Higher-than-normal levels of thryoid-stimulating hormone (TSH) are relatively common among older people, but don't necessarily signal thyroid failure. Should they be treated? The experts say

Yes, if
- they have symptoms of low thyroid function.
- tests show the immune system is attacking the thyroid (high titers of microsomal autoantibodies).

No, if
- they have heart disease and no other indications.
- they have clinical osteoporosis.

The lowest possible levels of thyroxine should be used for treatment. Thyroxine should not be used to treat
- high cholesterol.
- obesity.
- fatigue not due to thyroid deficiency.

**Thyrotoxicosis
in Older
People** [56]
Most elderly people
with excess thyroid
hormone have
symptoms like
those of younger
patients. Some,
however, show the
following atypical
symptoms:
- apathy
- loss of appetite
- congestive
  heart
  failure
- constipation
- dementia
- depression
- rigidity

thyroid hormone as the body needs, so the logical treatment is to give thyroid. For years, doctors prescribed actual ground-up dried thyroid from cows or pigs. Although these products are still available, natural variability in the animals they come from means variability in the dose from one batch to another. Synthetic T_4, known as levothyroxine (**Synthroid**, **Levothroid**), is effective, consistent, and comes in a wide range of doses.[50]

The variety of doses available, especially of low doses, is very important. People starting thyroid treatment need to begin with a low dose and gradually work their way up to the lowest dose of levothyroxine at which they feel good again. This calls for close cooperation between the doctor and the patient, with testing every four to six weeks while the dose is being established.[51]

It is important to take the lowest amount of thyroid replacement hormone that reverses symptoms, because over the years, too much thyroxine can make people more susceptible to heart disease and can weaken the bones, making osteoporosis more serious. Older people may need less thyroxine than they did in earlier years, especially if they develop heart problems. Taking too much thyroxine can even result in symptoms of thyrotoxicosis (hyperthyroid).

How much thyroxine is appropriate? Doctors now think there is no single dose that is right for everyone, underscoring the importance of this "titrating" phase of testing to see if the prescribed dose has corrected the problem. A target dose of around 1.6 or 1.7 micrograms thyroxine for every kilogram of body weight (around 110 or 115 micrograms daily for an adult weighing 150 pounds) has been suggested,[52,53] but many factors affect dosing. Since most hypothyroid people will have to take thyroxine for the rest of their lives, it makes sense to take the time and effort to establish the proper dose on an individual basis. Certain other medications can interact with thyroxine, and may mean the dose needs to be adjusted even more carefully than usual.

TOO MUCH THYROXINE

As uncomfortable as it can be to have too little thyroid

hormone in the system, it is just as bad to have too much. Thyrotoxicosis, as this condition is called, is in some ways the opposite of the underactive thyroid syndrome. Instead of being easily chilled, a person with too much thyroxine may find it hard to stand hot weather. Her skin may be excessively sweaty rather than dry, and she may suffer from insomnia rather than drowsiness. Nervousness or even severe anxiety may appear.

One thirty-year-old woman had started feeling extremely anxious and afraid to drive eight years earlier, shortly after the birth of her first child. During each subsequent pregnancy she felt much less threatened by the outside world, more at peace with herself, and was better able to function. However, her symptoms returned and worsened with each birth; besides not driving or going out even for grocery shopping, she even refused to go along on the annual family vacation. After delivering her third child, she was even more anxious about leaving her home. However, she also felt lethargic and weak, was losing weight rapidly, and had a visibly enlarged thyroid gland. Although going to the doctor required leaving home and was extremely threatening to her, her family took her to a physician who found she had clear thyrotoxicosis. Treatment resolved her medical problems. At the same time, almost like magic, the agoraphobia disappeared.[55]

Not everyone with agoraphobia suffers from thyrotoxicosis. And not all patients with excess thyroxine coursing through their veins will be handicapped by anxiety. But someone who

---

Drugs that Interact with Thyroid Hormone[54]

Cholybar
  (cholestyramine)

Colestid
  (colestipol)

Coumadin
  (warfarin)

Lanoxin
  (digoxin)

Questran
  (cholestyramine)

Tofranil
  (imipramine)

Signs of Excessive Thyroid Activity

fatigue	palpitations
insomnia	heat intolerance
weakness	agitation
nervousness	change in weight
increased appetite	(often weight loss)
rapid heartbeat	shortness of breath
reduced or absent menstrual periods	eye complaints
frequent bowel movements	loosened fingernails
increased systolic blood pressure	finger tremor
increased sweating	

**Propyl-
thiouracil**

Not a cure for
thyrotoxicosis;
suppresses
thyroxine produc-
tion.
Safer than
methimazole for
pregnant or nursing
mothers.

★

feels very anxious without apparent cause and has some of the other symptoms of thyrotoxicosis might wish to ask his doctor to run the blood tests. The TSH level will be extremely low, maybe undetectable even by the new IRMA test. The doctor may need to do further testing to help him or her decide whether the elevated level of thyroxine is likely to be temporary or permanent, what is causing it, and how to treat it.

Treating Thyrotoxicosis

Treatment depends on the cause for elevated thyroid hormone. If a person has thyroiditis (which can be caused by exposure to iodine, as in X-ray contrast materials), the best approach is often "watch and wait." A beta-blocker such as **Inderal** (propranolol) or **Tenormin** (atenolol) may keep symptoms of rapid heartbeat, tremor, and anxiety under control.[57]

When the thyroid gland is overproducing, treatment can be tricky. The goal is to modulate the amount of thyroid hormone being manufactured so there is neither too little nor too much, but in this instance the doctors' tools are crude. They can remove some of the thyroid tissue surgically; they can try to destroy some of the tissue with radioactive iodine; or they can suppress the gland's function with an antithyroid drug, either propylthiouracil or **Tapazole** (methimazole). Each method has some drawbacks and requires extensive follow-up. Women who must be treated during pregnancy should take propylthiouracil, if possible, rather than **Tapazole**, because it is less likely to cross the placenta and affect the fetus.

Diabetes Dilemmas

We usually think of diabetes mellitus (a term describing abnormal insulin and sugar metabolism) as a disease. In fact, diabetes is several different diseases that produce a similar consequence: In the untreated diabetic, the simple sugar glucose that provides most of the energy for the human body cannot get into the cells that need it, so blood levels of sugar soar. If blood levels are high enough, the kidney can't filter this sugar efficiently, and some gets into the urine. (That, by the way, is how the name diabetes mellitus, which means "sweet-tasting urine," came about, back in the days of the ancient Greeks.) Needless to say, this puts quite a strain on the kidney, and in fact organs throughout the body suffer when blood sugar and insulin aren't kept in the proper balance. Fortunately, patients today don't have to rely on crude measures like tasting or testing the urine. Today's technology makes it possible for people to determine the level of sugar in the blood long before it gets so dangerously high that it shows up in the urine or so low that they feel near collapse.

SELF-MONITORING OF BLOOD GLUCOSE

Regardless of the underlying disease, most diabetes experts now recommend that patients keep track of their own blood glucose. Doctors now believe that the risks of chronic high blood sugar are so serious that even people who don't require insulin injections should be measuring their blood glucose on their own, between doctor visits.[58] They may not need to take a reading as often; after the treatment is stabilized, once a day may be adequate for non-insulin-dependent patients, in contrast to the several times daily needed by a person who must use insulin.

The machines used for self-monitoring of blood glucose all read a chemical reaction of a drop of blood from a finger prick with a specially prepared paper strip. They vary considerably in size, features, and price, with some as small as a ballpoint pen, and others closer in size to a desktop calculator. Some can be operated at a wide range of temperatures, essential to a person who spends much of the working day outside. Some are easier to read than others, and a few even announce the results out loud, for people who have difficulty seeing. Many have a memory for past readings, so that patient or doctor can review the trends over a period of time. Before plunking down what may be considerably more than a hundred dollars, it makes sense to think carefully about what features you need and what machine seems most logical and easiest for you to operate. Talk this over, if you can, with a diabetes educator to get an idea of your options and what is best for you.

Recent tests have consistently shown the **Accu-Chek** (models: bG, II, IIm) device to be reliable.[60–62] However, most experts feel there is little difference clinically in the accuracy of home blood glucose monitors. The most important issues have to do with their use:

1. All such devices should be calibrated in the doctor's office periodically with a known "standard." This minimizes the risk of serious inaccuracy.

2. Learn how to use your equipment. Read the instruction manual, or better yet, get your health-care person to demonstrate. Then make sure that you show them that you can do it, too. Your doctor, nurse, or diabetes educator may ask you to demonstrate your technique from time to time, just to make sure that you are still able to measure your blood sugar accurately.

Picking the Best Monitor[59]

No one machine will work for everyone, so you have to pick out the best one for you. This is no time for a mail-order purchase. You need to actually see, touch, and try the options you are considering. Think about

- How big is it? Will it fit in my shirt pocket or handbag if I'm often on the go?
- How "fussy" is it? Will it still work at my beach cottage with no air conditioning?
- What is the range of blood sugar it will measure? Is this appropriate for my needs?
- Can I do all the steps it requires? Does it feel overwhelming?
- Can I read the results? Are the numbers big enough, and do they have enough contrast?
- Does it offer memory? Do I need a memory feature?
- Is it reliable?
- Are the supplies available?

For advice and assistance in picking out the best machine as well as trouble-shooting later, a diabetes educator is invaluable. If you don't know of one near you, you can contact

American Association of Diabetes Educators
500 N. Michigan Ave., Suite 1400
Chicago, IL 60611

(3) Write your results down, unless your machine has an automatic memory feature. And don't give in to the temptation to put the best "spin" on your readings. If your treatment program isn't working to bring your blood glucose down, your doctor needs to know that so it can be adjusted.

The doctor will probably also order a glycosylated hemoglobin (HbA$_1$) test periodically. This indicates long-term blood glucose control, just as your monitor shows short-term control.

Blood Glucose Goals[63,64]			
Index	Desirable	Acceptable (Type II)	Dangerous
Blood glucose: before meals	70–120 mg/dL	140 mg/dL	over 200 mg/dL
Blood glucose: after meals	140–180 mg/dl	under 200 mg/dL	over 235 mg/dL
Blood glucose: two a.m.	70–120 mg/dL		
Glycosylated hemoglobin	6 percent	8 percent	over 10 percent

DIET AND EXERCISE

No question about it, diet and exercise are the cornerstones of treatment for diabetes. In insulin-dependent diabetes, which occurs when the beta cells of the pancreas are unable to produce any insulin, careful attention to diet is essential for the insulin to work properly and keep blood sugar within normal bounds. Exercise also reduces insulin requirements. Paying attention to diet and to exercise can help stabilize blood sugar and help insulin-dependent diabetics feel better if they are careful with self-monitoring. An exercise program can also encourage young people to improve their self-monitoring and glucose control.[65]

In so-called type II diabetes, in which body tissues do not respond normally to insulin by taking up sugar, diet is often the first prescription.[66] Dietary tactics alone work for type II diabetes for about one person in ten; the others require further therapy in addition to diet.

Exercise also offers benefits in type II diabetes; one thirty-minute exercise session can lower blood sugar for several hours, and regular exercise can improve glucose handling noticeably.[67] Another consideration is weight loss. Many type II diabetics are overweight, and sometimes losing ten or twenty pounds can decrease insulin resistance and improve blood-sugar levels.[68] Anyone who's ever tried to lose weight by dieting knows it's not easy. Exercise may help with weight loss, offers better blood-sugar handling immediately, and may provide long-term cardiovascular benefits as well. But exercise without attention to diet can precipitate a low blood glucose (hypoglycemic) reaction—a terrifying situation that requires extra calories to reverse it.

What to Eat

Despite the fact that diet is key to the diabetic's health regimen, there is an enormous amount of controversy over the appropriate diet. Some of the conventional diabetic commandments, like "avoid sugar," seem to make sense but haven't been thoroughly tested on diabetics. According to Dr. Joyce Wise, a pediatrician at the University of Illinois, "Many patients think that as long as they don't eat sugar, they can eat anything they want." She conducted a very small, preliminary trial that suggests sugar may not be as dangerous as has been thought. Camp counselors with type I diabetes were split into two groups. One was allowed two snacks per day of treats such as "real" cookies and ice cream, while the others had snacks sweetened with aspartame. At the end of one week, both groups had improved blood glucose control, with no significant differences between them.[69] Dr. Wise thinks average blood sugar readings probably dropped for these young people because they were monitoring more frequently, taking greater care figuring out how much insulin they'd need, and getting more exercise.

It is astonishing that researchers still haven't figured out how much carbohydrate is optimal in the diabetic diet, considering that doctors have been arguing over this at least since the late eighteenth century.[70] Current recommendations stress unrefined carbohydrates associated with fiber, found in foods such as fruits, vegetables, whole grains, and beans. The American Diabetes Association advises diabetics to get 60 percent of their daily calories from these carbohydrate-rich sources.

But while this may work well in the case of type I diabetes, scientists like Ann M. Coulston of Stanford University question whether it is the most appropriate diet for insulin-resistant type II diabetes: "When patients who have non-insulin-dependent diabetes are given this so-called 'good' diet, they have marked increases in triglycerides and a significant decrease in HDL cholesterol. And in patients with diabetes, a rise in triglycerides is associated with an increased risk of cardiovascular disease."[71] Coulston and a few other diabetic-diet renegades believe that people with type II diabetes would do better on a regimen getting only 40-45 percent of its calories from carbohydrates. Such a diet would also include 15–20 percent of calories from protein. It could get as much as 35–40 percent of calories from fat—not bad-guy cholesterol- and triglyceride-raising saturated fat, but primarily monounsaturated fats, like those found in olive oil.[72]

It may be splitting hairs to quibble about the proportion of calories derived from carbohydrates or proteins, in any event. Within the past several years, scientists have found that some foods don't have the expected effect on blood sugar. Just to complicate matters even more, the way foods are cooked seems to affect their propensity to make blood sugar soar. Moreover, eating a food all by itself can have a different impact from eating the same food in combination with others, in a meal.

The best advice: Eat sensibly, not dogmatically. Keep track of your blood sugar and how you respond to certain foods. If certain kinds of meals have a negative impact on your blood sugar, keep them to a minimum. For help in figuring out how to plan meals that fit your recommended diet, it might be worthwhile to consult a registered dietitian.

When to Eat

One of the most important questions for the type I diabetic is "When do we eat?" People who must use insulin to control blood sugar have to take their meals and snacks at regular predictable times to maximize the effectiveness of the insulin

The Olive Oil Bonus

A large study by the Italian National Research Council found that olive oil consumption was associated with lower blood levels of cholesterol and glucose, as well as lower systolic blood pressure, in nondiabetic men and women.[73] If this holds up for diabetics as well, it should be good news indeed.

and minimize the possibility of blood sugar dropping too low.[74]

Type II diabetics who are not using insulin do not usually need to be quite as punctual at the dinner table. In fact, there is a possibility that they should avoid sitting down for a classic big dinner. Instead, they may benefit from spreading their day's calories out over a multitude of small snacks every few hours. Healthy volunteers who ate seventeen snacks a day (one every waking hour or so) made less insulin and had lower serum insulin levels than other study volunteers eating the exact same number of calories, from the same food sources, in the traditional three meals a day.[75] Whether or not people with type II diabetes will experience the same benefits remains to be studied. Trying to snack every hour is time-consuming and inconvenient; but if a "grazing" pattern proves to be an advantage for insulin-resistant diabetics, it may be worth considering eating six or eight tiny meals a day instead of two or three big ones. The biggest pitfall, of course, could be going overboard and eating a lot more calories a little bit at a time.

Dietary Supplements

Certain minerals are sometimes recommended as possible diabetes-fighters. Although a number of elements are crucial in the manufacture of insulin and others may have an impact on insulin resistance, there is unfortunately no solid evidence suggesting that any mineral can reverse diabetes. However, it is possible that adequate chromium in the diet might delay the development of type II diabetes in susceptible individuals. In several studies, chromium supplements have been associated with improved glucose tolerance in nondiabetic people, both old and young.[76] There is no evidence that chromium can counteract diabetes once the disease sets in, but there's also no reason why a diabetic who is monitoring blood glucose on a regular basis should be discouraged from taking chromium supplements. The diets of many Americans are low in this essential element, and supplements of 50–200 micrograms (μg) daily are considered safe. One of the best dietary sources of chromium is brewer's yeast.

Magnesium is of some interest to diabetics, because it is

crucial to the metabolism of glucose. No studies suggest that magnesium supplements have any impact on insulin requirements or glucose tolerance, though, and a balanced diet that includes plenty of green vegetables, seafood, meat, and dairy products should supply most of the 300–350 mg of magnesium needed every day. Regular exercisers may lose more magnesium and more chromium than other people and could benefit from supplements.

Manganese is sometimes suggested as a supplement for diabetics because when animals are kept on a very low manganese diet, they develop blood sugar disturbances. This does not seem to be relevant to the development of diabetes in humans, however, and there's no evidence that manganese supplements would benefit diabetic people more than anyone else. The National Research Council of the National Academy of Science has concluded that 2.5–5 mg of manganese daily is a safe and adequate intake for adults.

Vanadium in the form of vanadate has aroused interest because in some laboratory animals it can counteract chemically induced diabetes. According to Dr. Sheldon Hendler, however, "Recommendation of vanadium to treat glucose intolerance and elevated cholesterol at this time is inappropriate and unacceptable."[77]

> **Vanadate**
> Claims for benefit in diabetes unproven. May provoke manic-depression in susceptible individuals. Not recommended.

DRUGS FOR DIABETES

Insulin

Even with careful attention to diet and exercise, the vast majority of diabetics require some medication to keep blood sugar under control. For approximately ten percent of the diabetics diagnosed every year, there is no substitute for life-saving insulin. Beta cells in their pancreas have been destroyed, and their bodies can't make any insulin. These people have no choice but to learn to inject themselves with insulin on schedule, monitor their blood sugar several times a day, and adjust food intake and exercise accordingly. It may take some time and close cooperation among doctor, patient, and diabetes educator to work out the proper balance of short-, medium-, and long-acting insulins. The possibility of blood sugar dropping too low early in the morning before breakfast time may require blood sugar monitoring at two or three a.m.

The goal is to avoid wide swings of blood glucose, either too high or too low. Doctors now believe that repeated blood sugar peaks high above normal are largely responsible for the serious long-term complications, especially kidney damage, that can occur in diabetes. One study has shown that poor long-term blood-sugar control is the major factor in the development of diabetic kidney failure and the second most important factor (after duration of diabetes) in the development of diabetic retinopathy.[78]

Because insulin must be injected rather than given by mouth, many patients have welcomed the innovation of the insulin "pen." This looks more like a ballpoint pen than a syringe, and it makes the injection process easier. It requires the same dedication to self-monitoring of blood glucose, however, to be able to adjust the amount of insulin injected two, three, or four times a day. It is not a magic wand that will allow any diabetic to ignore diet and exercise with impunity.[80]

Oral Diabetes Drugs

The person who still has beta cells functioning in the pancreas may benefit from a medicine that makes beta cells more sensitive to glucose, so they release more insulin. Such a drug may also make tissues more sensitive to insulin, and reduce the amount of insulin the liver pulls from the bloodstream.[82] These drugs include both fairly old agents, including **Orinase** (tolbutamide), **Dymelor** (acetohexamide), **Tolinase** (tolazamide), and **Diabinese** (chlorpropamide), and two relatively recent arrivals, **Glucotrol** (glipizide) and **DiaBeta** or **Micronase** (glyburide). None of these medications is appropriate for a person who is allergic to sulfa drugs, as they all have a sulfa component.

Probably because it can be given once a day, **Diabinese**

(chlorpropamide) is more widely prescribed than the other "old" oral hypoglycemics, as these drugs are called. Unfortunately, however, serious side effects are more common on chlorpropamide,[83] and it should not be used by anyone whose kidneys are not functioning properly.[84] Both chlorpropamide and tolbutamide interact adversely with a variety of other medications.[85]

Many doctors are turning to the newer and more potent medications, **Micronase** or **DiaBeta** (glyburide) and **Glucotrol** (glipizide). Both may be given on a once- or twice-a-day schedule, and either should be taken fifteen to thirty minutes before meals for maximum absorption and effectiveness.[86] High blood sugar (hyperglycemia) interferes with the absorption and efficacy of these medications,[87] but blood sugar is likely to be at its lowest shortly before a meal. Perhaps because glyburide is eliminated from the body more slowly, it is almost twice as likely as glipizide to cause a life-threatening low blood sugar reaction, although such an event is rare on either of these medicines.[88]

Herbs

Blood glucose should be closely monitored by any diabetic using herbal medications for any purpose, because some herbs can have an impact on blood sugar and may alter a person's requirement for insulin or an oral diabetes drug. Glucomannan, for example, is found in a variety of herbal preparations purported to promote weight loss. Although its effectiveness at reducing appetite or speeding weight loss is unproven, this soluble fiber derived from konjak tubers has been shown to lower average fasting blood-sugar levels in diabetics and improve glucose tolerance in nondiabetic people. The word from the experts: "Glucomannan use is associated with a reduction in the need for hypoglycemic agents, and the product may result in a loss of glycemic control in diabetic patients. It should be used [only] with great care by diabetic patients."[89]

Another herb that appears to have hypoglycemic power is Gymnema. Animal studies on Gymnema extracts show that it can lower blood sugar in artificially induced diabetes. It prob-

Glucotrol
(glipizide)
May offer blood-sugar control when older oral drugs can't.
Less likely than other oral hypoglycemics to react with drugs for other conditions. Lower likelihood of severe hypoglycemia.

★ ★ ★

ably acts in a manner similar to the oral diabetes drugs, but unlike them, dose is variable and safety for humans has not been thoroughly tested.[90] Any diabetic person taking this traditional Ayurvedic medicine (found in "tribang shila") would be well-advised to monitor blood glucose carefully.

Some European herbal preparations marketed for the treatment of diabetes contain lavender oil. Animal studies suggest that it may have some effectiveness in lowering blood sugar, at least when the pancreas contains active beta cells.[91] Safety has not been well-studied; in small quantities to flavor food or scent cosmetics, it has traditionally been used without any noticeable problems. But we can't recommend its use for the treatment of diabetes unless the person with mild type II diabetes were willing to undertake the kind of intensive blood-sugar monitoring that is usually associated with more severe disease.

STRESS CONTROL FOR BETTER BLOOD-GLUCOSE LEVELS

Stress gets blamed for a lot of ills these days. It may not always deserve its nasty reputation, as some people seem to thrive on high-pressure jobs or risky hobbies. But when it comes to diabetes, stress is a bad actor. Doctors have long known that the physiological stress of illness can throw a serious monkey wrench into the balance of insulin and blood sugar. Psychological stress can also exact a high price.[92]

Dr. Richard Surwit at Duke University has shown that people who undergo biofeedback-guided relaxation training have better control over blood glucose. And although we're generally very cautious about recommending antianxiety agents, Dr. Surwit has found that short-term use of benzodiazepines like **Xanax** (alprazolam) can also temporarily improve glucose tolerance. But there are dangers to long-term use of such drugs and it is unlikely that the benefits will outweigh the risks.

There are many ways to deal with excessive psychological stress other than **Valium** or **Xanax**, of course. Some people find exercise most helpful, while others swear by a hot bath or listening to music. If you haven't yet found your own best stress-fighter, relaxation tapes or training may help.

FUTURE DEVELOPMENTS

Even without the invention of brand-new drugs, the treatment of diabetes is changing. Intensive early therapy of newly diagnosed diabetics, now being studied in several medical centers, may provide ways to slow the progression of the disease. For type II diabetics, the experimental approach focuses on severe caloric restriction under strict supervision.

For type I diabetics, however, such an approach would be disastrous. Early treatment has focused on attempts to preserve the insulin-producing beta cells, with a short course of very high-dose insulin therapy[93] or with **Sandimmune** (cyclosporine), a drug that suppresses the immune system and reportedly saves the beta cells from attack.[94–96] Because of the inherent risks of both these therapies, they may continue to be confined to high-tech medical centers.

Changes in insulin therapy probably lie ahead. Recent reports suggest that a synthetic insulinlike chemical (B9AspB27Glu) may actually work more like insulin in diabetics than human insulin does.[97] The technique of giving insulin may also be improved. Most people don't like shots very much, although diabetics who use insulin must inject themselves regularly, often several times a day, carefully rotating injection sites to avoid complications. It may be possible that in the future patients won't have to use injections, for insulin may become available in a nasal spray or even in a pill covered with a protective coating that prevents it from being digested in the stomach or small intestine, yet allows it to be absorbed into the bloodstream from the large intestine.[98] Don't hold your breath, however, as these forms of insulin are not likely to show up on drugstore shelves anytime soon. What may appear sooner is an implantable insulin delivery device with a glucose sensor attached, for continuous self-correcting adjustment of the quantity of insulin released.[99]

One drug that may well be approved within the next few years is metformin, which is already available in parts of Europe and in Canada and Mexico. It is an oral diabetes drug that increases the action of insulin. Unlike the current diabetes medications, metformin does not lead to weight gain. It also helps to improve levels of cholesterol and other blood fats and lowers glycosylated hemoglobin levels, suggesting good long-term blood-glucose control. It also offers some promise in combination with current oral medications when one is only partly effective at bringing blood sugar under control.[100]

Other medications under development include midaglizole, currently in clinical trials for its ability to stimulate beta cells to produce more insulin. A number of drugs that interfere with carbohydrate digestion and absorption are also being tested: acarbose, emiglitate, and miglitol. Acarbose has been better studied, and seems to improve blood-sugar control in about half of the type II diabetics who have taken it. The price, however, is flatulence and other gastrointestinal symptoms.[101] Researchers are just beginning to study medications that prevent the body from turning fatty acids into glucose. Drugs with an impact on fat metabolism, etomoxir and acipimox, will have to be thoroughly tested to determine their effectiveness and potential toxicity.[102]

Alredase (tolrestat) is already awaiting approval by the FDA, not because it improves blood-sugar control, but because it seems to prevent the formation of biochemicals that might be responsible for diabetic complications such as retinopathy and neuropathy. Unfortunately, although **Alredase** appears to be reasonably safe, there is no good evidence yet that it can actually prevent the development of these serious consequences of the disease.[103]

Another interesting diabetes development comes from a small startup company, Geritech, in Northvale, New Jersey. It has convinced a huge Japanese firm, Yamanouchi Pharmaceutical, to underwrite trials of its new medication aminoguanidine. Results in animals are promising, but it will be several years before we know if this compound actually will reduce the complications of diabetes and retard aging.

The most exciting advance for diabetics would be the possibility of supplying new insulin-producing cells. Fetal tissue research, if it proceeds, may someday offer type I diabetics the possibility of beta-cell transplants without immunological markers. (This would make the new cells "invisible" to the

immune system marauders that destroyed the person's original beta cells.) Another possibility is that genetic engineering
may enable other, nonbeta, cells to produce insulin when
transplanted into the body. This technology has already been
smoothed out before it's ready for humans: some of the newly
transplanted insulin-producing cells kept on pouring out the
hormone indefinitely, and a few of the experimental mice died
of low blood sugar.[104]

Quick Takes

- Both men and women are susceptible to osteoporosis as they
  age. Preventive strategies include lifelong adequate calcium
  intake, weight-bearing exercise, avoidance of smoking and
  cortisonelike drugs, and use of thiazide diuretics if high
  blood pressure requires medication.

- A history of irregular periods suggests low estrogen levels.
  Replacement estrogen can delay bone loss in postmenopausal women; it also helps protect against heart attack.
  However, it increases the risk of endometrial cancer, and its
  impact on breast cancer risk is not yet clear.

- Etidronate given in cycles and calcitonin work as well as
  estrogen at preventing bone loss. All three medications are
  most effective in combination with calcium (1000–1200 mg/
  day) and vitamin D (400 IU/day), but calcium supplements
  may interfere with etidronate absorption and should not
  be taken at the same time.

- Activated vitamin D has been approved in Australia, New
  Zealand, Japan, and several other countries for treatment of
  osteoporosis, but clinical trials in the United States do not
  indicate a strong protective effect against fractures.

- Excess thyroid hormone can weaken bones. Those who
  need thyroid replacement therapy should take the lowest
  effective dose.

- Synthetic levothyroxine (**Levothroid** or **Synthroid**) is reliable, relatively inexpensive, and effective for treatment of the hypothyroid condition.

- Too much thyroid hormone is as bad as too little; it may cause psychological problems like agoraphobia as well as physical symptoms such as weakness, rapid heartbeat, shortness of breath, fatigue, or insomnia.

- Good control of diabetes often calls for self-monitoring of blood-sugar levels. A blood-glucose monitor for home use should go through a hands-on trial before selection. Mail-order savings don't make sense in this case.

- Diet and exercise are the key to good treatment for all diabetics. In type I diabetics, proper diet and appropriate exercise can maximize insulin effectiveness and minimize the dose needed. Many type II diabetics could control their blood sugar with close attention to good diet and daily exercise.

- Fat, especially saturated fat, may be as dangerous for diabetics as sugar. Frequent small meals and the use of olive oil instead of butter or cheese may help control blood-sugar and cholesterol levels. Type I diabetics must coordinate the timing of meals with insulin administration.

- Chromium (50–200 micrograms daily) may delay the onset of type II diabetes.

- The insulin pen offers convenience for diabetics who require injections several times a day. For more information, contact: Squibb-Novo, Box 4000, Princeton, NJ 08540. (**NovoPen** and **NovolinPen**) or Owen Mumford Mfg., Ulster Scientific, Inc., P.O. Box 902, Highland, NY 12528 (**Accupen**).

- Stress may aggravate blood sugar problems. Meditation, relaxation, or short-term use of antianxiety drugs such as **Xanax** may help at a particularly difficult point.

References

[1] Williams, T. Franklin. "Editorial: Osteoporosis and Hip Fractures: Challenges to Investigators and Clinicians." *JAMA* 1990; 263:708.

[2] Rudy, David R. "Osteoporosis: Overcoming a costly and debilitating disease." *Postgraduate Medicine* 1989; 86:151–158.

[3] Cummings, Steven R., et al. "Appendicular Bone Density and Age Predict Hip Fracture in Women." *JAMA* 1990; 263:665–668.

[4] Seeman, Ego, et al. "Reduced Bone Mass in Daughters of Women with Osteoporosis." *N. Engl. J. Med.* 1989; 320:554–558.

[5] LaCroix, Andrea Z., et al. "Thiazide Diuretic Agents and the Incidence of Hip Fracture." *N. Engl. J. Med.* 1990; 322:286–290.

[6] Ray, Wayne A., et al. "Long-Term Use of Thiazide Diuretics and Risk of Hip Fracture." *Lancet* 1989; 1:687–690.

[7] Drinkwater, Barbara L., et al. "Menstrual History as a Determinant of Current Bone Density in Young Athletes." *JAMA* 1990; 263:545–548.

[8] Hendler, Sheldon Saul. *TheVitamin and Mineral Encyclopedia*. New York: Simon & Schuster, 1990, p. 306.

[9] Baran, Daniel. "Diagnosis and Management of Osteoporosis." *Modern Medicine* 1989; 57:114–118.

[10] Licata, Angelo A. "New Ideas in Diagnosis and Treatment of Osteoporosis." *Modern Medicine* 1987; 55:95–102.

[11] Ravnikar, Veronica. "A Strategy for the Management of Osteoporosis." *Modern Medicine* 1988; 56:62–69.

[12] Rudy, op. cit. p. 155.

[13] Tessler, Sandra Rubin. "Call for Building, Preserving Bone Mass Intensifies." *Med. World News* 1988(June 27); 26–28.

[14] Keil, Douglas P., et al. "Hip Fracture and the Use of Estrogens in Postmenopausal Women: The Framingham Study." *N. Engl. J. Med.* 1987; 317:1169–1174.

[15] Bush, Trudy, et al. "How ERT Affects Heart Disease." *Patient Care* 1989(May 30); 67–82.

[16] Charles, Allan G. "Estrogen Replacement after Menopause. When is it Warranted?" *Postgraduate Medicine* 1989; 85:101.

[17] Ibid.

[18] Bush, op. cit. p. 80.

[19] Bergkvist, Leif, et al. "The Risk of Breast Cancer after Estrogen and Estrogen-Progestin Replacement." *N. Engl. J. Med.* 1989; 321:293–297.

[20] "Breast Cancer and Estrogen Replacement." (Six letters and reply) *N. Engl. J. Med.* 1990; 322:201–204.

[21] Speroff, Leon. "Breast Cancer and Postmenopausal Hormone Therapy." *Contemporary Ob/Gyn* 1990; 35:71–82.

[22] Barnes, Deborah M. "Close Encounters with an Osteoclast." *Science* 1987; 236:914–916.

[23] Morrison, Nigel A., et al. "1,25-Dihydroxyvitamin D-Responsive Element and Glucocorticoid Repression in the Osteocalcin Gene." *Science* 1989; 246:1158–1161.

[24] Gruber, Helen E., et al. "Long-Term Calcitonin Therapy in Post-menopausal Osteoporosis." *Metabolism* 1984; 33:295–303.

[25] MacIntyre, I., et al. "Calcitonin for Prevention of Postmenopausal Bone Loss." *Lancet* 1988;1:900–902.

[26] Product News in Brief. "SK&F Introduces Carbicalcin Nasal Spray in Italy." *Scrip* 1989; 1459:30.

[27] Editorial. "Calcitonin." *Lancet* 1989; 2:1409.

[28] Storm, Tommy, et al. "Effect of Intermittent Cyclical Etidronate Therapy on Bone Mass and Fracture Rate in Women with Postmeno-pausal Osteoporosis." *N. Engl. J. Med.* 1990; 322(18):1265–1271.

[29] Hodsman, A. B. "Effects of Cyclical Therapy for Osteoporosis Using an Oral Regimen of Inorganic Phosphate and Sodium Etidronate: A

Clinical and Bone Histomorphometric Study." *Bone Miner* 1989; 5:201–212.

[30] Horwitz, Nathan. "In Open Trial, 76% Amass Bone—Gains of Up to 10%." *Med. Tribune* 1988; 29(35):6.

[31] Mallette, L.E., et al. "Cyclic Therapy of Osteoporosis with Neutral Phosphate and Brief, High-Dose Pulses of Etidronate." *J. Bone Miner. Res.* 1989; 4:143–148.

[32] Watts, Nelson B., et al. "Intermittent Cyclical Etidronate Treatment of Postmenopausal Osteoporosis." *N. Engl. J. Med.* 1990; 323(2):73–79.

[33] Ibid. p. 79.

[34] Mallette et al., op. cit. p. 317.

[35] Orwoll, E.S., et al. "The Rate of Bone Mineral Loss in Normal Men and the Effects of Calcium and Cholecalciferol Supplementation." *Ann. Intern. Med.* 1990; 112:29–34.

[36] "Calcitriol's osteoporosis approval." *Scrip* 1989; 1456:26.

[37] Gallagher, J.C., et al. "The Effect of Calcitriol on Patients with Postmenopausal Osteoporosis with Special Reference to Fracture Frequency." *Proc. Soc. Experimental Biol. and Med.* 1989; 191(3):287–292.

[38] Ott, Susan M., and Chesnutt, Charles H., III. "Calcitriol Treatment Is Not Effective in Postmenopausal Osteoporosis." *Ann. Internal Medicine* 1989; 110:267–274.

[39] Bishop, Jerry E. "New Vitamin D Undergoes Human Osteoporosis Tests." *Wall Street Journal,* August 14, 1989, B3.

[40] Reginster, J.Y., et al. "Prevention of Postmenopausal Bone Loss by Tiludronate." *Lancet* 1989; 2:1469–1471.

[41] "Pamidronate—'a major step forward.' " *Scrip* 1989; 1438:22.

[42] Cotton, Paul. "Peptide Portions May Hold Key to Amplifying Bone against Porosis." *JAMA* 1990; 263:621.

[43] Salman, Karl, et al. "Selection of Thyroid Preparations." *American Family Physician* 1989; 40:215–219.

[44] Bansal, Sudhir. "A New TSH Assay." *Postgraduate Medicine* 1989; 86:98.

[45] Hershman, Jerome M., et al. "Getting the Most from Thyroid Tests." *Patient Care* 1989(Apr. 30); 88.

[46] Hamburger, Joel I., and Kaplan, Michael M. "Hypothyroidism: Don't Treat Patients Who Don't Have It." *Postgraduate Medicine* 1989; 86:72.

[47] Bansal, op. cit.

[48] "Effects of Drugs on Thyroid Function Tests." *Medical Letter* 1981; 23:31.

[49] Felicetta, James V., "Effects of Illness on Thyroid Function Tests." *Postgraduate Medicine* 1989; 85:213–220.

[50] Salman et al., op. cit. p. 217.

[51] Ibid., p. 219.

[52] Sakiyama, Roland. "Common Thyroid Disorders." *American Family Physician* 1988; 38:227–238.

[53] Salman, et al., op. cit. p. 218.

[54] Covington, Timothy R. "Patient Information: Thyroid Hormones." *Facts & Comparisons Drug Newsletter* 1989; 8:39.

[55] Emanuele, Mary Ann, et al."Agoraphobia and Hyperthyroidism." *Am. J. Med.* 1989; 86:484–486.

[56] Sakiyama, op. cit. p. 229.

[57] Ibid. p. 230.

[58] Cohen, Margo P., et al. "Glycemic Control in Type II Diabetes." *Patient Care* 1988(Sept. 30); 47–66.

[59] Peggy Yarborough, R.Ph., M.S., C.D.E. Personal communication.

[60] Clarke, W.L., et al. "Evaluating Clinical Accuracy of Systems for Self-Monitoring of Blood Glucose." *Diabetes Care* 1987; 10:622–628.

[61] Koschinsky, T., et al. "New Approach to Technical and Clinical Evaluation of Devices for Self-Monitoring of Blood Glucose." *Diabetes Care* 1988; 11:619–629.

[62] North, D.S., et al. "Home Monitors of Blood Glucose: Comparison of Precision and Accuracy." *Diabetes Care* 1987; 10:360–366.

[63] Cohen et al., op. cit. p. 49.

[64] Spencer, Martha. "Type I Diabetes." *Postgraduate Medicine* 1989; 85:201–209.

[65] Marrero, D., et al. "Improving Compliance with Exercise in Adolescents with Insulin-Dependent Diabetes Mellitus: Results of a Self-Motivated Home Exercise Program." *Pediatrics* 1988; 81:519–525.

[66] Hollander, Priscilla. "Type II Diabetes." *Postgraduate Medicine* 1989; 85:211–222.

[67] Medical Meeting Digest. "Exercise Improves Glucose Disposal in Type II Diabetics." *Modern Med.* 1988(May); 56:41.

[68] Hollander, op. cit. p. 217.

[69] Bankhead, Charles D. "Diabetics Do Fine on Sugar Snacks in Short-Term Trial." *Med. World News* 1989(Aug. 14); 50.

[70] Gwynne, John T., and Richardson, Lyn. "The Carbohydrate Controversy: An Overview." *Modern Medicine* 1989(June); 57:97.

[71] Fackelmann, K.A. "High-Carbohydrate Diet May Pose Heart Risks." *Science News* 1989; 136:185.

[72] Ibid.

[73] Trevisan, Maurizio, et al. "Consumption of Olive Oil, Butter, and Vegetable Oils and Coronary Heart Disease Risk Factors." *JAMA* 1990; 263:688–692.

[74] Gwynne, John T., and Richardson, Lyn. "The Role of Nutrition in the Management of Diabetes." *Modern Medicine* 1989(June); 57:94–100.

[75] Jenkins, David J.A., et al. "Nibbling versus Gorging: Metabolic Advantages of Increased Meal Frequency." *N. Engl. J. Med.* 1989; 321:929–934.

[76] Hendler, op cit. p. 125.

[77] Ibid., p. 195.

[78] Chase, H. Peter, et al."Glucose Control and the Renal and Retinal Complications of Insulin-dependent Diabetes." *JAMA* 1989; 261:1155–1160.

[79] Mullen, Lucy, and Hollander, Priscilla. "A Practical Guide to Using Insulin." *Postgraduate Medicine* 1989; 85:227–232.

[80] Editorial. "Insulin Pen: Mightier than Syringe?" *Lancet* 1989; 1:307–308.

[81] Molitch, Mark E. "Diabetes Mellitus: Control and Complications." *Postgraduate Medicine* 1989; 85:182–194.

[82] Gerich, John E. "Oral Hypoglycemic Agents." *N. Engl. J. Med.* 1989; 321:1231–1245.

[83] Ibid. p. 1236.

[84] Garber, Alan J., and Huffman, David M. "Sulfonylureas: New Therapeutic Approaches to the Management of Diabetes Mellitus." *Modern Medicine* 1988(April); 56:58–69.

[85] Ibid. p. 60.

[86] Ibid.

[87] Groop, Leif C., et al. "Hyperglycaemia and Absorption of Sulphonylurea Drugs." *Lancet* 1989; 2:129–130.

[88] Gerich, op. cit. p. 1237.

[89] "Glucomannan." *Lawrence Review of Natural Products.* St. Louis: Facts & Comparisons, 1986.

[90] "Gymnema." *Lawrence Review of Natural Products.* St. Louis: Facts & Comparisons, 1989.

[91] "Lavender." *Lawrence Review of Natural Products*. St. Louis: Facts & Comparisons,1989.

[92] Minuchin, Salvador, et al. *Psychosomatic Families*. Cambridge, Mass.: Harvard University Press, 1978, pp. 23–29.

[93] "Beta-Cell Break Benefits Diabetics." *Science News* 1989; 135:156.

[94] Kahan, Barry D. "Cyclosporine." *N. Engl. J. Med.* 1989; 321:1725–1738.

[95] Bougneres, P.F., et al. "Factors Associated with Early Remission of Type I Diabetes in Children Treated with Cyclosporine." *N. Engl. J. Med.* 1988; 318:663–670.

[96] Rosenberg, Stuart A., et al. "Advances in the Management of Type I (Insulin-Dependent) Diabetes Mellitus." *Modern Med.* 1988(Feb.); 56:51–53.

[97] Kang, Steven, et al. "Comparison of Insulin Analogue B9AspB27Glu and Soluble Human Insulin in Insulin-Treated Diabetes." *Lancet* 1990; 335:303–306.

[98] Saffran, Murray, et al. "A New Approach to the Oral Administration of Insulin and Other Peptide Drugs." *Science* 1986; 233:1081–1084.

[99] Feinglos, Mark, MD. Personal communication.

[100] Bankhead, Charles D. "Options and Optimism Growing: Type 2 Diabetes." *Med. World News* 1989(Oct. 9); 35–40.

[101] Ibid.

[102] Ibid.

[103] "Tolrestat." *Drug Facts and Comparisons*. St. Louis: J.B. Lippincott, 1990, p. 2476.

[104] Rosenberg, op. cit. p. 53.

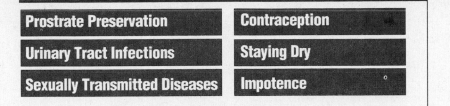

Plumbing Problems

9

Chances are you don't pay much attention to the plumbing at your house—at least, not unless the pipes shudder and knock when you turn off the water, or the toilet overflows, or no water comes out when you turn the faucet. Just like your household plumbing, your personal plumbing may not really get your attention unless something goes wrong. The difference between the two is that your plumbing often hurts when something is wrong. With both, however, delaying a needed service call can lead to more problems and get very costly.

For our purposes, plumbing comes in two types—reproductive and urinary. Each type has two models—male and female. In some cases, men and women get exactly the same problems, but often their plumbing problems are distinctive. Let's start by taking a look at one that almost all men face eventually and women can never have.

Prostate Preservation

At last there is good news about the prostate. Since this gland is enlarged in half or more of the men over the age of fifty,[1] a new drug capable of preventing prostatic overgrowth will be welcome indeed. In many men, prostate enlargement causes discomfort and eventually requires treatment—usually surgery. In an average year more than four hundred thousand prostate operations are performed; Medicare alone shells out more than $1 billion annually to the nation's urologists for their surgical efforts,[2] and prostate resections are the most common operation on men over the age of sixty-five.[3]

PROSTATE BASICS

In a boy the prostate gland, which surrounds the urethra (the tube that carries urine out of the bladder), is the size of an almond. As he grows, so does the prostate, reaching the size of a walnut in a young man. However, though everything else stops growing, the prostate keeps on slowly getting bigger, especially from the mid-thirties on. What was once a walnut-sized organ may swell to the size of a lemon or an orange. (Prostate researchers, for reasons undetermined, are very big on citrus fruit comparisons.) In really extreme cases, an older man may end up with a prostate as large as a grapefruit. No matter how big it gets, the urethra must still go through the middle of the prostate to get urine out of the body.

Unlike hidden body parts that seem to exist only to cause us problems, such as the appendix, the prostate does have its purpose. It manufactures most of the fluid comprising a man's ejaculate. Prostatic fluid nourishes the sperm and speeds them along on their journey to the uterus and Fallopian tubes.

Scientists are finally beginning to understand what pro-

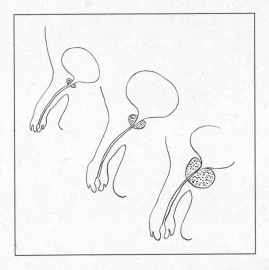

*Change In
Prostrate With Age*

vokes the prostate to reach such unreasonable dimensions in many men. The prostate is hormonally driven. The clearest evidence for this is the fact that men who have been castrated never have enlarged prostates. Needless to say, however, few men are clamoring for castration as a treatment option, though it was practiced in the late 1800s. This overgrowth is technically referred to as benign prostatic hypertrophy (BPH to those in the know), even though it's not really all that wonderful, just to distinguish it from prostatic cancer. BPH is rarely life-threatening, unless the urethra becomes completely blocked and the bladder cannot be emptied. Most of the time it is just annoying. The diagnosis of BPH is completely separate from a diagnosis of cancer.

Although the vast majority of men develop an enlarged prostate as they age, not every enlarged prostate causes symptoms. In fact, one of the things that continues to perplex urologists is that there is no correlation between the size of a prostate and the amount of trouble it causes. Small glands sometimes wreak large amounts of havoc, while some real giants provide nothing more than amazement for the doctor whose probing finger finds them during an annual rectal exam.

Remember, the prostate surrounds the urethra. As it swells, it may just expand outward, leaving the urethra clear. But all too frequently, it enlarges in a direction that compresses the

The only other animal besides man that suffers the discomfort and indignity of a spontaneously enlarged prostate is the dog.

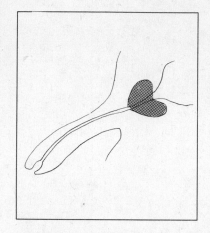 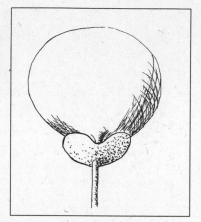

urine pathway, making urination difficult. Imagine, if you will, a doughnut surrounding a garden hose. If the doughnut gets twice as big, uniformly, without changing position, it will not only take up more space around the outside, but the doughnut

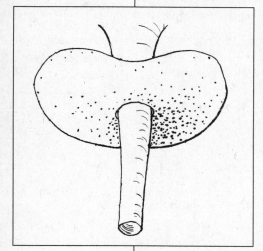

hole in the middle will be smaller. If the garden hose was a snug fit to start with, the swelling doughnut will crimp it and constrict the flow.

SURGERY

Timing

A man who develops troublesome symptoms as a result of this blockage has had few options other than surgery until very recently. However, usually he and his urologist can pick and choose the timing for the operation, as it is not generally considered urgent. If the urine stream is completely stopped, emergency treatment is necessary to empty the bladder. But in other cases, there is no single test a urologist can do or symptom he can count on to determine precisely when surgery is needed.[4] It depends to a significant extent on a patient's level of discomfort with his symptoms and his willingness to go through with a major operation. Indeed, one group of doctors comparing the "watchful waiting" approach to immediate surgery found that the scales were tipped primarily by the men's self-assessment of their quality of life. They conclude "that patient preferences should be the dominant factor in the decision whether to recommend prostatectomy."[5]

The treatment of choice for an unbearably swollen prostate used to be complete removal of the gland via a procedure called an open prostatectomy. It's an operation that calls for opening the abdomen—always a major procedure—and it can lead to a number of nasty side effects. One study found there was a 20 percent chance of an infection after surgery, a 24 percent chance the patient would be back in the doctor's office for a prostate-related problem within three months, and an 8 percent chance the patient would wind up back in the hospital within that same period. Perhaps most discouraging, 4 percent ended up with persistent inconti-

> A sudden constriction may be caused by certain medications that ought to be avoided by men with BPH: over-the-counter cold and allergy remedies (for example, **Actifed** or **Benadryl**) are notorious for provoking the prostate. Some antidepressants (such as **Elavil** or **Norpramin**), digestive tract drugs (especially **Donnatal**), narcotic analgesics, anticonvulsants, or Parkinson's disease medications may also cause difficulties. Anyone with prostate problems should not take any over-the-counter or prescription drugs without first checking with the physician or pharmacist.

The Symptoms of BPH

Not every man will have all (or any) of these symptoms even if he has an enlarged prostate, and there can be other causes for these problems. Some of the symptoms, such as urgency, frequency, and the need to get up at night, are common; others are less frequent:

- urgency—a sense of needing to urinate.
- an inability to urinate despite a sense of urgency.
- difficulty in starting the urinary stream, or a stream that barely dribbles despite a sense that the bladder is full.
- frequent urination.
- the need to get up at night in order to urinate.
- the sensation that, even immediately after voiding, the bladder is still not empty.
- decreased size or force of the urinary stream.
- uncontrollable dribbling after urination.
- blood in the urine.
- a stream that starts and stops.
- incontinence.
- urinary tract infections.

nence and 5 percent wound up impotent.[6] The fear of impotence kept many men from having their prostates removed until complete closure of the urethra made it a no-choice situation.

Troubles with TURP

Then along came the era of miniaturization, and a technique called TURP—transurethral resection of the prostate, in which the physician passes an electric cautery up through the penis and uses it to destroy the tissue that has invaded and blocked the urethra. This is referred to, colloquially and perhaps a bit cruelly, as a prostatic Roto-Rooter job. This is not one of life's peak experiences, but it avoids an abdominal incision so there's less pain after the anesthesia wears off. Working from the inside out seems much neater. Hospital stays are shorter. The risk of dying during or right after the operation is lower (only about two chances per one thousand, as compared with one out of one hundred). Doctors also assumed the rates of impotence following this type of operation would be lower. (Data now indicate that up to 6 percent of patients will become impotent after TURP, and incontinence occurs in 1 percent or fewer.[7]) In the vast majority of men who retain sexual potency, however, TURP causes retrograde ejaculation, in which the semen is squirted back into the bladder. Although disconcerting, it does not affect sexual enjoyment and is not dangerous.

How TURP Is Done

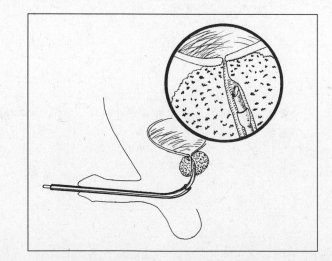

TURP caught on quickly. By 1985, 95 percent of the prostatectomies being performed on Medicare patients were done using this procedure.[8] It seemed so much better than the open procedure that nobody really took the time to assess it. It simply became the procedure of choice.

Then a bomb landed. Or, as the prestigious British medical journal *Lancet* said, "A boulder has just rolled in."[9] In the spring of 1989, the results of a large study comparing the two procedures in three different countries were published in the *New England Journal of Medicine*.[10] The results of four hundred thousand prostate operations were tallied, and the researchers found that those who'd had a TURP were much more likely to need another prostate surgery within five years. Worse, they were more likely to die within five years than those who had an open prostatectomy. Even after adjusting for preexisting heart disease, the risk of a fatal heart attack was two and a half times higher in the years following a TURP. It didn't seem to be a fluke, either. "The evidence for increased rates of reoperation and for reduced survival after transurethral prostatectomy as compared with open prostatectomy was consistent over time and place," the researchers concluded.[11]

This might seem like the strongest argument yet for a wait-and-see attitude toward surgery for BPH. In fact, even before the long-term mortality data were collected, doctors had estimated that having surgery promptly upon the development of symptoms (instead of waiting) would result in less than three "quality adjusted" months.[12] Fortunately, medically-supervised watchful waiting is rapidly becoming easier.

DRUG TREATMENTS

There is considerable excitement these days over a couple of drugs that hold the very strong promise of being able to help a sizable percentage of those with prostate troubles. Needless to say, trading the knife (or the transpenal needle) for a pill has a lot of attraction.

Potential Advantages of Prostate Drug Treatments

1. No surgery, with its attendant risks.
2. Temporary relief for those needing surgery but who can't have it done at the time, for a variety of reasons.
3. Long-term relief for those who can't have surgery.
4. Lower cost.
5. Fewer long-term side effects.

Proscar
(finasteride)

If this drug lives up to its potential to shrink prostates with few if any serious side effects, it will be a breakthrough.
Potential other uses: reversal of male pattern baldness, treatment of hirsutism in women, acne cure.
Currently in clinical trials.
Manufacturer: Merck.

★ ★ ★ ★

Proscar

The drug that's currently getting the most attention is **Proscar** (finasteride). Known as MK-906 during the early stages of testing, it has caused an enormous buzz in research circles, not to mention in a few stock brokerage offices. Because of the near-universality of prostate trouble in older men, any drug that proves useful and garners the FDA's stamp of approval is likely to reap its lucky maker a fortune. In this case, the maker is Merck, and the fortune is estimated as being up to a billion bucks a year!

Proscar works by blocking the action of an enzyme that converts the male hormone testosterone to a form called dihydrotestosterone.[13, 14] Remember we said that the prostate is a hormone-driven organ. Take away testosterone, through castration, and bingo, no BPH. Take away dihydrotestosterone, by eliminating the enzyme needed to make it, and a significant number of prostates should reduce their size.

How many? The final numbers aren't in yet. Preliminary tests, which began on the toughest cases, showed about one third of the men getting measurable reductions in their prostate size and relief of symptoms.[15] The reduction begins within about three months of starting on the drug, and continues to accumulate until it gets as far as it's going to go for each man, usually at about the six month mark. Once started on it, a man must continue taking **Proscar** or the prostate will again start responding to dihydrotestosterone and begin to swell.

Although it's no sure cure, **Proscar** is certainly going to be worth a try for many men if it survives the final phase of testing unscathed. The drug is currently in what is called Phase III testing—the final trial, on a large group of men, in which both the safety and the efficacy of the drug are probed. Just how long that will take, and how long it will take the FDA to evaluate the results, is anyone's guess, but you can bet the pressure is on for the promptest possible decision. "It will come faster than most people think," according to Merck & Company's chairman, Roy Vagelos.

Unlike some other drug treatments that have been tried over the years for BPH, **Proscar** shows no signs of lowering a man's sex drive. In fact, the Merck chairman says the drug shows "essentially no side effects thus far." Of course, we've heard that before about a lot of drugs that later turned out to have plenty of problems. But so far, so good with **Proscar**.

> In a briefing for financial analysts in 1988, Merck chairman Vagelos responded tongue in cheek to a question about adverse effects: "Thus far the things that we have seen are the things that you would anticipate from a drug that cuts off dihydrotestosterone. In other words, it is a teratogen [causes birth defects]. It has to be, because you are cutting off a hormone that is required for the formation of a normal penis. So, if you don't have a penis yet, you shouldn't be on this drug."

Alpha-Blockers

Proscar may have Merck shareholders aquiver, but it is strictly future tense for most men with enlarged prostates at this time. That doesn't necessarily mean, however, that surgery or suffering are their only options. Another category of drugs, called "alpha-blockers" for technical pharmacological reasons, also show promise for shrinking prostates. These drugs seem to work not by shrinking the prostate per se, but rather by relaxing the muscles around the urethra and prostate.

Phenoxybenzamine (sold as **Dibenzyline**) was the first alpha-blocker to be tested for prostate shrinking. Studies have indicated improvement in urinary flow with phenoxybenzamine,[16,17] but a substantial number of people taking it suffer side effects, including dizziness, very low blood pressure, tiredness, nasal congestion, visual problems, and impaired ejaculation. In addition, the drug is carcinogenic in animals and questions have been raised about its safety in humans. Given the difficulties, this little-used blood-pressure medication is not likely to catch on for treating the prostate.

The research on phenoxybenzamine got doctors looking at other alpha-blockers for relaxing the prostate, and they have come up with a few that show promise. Both are currently approved in this country for high blood pressure: **Minipress** (prazosin) and **Hytrin** (terazosin).[18–20] Studies have shown that men taking **Minipress** increase their urinary flow rate and reduce the number of visits they must make to the lavatory in a day.[21] As a blood pressure medication, **Minipress** is less likely than the diuretic hydrochlorothiazide to cause sexual difficulties.[22] However, it must be taken two to three times a day and may cause marked dizziness after the first dose.

Hytrin (Abbott Laboratories and Burroughs Wellcome) is now undergoing a major multicenter U.S. trial to test its effectiveness against BPH.[23] Although it can also cause severe dizziness due to a sudden drop in blood pressure, **Hytrin** has the advantage of once-a-day dosing. One urologist starts patients on a low dose at bed time, carefully monitors blood pressure and dizziness the first day, and continues measuring blood pressure and prostate symptoms over the next few months as the dose is gradually increased.[24]

According to Dr. Herbert Lepor, an expert on drug treatment for prostate enlargement, the ten European studies that have been done on such alpha-blockers have reached generally positive conclusions, but they have not been sufficiently rigorous for urologists to count on. He hopes that the current U.S. trial of **Hytrin** will show clearly how well this type of drug works for BPH.[25] In another study, a new alpha-blocker, **Cardura** (doxazosin), a once-a-day, blood-pressure medication awaiting approval by the FDA, is being examined for its effectiveness against prostate symptoms.[26] The manufacturer is Pfizer.

None of the alpha-blockers is likely to provide a permanent solution to prostate problems. The jury is still out on how much relief they can provide. But for a man who wants to buy a little time until **Proscar** becomes available, or to postpone surgery, these medications might be worth discussing with the urologist, especially if you have high blood pressure that must be treated.

BALLOON DILATION

One new technique being scrutinized as an alternative to surgery is balloon dilation. It's an adaptation of the balloon angioplasty treatment that has proved effective for flattening arterial plaque and sparing many people from a heart-artery bypass.

In the prostate version, a catheter is inserted into the

urethra. A balloon is then passed to the point where the prostate is getting in the way. When it's inflated, it forces the passage open.[27] It's an outpatient procedure, accomplished in about 20 minutes under a local anesthetic. Its speed, lower cost, and lack of need for hospitalization are appealing, but of course the proof of the pudding is in the peeing, and there the results are unclear so far.

A few thousand patients have been treated this way to date. There's no doubt that urethral diameter does increase, but the evidence is still being gathered on whether or not that translates into an improvement, either short- or long-term, in symptom relief. Initial reports were uniformly optimistic,[28,29] but didn't have the kind of objective data that doctors like to see before they turn to something besides surgery.

Another highly experimental treatment that's neither surgery nor medication is heat. A catheter is used here too, to pass the heating element up the urethra to the vicinity of the prostate. Then microwaves are turned on, prostate tissue is heated (but not so much that the patient needs anesthesia), and then theoretically it shrinks and stops causing trouble. This treatment is, if anything, even more experimental than balloon dilation.[30,31] If either of these procedures proves successful, though, it could be a helpful option for a patient who'd rather not be treated with TURP.

Urinary Tract Infections

When a bacterial bug lodges in the urinary tract and multiplies out of control, the result is a urinary tract infection and that means a lot of discomfort for the patient. Urinary tract infections—UTIs, in doctorspeak—are usually thought of as a female problem, but they aren't confined to women. Men get them too, although they're most often caused by different bacteria than the ones bugging women.

Here's the anatomy. Everyone, male and female, has kidneys, most often two per person. The kidneys process liquids, with waste—urine—extracted and sent via two tubes called ureters to the bladder, where it is stored. Any infection in the kidneys or ureters is an upper urinary tract infection. If the infection is in the bladder, it's called cystitis.

The urine leaves the bladder via a tube called the urethra (you remember it from the discussion of prostate problems on p. 326). Here is where men and women differ. For women, the road from bladder to the outer world is relatively short. The urethra is typically about an inch-and-a-half long. For men, the urethra traverses the length of the penis as well, making its total length in the neighborhood of seven or eight inches. Any infection between the bladder and the outside is a lower urinary tract infection.

WOMEN'S UTIS

What a difference a few inches makes! The nasty reality is that women frequently get UTIs, whereas men rarely do. There seem to be several reasons for that, beyond the fact that there's less distance for bacteria to travel.

For one thing, the thrusting involved in intercourse may give bacteria a head start up the urinary tract. Indirect evidence for this can be found in the fact that women who urinate within ten minutes of intercourse have substantially fewer UTIs than women who do not.[32]

Preventing Post-Sex UTIs [33]

If intercourse is often followed by the burning and urgency of a UTI, here are some hints to make that aftermath less likely:

- Always drink plenty of fluids, at least eight cups a day. This may help "wash" the bugs out, and is good for the kidneys in any event.
- During intercourse, avoid vigorous up-and-down thrusts that could irritate the urethra. A rocking motion might be just as pleasurable with less painful consequences.
- Using a diaphragm boosts the risk of a UTI. Use another contraceptive method, or have the diaphragm's fit checked.
- Urinate after intercourse—within ten minutes is best.
- If UTIs are a frequent consequence of intercourse, check with the doctor about prophylactic antibiotics to take after sex.
- Recurrent infections may indicate that your partner is a reservoir. Have him see a doctor, too.

There's also the fact that in women the urethral and anal openings are close to one another. The usual cause of UTIs is the colon bacteria named *E. coli,* and the simple explanation of UTIs used to be that women who "wiped the wrong way" were sweeping these bacteria into the urinary tract. However, the truth appears to be considerably more complicated.

First, although the bacteria that cause most female UTIs are indeed *E. coli,* they are usually a subtype that differs in important ways from the kind usually found in the colon.[34] It is not at all clear that the bacteria are coming from the colon, and it may not make the least difference which way a woman wipes. In fact, there are no controlled studies establishing that as a factor; it appears to be one of those "old doctors' tales" that somehow go from speculation to medical fact without passing through a truth filter.

One of the unique properties of these urinary *E. coli* is their affinity for certain cells normally found in the urine. Those cells contain receptor sites for a sticky surface protein on this particular subtype of *E. coli,* and the attraction between cell and bacteria is sort of like static cling. Once they get stuck together, it's hard to pry them apart. Some women seem to be genetically inclined to have more receptor sites on their cells, and thus are more susceptible to bacterial reruns.

Nondrug Treatment

Cranberry juice has long enjoyed a reputation against urinary tract infections. Physicians have argued about its effectiveness for years. At first, it was believed that cranberry juice made the urine acid, discouraging bacterial growth. That theory has fallen by the wayside, to be replaced by an hypothesis that cranberry juice can keep bacteria from sticking to urinary tract cells. It is still unclear how long this benefit lasts, or whether it makes any practical difference. However, it is a time-honored remedy that is not likely to do any harm so long as it's not substituted for medical treatment.

Differentiating just where an infection is located can be difficult. With the exception of infections that have settled in and made themselves comfortable—and you uncomfortable—

in the bladder, most urinary invasions will simply be called a UTI, and then treated with an antibiotic.

Antibiotic Treatment

Which antibiotic you need depends partly on whether your infection is a one-shot proposition or a recurrent problem. Most women will have a UTI occasionally, and the infrequent guest is pretty easily battled with a drug that combines trimethoprim and sulfamethoxazole (**Bactrim**, **Septra**). This one-two punch has been shown to be effective in simple UTIs. Once upon a time, it was given as a ten- or fourteen-day course of treatment, but then doctors made the discovery that a single larger dose, given only once, was about as effective.

In one recent study, 89 percent of those given the one-shot treatment were either improved or entirely symptom-free by the third day after treatment, while 92 percent of those on a ten-day course showed a cure or improvement three days after they finished their pills.[35] At two weeks and six weeks after treatment, cure rates were not significantly different for the single-dose treatment or the ten-day. This was good news, because the single-dose approach caused a lot less bellyaching—literally. One of the side-effect complaints with most antibiotics is that they do a number on the gastrointestinal system, causing an upset stomach. While 25 percent of those taking the longer course complained of adverse effects, only half as many on the short course had a gripe.

Other effective drugs on the bacteria-busting list include **Augmentin** (a combination of amoxicillin and a chemical to counteract an enzyme that might otherwise reduce the drug's effectiveness), **Keflex** (cephalexin), **Cipro** (ciprofloxacin), and **Noroxin** (norfloxacin).

For a small but unfortunate percentage of the populace, it won't be quite that easy. These women suffer from recurrent UTIs, probably because of the genetic susceptibility we mentioned above. They get one infection after another; anything more than two UTIs a year is considered a recurrent UTI. For many of these women, it makes sense to try to suppress the bugs with a small dose daily or several times a week of a drug such as

---

Bactrim
or **Septra**
*(trimethoprim/
sulfameth-
oxazole)*

Single large dose, or ten-day course. Side effects: gastrointestinal upset, rash. Rare reactions: headache, dizziness, insomnia, depression, seizures.

★ ★ ★

Macrodantin (nitrofurantoin), **Cipro**, or **Noroxin**. These drugs, taken on a regular basis, seem to hold the bacterial count down to the point where it doesn't cause symptoms or get out of hand. Another tack that works for some is to take an antibiotic prophylactically, following intercourse. And in some cases, the doctor will provide the patient with antibiotics to be used for single-dose treatments under appropriate guidelines.[36]

MALE UTIS

While UTIs and women are thought to be synonymous, men can suffer as well. It's not real frequent, but it is real uncomfortable. In men, infections are more usually in the urethra than the bladder, and men are more likely to have an asymptomatic infection.

In older men, the source is very often an infection of the prostate. Prostate enlargement that has interfered with bladder emptying may also contribute to a urinary tract infection. For younger men, the cause is most likely to be a sexually transmitted disease (for more details, turn to p. 340). The next most common culprit is a bacterium called *Gardnerella vaginalis*, the bacterium frequently implicated (as its name tells you) in the vaginal infections that plague many women. By the way, although men readily catch either *Gardnerella* or another vaginal bacterium, *Trichomonas*, they rarely seem to be infected by any of the fungi, such as *Candida*, even when their sexual partners have raging infections.

Now, don't be hasty and conclude that sexual intercourse is to blame for most male urinary tract infections. 'Tain't so. A bigger danger is the doctor! It's not unusual for a man to come down with a UTI after catheterization, cystoscopy, TURP, or some other instrumentation of the urinary passage. "Urethral catheterization," according to one study, "is the single most important predisposing factor in the development of nosocomial [hospital-acquired] urinary tract infection."[37]

Cystitis (a bladder infection) is rare in men, which means most male UTIs are infections of the lower tract.[38] Unfortunately, men's infections tend to be stubborn devils to eradicate, probably because a fair proportion of them also involve infection of the prostate, where many antibiotics don't work well.[39]

Several things usually will get the job done, including the **Bactrim** or **Septra** (trimethoprim/sulfamethoxazole combination) that works for women. Also effective are the tetracyclines (such as minocycline and doxycycline), and **Geopen** or **Geocillin** (carbenicillin). The one-shot treatment of UTIs is not nearly as likely to be effective in men as in women. Don't be surprised, in fact, when the doctor tells you to stay on the drug for what seems a long, long time . . . up to thirty days! The aim here is to clear up the infection, first, then keep it from becoming a chronic prostate infection that is *really* hard to dislodge.

Sexually Transmitted Nasties

Venereal disease used to be fairly simple: there was syphilis, "the clap," and crabs (pubic lice). None of these was pleasant, but once antibiotics were invented, syphilis and gonorrhea could be cured. (The lice were more of a nuisance than a real hazard.) As long as you got treatment promptly, there was little to worry about from any of them. No more. Today's venereal diseases are a lot more challenging and complex.

First off, it's no longer *venereal disease*. That sounds a little too old-fashioned. The new nomenclature is *sexually transmitted diseases*, or STDs, even if that does sound like a motor-oil additive that Andy Granatelli should be selling on the pages of *Popular Mechanics*. "The concept now is that any microbial agent or syndrome that is passed from person to person through close intimate contact qualifies as an STD."[40]

Second, the nature of the infections that are around these days has changed. Now you can catch herpes, which is permanent but controllable, or AIDS, which is permanent and almost always fatal. There is a whole fistful of other infections as well, most of which were not really recognized a generation ago.

Third, STDs are no longer (if they ever were) something you can avoid by making love only to "nice" people. STDs are not a whorehouse exclusive. Teenagers get STDs. So does the geriatric set. Poor people get them. So do the rich and famous. Almost the only people not at risk of STDs are those rare individuals, the celibate. One of the most difficult misconceptions to combat is that STDs are the exclusive province of some particular group—usually any group except the one you belong to. But in this epidemic, everyone is eligible.

The statistics are impressive. Four to five million people a year get chlamydial infections,[41,42] and close to that many get gonorrhea.[43] Other STDs fell large numbers of people as well. Keep in mind that these numbers are estimates based on what's reported. You can bet your last dime that a lot of people go untreated, and thus untallied. All the major STDs except for

---

Words of Wisdom

It's not always easy for people to stroll casually into their doctor's office and say, "Tell me all about sexually transmitted diseases." Even after contracting one, most folks are too embarrassed to do much more than sneak in, get whatever they need to get better, and slink out. They're often no wiser for the experience.

So, friends, in the interest of education and perhaps even prevention, we suggest

1. Write or call for an excellent booklet called "Genital Self-Examination." It will literally tell you where it's at when it comes to detecting STDs. Just like it says on the little piece of paper they send along with newly imprinted checks, "You're the final inspector."

   For a copy of "Genital Self-Examination," write GSE, Box 4088, Woburn, MA 01888–4088 or call (800) 234–1124. The booklet, which is free, is published by a drug manufacturer and several of the professional medical societies concerned with STDs.

2. If you have a specific question about an STD, you can call the toll-free **STD National Hotline** Monday through Friday, eight a.m. to eleven p.m. eastern time, at (800) 227–8922.

3. If your concern is with herpes, there is a **National Herpes Hotline**, available Monday through Friday nine a.m. to six p.m. eastern time at (919) 361–2120.

4. And if you have any questions about AIDS, the **National AIDS Hotline** is staffed twenty-four hours a day, seven days a week. Call (800) 342–AIDS.

AIDS are at least controllable, and most are curable. Recent pharmaceutical advances have made treatment for several easier or more effective.

What hasn't changed for at least fifteen years, despite publicity about AIDS and other STDs, is people's sexual behavior. A study of women students at a northeastern university in 1975, 1986, and 1989 reveals that the same proportion of young women are sexually active now as in the mid-1970s—about 90 percent by the age of 21.[44] Nearly 25 percent of those surveyed (with an anonymous written questionnaire) had had intercourse with six or more men. And approximately one-tenth of these young women engage in anal sex, just as in 1975, although this practice has gotten media notice as a high-risk behavior for the transmission of HIV (human immunodeficiency virus, linked to AIDS).

If it takes two to tango, as they say, it certainly requires two partners to practice intercourse. Presumably the sexual activity these young women report is matched by patterns of sexual behavior in young men, although the study did not include questionnaires for males. The take-home lesson is this: *condoms are crucial*. Since people seem unlikely to change their behavior and actually practice safe sex (abstinence is safe; so is mutual monogamy), it's important to make it safer by using barrier contraceptives, especially condoms. Adding a spermicide containing nonoxynol 9 may add a measure of antiviral and antibacterial protection.

Condoms are not perfect, but they do provide a measure of protection against many of the bad bugs out there nowadays, including to a limited extent HIV. The good news in the recent study is that more young women now are insisting that their partners always use a condom for intercourse. Back in 1975, only 12 percent said they did; that rose to about 20 percent by the mid-1980s, and at the end of the decade nearly half said their partners always or almost always used a condom.[45] With luck, repeating the survey in the early 1990s will find that proportion skyrocketing. Then fewer people will have to worry about the STDs we are talking about here.

CHLAMYDIA

Most people have trouble even saying it (kla-MID-y-ah). They should start practicing, because this is now the number-one STD, and still growing. It's estimated that the financial toll for chlamydial infections is now $1.5 billion a year.[46]

Caused by the microorganism *Chlamydia trachomatis*, this STD has zoomed from almost nothing to being at the top of the chart. The offending organism is a tricky one, with traits of both bacteria and viruses, and until very recently the only lab test for chlamydia was long, involved, and slow. There is now a quick in-the-office test,[47] and several new lab tests that are faster and cheaper have come along.

Most authorities now rate chlamydia as epidemic. Treated early, it's fairly easy to combat. Left to fester, it can have catastrophic effects, especially for women, who are often left with damage to their reproductive organs that makes them infertile.

The Three Questions

Chlamydia infections, especially in women, are often without symptoms, at least until they are fairly advanced. Yet it is probably impractical to test everyone for chlamydia.

What do we do? One study concluded that certain risk factors were so strongly associated with chlamydial infections that these people should automatically be tested for the disease any time they presented themselves to a gynecologist or GP.[48]

The three questions are

(1) Is the patient's level of education high school or less?

(2) Has her partner had other sexual partners in the last three months?

(3) Does the cervix bleed when swabbed?

Other known risk factors include being under the age of twenty-five, having multiple sex partners or partners with genital symptoms, having a new partner, or having a cervical discharge. Having one of the risk factors puts the danger at about 8 percent; having two or more raises the ante to about a 19 percent chance of being infected.

Antibiotic Treatment

The treatment of choice is one of two old standbys, doxycycline (**Vibramycin** and other brand names), or tetracycline (**Sumycin** and others). If you can't tolerate those drugs, erythromycin is the alternative. It's a good idea for both people (the sufferer and the sex partner) to be treated simultaneously, since upwards of half the partners will prove to be infected.[49] This reduces the likelihood of reinfection.

While treatment of chlamydia relies on some very old-fashioned drugs, one new one that has recently appeared on the horizon is ofloxacin. It appears very effective against chlamydia, and has the added advantage of also dousing gonorrhea infections.[50] Since these two infections are often found together, this drug offers the prospect of successfully killing two birds with one stone when it becomes available.

GONORRHEA

Speaking of gonorrhea, here's a disease that's been around a l-o-n-g time. It is still very big, although (who knows why) the head count on this one has been dropping slightly over the past few years. It is still a threat to plenty of people, with over 140,000 new cases reported in the first three months of 1990 alone.[51] The difference now is the drug used to combat it.

Penicillin is no longer the front-line warrior against this very prevalent STD. The versatile *Neisseria gonorrhoeae* (the bacterium that causes the disease) now comes in forms that are pretty resistant to penicillin and tetracycline.[53] The recommended drug is now **Rocephin** (ceftriaxone), which belongs to a group of drugs known as third-generation cephalosporins. As you might expect for something with such a fancy title, you will pay dearly for the privilege of this cutting-edge technology. Ceftriaxone is ten or fifteen times more expensive than either of the old (and off-patent) favorites. Of course, when you're standing there at the doctor's office with a painful STD, there's usually little room for arguing about the

---

Naming the Clap

Obviously "the clap" is easier to say (and spell) than gonorrhea, but where does the term come from? "According to legend," says one authority, "medieval Parisian prostitutes were restricted to buildings called 'clapiers,' thus explaining the term 'clap.' "[52]

price of relieving what can often be the very considerable discomfort caused by having gonorrhea.

Another closely related drug, **Cefizox** (ceftizoxime) also has been shown to be effective against gonorrhea, and at a dose that reduces treatment cost considerably.

PID

Pelvic inflammatory disease (PID) is an infection that gets into a woman's reproductive machinery and peritoneal cavity, often reaching the Fallopian tubes. This is serious business. Left untreated for even a little while, PID can lead to sterility. Even a single bout of PID means a 14 percent chance of infertility; a second episode raises the likelihood of fertility damage to 35 percent, and if a woman has a third episode of PID, it's no better than fifty-fifty that she will ever be able to bear children.[54] The result of the infection may well

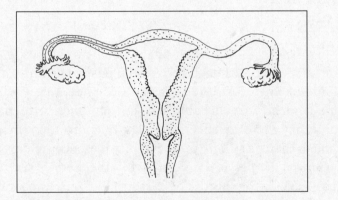

Organs Susceptible to PID

be scarring of the Fallopian tubes leading from the ovaries to the uterus, which can block the tubes and not let eggs pass through for fertilization. Infection-scarred tubes may also increase the risk of a tubal pregnancy.

The symptoms of PID include pelvic tenderness and pain, sensitivity to motion of the cervix (the opening of the uterus into the vagina), and fever. About a million women each year are treated for PID. A quarter of them will require hospitalization, and half of those will have surgery.[55]

The cause of PID may be *Chlamydia*, *N. gonorrhoeae*, or one of dozens of other nasty bugs. At one time it was thought that gonorrhea was the major problem, but further research has revealed that although the gonorrhea bacterium is often present in the lower reproductive tract, that the infection higher up, in the cervix, uterus, or Fallopian tubes, exhibited a much wider range of bacteria.[56]

That could pose a dilemma: Which drug will work? In the last few years, however, the third generation cephalosporins have proved effective against a wide range of organisms likely to cause PID, including those that had developed resistance to the prior antibiotic bug-fighters. The official Centers for Disease Control recommendation for treating PID is to go with **Mefoxin** (cefoxitin sodium), which can do battle with the gonorrhea bacterium and a wide range of others. An alternative is **Cefotan** (cefotetan) plus the older antibiotic doxycycline. Either way, these offer the best chance of fending off the long-term consequences of having contracted PID.

HERPES

Just before AIDS hit national awareness, herpes was the scare buzzword. Although it has been pushed aside by all the attention being paid to AIDS, it is still very definitely with us. Unlike the early days of public recognition, when little could be done, today there are effective means of controlling the virus, although there is still no drug that provides a complete cure.

Genital herpes is infection with the herpes simplex II virus—HSV-2, for short. The reason HSV-2 is impossible to eradicate is that it hides in certain areas of nerve cells. There it lies in wait, sometimes for days or weeks, sometimes for months or years. Some people suffer frequent recurrences; others have one attack and never see the signs of herpes again. Although street lore has it that stress will cause a herpes outbreak, this appears true for only a small percentage of the people who are infected.[57] When active, the virus produces painful blisters on the genitals. They are not only embarrassing but painful, and can put a chill on a new relationship.

The big breakthrough in treating herpes came with the discovery of **Zovirax** (acyclovir), a prescription drug that is

---

Zovirax
(acyclovir)

Aborts attack of genital herpes if taken before lesions fully appear.

Can be used to prevent outbreaks.

Does not cure herpes.

Side effects: extremely rare— diarrhea, dizziness, headache, nausea, joint pain.

★ ★ ★

available both as an ointment and to be taken orally. The ointment has had a mixed record at best, but the oral preparation is effective for the majority of people, provided it is taken early enough. Acyclovir *cannot* eradicate the herpes virus, but it does interrupt replication, thus short-circuiting an attack. Those who suffer frequent recurrences can be put on a daily regimen of **Zovirax** and greatly reduce or completely eliminate new outbreaks. It has been used in some people for several years now, with negligible side effects. Be forewarned, however, that some people report "rebound" attacks when they go off suppressive **Zovirax**.

For a first attack, or if suppression doesn't work, a new drug called alpha-interferon gel seems to hold promise. When the gel was tried on ninety-nine herpes sufferers who had a history of suffering at least three attacks a year, those who used the drug as soon as they felt recurrences coming on had the time during which they were symptomatic shortened by a third.

GENITAL WARTS

We'll bet you've never heard of human papillomavirus (HPV). Most people haven't, yet this sexually transmitted disease now rivals gonorrhea in frequency.[58] Worse yet, it is the most common STD in teenage girls.[59] HPV causes genital warts. These can take a number of forms. Some look just like the warts people get on their hands or feet, while others have distinctive forms or coloration. Some are external, some internal. There are at least fifty-six variations of HPV, of which about ten cause genital warts.[60]

Obviously, having warts on one's penis or vulva (or anywhere else) is a bit distressing. What's really scary is the finding that there is an association between genital warts and cervical cancer.[61] Anywhere from 5–15 percent of the women with persistent genital warts may develop cancer, usually of the cervix. Most researchers aren't convinced that any variant of the human papillomavirus causes cancer in and of itself, but it may combine with other factors to trigger cancerous growth.

These warts are clearly something to be rid of, but quick. Just as with herpes, you can't completely eliminate the virus, but the warts can be eradicated. Until very recently, the two major techniques for banishing genital warts were cutting them off, or attempting to destroy them with trichloroacetic acid. The former worked only if the warts were relatively few in number and fairly large in size. The trichloroacetic acid worked fairly well on warts in mucosal tissue, but did less well when the site was the exterior skin.

A third agent—podophyllin, a plant resin—was available, but used infrequently. "There is little enthusiasm for its use," say experts, "because it carries a high risk of local and systemic toxicity; the risk is increased when podophyllin is used on large areas. Moreover, because podophyllin is a mixture of compounds that vary enormously in biologic activity, individuals may have highly idiosyncratic responses to it."[62]

That's why many specialists in the treatment of STDs are hailing the appearance of a drug called **Podofilox**. **Podofilox**, also known as podophyllotoxin, is one of the active compounds in podophyllin and is thought to be the part of the natural resin that does the most good against genital warts.[63] The new drug (if something extracted from a plant that has been around for millennia can be said to be "new") has several advantages over podophyllin. First, it is more effective. In one study, 74 percent of the warts were gone by the end of the experiment, versus only 8 percent that disappeared in the placebo group. Overall, a cure rate (people showing no warts—remember, the virus itself lingers and can't be eliminated) of around 50 percent to as high as 88 percent has been reported in a number of studies of **Podofilox**,[64,65] whereas the cure rate with traditional podophyllin treatment hovers around the one-third mark.

Second, the drug is not as caustic as podophyllin, which doctors almost always apply themselves for fear patients will smear it around and do great damage. In most of the studies on **Podofilox**, patients do it themselves. Third, and certainly encouraging, is the fact that there have been no reported systemic reactions to podofilox, and very little is absorbed because the concentration used for treatment is very low. "Patient-applied podofilox," one group of researchers says, "offers promise as a safe and effective first line therapy for patients with genital warts."[66]

Future treatments include laser eradication and interferon, a protein that provokes the body into antiviral activity. Early studies on both offer encouragement that there may soon be a whole bag of tricks to use against the nasty HPV. And if interferon works, there's even the hope that it might be possible to completely eradicate the bug from the body.

VAGINAL INFECTIONS

The human vagina is just the sort of place bacteria and yeast like to live. It offers warmth, nourishment, and the right pH. As a matter of fact, both bacteria and yeast are perfectly normal inhabitants of the vagina. But when they get a bit rambunctious and out of control, a woman winds up with a discharge, irritation, pain on urination, and possibly itching.

Although many of the things that cause vaginal infections can be passed back and forth between men and women, it is far from clear whether any of the vaginal infections are in fact truly sexually transmitted diseases. As often as not, they may simply result from a disruption in a woman's physiology or biochemistry sufficient to slightly alter the vaginal environment.

There isn't a whole lot new to offer in the way of treating various vaginal infections, but that isn't bad news because most of what we have works pretty well. The key to getting cured is finding out what you really have. If that sounds obvious, be aware that docs sometimes make an armchair diagnosis based on a few quick questions, and that doesn't always tell the whole story. Not everything that itches or irritates is a vaginal infection. Allergies to douches and deodorants, for example, can produce vaginal irritation, and increased vaginal secretions can be stimulated by anything from ovulation and pregnancy to increased sexual activity.

There are three major causes of vaginal infections: bacteria, yeast, and a protozoan called *Trichomonas*.

Bacteria

Bacterial vaginosis is the term of choice for a bacterial infection of the vagina. But medical science has shifted from one conclusion to another on what causes it. A genus of bacteria called *Gardnerella* was once the confirmed enemy, so it was *Gardnerella* vaginitis. While some authorities still think *Gardnerella* is the major offender,[67] others are less sure, thinking it may in fact be caused by a disruption and rearrangement of the normal vaginal flora where one of several bacteria get the upper hand and multiply out of control.

Whatever the cause, the most frequent cure is **Flagyl** (metronidazole), which does an excellent job the vast majority of the time, even though it is only moderately effective against *Gardnerella* bacteria. Perhaps it holds down the activity of *Gardnerella* while permitting the normal flora to regrow. A recent innovation with **Flagyl** is a short-course treatment consisting of 2 grams of metronidazole given twice a day on days one and three. That's it. The older and more conservative approach is 500 mg twice a day for a week.

Trichomonas

Number two on the list of vaginal infections is trichomoniasis ("trich"). Trich is a protozoan, a little organism that lodges on the cells lining the vagina and damages them. This produces irritation and inflammation, along with a characteristic discharge. Just as in a bacterial infection, trichomonads respond to **Flagyl** (metronidazole). In trichomoniasis, however, it is important that the sexual partner also be treated or the likelihood of reinfection is great.

Yeast

The final player in this vaginal drama is a yeast called *Candida*. Sufferers are said to have candidiasis, and suffer they do, since the cardinal symptom is an intense, almost unbearable itch. Here again, we emphasize that *Candida* is a normal occupant of the vaginal vault. Very frequently, however, when women are given systemic antibiotics, they will develop a vaginal *Candida* infection. The antibiotics have no effect on *Candida*, but they do seem to wipe out the other occupants, and the yeast cells rush to fill the vacancies. Oral contraceptives have the same effect for some women.

There are lots of cures available, all of them pretty likely to work. **Monistat** (miconazole), either as a cream or a vaginal suppository, usually gets the nod. Alternatives include clotrimazole (**Gyne-Lotrimin; Mycelex-G**), **Femstat** (butoconazole), or **Nizoral** (ketoconazole). All have an 80–90 percent cure rate.

For reasons that are poorly understood (that means physicians don't have the foggiest notion why it happens), some women suffer recurrent attacks of candidiasis, despite an apparently complete cure each time. That's what happened to one of our readers, who finally found the solution in a bottle of ordinary vinegar:

> *OTC Savings*
>
> **Monistat** is a pretty pricy drug, but it is in other respects identical to the nonprescription antifungal cream **Micatin**. The **Monistat** applicatior even fits a **Micatin** tube. Vaginal yeast infections require professional diagnosis; but if a second tube of **Monistat** is called for, there's no reason **Micatin** couldn't be substituted at several dollars less.

> After the birth of my son, I developed a yeast infection. I did the usual things and it got better in a week, only to come back again the next week. It lasted a year and a half, at the expense of almost $2000 in office fees and medication. My husband was put on some of the same medication because yeast infections can be passed back and forth.
>
> The last OB/GYN I went to told me I'd just have to live with it; he didn't know why they couldn't "fix" me.
>
> In a final attempt, and in desperation, I went to a GP on the advice of a friend. He was my salvation! He prescribed douching with 2 tablespoons of vinegar in a quart of water in a regular douche bag. Douche up to three times a day for a week, then twice a day for a week, then down to one time for a week. The day after sex helps, too.
>
> My case was extreme, but it's worked for all my friends who've suffered. Maybe you can pass this along to your female readers.

Well, female readers, there it is. It's an inexpensive home remedy that worked for one woman. We caution you, however, that routine and vigorous douching may increase your risk of PID and ectopic pregancy. The disposable vinegar douching product may be somewhat safer in that they should be sterile and the throw-away bottles do not create as much force.

Another home remedy that has some validity is yogurt. Instead of douching with it, though, spoon it up. Dr. Eileen Hilton, a specialist in infectious disease, studied women who had suffered recurrent bouts of vaginitis. Women who ate a cup of yogurt every day were three times less likely to come down with another yeast infection during the study than those who skipped the stuff. To be effective, though, the yogurt has to contain active *Lactobacillus acidophilus* culture. Check the fine print on the carton, or make your own yogurt with active *L. acidophilus*.

Contraception

It is now the 1990s. We remind you of this because were you to try to estimate the date by the methods of contraception that are available, the answer might come up 1960s—or maybe 1860s.

If you think we live in the most advanced, most high-tech country in the world, then ask yourself why America is so far from the cutting edge of contraceptive technology. While Euro-

Contraception in the United States Today

Method	Percent Using	Percent Failure/Year
vasectomy	14	0.15
female sterilization	19	0.4
oral contraceptives	32	3
IUD	3	6
condoms	17	12
diaphragms	4–6	2–23
contraceptive sponge	3	18
rhythm ("natural") method	4	20
foam	2	21

Source: "Developing New Contraceptives," National Academy of Sciences, 1990. "Percent using" figures are for 1988, "percent failure/year" are for 1987.

peans contemplate a plethora of exciting and safer new options, such as reversible sterilization for both men and women, methods to block sperm production, a once-a-month pill, and time-release contraceptives, the United States sits dead in the water. Paralyzed by legal and political battles, the birth-control researchers have gone into hiding, and show little sign of emerging any time in the future. "It is unlikely," according to Dr. Daniel Mishell, Jr., "that any new method of contraception, other than different oral steroid formulations, will be available in the United States during the next decade."[68]

That is a tragic situation, because it translates directly into unwanted pregnancies—as many as three million in this country last year. This is likely to happen to three million more women this year, and next year, and every year thereafter until contraceptive research gets going again.

In a recent and devastating look at the state of contraception in this country, a panel of sixteen experts from the prestigious National Research Council of the National Academy of Sciences concluded that "The current array of contraceptives fails to meet the needs of a substantial number of men and women in the U.S."

"We are very far behind the rest of the world," said the panel's chairman, Luigi Mastroianni, Jr., at a press conference when the report was released. "Despite a potential market of more than a half-billion people worldwide, the outlook for new contraceptive development under the current regulatory and legal climate in the United States is bleak," he said.

Even though birth control could be big business, few pharmaceutical companies are actively engaged in contraceptive research in the United States. Fear of being sued has discouraged many manufacturers from developing new contraceptive compounds.

The table demonstrates the problem. With the exception of

Driving with an Expired Condom?

Most condom failures are probably a result of improper use (putting it on wrong, failure to withdraw promptly after orgasm so that the condom comes off, and so on), but there is the occasional burst balloon.

Now manufacturers have announced they will place an expiration date on their product, just like there is on a milk carton. That way you can be certain the goods are still good.

Condom makers are now in the process of testing to see how long they can guarantee the safety of their products. It's generally believed that a reasonable shelf life is three to five years, but if they're going to start saying it on the label, the manufacturers want to be sure.

Get pregnant while on the Pill?

Once thought to be practically a perfect contraceptive as long as a woman remembered to take it, there is increasing evidence that the pill is letting women down.

Why? Two reasons. First, the current "low-dose-pill" contains lower levels of hormones. That means less slack in the system, so a missed pill is a lot bigger deal, and more likely to result in exposure to pregnancy.

Second, and most often overlooked because it's unknown, many kinds of prescription and OTC drugs can diminish the power of the Pill. It's a difficult thing to prove with a high degree of certainty, but there are studies that seriously raise the question about the following:

- antibiotics (ampicillin, tetracycline, rifampicin, griseofulvin).
- nonsteroidal anti-inflammatory drugs (see p. 27 for list).
- clofibrate.
- **Valium** (diazepam) and **Librium** (chlordiazepoxide).
- antihistamines and decongestants in cold remedies.
- many anticonvulsants (phenytoin, phenobarbital, primidone, butabarbital, carbamazepine).
- antitubercular drugs.

Source: D'Arcy, P.F. "Drug Interactions with Oral Contraceptives." *Drug Intelligence and Clin. Pharm.* 1986; 20(5):353–362.

surgical sterilization procedures, other available methods are either associated with substantial questions of long-term safety, or have a high failure rate.

SAFETY

The safety issue is a tough one, and of course it underlies the legal problem that has driven the pharmaceutical companies away from contraceptive innovation. Is the Pill safe? After thirty years of extensive use, the debate continues—no, make that rages—over the safety of oral contraceptives in their various forms and formulations. Whatever you would like to say or prove about the Pill—it does or doesn't increase the risk of breast cancer, cervical cancer, or rain in Iowa—you can find a study to "prove" it. The truth? The truth is that the human hormonal system is a very complex thing, and that's the reason so many studies, involving so many women, have yielded so much seemingly contradictory information.

The Pill has changed a lot since its introduction in the 1960s. By today's standards, the amount of hormones in those pills was gargantuan, and may account for the many adverse effects reported over the years. One of the great difficulties in evaluating cancer danger is the long latency period for many types of cancer. We may just now be seeing the effects of the *old* Pill. We hope that the minipill now in use will be safer, but proving that is not going to happen any time soon.

As for IUDs, yes, there are still two available: the Population Council's copper T380A, and a progesterone-releasing, T-shaped device from Searle (**Progestasert**). The IUD has had a lot of bad press, and it certainly has had problems associated with it.

Just the process of insertion and removal itself poses some risks.

It's not a pretty picture. On the one hand, there's the risk of pregnancy. And pregnancy *is* a risk. Even if it is planned, there are dangers associated with having a child. And if the pregnancy was unwanted, there are the psychological dangers of having a child under adverse circumstances, or the physical and psychological difficulties of having an abortion.

FUTURE OPTIONS?

About all we can do is look enviously toward Europe, to see what contraception might look like some day in this country. Among the things currently available there:

(1) **Norplant** (levonorgestrel). **Norplant** is a small set of progestin-containing tubes which, when implanted under the skin, provide up to five years of contraceptive protection. Removing the device restores fertility. Although originally invented in the United States, **Norplant** is manufactured by Leiras of Finland. It is also available in Sweden, Czechoslovakia, and a number of South American countries. At the time of this writing United States approval is expected imminently.

(2) **Filshie Clip** (fallopian ring). Some fallopian clips are available in the United States but don't offer many advantages to tubal ligation. Cutting the tubes must be considered permanent sterilization, even though this procedure can sometimes be undone with microsurgery. The **Filshie Clip** can be inserted with minimal scarring, and is much more reversible than the devices currently available in this country. It is approved in the United Kingdom, Canada, Australia, and South Africa.

(3) **RU-486** (mifepristone). This is the hottest item, in more ways than one. Often called "the morning-after pill," **RU-486** can be used to terminate a pregnancy within forty-five days of fertilization. It was recently approved for use in France, and is already in use in China.

Staying Dry

Bedwetting has been a battleground for generations of parents and their children. It has also been a battleground for legions of experts, each of whom had an opinion on what caused the problem and how to cure it. Neither the explanations nor the cures have turned out to be very correct.

Bedwetting—enuresis, to the doctor—is an extremely distressing problem. No doubt about that. Children who can't stay dry at night face shame, ridicule, and an enormous loss of self-esteem. This damage sometimes persists for life. Sadly, the psychological scars are mostly unjustified and unnecessary. Both new treatments and new understanding are helping us put bedwetting in its place.

One of the things we now understand more fully is that kids don't all have plumbing that comes to maturity at the same time. While age five is generally used as a cutoff point, by which time a child should be physiologically capable of attaining bladder control both day and night, a lot of kids just don't have the musculature for it by that age.

In reality, 15–20 percent of five-year-olds still wet the bed at night.[69] Now, think about it for a second. If, as was once believed, bedwetting was a symptom of some deep, underlying psychological problem, does that mean that a fifth of the five-year-olds on the playgrounds of America (between five and seven million kids) need to be seeing a psychiatrist? A parent who thinks that bedwetting is usually caused by psychological problems is much more likely to engage in a psychological tug-of-war with a kid whose only fault is that his or her muscles and nerves didn't mature quite as fast as those of the kid down the street.

And why, pray tell, might that be? Quite possibly for genetic reasons. One study found that when both parents had a history of enuresis, 77 percent of their children were bedwetters.[70] When only one parent was a bedwetter, the number of affected children dropped by almost half, and with neither parent could remember having been a bedwetter, only 15 percent of the kids were.

So let's throw some old myths out. A child who is a bedwetter is most likely *not* afflicted with some grave personality problem (which is not to say that psychological factors aren't at play some of the time—but not very often). They don't hate their parents, they're not social deviants, they aren't "babies," and they don't want to wet the bed.

While we're myth tossing, let's move a few myths about "cures" out of the way. Withholding fluids in the evening, awakening the child to urinate, and punishment have never been proved to be effective,[71] despite the testimony of hundreds of well-meaning grandmas. Obviously, if there's less liquid a child will wet the bed less, but less fluid does not make the muscles more capable of holding onto whatever they have. Urinating, or not urinating, is a pretty complex operation. It involves competing sets of muscles, which must be coordinated just so in order to retain or expel urine. Until the muscles are up to it, no amount of potty training, pleading, threatening, rewarding, or other action is going to keep the child dry.

But enough pressure and hassle *can* keep a child wet. Once staying dry becomes an issue, things can come unraveled pretty quickly, to the detriment of all the players in the drama. Why humiliate kids in front of adults and peers for something over which they literally don't have any control?

So rule number one for solving the bedwetting problem, parents, is to *lighten up*. Don't call your child a baby, add to his or her embarrassment in any way, or place blame. After all, would you criticize or sympathize with a friend or spouse who had tennis elbow? Well, it's no different for the child who's a bedwetter. Now the really good news is that there are a lot of things that can help.

NONDRUG APPROACH

One low-key approach that has proved useful is wetness alarms. These consist of a detector, usually connected to a small sensor in a pocket on the child's underwear and hooked to a buzzer. When the child begins to urinate at night, the buzzer sounds and the child is awakened to finish voiding in the bathroom. The cost is modest ($50-75), no prescription is required, and studies have shown these alarms to be reasonably effective (about 70 percent). Some children experience relapses when the devices are discontinued. Two brand names you might look for are **Wet-Stop** and **Wee-Alert**.

DRUG TREATMENTS

The newest and most interesting discovery for the treatment of bedwetting is a drug called desmopressin. This compound is a synthetic version of a naturally occurring hormone whose job in the body is to slow urine production. In the plumbing system, as with many body systems, things work by a balance between two or more muscles or chemicals. In this case, there is a diuretic (urine-making) hormone, and an antidiuretic hormone (ADH). Evidence is accumulating rather rapidly that the only thing wrong with a lot of kids who are bedwetters is slight underproduction at night of the antidiuretic hormone. In most people, ADH levels rise at night. That doesn't happen for bedwetters, so they go on creating urine at the daytime rate, resulting in bedwetting.

In one study, a rather impressive 80 percent of the children treated with desmopressin either greatly reduced or eliminated bedwetting episodes.[72] Other investigators have reported similarly encouraging results.[73] It remains to be seen whether the benefits are long-lasting or whether wet nights return once the medicine is discontinued. Dr. George T. Klauber, of Tufts University, has found that if the medicine is used continusously for three months or more, relapse is less likely when **DDAVP** is stopped.[74]

This drug was approved by the FDA in late 1989. Worried your child won't swallow a pill? Then here's the best news yet—the medicine, sold as **DDAVP**, is a nasal spray!

Most children will eventually grow out of their bedwetting problem. But if an alarm device is unsuccessful and psychological problems are starting to develop, a discussion about **DDAVP** with a urologist or pediatrician may be in order. This medicine can be especially helpful when children need short-term protection—say when they are invited to spend the night at a friend's house or go to camp.

On the other hand, we can see nothing but reasons why a child *shouldn't* be placed on antidepressants, which has become a popular way to attempt to deal with bedwetting. It's hard to defend giving that kind of a drug to a child in order to deal with bedwetting by any argument except sheer desperation. This may be the classic case of hunting mosquitoes with an elephant gun.

The most widely used antidepressant in treating bedwetting is imipramine (**Tofranil, Tipramine, Janimine** and others), although desipramine (**Norpramin, Pertofrane**) has also been used.[75,76] Given the substantial side effects that can accompany antidepressants, the difficulty of adjusting dosages to small bodies, the lack of adequate testing of these drugs for safety on children, and the wide differences in ability to metabolize the drugs that might be expected between children and adults, we can't recommend this kind of drug to deal with bedwetting, especially in view of the fact that "clinical response is not long lasting; relapse rate is high."[77]

> ### *Some Side Effects of Antidepressants* [78]
>
> How much is a dry bed worth? Would you subject your child to the following, all of which are possible side effects of the antidepressant drugs commonly used for treating bedwetting?
> - anxiety
> - blood pressure changes
> - blurred vision
> - diarrhea
> - dizziness
> - drowsiness
> - dry mouth
> - headache
> - insomnia
> - irregular heartbeat
> - nausea
> - vomiting

FUTURE

A medication for grownups who have bedwetting problems (incontinence, nocturia) has been submitted to the FDA for approval. If the agency approves it, physicians may test **Micturin** (terodiline) for bedwetting problems. The manufacturer is Forest Laboratories.

Impotence

There is probably no more personal nor more obvious problem than impotence—the failure to get and sustain an erection. It's not the kind of problem a man can hide except by

How Erections Happen

The penis represents perhaps the ultimate example of complex plumbing, which means there's a lot that can go wrong.

Arteries bring blood into the penis; veins drain the blood out. All the necessary plumbing, complete with a complex set of valves, is located in tissue called the *corpus cavernosa* that runs up the penis, amidst thick bundles of smooth muscle and a fiber framework of collagen and related materiels. If an artery is blocked, blood can't get in. No erection. If blood gets in but blood pressure in the local area is insufficient, no erection. If blood gets in, and blood pressure is sufficient, but a leaky valve in the vein lets it flow out, guess what happens? Right. No erection.

With that many possibilities for things to go awry, it's probably a miracle that anyone *ever* gets it straight!

avoiding sexual intercourse, which is just what many impotent men decide to do. "Not tonight dear, I've got a headache," is not a female exclusive. That's a shame, because today many cases of impotence can be straightened out. That's right. Not 5 percent, or 15 percent, or 50 percent, but (with very few exceptions) most men who want an erection can have one.

For many years the medical establishment was sold on the notion that most impotence was psychological. There is absolutely no doubt that some cases of impotence are psychological in origin, stemming from performance anxiety, sexual inhibition, fear of pregnancy or STDs, or a conflict in the relationship. However, the belief among most sexual experts now is that most cases of impotence are not in the man's head.

That's good news. Even better, many of the physiological reasons for impotence can be overcome. When they can't, medical science still may have a trick up its sleeve. Sometimes it's as easy as finding out that one or another prescription drug is causing a problem and switching to another. Other times, surgery may be required.

Here are some of the impotence options:

(1) Hormonal treatment. Checking a man's hormone levels is an obvious first step in the treatment of impotence, but most men with erection problems do not have low testosterone levels. The willy-nilly injection of testosterone is definitely not to be encouraged, since it may promote the growth of what had been a very slow-growing prostate cancer in middle aged and older men.[79]

(2) Erection injection. One of the greatest advances in treating impotence was the discovery that certain drugs, when injected directly into the penis, could cause an erection that will persist for thirty minutes to an hour or so. The drug

most frequently used is papaverine, which is sometimes given in combination with phentolamine (**Regitine**). Another drug that has recently shown signs of success is prostaglandin E1, which is a smooth-muscle relaxant,[80] but

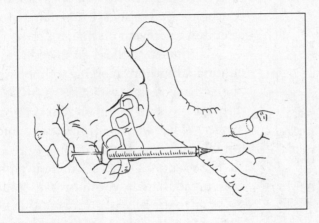

Self-Injection for Erection

more men report having pain and burning in their penis after injecting this drug, limiting its appeal considerably. A combination of the three may offer advantages (less likelihood of fibrosis) because the total volume injected is substantially lower.[81]

An experimental treatment, vasoactive intestinal peptide (VIP) is also being tested in combination with phentolamine. Senetek, the Danish company that is developing this medication, is negotiating for approval and marketing rights. A disposable auto-injector will make self injection easier.[82]

If the idea of injecting something into your penis makes you a bit squeamish, maybe the excellent and visible results will encourage you. The method works for men who have impotence from a wide variety of causes, including local nerve damage, some types of spinal cord injury, and even those whose impotence comes from psychological causes.[83] For most men the discomfort of the injection is minimal once they get used to the idea.

Nothing is perfect, of course. Some men develop a reaction to the injections in which they form fibrous tissue, and they may eventually have to forgo the drug treatment. (Prostaglandin

One vacuum device, the **ErecAid**, is available by prescription from Osbon Medical Supply, Department C, P.O. Drawer 1478, Augusta, GA 30903. Their number is: (800) 438-8592.

The company has printed a magnificent booklet written by Dr. Stephen Leslie titled *IMPOTENCE: Current Diagnosis and Treatment.* It provides an objective evaluation of all treatment options and is available free of charge by calling (800) 825-4215 or writing The Education Office, Department C, Geddings D. Osbon, Sr. Foundation, 1246 Jones Street, Augusta, GA 30901.

If your doctor wants to know more about the **ErecAid**, he can call for professional information: (800) 344-9688.

E1 seems safer in this regard.) Others, proving that you can have too much of a good thing, find themselves with erections that won't go down for prolonged periods. This condition, called priapism, is not only painful, but dangerous. It requires immediate medical attention to prevent permanent damage.

A number of these problems may be eliminated with an emerging technology that offers the possibility of carrying the drug through the skin using an "absorption enhancer." That would eliminate the uncomfortable necessity for injection.

(3) Vacuum Devices. There is probably no living adult male who did not at some time see an ad in the back of one or another men's magazine for a device that would allegedly make his penis bigger.

These dubious diddlers were suction devices of one sort or another, and what they produced was a very temporary illusion that the penis was bigger by swelling it with blood. The organ hadn't really grown, of course, and a six-inch penis was still a six-inch penis.

Now, however, vacuum devices have moved out of the men's magazines and become effective medical devices. With our increased understanding in the last several years of the mechanics of blood flow, it has been possible to effectively treat impotence by making vacuum devices that draw blood into the penis. Once there, the blood is entrapped by placing a constricting band at the base of the penis, thus impeding the outflow of blood. The result is an erection, good for a half hour or so, after which time the blood should be released to prevent untoward consequences.

(4) Surgery. As we said above, getting and keeping an erection is a complicated plumbing act. Sometimes the plumbing won't perform without a bit of tweaking, and doctors are getting amazingly skilled at repairing both large and small defects in the critical veins and arteries. It is now possible to

bypass blocked arteries, just as bad heart arteries are bypassed.

In another adaption of heart-surgery techniques, balloon angioplasty—inserting a catheter and inflating a balloon to crush substances blocking an artery and reopen the free flow of blood—has now been used on a few occasions to correct impotence. Since part of the time the problem is that veins let blood leak out, the balloon has also been used to carry substances that solidify and partially block the leaking vein.

The problem with the angioplasty technique as applied to arteries is that the arteries serving the penis are, relatively speaking, very small, and often the balloon just won't go. Look for advances in miniaturization, however, to solve that problem in the next few years.

(5) Penile Implants. When none of the above work, a man who is impotent and wants to have sexual intercourse is still not out of luck. Not any more, because he now has a wide range of implantable prostheses to choose from.

A penile prosthesis is a device implanted in the penis that allows a man to have an erection either because the device itself is semirigid (noninflatable), or because the device has some pneumatic rigging through which fluid is pumped by pressing on a reservoir implanted elsewhere (inflatable).

Implants have proved a real boon, and it's estimated that about twenty-five thousand of these operations are now performed in the United States every year. The best news is that an astounding 90 percent of the men report satisfaction with the prosthesis.[84] Since it's hard to get 90 percent of any bunch of people to agree on anything, this is strong testimony in favor of the implants. The techniques and materials are constantly improving, so things can only get better.

So the good news for men who are impotent is that lots of things work. All that's really necessary to get an erection is an interest in doing so, and a willingness to confront the problem with the assistance of a physician who is knowledgeable and experienced.

Quick Takes

- If you are a man and over forty, there is a very good chance your prostate is getting bigger. The older you get, the bigger it will grow. If you have been blessed with good genes or hormones, or something still undetermined, you won't have to worry. If urination gets tricky, start looking over your shoulder.

- Sometimes surgery is absolutely essential—as in a crisis. But if your doctor says you can comfortably watch and wait, that may make sense for now. New research suggests that prostate surgery of any sort carries some significant risks.

- **Proscar** could end up being the drug of the decade. Not only does it show great promise to shrink the size of the prostate, researchers are excited about its potential to reverse male pattern baldness, put an end to facial hair in women (hirsutism), and perhaps even cure acne.

- **Hytrin** and **Minipress** may offer stop-gap protection against urinary difficulties until we find out how good **Proscar** really is. Although these blood-pressure drugs have not yet been approved for enlarged prostate, there is some preliminary evidence that suggests they can be helpful.

- Preventing urinary tract infections can entail some effort. If a frequent result of intercourse, urinate within ten minutes after sexual activity. Drink eight cups of water a day. Avoid a diaphragm. Have your partner checked for infections—he may be a reservoir for bacteria.

- **Bactrim** and **Septra** are still the front-line defenders against UTIs. When they fail there are some newer and more potent antibiotics available. Your doctor will probably want to do a culture to determine which drug will kill your beasties.

- When it comes to STDs (sexually transmitted diseases) it's a jungle out there. There are microbes and viruses most of us never dreamed of and they can hurt like heck, not to   mention kill. Next to celibacy or monogamy with a "safe" partner, condoms are the only protection. Don't forget to check the label—condoms now carry an expiration date.

- Genital warts are hard to eliminate. Fears of cervical cancer have everyone nervous. Although not a cure, **Podofilox** looks like a promising new treatment. It should become available in the near future.

- Don't hold your breath for a new breakthrough in contraception any time soon. The United States lags far behind Europe in this regard. Aging baby boomers will be left high and dry—and maybe pregnant.

- Does the Pill cause breast cancer? Still anyone's guess. After thirty years we still don't have a definitive answer. Because breast cancer is so common—and lethal—anyone with a history of breast cancer in the family may want to think twice. It will be years before the jury is finally in, if ever.

- Bedwetting is common, not a sign of deep psychological problems, and will usually go away all by itself. Before any medications are started, a urologist should probably check to make sure there is not some anatomical abnormality.

- New treatments for bedwetting are starting to show up. **DDAVP** is now available for children in a nasal spray. We would discuss it with a urologist after everything else has failed and the child is desperate. The **Wee-Alert** and **Wet-Stop** alarms are a reasonable first line treatment—effectiveness runs up to 70 percent.

- Male sexual dysfunction can be treated. It takes some effort to shop around and find a sympathetic urologist who won't immediately push you in the direction of an implant. Implantation works, it is just the last resort. Discuss the "erection injection" and some of the other new alternatives. The right choices can only be made as a partnership—man, woman, and physician talking it out together.

References

[1] Bueschen, Anton. "Benign Prostatic Hyperplasia: Evaluation and Treatment." *Med. Aspects of Human Sexuality* 1989; 44–55.

[2] Lepor, Herbert. "Nonsurgical Approaches to BPH." *Patient Care* 1989; 23(20):46–55.

[3] Winslow, Ron. "Prostate Patients Get Choice of Treatments That Obviate Surgery." *The Wall Street Journal* 1990; 215(27):1.

[4] Zoler, Mitchel L. "Urologists Prop Up their Mainstay." *Med. World News* 1988(Sept. 26); 15–16.

[5] Barry, Michael J., et al. "Watchful Waiting vs. Immediate Transurethral Resection for Symptomatic Prostatism." *JAMA* 1988; 259: 3010–3017.

[6] Fowler, F.J., et al. "Symptom Status and Quality of Life Following Prostatectomy." *JAMA* 1988; 259:3018–3022.

[7] Winslow, op. cit.

[8] Wennberg, John E., et al. "An Assessment of Prostatectomy for Benign Urinary Tract Obstruction." *JAMA* 1988; 259:3027–3030.

[9] Editorial. "TU or Not TU." *Lancet*, 1989; i:1361–1362.

[10] Roos, Noralou P., et al. "Mortality and Reoperation After Open and Transurethral Resection of the Prostate for Benign Prostatic Hyperplasia." *N. Engl. J. Med.* 1989; 320(17):1120–1124.

[11] Ibid. p. 1123.

[12] Barry et al., op. cit.

[13] Rittmaster, Roger S., et al. "Effect of MK–906, a Specific 5a–Reductase Inhibitor, on Serum Androgens and Androgen Conjugates in Normal Men." *J. Andrology* 1989; 10(4):259–262.

[14] Vermeulen, A. "Hormonal Effects of an Orally Active 4-Azasteroid Inhibitor of 5 Alpha-Reductase in Humans."*Prostate* 1989; 14(1):45–53.

[15] Winslow, op. cit.

[16] Caine, M., et al. "A Placebo-Controlled Double-Blind Study of the Effect of Phenoxybenzamine in Benign Prostatic Obstruction." *Brit. J. Urol.* 1978; 50:551.

[17] Lepor, op. cit.

[18] Dunzendorfer, U. "Clinical Experience with Symptomatic Management of BPH with Terazosin." *Urology* 1988; Suppl. 6(32):27.

[19] Storr, Cynthia. "The Enlarged Prostate." *Drug Topics* 1989(Sept. 4); 46–49.

[20] Kirby, Robert S. "Alpha-Adrenoceptor Inhibitors in the Treatment of Benign Prostatic Hyperplasia." *Am. J. Medicine* 1989; 87 (Suppl. 2A):2A–26S–2A–30S.

[21] Ibid. p. 2A–28S.

[22] Scharf, Martin B., and Mayleben, David W. "Comparative Effects of Prazosin and Hydrochlorothiazide on Sexual Function in Hypertensive Men." *Am. J. Medicine* 1989; 86 (Suppl. 1B):110–112.

[23] Bankhead, Charles D. "More Nonsurgical BPH Options." *Med. World News* 1989(July 10); 22.

[24] Lepor, op. cit. p. 49.

[25] Lepor, Herbert. "Nonoperative Management of Benign Prostatic Hyperplasia." *J. Urology* 1989; 141:1283–1289.

[26] Storr, op. cit. p. 48.

[27] Ibid. p. 49.

[28] Quinn, S.F., et al. "Balloon Dilatation of the Prostatic Urethra." *Radiology* 1985; 157:57–58.

[29] Reddy, J.P.K., et al. "Balloon Dilatation of the Prostate for Treatment of Benign Hyperplasia." *Urol. Clin. N. Am.* 1988; 15:529–535.

[30] Winslow, op. cit.

[31] Storr, op. cit.

[32] Adatto, Kiku, et al. "Behavior Factors and Urinary Tract Infection." *JAMA* 1979; 241:2525–2526.

[33] Hoffman, Stephen A. "Everything You Need to Know about Urinary Tract Woes." *American Health* 1989; 8(3): 72–77.

[34] Schoolnik, Gary K. "How Escherichia coli Infects the Urinary Tract." (editorial). *N. Engl. J. Med.* 1989; 320:804.

[35] Fihn, S.D., et al. "Trimethoprim-Sulfamethoxazole for Acute Dysuria in Women: A Single-Dose or 10-Day Course. A Double-Blind, Randomized Trial." *Ann. Intern. Med.* 1988; 108:350–357.

[36] Johnson, M.A. "Urinary Tract Infections in Women." *Am. Fam. Physician* 1990; 41(2):565–571.

[37] Madsen, Paul O., et al. "Complications After Instrumentation of Urinary Tract." *Urology* 1985; 26(1):15–17.

[38] Manson, Alan. "Choice of Antibiotic for Lower Urinary Tract Infections in Men." *Postgrad. Med.* 1989; 85(2):224–226.

[39] Stamey, T.A. "Urinary Tract Infections in Males." in Stamey, T.A., ed., *Pathogenesis and Treatment of Urinary Tract Infections*. Baltimore: Williams & Wilkins, 1980, pp. 342–429.

[40] Spence, Michael. "Epidemiology of Sexually Transmitted Diseases." *Ob. Gyn. Clinics N. Am.* 1989; 16(3):454–466.

[41] Setness, Peter A. "Chlamydial Infections. Gaining Control of a Growing Epidemic." *Postgrad. Med.* 1989; 85(4):109–113.

[42] McGregor, James A. "Chlamydial Infection in Women." *Ob. Gyn. Clinics N. Am.* 1989; 16(3):565–592.

[43] Johnson, Larry W., and Heth, William L. "Infections of the Male Genitourinary System." *Primary Care* 1989; 16(4):929–940.

[44] DeBuono, B.A., et al. "Sexual Behavior of College Women in 1975, 1986, and 1989." *N. Engl. J. Med.* 1990; 322: 821–825.

[45] Ibid. p. 823.

[46] Schacter, Julius. "Why We Need a Program for the Control of Chlamydia trachomatis." *N. Engl. J. Med.* 1989; 320(12):802–803.

[47] Prescott, Lawrence M. "In-Office Chlamydia Test Unveiled." *Med. World News* 1988; 27(23):53.

[48] Phillips, R.S., et al. "Chlamydia trachomatis Cervical Infection in Women Seeking Routine Gynecologic Care: Criteria for Selective Testing." *Am. J. Med.* 1989; 515–520.

[49] Setness, op. cit.

[50] Schacter, Julius, and Moncada, Jeanne V. "In Vitro Activity of Ofloxacin Against Chlyamydia trachomatis." *Am. J. Med.* 1989; 87(Suppl. 6C):14–16.

[51] Table 1. *Morbidity and Mortality Weekly Report* 1990; 39(11):180.

[52] Johnson and Heth, op. cit.

[53] Higgins, Linda C. "Epidemic of Antibiotic-Resistant Gonorrhea Reshaping Treatment." *Med. World News* 1988; 29(22):12–13.

[54] Ansbacher, Rudi. "Recognition and Treatment of Pelvic Inflammatory Disease." *Modern Medicine* 1987; 55:79–86.

[55] Sweet, Richard L. "Pelvic Inflammatory Disease: Prevention and Treatment." *Mod. Med.* 1987; 55:64–68.

[56] Ibid.

[57] Rudlinger, Rene, and Norval, Mary. "Herpes simplex Virus Infections: New Concepts in an Old Disease." *Dermatologica* 1989; 178:1–5.

[58] Friedman-Kien, Alvin E., et al. "Genital Warts: Nuisance or Menace?" *Patient Care* 1988(Aug. 15); 36–42.

[59] "Study: Teen Girls' Risk of HPV Increasing." *Mod. Med.* 1989; 57:41.

[60] Friedman-Kien et al., op. cit.

[61] Peterson, Ila M. "Genital Warts. Newly Discovered Consequences of an Ancient Disease." *Postgrad. Med.* 1989; 86(3):197–204.

[62] Friedman-Kien et al., op. cit.

[63] Von Krogh, G. "Topical Treatment of Penile Condylomata acuminata with Podophyillin, Podophyllotoxin and Colchicine." *Acta Derm. Venereol.* 1978; 163–168.

[64] Von Krogh, G. "Topical Self-Treatment of Penile Warts with 0.5% Podophyllotoxin in Ethanol for Four of Five Days." *Sex. Transm. Dis.* 1987; 14:135–140.

[65] Edwards, A., et al. "Podophyllotoxin 0.5% versus Podophyllin 20% to Treat Penile Warts." *Genitourin. Med.* 1988; 64;263–265.

[66] Beutner, Karl R., et al. "Patient-Applied Podofilox for Treatment of Genital Warts." *Lancet* 1989; 1:831–834.

[67] Taylor, Robert N., and Callen, Karen R. "Common Problems in Office Gynecology: Vulvovaginitis." *Mod. Med.* 1988; 56:72–83.

[68] Mishell, Daniel R., Jr. "Contraception." *N. Engl. J. Med.* 1989; 320(12):777–787.

[69] Perlmutter, D. "Enuresis," in Kelalis, P.P., et al. (eds), *Clinical Pediatric Urology.* 2nd ed. Philadelphia: WB Saunders, 1985, pp. 311–325.

[70] Bakwin, H. "The Genetics of Enuresis," in Kolvin, I., et al. (eds), *Bladder Control and Enuresis.* London: Heinemann Medical, 1973, pp. 73–77.

[71] Rushton, H. Gil. "Nocturnal Enuresis: Epidemiology, Evaluation, and Currently Available Treatment Options." *J. Ped.* 1989; 114(4):691–696.

[72] Bankhead, Charles D. "Enuresis Therapy Targets Impaired Hormone Output." *Med. World News* 1989(June 12); 59.

[73] Kaluber, George T. "Clinical Efficacy and Safety of Desmopressin in the Treatment of Nocturnal Enuresis." *J. Pediatrics* 1989; 114(4):719–722.

[74] "Desmopressin Approved for Nocturnal Enuresis." *Patient Care* 1990(Apr 30); 24(8):23.

[75] MacLean, R.E.G. "Imipramine hydrochloride (Tofranil) and Enuresis." *Am. J. Psychiatry* 1960; 117:551.

[76] Rapoport, J.L., et al. "Childhood Enuresis. II: Psychopathology, Tricyclic Concentration in Plasma, and Antienuretic Effect." *Arch. Gen. Psychiatry* 1980; 37:1146–1152.

[77] Orsulak, Paul J., and Waller, David. "Antidepressant Drugs: Additional Clinical Uses." *J. Fam. Prac.* 1989; 28(2):209–216.

[78] Farley, Dixie. "Childhood Bed-Wetting: Cause for Concern?" *FDA Consumer* 1989(May); 8–11.

[79] Krane, Robert J., et al. "Impotence." *N. Engl. J. Med.* 1989; 321(24):1648–1659.

[80] Stackl, W., et al. "Intracavernous Injection of Prostaglandin E1 in Impotent Men." *J. Urol.* 1988; 140:66–68.

[81] "Impotence Rx Improved." *Medical Tribune* 1990(June 14); 31(12):1.

[82] "Senetek's Male Impotence Therapy." *Scrip* 1990(June 6); 1520:29.

[83] Krane et al., op. cit.

[84] Gregory, J.G., and Purcell, M.H. "Scott's Inflatable Penile Prosthesis: Evaluation of Mechanical Survival in the Series 700 Model." *J. Urol.* 1987; 137:676–677.

Allergy and Asthma | *10*

It's a war zone out there. We are besieged by enemies with every breath. For some, the adversary may be dust mites in the mattress or dander from a cat. Others are sensitive to cigarette smoke or mold from the air conditioner. Sulfite preservatives in food can do some people in, while others are allergic to one of the thousands of other chemical pollutants loose in our environment. Pollen, of course, is everywhere. There's no place to hide. No wonder our bodies often revolt. There are roughly twenty-five to thirty million Americans who suffer from seasonal hay fever.[1] Another twelve million people are allergic to things other than pollen and may suffer all year round.[2] Such allergies can increase our susceptibility to sinusitis and asthma.

Allergic Disorders

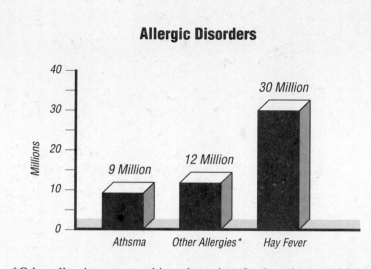

*Other allergies: eczema, hives, bee sting, food, or drug sensitivity.

Allergy and Hay Fever

It does not take an advanced degree in immunology to discover bad guys. If you start to sneeze and your eyes get red and itchy every time a cat sits in your lap, you do not need to go through an expensive series of skin tests to figure out that you are allergic to cats. If every spring and fall your nose starts to drip, itch, and become congested, allergies are a likely suspect, especially if your eyes begin to tear, and you feel sluggish and foggy. Doctors like to call it seasonal rhinitis (nasal inflammation). In plain English, that means your nose runs at certain times of the year. It is usually caused by allergens—pollen from timothy, orchard, blue, and Bermuda grasses, or oak, elm, and maple trees. Mold spores and of course ragweed pollen can also precipitate problems.

Chronic allergy victims have a harder time. Instead of suffering "only" twenty weeks out of the year they may be stuffed up and spaced out virtually all year long. They can be sensitive to dust mites, microscopic beasties that thrive in mattresses and upholstered furniture and hide by the millions in pillows, blankets, and carpets. It is actually these tiny creatures' fecal pellets that most people are allergic to. Mold can flourish anywhere there is humidity. Automobile air-conditioning ducts are a prime culprit. Cosmetics, pesticides, or even a beloved pet may be the hidden assailant. The workplace can serve up a soup of chemical fumes found circulating in the closed environment of a new high-rise office building (sick building syndrome). Tightly-insulated homes can also trap chemical gasses from carpets, cleaners, aerosol antiperspirants, and a host of other household products.

HOW IT HAPPENS

Once you are exposed to a foreign substance, or allergen, your immune system goes into gear to produce antibodies called immunoglobulin E—IgE for short. Each IgE antibody is tailored exactly to fit a tiny segment of the attacking allergen. These antibodies are like microscopic homing devices and they end up coating special mast cells that are found throughout the body, but in especially high concentrations in the eyes, nose, and lungs. These mast cells have been described as "floating mines" just waiting to come in contact with ragweed pollen, or some other allergen.

Once the invading allergen bridges the gap between two IgE antibodies on the surface of the mast cell, it is like a switch gets thrown on this cellular "mine." Quickly all hell breaks loose. Mast cells start releasing nasty chemicals—histamine and kinins (pronounced KYE-nins), which in turn lead to production of other rascals called leukotrienes, prostaglandins, bradyki-nins, and some unpleasant enzymes. These chemical shock troops cause all sorts of mischief including itching, sneezing, congestion, bronchial constriction (asthma), mucus secretion, swelling, and generalized yucky feelings. This is known as the "early phase" of the allergic reaction. Histamine and kinins also send out a signal that attracts white blood cells to the area. They in turn cause "late phase" infiltration and damage of tissues. All in all, it's a dirty little war that gets fought inside your nose, eyes, skin, throat, and lungs. There is growing evidence that asthma is firmly rooted in the allergy quagmire.

Why some people have hyper-reactive immune systems is still unclear, but genetics plays an important role. If both Mom and Dad are victims, then there is a high probability that the kids will be vulnerable too. But even people with no family history may develop allergic sensitivities, especially if they are exposed to a large number of allergens. Cold viruses may also trigger the immune system to overreact, which may explain why asthma often appears or becomes worse after upper respiratory infections in the winter.

NONDRUG TREATMENT

The best way to overcome allergies is to keep allergens like pollen, dander, or dust mites from ever completing the circuit on the surface of a mast cell. If this cellular mine never blows up, it can't release all those dreadful chemicals. If you could either banish the offending allergens from your environment, or do your best to insulate yourself from them once they are in the air, you could improve immeasurably your odds of weathering the pollen storm. Avoidance is undoubtedly the best possible therapy.

Air Filters

If fall hay fever is your nemesis, an ocean cruise is one way to reduce your exposure to ragweed. Even a vacation at the beach could be helpful. If that's not possible, air conditioning can do a lot to filter out the pollen. (Keep windows closed during spring and fall allergy season.) It is also a good idea to have an effective air filter installed. Now we are not talking about those largely ineffective fiberglass doodahs that most people have on their furnaces. These filters only capture really large dust particles and relying on them to trap pollen or other small allergens would be like trying to catch flies with a fishnet.

The best kind are HEPA filters—high-efficiency particulate-arresting filters—that are made of densely packed fibers. The filter itself is pleated and looks a little like an accordion that has been scrunched together. The prototype HEPA filters were developed to decrease radioactive dust escaping from atomic plants. Nowadays these high-efficiency filters are used industrially in hospitals, pharmaceutical plants, and "clean rooms" for computer chip manufacturing because they can trap very tiny dust particles.

HEPA filters for the home are available, but not widely used because they are more expensive than traditional filter systems. The best system filters air centrally, throughout the house. They usually have to be changed only once a year and actually become more efficient the dirtier they get. Check with a heating and air-conditioning expert. One brand that we have been pleased with is **Space-Gard** (available from Research Products, Corp., Madison, WI 53501). Portable room air purifiers are less effective, but *Consumer Reports* rated a number of models that do a good job. They run roughly $300–$500.

If you are allergic to dust mites or animal dander, an air filter won't help much. Remember that the dust mite is associated with upholstery, pillows, and mattresses. Allergists often recommend encasing mattresses in allergen-proof plastic and using a pillow made of hypoallergenic synthetic material (dacron or polyester). In Britain an exciting new polyurethane material called Ventflex (**Coverplus**) is being used on some mattress covers, pillows and other textiles. It allows water vapor to pass through, but traps mites inside. Preliminary testing shows that Ventflex-coated fabrics are 99 percent effective at trapping mite feces compared to conventional bedding. Researchers report that "Ventflex covers seem to be a novel, safe, convenient, and comfortable method of eliminating house dust mite antigen from bedding. The covering should prove useful in the management of house dust mite sensitive patients with asthma, rhinitis, and eczema."[4]

Some physicians recommend foam rubber pillows, but there are people who are even allergic to foam. If you do try foam, replace it periodically to make sure no mold starts growing. Wash sheets, blankets, and mattress pads frequently in hot water to kill any mites that may escape. Any mattress covering should be vacuumed weekly.

People who are allergic should never vacuum and should probably be out of the house when vacuuming is under way because paper or fabric dust bags do not trap all the material they collect. As a result, allergens are spread throughout the air for at least an hour. (What a great excuse to get out of this household chore!). Fortunately (or unfortunately, depending upon your viewpoint), there are several vacuum cleaners that are exceptions to this rule. They trap dust in a water canister or rely on HEPA (high-efficiency, particulate-arresting) filters. We suggest checking out the **Nilfisk Dustless HEPA** or the **Rainbow** brand vacuum cleaner. A cheaper, but less efficient alternative would be to retrofit your current vacuum cleaner with a more efficient filter. Such products are available from National Allergy Supply, Inc. If you are planning to build a house you might want to consider a centralized vacuuming system that vents the dust directly to the outside.

Eliminating carpets, rugs, upholstered furniture and other surfaces where dust can collect can also help. A plain wood "look" is a popular decorating approach for severely allergic individuals. If you can't bear to part with a pet, at least bar the animal from the bedroom!

Vitamin C

No matter how hard you try to reduce exposure to pollen, dust, mold, dander, and chemicals, it is impossible completely to eliminate allergens from the environment. Before reaching for medicine our first line of defense is vitamins, and ascorbic acid heads our list. Ever since Dr. Linus Pauling started recommending vitamin C for the common cold, doctors have been giving him grief. This is clearly one of the most controversial nutrients of all time, with the enthusiasts proclaiming its benefits for everything from cancer and cold prevention to combating gum disease and diabetes.

Unfortunately, there is a lack of excellent research on vitamin C and allergies. A number of articles in the medical literature suggest that large doses of this nutrient have anti-inflammatory and antiallergic properties, perhaps by preventing the antibody-antigen bonding.[5-8] Researchers at the University of California, San Francisco, found that patients who suffered from a severe allergic skin condition called atopic dermatitis benefited substantially from large doses of vitamin C (3000–5000 mg total daily dose—50–75 mg/kg of body weight).[9]

We have also been encouraged by some new studies conducted by one of the world's experts on the common cold. Dr. Elliot Dick at the University of Wisconsin has been studying cold viruses for years and recently discovered that it is the amount of vitamin C that gets into cells that is the most important factor in improving cold symptoms. For reasons that are not yet clear, this appears to differ tremendously from individual to individual and may account for the wide variability in vitamin C research results. Dr. Dick found that it takes around 2.5 grams of vitamin C a day to get reliable levels into cells and an anticold effect.[10] In our experience this dose (divided throughout the day in 500 mg amounts) seems to offer some relief against allergic symptoms as well. What we really need are some well-controlled scientific studies on the effects of vitamin C against allergies.

DRUG TREATMENTS

Walk into any pharmacy in the country and you will be overwhelmed by antihistamines, decongestants, combination allergy remedies, and nasal sprays. Some of the hottest items on the drugstore shelves were once available only by prescription.

There are major difficulties with nonprescription allergy treatments, however. Over-the-counter antihistamines are generally sedating (**Seldane** will be an exception if and when it becomes available OTC). Although people vary in their susceptibility to drowsiness, most of these medications do not make you feel terrific. Often overlooked or ignored is the warning on the label, "Do not drive or operate heavy machinery."

They're not kidding. Dr. Fran Gengo of the State University of New York at Buffalo noted that "50 milligrams of diphenhydramine [the ingredient in **Benadryl**] may cause the same impairment as a blood-alcohol level of 0.1, the standard for legal drunkenness. The impairment levels are the same; the consequences will be equally tragic." In California, the highway patrol can pull you over for DWI (driving while impaired) if

OTC Allergy Drugs
Actifed
Afrin
Benadryl
Chlor-Trimeton
Coricidin
Dimetane
Dimetapp
Drixoral
Sudafed

you are affected by over-the-counter antihistamines.

Nasal sprays are just as problematical. Products like **Afrin**, **Dristan Long Lasting**, **Duration**, **Neo-Synephrine 12 Hour**, and **Sinex Long-Acting** are so effective at opening congested nasal passages that many folks are tempted to keep using them beyond the three-day limit. Since allergies last a lot longer than three days, lots of people become hooked on their nasal decongestants. Every time they try to stop, their noses clog up and they feel so miserable that they go right back to the spray.

Weaning off Nasal Sprays

Dr. Ron Gerbe, an ENT (ear, nose, and throat) specialist, suggests that his patients turn to **Otrivin** spray. It comes in 0.1 percent strength for adults and 0.05 percent for children. He starts people on the adult dose and then suggests that they dilute it with water or saline (**Ayr Saline** or **NāSal** saline). By eventually switching over to the children's dose and diluting it every two or three days, patients can slowly reduce exposure until pure saline is being used. If this does not work, Dr. Gerbe prescribes a steroid nasal spray (like **Beconase** or **Nasalide**) and in really difficult cases, a short course of an oral cortisonelike medicine may be necessary. He prescribes **Medrol Dosepak** for five or six days.

PRESCRIPTION SOLUTIONS

In our humble opinion, most allergy sufferers would do well to avoid the over-the-counter antihistamines and nasal decongestants, pass go and head straight for the doctor's office. The prescription allergy medicines that are available are far more effective and lots safer than most non-prescription allergy remedies.

Nasalcrom and Opticrom

Our first line defense in the fight against allergies is cromolyn sodium (**Nasalcrom** spray for the nose and **Opticrom** drops for the eyes). This drug stabilizes the mast cells. Remember, these are the floating cellular mines loaded with histamine and kinins. **Nasalcrom** prevents these cells from releasing

---

Safe Nasal Sprays

Saline solutions are soothing and nonaddicting. They can help rinse the nose of irritants and relieve irritated membranes. We recommend any of the following:

Ayr Saline

HuMIST Saline Nasal Mist

NāSal

Ocean Mist

★ ★ ★

these chemicals in the nose. What makes it special is that it works both against the early- as well as the late-phase allergic reaction.

The only problem with cromolyn is that you must use it daily to prevent problems. It is purely prophylactic and will not reverse an allergic reaction once it is under way. If you have to visit grandma and you are allergic to her cat, use the **Nasalcrom** and **Opticrom** several hours before visiting and you may be able to make it through dinner without sneezing. The other advantage of cromolyn is its extraordinary safety record. Although some people complain of temporary sneezing, stinging, irritation, and a bad taste in the mouth, most people find they can tolerate this medicine very well.

Prescription Antihistamines

Perhaps the greatest revolution in allergy treatment comes in the form of nonsedating antihistamines. **Seldane** (terfenadine) was the first to hit pharmacy shelves and quickly went on to dominate the prescription antihistamine market. The usual dose is 60 mg twice a day. Adverse effects are rare, though hair thinning and hair loss have been reported. Other rare, but possible side effects include digestive tract upset, dry mouth and throat, and depression. More disturbing are recent reports that **Seldane** may affect electrical conduction within the heart and lead to irregular rhythms. Although apparently rare, this disturbance may be more likely to appear in cases of overdose or when the antihistamine is taken simultaneously with the antifungal drug **Nizoral** or certain antibiotics. For someone with heart disease, such a reaction might be life-threatening. This unexpected complication has delayed the launch of **Seldane** for nonprescription use.

Hismanal (astemizole) was the second nonsedating prescription antihistamine to receive FDA approval. It is longer-acting than **Seldane,** and once-daily dosing is all that is necessary. It provides twenty-four-hour coverage so allergy victims will be pleased to discover that they don't wake up in the early-morning hours all stuffed up. **Hismanal** is especially effective at relieving itching and eye tearing and may

---

Nasalcrom, Opticrom *(cromolyn)*
Effective allergy prevention. Stabilizes mast cells to prevent histamine release. Very safe!

★ ★ ★ ★

be slightly superior to **Seldane** in this regard.[11] It also works reasonably well against hives.

Hismanal may take four or five days to begin working, though. Someone who is in a big hurry might want to follow the recommendation (under a physician's supervision) of "taking a single dose of 30 mg on the first day, followed by a single dose of 20 mg on the second day and 10 mg thereafter."[12] This medication does not cause drowsiness and changes in mood, or affect the ability to drive or operate machinery. To date we have not seen any report that it causes hair thinning. All in all, **Hismanal** is our first choice of oral antihistamines.

Steroid Sprays

If all else fails there is still hope. Our ace in the hole is a steroid nasal spray. These cortisonelike medications are surprisingly safe and effective. Most people shudder when they hear the words steroid or cortisone. In this case there is little reason to worry, though. The medications are barely absorbed into the body and therefore there is no concern about the systemic side effects typical of oral corticosteroids. There are two basic ingredients to choose from, beclomethasone (**Beconase** and **Vancenase**) and flunisolide (**Nasalide**).

These medications are comparable, although some people complain that **Beconase** smells funny while others say **Nasalide** stings a little bit. A new aerosol canister called a "compact actuator" has been designed for **Beconase** and may make it easier for some people to use. For those who like a liquid spray, there is **Beconase AQ.** Trial and error is really the best way to determine which steroid spray and delivery system suits your needs. These products can reduce congestion, itching, inflammation, and sneezing, although there may be a little irritation at first. Nosebleeds occur in about five percent of patients. It can take about a week of regular use to produce noticeable benefit, so be patient.

Hismanal
(astemizole)

A long-acting, nonsedating oral antihistamine. Provides excellent protection, but requires up to five days to go to work. Should be taken on an empty stomach for maximal absorption. Does not appear to cause hair loss.
Side effect: Weight gain has been reported in about 4 percent of patients.

★ ★ ★ ★

FUTURE DRUGS

The future looks great for allergy sufferers. There will be new, and perhaps even better, long-acting nonsedating antihistamines entering the market. The one that is most likely to arrive any time now is **Claritin** (loratadine) from Schering-Plough. Like **Hismanal**, **Claritin** is a once-daily medication, which will make it slightly more convenient than **Seldane**. Another long-acting antihistamine undergoing investigation is **Zyrtec** (certirizine). It has done very well in Europe (marketed by Allen & Hanburys in the United Kingdom under the name **Zirtek**). It is being developed by Pfizer in the United States. Burroughs Wellcome also has an entry, **Sempex** (acrivastine), and Janssen Pharmaceutica is working on an interesting antihistamine nasal spray called levocabastine.

New topical steroid sprays are also in the works. Dr. Elizabeth Juniper of McMaster University in Hamilton, Ontario, Canada, has found that a new medication called budesonide is better than allergy shots at controlling hay fever symptoms. It is being sold in Sweden by Astra as **Pulmicort** for asthma. Early reports are impressive. Most exciting of all, researchers at the University of California, San Diego, and Northwestern University are coming up with powerful new allergy shots that may have to be given only for short periods of time and may offer unprecedented relief.

The majority of allergy victims can now live more-or-less normal lives. Obviously, the best approach is still, and always will be, the elimination of offending allergens. But with the medicines at hand and new ones in the pipeline, there is no reason to have to settle between the sneezes and sniffles of hay fever on one hand or the sedation and spacey feeling of over-the-counter antihistamines on the other.

Sinusitis

There's a wonderful old spiritual that starts, "Nobody knows the trouble I've seen, nobody knows but Jesus." Well,

---

Steroid Nasal Sprays
beclomethasone
(Beconase, Vancenase)
flunisolide
(Nasalide)

These medicines are very effective at relieving sneezing, congestion, itching, and inflammation. May take several days to produce benefits. Can cause drying of the nose and nosebleeds. Prolonged use may cause fungal infections (*Candida*) in the nose.

★ ★ ★

when it comes to sinusitis, you almost have to experience it to really know the true sorrow of the sinus victim. Sinusitis (inflammation of the sinuses) can leave you feeling congested, disoriented, swollen, headachy, and generally miserable. The pain can be mild to severe. Your nose, forehead, eyes, and teeth may hurt. Even your vision can be affected. It is hard to think or function when you have a sinus infection.

Location of Sinuses

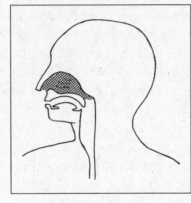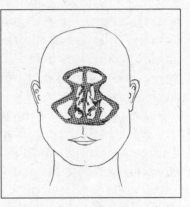

Often there are yellowish green mucus discharges from the nose. Some of this gunk may cause you to gag as it gradually works its way down the back of your throat (postnasal drip). But if you develop severe facial pain and headache without mucus, that can even be worse: the pressure can build up because there is no drainage. You may feel tempted to call the Roto-Rooter man to come and unplug your personal drain.

The sinus cavities make up almost one third of the frontal part of the head. No one really knows why we even have sinuses. Some ENT experts have speculated that they were an evolutionary adaptation to protect us from head injury during the time of the cave men. These days, they cause us a lot of grief. Anything that blocks sinus drainage can lead to big trouble. A simple cold that causes mucus to accumulate can evolve into fullblown sinusitis. Allergy victims are especially vulnerable to sinus infections because when the nasal passages become congested and you can no longer breathe through your nose, conditions become ripe for bacterial invasion.

PREVENTION

As always, prevention is the best medicine. If your sinusitis is related to allergies, you may be able to avoid an infection if you can keep those nasal passages open and draining. See the discussion of allergies (p. 380) for various options. Avoid as many chemical irritants as possible, as they too can aggravate this condition.

It is important to keep the mucus in the sinuses relatively thin and moving. The thicker the mucus, the more likely bacteria will start to grow. Drink plenty of fluids—eight glasses of water a day if you can stand it. And try to avoid alcohol. It can cause nasal congestion. Avoid regular use of topical decongestants (three-day limit). Nasal spray addiction can lead to rebound congestion, which in turn can set up conditions for a vicious cycle. Saline nose sprays (**Ayr Saline, HuMIST Saline Nasal Mist, NāSal,** and **Ocean Mist**) may be helpful by keeping the tissues moist. If there is some kind of anatomical abnormality, such as a deviated septum (crooked cartilage) or sinus blockage, surgery is really the best prevention for future sinusitis.

DRUG TREATMENT

But what do you do when it's too late to prevent problems? If your head feels about the size of a basketball, the yellowish green mucus is nonstop, and you think the pain will never go away, the chances are good you have a sinus infection. First things first. It is essential your doctor clears up the underlying bacterial infection. A first-ever sinus infection may be caused by such bugs as *Pneumococcus*, *Streptococcus* (the same nasties that cause strep throat), *Branhamella catarrhalis*, and *Hemophilus influenzae*. Chronic infections may be brought on by *Staphylococcus aureus*.[13] But there are literally dozens of microbes that are willing and able to set up housekeeping in your sinuses.

Getting the right antibiotic for the beastie causing your misery may require a sinus culture, though this can be complicated and is more appropriate in resistant cases. If it is your first infection, the doctor may decide to go ahead and treat immediately with ampicillin, amoxicillin, **Augmentin** (amoxicillin/

> ## Cephalosporin Antibiotics for Bacterial Sinusitis
> ### Ceclor (cefaclor)
> ### Ceftin (cefuroxime)
> ### Cipro (ciprofloxacin)
>
> These medicines are usually well-tolerated but some people may be especially susceptible to side effects. Some that you should be alert for include nausea, diarrhea, gas, stomach upset, headache, insomnia, mental confusion, rash, itching, fever, jaundice.

clavulanate), erythromycin, or tetracycline. People who are allergic to penicillin may get **Bactrim** or **Septra** (trimethoprim/sulfamethoxazole). It may take as long as six weeks of conscientious treatment to make any progress.[14]

If these basic antibiotics don't do the job, or if you have been battling chronic sinusitis for weeks or months, it could be time to bring on the heavy artillery. Cephalosporin antibiotics can work wonders where other drugs fall by the wayside. They are, unfortunately, very expensive. A single pill can cost anywhere from $1–2 and a month's treatment may run well over $60.

Anyone who suffers chronic sinus infections (more than two or three a year) should bite the bullet and have an ear, nose, and throat specialist do some careful examination of the old proboscis. If there is an anatomical abnormality, such as a deviated septum, a little corrective surgery can go a long way toward ending sinusitis forever.

Asthma

There is something bad happening to asthmatics and no one knows why. All around the world asthma is becoming more common and more severe.[15] Hospitalizations are up, and more people are dying. During the 1980s, the death rate increased 25 percent in five years.[16] Urban areas have been hardest hit, with older people, African-Americans, and Hispanics especially vulnerable.

There are seasonal patterns that are hard to explain. Children are more likely to die during the summer, while older people (over sixty-five) are most susceptible in the winter.[17] More than four thousand Americans succumbed to asthma last year despite new and better medicines. Is it air pollution? Do people have too many pets? Are asthmatics overusing their inhalers or are they underusing them? Are the drugs relieving symptoms better but increasing the death rate? Are people trying to self-medicate when they should really be seeing a physician? At this point there are no answers to these important questions.

Some suggest that the reason deaths are rising so rapidly is that patients are more "noncompliant" these days. That is, they aren't following doctor's orders. We don't buy it. Someone who is having difficulty breathing is motivated to get relief. Believe us; we know because we've been there (JG suffered from asthma as a teenager). When you are lying in bed late at night gasping for breath, you follow whatever recommendations   have been offered. And you take your medicine because the memory of that attack does not go away. We can't think of a more committed group than asthmatics when it comes to trying to comply with the appropriate regimen. Compared to people with high blood pressure, we'd bet that patients with asthma would win hands down when it comes to following directions. But part of the problem might be that instructions are not clear. Drug side effects may also be a problem that interferes with successful treatment.

A recent survey of 1,150 asthmatics and the people involved with their treatment has revealed some startling statistics.[18] During the 1970s asthma increased 58 percent in six- to eleven-year-old children. "Nearly half (46 percent) of the surveyed pediatricians are treating more asthmatic children today than they were just five or ten years ago." Almost 50 percent of children with asthma suffered emotional trauma from their condition. Side effects from medicine are common.

> ### Medication Problems
>
> Eighty-one percent of surveyed pediatricians reported that parents of asthmatic children complain about side effects.
>
> Parents mention restlessness (59 percent) and difficulty in concentrating (27 percent) as among the more common adverse reactions to medicine.
>
> Pediatricians report that upset stomach caused by theophylline is reported to them 38 percent of the time. Hyperactivity is also more common with theophylline.

It is essential that researchers start investigating the reasons behind the rapid increase in asthma severity and deaths. If pollution and chemical exposure are to blame, we had better redouble our efforts to clean up the environment. If the increasing use of potent medicines is responsible, physicians will need to rethink their reliance on multiple prescriptions. The impact of combinations of different asthma drugs on other body systems, particularly the heart, needs closer scrutiny. Unless we can pinpoint the cause, we have little hope of reversing the scary increase in asthma deaths.

NONDRUG TREATMENTS

The first goal of a successful treatment program should always be the elimination of any triggers that may bring on an attack. If pets are a source of trouble, then it is essential they be moved outdoors. If smoke, dust, or chemical pollution causes wheezing, then the offending allergen should be controlled as well as possible. The workplace is often a source of trouble. Sick-building syndrome can lead to asthma because of fumes given off by synthetic building materials which may not be able to escape due to tight insulation. If health becomes threatened by the job environment, a change may be in order.

HERBAL REMEDIES

For an occasional case of mild asthma, herbal treatment might work in a pinch. Ephedra is an ancient Chinese medicine dating back at least five thousand years. The active ingredient, ephedrine, has been used for decades to dilate constricted airways. Unfortunately, the benefits of this medicine are lost if it is used too frequently. It can also cause a number of unpleasant side effects, including anxiety, insomnia, difficult urination, stomach upset, and heart palpitations. People with high blood pressure and prostate problems should avoid ephedrine. Here is a clear case where an herbal remedy may be less effective and more toxic than most prescription asthma medications.

Ginkgo

Another ancient Chinese herbal remedy comes from the leaves of the ginkgo tree. Healers have used an extract from these leaves for thousands of years to treat asthma, allergies, coughs, and bronchitis. Scientists have finally isolated the active substance from ginkgo and what do you know, it works.

Organic chemists at Harvard have made ginkgolide B in the laboratory and there is excitement that it may open up the door to a whole new class of therapeutic compounds.[19] Unfortunately, the ginkgo products available in many health-food stores do not contain enough of the active ingredient to do much, if any, good. Although this substance appears to be quite safe, it will probably be some time before its true therapeutic potential is realized.

Caffeine

We received a letter not too long ago from a very happy woman. She wrote to tell us how we saved her honeymoon:

> My husband and I left for Hawaii immediately after the wedding. In all the excitement I forgot my asthma medicine. Although I don't have to take it everyday I always keep some on hand.
>
> The day after we arrived we took a long walk on the beach and by the time we got back I was wheezing. I almost panicked until I remembered reading in your newspaper column that coffee can act as an emergency treatment for asthma.
>
> Three cups controlled my attack and I didn't have any more trouble. The rest of the honeymoon was great.

Caffeine is chemically related to a classic asthma medicine called theophylline, so it's no wonder that several hundred milligrams (two to three cups of regular coffee) can partially open airways. This is not the appropriate treatment in a real emergency, but as a stopgap measure to control a mild wheeze, caffeine may buy you enough time to get to your real medicine.

VITAMINS

Vitamin C is just as controversial for asthma as for allergy treatment. The most that can be said is that there are conflicting studies. Some suggest 500–1000 mg protect the airways from spasm, but others state unequivocally that ascorbic acid is useless. None of the studies were really well done, however, and none took into account Dr. Elliot Dick's recent finding that intracellular vitamin C levels are highly variable from individual to individual.

One of the more intriguing findings on vitamin C comes from analysis of the second National Health and Nutrition Examination Survey (NHANES II). This analysis of ninety-one hundred adults revealed that an "above average intake of vitamin C—200 mg more than the 98-mg average—was associated with about a 30 percent lower incidence of bronchitis and wheezing. Greater serum niacin levels were associated with a reduction in wheezing."[20]

In 1985 a fascinating article in the *American Journal of Clinical Nutrition* reported that fifteen asthmatics had significantly lower levels of vitamin B_6 (pyridoxine). Seven of the subjects were given 50 mg of pyridoxine and bingo, they experienced a "dramatic decrease in the frequency and severity of the wheezing attacks" while on the supplement.[21] Unfortunately, we have been unable to locate any follow-up of this research. We need a good double-blind and controlled study to confirm these tantalizing results. For the moment, however, we do not see any great harm in asthmatics doing a little personal experimenting with 50 mg of vitamin B_6.

NONPRESCRIPTION REMEDIES

Shopping for over-the-counter treatments is risky business. It could be one of the biggest traps that an asthmatic can fall into. The promise is great—instant relief from wheezing. But the likelihood for problems is much greater than with prescription treatment. If you have asthma it is worth treating right.

THE RIGHT RX STUFF

Asthma seems to occur because the airways are supersensitive to irritation. This hyperresponsiveness leads to inflammation and constriction. The goal of treatment, then, is to prevent or reduce the inflammatory response and dilate the bronchioles so people can breathe freely again.

Avoid reliance on epinephrine inhalers:

AsthmaHaler
AsthmaNefrin
Bronitin Mist
Bronkaid Mist
Medihaler-Epi
Primatene Mist
Vaponefrin

Dilators

One of the first-line treatments for the intermittent wheeze of bronchial asthma is the beta-booster, otherwise known as a bronchodilator. These medications stimulate beta receptors—just the opposite of heart and high blood pressure beta-blockers, which can actually bring on asthma. Aerosol inhalers like albuterol (**Ventolin**, **Proventil**), fenoterol (**Berotec**), terbutaline (**Brethaire**), metaproterenol (**Alupent**, **Metaprel**), and bitolterol (**Tornalate**) can all open the airways rapidly during a mild to moderate asthma attack. They can be used before exercise to prevent exercise-induced asthma.

The only downside to these medications is their short-lived action—three to six hours. As the wheeze returns, people may get carried away with their inhaler and that can lead to overdosing. A longer-acting, twelve-hour inhaler, salmeterol, should soon become available from Allen & Hanburys, a division of Glaxo, Inc. It could make nighttime asthma treatment much easier.

Inhalers are less likely to cause side effects than oral medicine. When these same medications are taken in pill form, such as terbutaline (**Brethine**, **Bricanyl**), albuterol (**Ventolin**, **Proventil**), and metaproterenol (**Alupent**, **Metaprel**), they can cause tremor, palpitations, and rapid heart rate.

Theophylline

The United States is slowly catching up with its neighbors across the ocean. Whereas we used to use theophylline as a first-line treatment, asthma experts now are keeping it in reserve (mostly as a third line) because of its likelihood to cause side effects.[22] Many patients complain of nausea, stomach pain, loss of appetite, headache, insomnia, and irritability. At higher doses irregular heart rhythms and seizures may become problems. Children have been reported to have a hard time concentrating and may develop learning difficulties while on theophylline.[23] The FDA has called for further studies on this issue.

Theophylline can interact adversely with a number of other medications. Although it is not uncommon for theophylline to

---

Theophylline Medications

Bronkodyl
Elixophyllin
Somophyllin-T
Slo-bid
Slo-Phyllin
Theo-Dur
Theo-24
Theobid
Theolair
Uniphyl

be added to bronchodilators like **Ventolin** or **Alupent**, some experts now believe such combinations are generally inappropriate.[24] Certain antibiotics (erythromycin) or ulcer medications (**Tagamet**) can also interact with theophylline. And if someone comes down with a viral infection, the dose of theophylline may have to be temporarily lowered.

When necessary, theophylline can be used to control nighttime asthma attacks. A sustained-release product such as **Theo-Dur** or **Uniphyl** taken at suppertime can often prevent an early-morning wheezing attack. If daytime asthma is not a problem, some doctors believe it may be unnecessary to even take another theophylline dose until the next evening.[25]

Anti-inflammatory Agents

Now that allergists and pulmonary experts appreciate that inflammation is at the heart of asthma, they are concentrating on calming down the hyperresponsive lung tissues. Although these drugs can't stop an asthma attack once it starts, they are extremely effective at preventing one if they are used conscientiously. This means they will have to be used daily, even when asthma appears to be under control. Many physicians now consider these medicines the second step in asthma treatment after bronchodilators.

One underprescribed, extremely safe medication is our old allergy friend cromolyn (**Intal** inhaler for asthma). Children seem to respond somewhat better than adults, but it may be worth an initial try for almost anyone, given the drug's extraordinary safety record. It is thought to work by stabilizing mast cells in the lungs. **Intal** is beneficial both for the early and late phase of asthma hyperreactivity. This is one of our first choices in asthma treatment, especially for children.[26]

Speaking of children and asthma, we encourage parents to invest in a peak flow meter. Just as you have a thermometer on hand to measure a child's temperature, you should have a flow meter to monitor the general state of the lungs. As airways constrict, asthma tends to get worse, but the patient may not always realize how severe the situation has become. When a child (or adult, for that matter) inhales deeply and

---

Intal
(cromolyn sodium)

Prevents asthma attacks when used daily. (Cannot abort an acute attack—is purely prophylactic.) Works well to prevent exercise-induced asthma. Side effects: Extremely rare. May leave a bad taste and irritate throat. Occasional cough.

★ ★ ★

Peak Flow Meter

then blows into a peak flow meter, it is possible to get a measurement of lung capacity. Parents can keep a numerical record and plot it on a chart to keep track of response to asthma medication. This can be especially useful for children whose asthma reacts to exercise and can help determine whether they are ready for an athletic event. You can order a peak flow meter from Mothers of Asthmatics (10875 Main Street, Suite 210, Fairfax, VA 22030). Our preferred brand is the Mini-Wright Peak Flow Meter.

Steroid Sprays

Adults (and some children) who do not benefit from **Intal** are usually tried on a corticosteroid inhaler. There used to be a fear that such drugs would cause cortisonelike side effects, but after years of experience those concerns are finally fading. Most pulmonary experts believe that these medications are very safe in low doses and should be first-line anti-inflammatory choices. They represent one of the greatest advances in asthma therapy in recent years.[27] British specialists have long relied on these inhalers instead of oral theophylline with excellent results.

When steroid inhalers like beclomethasone (**Beclovent**, **Vanceril**), flunisolide (**AeroBid**), and triamcinolone (**Azmacort**) are used carefully, they can slowly calm a hyperactive lung response. They also help control exercise-induced asthma. As long as such medicine is not overused, there is little likelihood of serious systemic side effects, since very little gets absorbed into the body.

One common complication of such medicine, however, is yeast infection (*Candida*) in the throat. One way to reduce this side effect is to rinse the mouth with water every time the aerosol is used. Spacers can also be a big help in cutting down the likelihood of this adverse reaction. These simple devices fit on the inhaler and provide a chamber from which the medicine can be more easily inhaled in two or three breaths. This allows the medicine to be absorbed into the lungs more effectively and cuts down on the possibility of it accumulating on top of the mouth, tongue or throat. Several brands to look for in your pharmacy include **AeroChamber** (Forest Laboratories), **InhalAid** (Schering/Key), and **InspirEase** (Schering/Key).

FUTURE DRUGS

One of the most successful asthma drugs in the world has been denied the American public because the U.S. Food and Drug Administration has such an inflexible attitude about drug testing. **Zaditen** (made by Sandoz) has been available in Canada and Europe for years. It is roughly equivalent to an oral cromolyn and also has an excellent safety record. We're afraid the wait for **Zaditen** will go on and on.

One advance that we can expect in the near future is long-acting aerosol bronchodilators. Ciba-Geigy has formoterol, Astra is developing bambuterol, and Allen & Hanburys (a Glaxo subsidiary) has salmeterol. This oral product should soon become available under the brand name **Volmax**. It offers twelve-hour asthma relief, but is likely to have many of the side effects of other beta-boosting bronchodilators (see page 391). A long-acting steroid inhaler from Glaxo is also quite promising—fluticasone is now in the pipeline and should reach the marketplace sometime in the 1990s.

The future of asthma research looks incredibly bright. Scientists have identified exciting new compounds that block leukotrienes, chemicals that are thought responsible for the inflammatory reaction of asthma. We suspect that by the year 2000 we will have a whole new set of therapeutic agents that will make asthma pretty much a thing of the past.

For excellent information on all aspects of asthma treatment, we highly recommend the publications from Mothers of Asthmatics. The information is useful for everyone, not just parents! We especially recommend their newsletter, MA *Report* and a wonderful book by Nancy Sander called *A Parent's Guide to Asthma* (Doubleday, 1989). All their publications and various devices can be ordered directly.

> **Mothers of Asthmatics, Inc.**
> 10875 Main Street, Suite 210
> Fairfax, VA 22030
> (703) 385–4403
> (800) 878–4403

Quick Takes

- An allergy is almost always caused by something. Figuring out what it is sometimes requires super sleuthing. The best allergy treatment eliminates the offending allergen from the environment.

- Air conditioning, HEPA filters (high-efficiency, particulate-arresting filters), mattress covers, and dustless vacuum cleaners may all help to cut down on environmental pollutants.

- Pass go, do not spend $200, do not spend money on over-the-counter allergy remedies. These products are less effective and more likely to cause side effects than prescription allergy medicines. Nasal spray addiction is always a worry and sedating antihistamines can make you a hazard on the highways!

- Our initial choice for safe and effective symptom relief is cromolyn—**Nasalcrom** for the nose and **Opticrom** for the eyes.

- Second choice for backup protection is one of the new nonsedating oral antihistamines. **Hismanal** gets the nod. An alternative is **Seldane,** which may soon become available over the counter.

- If you are still suffering, a steroid nasal spray can round out the program. **Beconase** or **Nasalide** should do the trick.

- Sinusitis is not a do-it-yourself affair. First, make sure the right antibiotic has been prescribed for your infection. A culture may be called for. Once the infection is cured, have an ENT specialist check you out. It may be that allergies are the culprit, but if you have recurrent sinus infections, an operation may be in order.

- Asthma is killing people. Never take your asthma for granted. If you start losing control, head for the nearest emergency room!

- Avoid over-the-counter asthma remedies. Like the allergy drugs, they are less effective and potentially more dangerous than prescription medicines.

- The first-line treatment usually involves a bronchodilator. Drugs like **Ventolin** can control a mild to moderate acute attack. They are also helpful against exercise-induced asthma when used before a workout.

- Our favorite anti-inflammatory agent is still cromolyn (**Intal**). Safe and effective when used on a regular daily schedule, it too can prevent exercise-induced asthma. This drug can work for both children and adults. Always worth a first try.

- Steroid inhalers like **Beclovent** and **AeroBid** are finally coming into their own in this country. They can calm down hyperactive lung tissue when used regularly. Side effects are usually minimal as long as the inhalers are not overused.

- The future looks bright. New research is unlocking the mystery of asthma. We fully expect a whole new set of breakthrough medications over the next decade.

References

[1] Flieger, Ken. "It's Spring Again and Allergies Are in Bloom." *FDA Consumer* 1989(May); 17–20.

[2] Blaiss, Michael S., and Springgate, Clark F. "Human Immune System Response to Allergens and Anti-allergenic Agents." *Modern Medicine* 1988; 56(3):52–55.

[3] "Air Purifiers." *Consumer Reports* 1989; 54:88–93.

[4] Owen, Stephen, et al. "Control of House Dust Mite Antigen in Bedding." *Lancet* 1990; 335:396–397.

[5] Jackson, James A. "Ascorbic Acid Versus Allergies." *N.Y. J. Digestive Dis.* 1973; 51:218–226.

[6] Anderson, R. "The Immunostimulatory, Antiinflammatory and Anti-allergic Properties of Ascorbate." *Adv. Nutr. Res.* 1984; 6:19–45.

[7] Cathcard, R.F., 3d. "The Vitamin C Treatment of Allergy and the Normally Unprimed State of Antibodies." *Med. Hypotheses* 1986; 21(3):307–321.

[8] Galland, L. "Biochemical Abnormalities in Patients with Multiple Chemical Sensitivities." *State Art Rev. Occup. Med.* 1987; 2:714–720.

[9] Briefs. "Severe Atopic Dermatitis Responds to Ascorbic Acid." *Medical World News* 1989(Apr. 24); 41.

[10] Dick, Elliot. Personal communication, Jan. 25, 1990.

[11] Bussche, Gabriel Vanden, et al. "Clinical Profile of Astemizole. A Survey of 50 Double-blind Trials." *Ann. Allergy* 1987; 58:184–188.

[12] "Astemizole—Another Non-sedating Antihistamine." *Medical Letter* 1989; 31:43–44.

[13] Jafek, Bruce W., et al. "Bacterial Sinusitis: Rapid, Accurate Evaluation of Patient Complaints." *Modern Medicine* 1989; 57(11):56–64.

[14] Davidson, Terence M., and Cueva, Roberto A. "Sinusitis: State-of-the-art Evaluation." *Modern Medicine* 1988; 56(5):92–104.

[15] Williams, M. Henry, Jr. "Increasing Severity of Asthma from 1960 to 1987." (letter) *N. Engl. J. Med.* 1989; 320:1015–1016.

[16] Weiss, Kevin B. "Seasonal Trends in US Asthma Hospitalizations and Mortality." *JAMA* 1990; 263:2323–2328.

[17] Ibid.

[18] Research & Forecasts, Inc. "The American Asthma Report." 1989.

[19] Jamison, David C., ed. "Herbal Remedy for Asthma." *Asthma Update* 1988; 4(2):1.

[20] Clinical News. "Vitamin C, Niacin may Affect Bronchitis." *Modern Medicine* 1989; 57(9):17–23.

[21] Reynolds, R.D., and Natta, C.L. "Depressed Plasma Pyridoxal Phosphate Concentrations in Adult Asthmatics." *Am. J. Clin. Nutr.* 1985; 41:684–688.

[22] Barnes, Peter J. "A New Approach to the Treatment of Asthma." *N. Engl. J. Med.* 1989; 321:1517–1527.

[23] Rachelefsky, G.S., et al. "Behaviour Abnormalities and Poor School Performance Due to Oral Theophylline Use." *Pediatrics* 1986; 78:1133–1138.

[24] Cockcroft, Donald W. "A Stepwise Approach to the Outpatient Management of Asthma." *Modern Medicine* 1990; 58(5):50–60.

[25] Galant, Stanley P. "Treatment of Asthma." *Postgraduate Medicine* 1990; 87(4):229–236.

[26] Barnes, op. cit.

[27] Ibid.

Medicine Chest 11

Every home has a medicine chest in the bathroom. More often than not, it is filled with a haphazard assortment of old pill bottles, shaving stuff, gargles, frayed toothbrushes, antiperspirants, and adhesive bandages in mostly unusable sizes. If your bathroom cabinet is anything like ours, you have to open it carefully so nothing falls out into the sink. One thing you won't find in our medicine chest, however, is medicine. The bathroom is a terrible place to store pills.

Many medications are vulnerable to damage from heat and humidity In some cases, this could be disastrous. A study commissioned by the Food and Drug Administration examined the effects of humidity on the anticonvulsant medicine carbamazepine, often prescribed by the brand name **Tegretol**. Researchers discovered that this drug "may lose one-third or more of its effectiveness if stored in humid conditions."[1] An epileptic relying on this medicine could be in serious danger of a seizure if it were kept in the bathroom cabinet.

Don't worry about storing deodorant, razors, dental floss, or other health and beauty aids in the bathroom. But medicine should always be removed to a safe, dry spot well out of the reach of children. A kitchen cupboard or special shelf in a closet is acceptable as long as it is away from heat and sunlight. Always ask your pharmacist about proper storage conditions and insist that she write the expiration date on the label of all prescription medications.

Basic Supplies

Every family has to tailor its medicine chest to its own special needs, but there are some basics that almost everyone will want to have on hand. First-aid supplies top most people's list. Yet it always seems as if the bandages are the wrong size whenever someone gets a cut or a scrape. And you can be sure that when you need cough medicine in the middle of the night, the bottle will be almost empty. It is a good idea to review your medical supplies at least every three months to make sure an emergency doesn't catch you unprepared. This is a chance to weed out expired pills and potions that may no longer work and might even cause harm. All over-the-counter products have an expiration date stamped somewhere on the container. When in doubt, throw it out!

PERSONAL CARE

Selecting soap, skin cream, shampoo, and other hygiene products is largely a matter of personal preference. One individual may swear by a particular brand of strawberry-scented shampoo while someone else may find it repulsive. We are including general guidelines, but your own tastes will dictate precisely which products are best for you.

Soap

For washing hands, liquid soap is best. Soggy bar soap can become a breeding ground for germs.[2] *Consumer Reports* rated **Liquid Dial Antibacterial** as the best liquid soap on the market.[3] For bathing, **Dove** heads our list. Research by renowned dermatologist Dr. Albert Kligman has shown that it is one of the mildest soaps on the market and is especially good for people with dry skin.[4] The testers at Consumers Union also rated **Dove Unscented White** best for "cleaning, feel, lathering, and rinsability."[5]

Shampoo

In an impartial evaluation, experts for *Consumer Reports* lathered up for a comprehensive test of fifty-nine top-selling shampoos. The bottom line: all the shampoos got hair clean, just like **Ivory** Dishwashing Liquid. There were no consistent differences between brands labeled "for dry hair" or "for oily hair." The biggest differences between brands were cost and aroma. So, while CU's testers rated **Pert Plus** highest, you can follow your nose and your pocketbook for your personal choice.[6]

Moisturizer

Ignore the ads implying that any nonprescription skin cream will keep you wrinkle-free and youthful-looking. Though **Retin-A** may reverse some damage caused by sun exposure, nothing else has been proven to work. The most effective moisturizers for dry skin are greasy. Dr. Kligman recommends petroleum jelly (**Vaseline**).[7] **Eucerin** or **Nivea** are also high on his list. *Consumer Reports* gave **Nivea Moisturizing Lotion** and **Sea Breeze Moisture Lotion** high ratings and found them reasonably priced.[8] Another option for an inexpensive moisturizer is a "bovine beauty aid" such as **Udder Cream**, **Bova Cream**, or **Bag Balm**. See page 145 for order information.

Deodorant

The aluminum controversy (see page 20) has lots of people worried about spritzing their pits. We don't know if there is any real hazard, but we certainly suggest that you avoid breathing any fumes from aerosol antiperspirants. **Right Guard** deodorant does not contain aluminum and has been a staple in men's locker rooms for decades. A do-it-yourself home remedy can be made by mixing baking soda and corn starch and applying the powder to underarms with cotton balls.

Sunscreens

A good sunscreen is a medicine chest essential except for people whose skin is naturally dark. Use it whenever you go outdoors, but remember that very few sunscreens block significant amounts of ultraviolet-A, the source of much long-term damage. This means that if you use your sunscreen to spend hours in the sun, you are asking for trouble.

Any high rated (SPF 15 or above) blocker should protect against sunburn. If you have oily skin, we have found that **Shade 25 Gel** or **Clinique Oil-Free Sunblock** are excellent. For activities that involve water, we have found that waterproof products like **Shade 45 Lotion** or **PreSun 29 Sensitive Skin Sunscreen** are excellent. House brands also work well and are usually more economical.

BASIC DRUGS

Pain Relievers

Unless you have a sensitivity to it, aspirin is still our first choice for minor aches and pains, sprains and strains, mild fever, and garden-variety headaches. It is cheap and effective. (Do not give aspirin to children or teenagers with chicken pox or flu.) Smell your aspirin bottle periodically to see if it has started to go bad. A strong vinegarlike odor is a giveaway that deterioration has started.

☐ Aspirin,
OTC Acetaminophen,
or Ibuprofen

Ibuprofen (**Advil**, **Medipren**, **Motrin IB**, **Nuprin**, etc.) is a reasonable alternative, but not much easier on the digestive tract than aspirin. People with aspirin allergies or a sensitive stomach should stick with acetaminophen (**Anacin-3**, **Panadol**, **Tylenol**, etc.). Severe pain may require a prescription medication containing codeine such as **Tylenol with Codeine No. 3** or **Empirin with Codeine No. 3**.

Digestive Aids

Heartburn

Occasional indigestion calls for an antacid. We prefer a calcium-based product such as **Tums E-X** tablets or **Titralac** liquid. A home remedy that just might do the job is a banana. Indian researchers have found that banana powder is surprisingly effective against heartburn.[9] We also believe that **Pepto-Bismol** belongs in most medicine kits. Although the scientific data supporting its use against indigestion and diarrhea are not compelling, millions of families have relied on it for decades and new research suggests that the active ingredient (bismuth subsalicylate) may work against the germ that leads to ulcers and gastritis as well as those that cause travelers' diarrhea.

☐ OTC *Tums, Titralac, or other antacid*

☐ OTC *Pepto-Bismol*

Diarrhea

It is always best not to overreact to minor diarrhea. It may be something you ate, and your GI tract is merely doing its best to eliminate the problem. But when you need relief from the runs, it's a good idea to keep **Imodium A-D** (loperamide) or an over-the-counter remedy containing polycarbophil, such as **Mitrolan**, **Equalactin**, or **FiberCon**, on hand. (Do not give **Imodium A-D** to very young children without medical supervision.)

☐ OTC *Imodium A-D*

☐ OTC *Mitrolan, Equalactin, or FiberCon*

Constipation

Fluids and fiber are the first-line approach. If they fail, psyllium (**Fiberall**, **Metamucil**, **Perdiem Plain**, **Serutan**, etc.) is an excellent adjunct. An added bonus is that psyllium can help bring down elevated cholesterol levels. An alternative is polycarbophil (**Mitrolan**, **Equalactin**, or **FiberCon**) which does double-duty against diarrhea or constipation.

☐ OTC *Fiberall, Metamucil, Perdiem Plain, or Serutan*

or

☐ OTC *Mitrolan, Equalactin, or FiberCon*

COLD REMEDIES

Our first choice is vitamin C. Although there is no good evidence that it will prevent colds, 500 mg taken four times a day does seem to reduce symptoms and suffering.

☐ OTC *Vitamin C*

Sniffles and Sore Throat

Beware the seduction of advertising for multi-symptom cold and cough remedies. Most contain antihistamines, which may work against allergies but not colds. Treat each symptom as it arises. For a sore throat, a salt-water gargle (one-half teaspoon salt in eight ounces of water) is soothing. Nasal congestion will respond magnificently to a nose spray, but more than three days of continuous use can lead to dependence and rebound congestion. Oral decongestants such as pseudoephedrine (**Sudafed** or house brands) may be less likely to cause problems.

Cough

A dry cough that is annoying and keeps you awake at night calls for an effective cough suppressant. We prefer codeine (15 mg) if it is available. Some states sell codeine-containing cough remedies without a prescription (**Cheracol Syrup**, **Robitussin A-C**, **Tussi-Organidin Liquid**). If you have **Tylenol w/Codeine No. 3** on hand for pain, you could take half a tablet. Dextromethorphan is another alternative. Single-ingredient products include **Delsym**, **Hold**, **Sucrets Cough Control Lozenges**, and **St. Joseph Cough Syrup**.

FIRST AID

Cuts and Scratches

For ordinary household emergencies, a wide assortment of adhesive bandages should always be on hand. Along with standard shapes and sizes, we find the butterfly- and *H*-shaped varieties helpful for fingertips and knuckles. A skinned knee or larger abrasion needs a nonstick gauze pad and adhesive tape. If someone is allergic to tape, use one of the hypoallergenic varieties.

Mild soap and lots of water are best for cleaning most wounds. Forget alcohol or iodine; they hurt and may do more harm than good. If you want something to impress your patient, try a little hydrogen peroxide. It creates a foaming action that looks exciting without damaging abraded tissues and can help

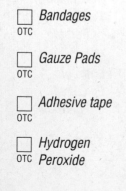

☐ **Cheracol Syrup,**
OTC **Robitussin A-C,**
or Tussi-
Organidin Liquid

or

☐ **Delsym, Hold,**
OTC **Sucrets Cough**
Control Lozenges
or St. Joseph
Cough Syrup

☐ *Bandages*
OTC

☐ *Gauze Pads*
OTC

☐ *Adhesive tape*
OTC

☐ *Hydrogen*
OTC *Peroxide*

clean out dirt and debris. A bit of antibiotic cream, such as **Polysporin**, helps prevent infection. (See p. 128.)

Sprains and Strains

First aid for bruises, sprains, and strains is a cold pack. This doesn't need to be much more elaborate than crushed ice cubes in a dishtowel, but instant cold packs such as **Ace Instant Cold Compress**, **Jack Frost Instant Cold Pack,** or **3M's Cold Comfort** don't take up room in the freezer. After chilling, sprains need compression. A familiar **Ace** bandage will work, but newer options such as **Coban ActionWrap** or **Fiberflex Wrap** may be easier to apply.

Splinters

To remove splinters and slivers there is no substitute for high-quality, fine-point tweezers (called forceps). Don't settle for the eyebrow-pluckers you'll find in the dimestore or even most pharmacies. Check a surgical supply house or order the **Splinter Removal Kit** from the *SelfCare Catalog* (800) 345–3371).

☐ OTC *Bactine First Aid,* *Lanabiotic,* *Mycitracin Triple, N.B.P.,* *Neosporin,* *Polysporin,* or *Triple Antibiotic*

☐ OTC *Ace Instant Cold Compress,* *Jack Frost Instant Cold Pack or* *3M's Cold Comfort*

☐ OTC *Ace bandage,* *Coban ActionWrap or Fiberflex Wrap*

Traveling Medical Kit

They say the cobbler's children often go barefoot. On one of our Cub Scout outings we came up with an unwelcome variation. Soon after we arrived, our son came hopping on one foot with a large splinter firmly embedded in the other heel. The rest of the adults naturally assumed we would have come well equipped for such emergencies. To our great embarrassment, we had left the first-aid kit at home. We ended up resorting to a safety pin and an old Scout knife to try to dislodge the splinter.

We learned our lesson the hard way. Now we have a well-stocked traveling medicine kit. For camping, we pack it into a fishing-tackle box. It makes a great first-aid kit even at home because everything has its place and is easily accessible. For backpacking or airplane trips, the essentials can be stored in a zippered pouch.

BLISTERS AND BURNS

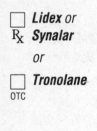

□ *2nd Skin*
OTC

Besides the first-aid supplies listed above, we also take along **2nd Skin**. This stuff is great for burns, blisters, and minor abrasions. It is 96 percent water in a gellike film. A bandage goes on over the top to hold the **2nd Skin** in place. There is nothing like this stuff if you get a blister on a long hike and need relief to make it back to camp.

ITCHES AND BITES

□ *Lidex* or
Rx *Synalar*

or

□ *Tronolane*
OTC

We always take along an anti-itch cream. We usually ask our dermatologist for sample tubes of an intermediate-strength steroid cream such as **Lidex** (fluocinonide) or **Synalar** (fluocinolone). **Tronolane** (pramoxine) is intended primarily for hemorrhoids, but it has an effective anesthetic so we often rely on it for itches.

□ *Insect Repellant*
OTC

Insect repellants are always a good idea during the summer, but we do not recommend a 100 percent DEET product. Reports of toxicity, especially when repellant is smeared too liberally on children, have scared us off. You can put your DEET bug spray on clothing to reduce risk or consider **Avon Skin-So-Soft**. This bath oil has a devoted following among Marines, forest rangers, hunters, and fishermen. It smells pretty strong, but may actually help keep mosquitoes and biting flies away.

MOTION SICKNESS

□ *Dramamine*
OTC

or

□ *Ginger*
Herb

Our children get motion sickness whether traveling by car, air, or boat. They are old enough to use **Dramamine** (dimenhydrinate) or its generic equivalent. (This medication should not be given to babies or toddlers.) The chewable tablets are especially convenient, and can do double-duty if jet lag makes it hard for an adult to get to sleep. (Children may develop insomnia on dimenhydrinate.)

A home remedy that might help is ground ginger. A capsule containing roughly 900 mg proved more helpful than **Dramamine** in a double-blind controlled test simulating an amusement park ride.[10]

Another product we recommend for motion sickness is

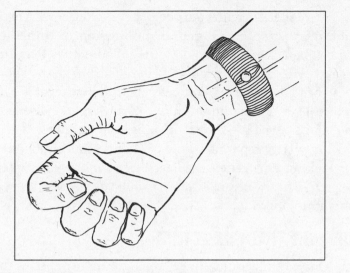

TRAVEL GARDE Acupressure Wrist Band. The elastic band has a small plastic button embedded in it which the user positions over the traditional Chinese acupressure point that controls nausea. Scientific studies are currently under way to test actual effectiveness. Since there are no side effects to worry about, we consider these wrist bands a safe alternative to medication. (An identical product called **MORNING GARDE** is sold for morning sickness and may be worth a try during pregnancy.) If you can't find it in your local pharmacy, you can call Marine Logic, Inc. (800–323–7853) or write to 400 Australian Ave, Suite 725, West Palm Beach, Florida 33401.

☐ *Accupressure*
OTC *Wrist Band*

TRAVELERS' DIARRHEA

Travelers' diarrhea may be a problem on international journeys no matter how careful you are about avoiding tap water, fresh fruits, and uncooked vegetables. Food handlers in many countries have a host of gastrointestinal problems ranging from *E. coli* and *Salmonella* to *Shigella* and *Campylobacter jejuni*. These are readily, if unwittingly, shared with innocent diners. **Pepto-Bismol** taken at recommended strength throughout the visit helps reduce your risk of getting the runs. Tablets are easier to pack and not as messy as the bottles. The recommended dose is two tablets in the morning and two at night.

☐ *Pepto-Bismol*
OTC *(tablets)*

☐ *Bactrim*
Rx *or Septra*

Also, check in with your doctor before you leave. A prescription medication containing a combination of trimethoprim and sulfamethoxazole, sold by the brand names **Bactrim** and **Septra**, will cut an attack of travelers' diarrhea short. The usual dose for adults is one **DS** (double strength) or two regular-strength tablets every twelve hours for five days. Serious side effects are rare but may be life-threatening. Be sure to review with your doctor what symptoms would call for discontinuing the drug or seeking emergency medical attention. If you have ever experienced an allergic reaction to sulfa drugs, you must avoid this antibiotic.

URINARY TRACT INFECTION

One advantage of taking along **Bactrim** or **Septra** is that either can also be used to treat a urinary tract infection (UTI), if one arises. While men don't generally need to worry about this contingency, a woman with a history of UTI should make sure to get dosing instructions from her doctor along with the prescription.

PACKING UP

Don't forget to take enough of your regular medications to get through any trip, as it might be difficult to pick up more high blood-pressure pills, heart medicine, or ulcer medication. Even in the United States, trying to get a refill on a prescription in an unfamiliar community where you are unknown can prove frustrating and take up valuable travel time. In addition to checking your supplies before departure, make sure they're packed in carry-on luggage so they don't end up sitting on the runway in Phoenix while you are looking for your suitcase in Milwaukee. And if your medicine requires refrigeration, you might want to consider investing in an insulated lunch bag with a chill pack to keep it cool until you can stash it in the mini-fridge in your hotel room.

Beyond the Basics

A truly well-stocked home medical inventory would contain a number of devices and drugs beyond the essentials listed above. Such a complete home kit would not only avoid a frantic two a.m. run to the round-the-clock pharmacy for cough syrup, but would also allow you to participate more fully in your own health care. Exactly which of the following suggestions you'll want to adopt will depend on your household. Some of the equipment will require training or practice to master, so you may need your doctor's help. When he sees that you're able to keep track of your findings and report them accurately, he'll probably be delighted to have such an involved patient.

Remember, the most important ingredient in any home medical cabinet doesn't fit on the shelf—it's common sense. If you understand the medicine you are using and what its consequences could be, you'll be in a better position to detect trouble before it becomes an emergency. Before you take any medication, prescription or over-the-counter, check to make sure it isn't incompatible with an underlying medical condition or another drug. Your physician and pharmacist can help you with this, so be sure to consult them when you have questions. And of course, always check with a physician before using any prescription medication.

PERSONAL CARE EXTRAS

Certain Dri (aluminum chloride)   OTC

A major sweating problem may not respond adequately to the usual antiperspirants. A person who drenches his shirt or her blouse in a normal day may find an aluminum chloride solution helpful. It should be applied to *dry* skin at night. (Daytime application could damage clothing.) One application may be effective for several days. For order information: (800) 338–8079.
Alternate brands: **Drysol** or **Xerac AC** (prescription only). **Fresh**, **At Last**, **Mon-Ray** (OTC).

☐ OTC *Certain Dri, Fresh, At Last, or Mon-Ray*

or

☐ Rx *Drysol or Xerac AC*

□ *Clinique Self-*
OTC *Tanning*
Formula,
Coppertone
Sunless Tanning
Lotion, or Estée
Lauder Self-
Action Tanning
Creme

□ *Lac-Hydrin*
R_X
  or

□ *Aqua Glycolic*
OTC *Lotion, Lac-*
Hydrin Five, or
LactiCare

□ *Nizoral*
Abroad *Shampoo*

□ *Witch Hazel*
OTC

Clinique Self-Tanning Formula (dihydroxyacetone)   OTC

If you want a tan without risking exposure to ultraviolet radiation, a tanning lotion like this one offers an alternative that many people find cosmetically acceptable.

Alternate brands: **Coppertone Sunless Tanning Lotion**, **Estée Lauder Self-Action Tanning Creme**.

Lac-Hydrin (ammonium lactate) R_X

If the moisturizers you have tried still leave your skin peeling, flaking, or itching with dryness, consider a prescription treatment called **Lac-Hydrin**. It makes the outer layer of the skin less vulnerable to moisture loss. It may sting or burn when first applied to irritated, cracked skin, but it does make a major difference.

OTC Alternatives: **Aqua Glycolic Lotion**, **Lac-Hydrin Five**, or **LactiCare** contain the same active ingredient, but at a lower concentration.

Nizoral Shampoo (ketoconazole)   Abroad

This medicated shampoo is fantastic for seborrheic dermatitis, banishing itchy flakes by killing the yeast that provokes them. For best results, this prescription lather should be left on the scalp for five minutes before thorough rinsing. It is awaiting approval for marketing in the United States. **Nizoral** cream may be prescribed to treat itchy red patches of seborrheic dermatitis on the face.

Witch Hazel   OTC

This astringent cleanser is often useful in preventing "itchy bottom." *Gently* patting the anal area clean with witch hazel–moistened cotton balls after a bowel movement can provide a measure of relief whether hemorrhoids are involved or not.

Alternate brands: **Tucks**, **Mediconet**, **Preparation H Cleansing** (OTC).

TOOLS FOR SELF-CARE

Blood-Glucose Monitors for Diabetics   OTC

All the machines used for self-monitoring of blood glucose use a drop of blood from a finger prick with a specially prepared paper strip. They vary considerably in size, features, and price. No one model is best for everyone. Before investing more than a hundred dollars, make sure that you try it out. Is it easy for you to operate? Can you read the results, or do you need one with a speaker? Will it adapt to your life-style? Your diabetes educator should be able to help you make the right decision so you and your doctor can track your blood glucose over the course of days and weeks (see p. 303–5).

☐ ***Blood-Glucose***
OTC ***Monitor***

Blood-Pressure Monitors   OTC

Digital devices have revolutionized the measurement of blood

☐ ***Blood Pressure***
OTC ***Monitor***

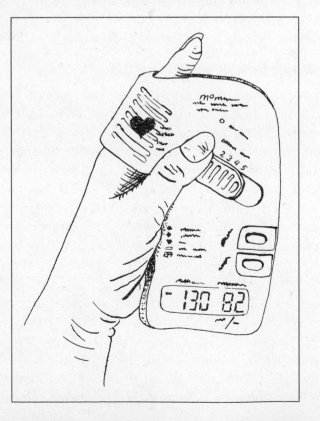

pressure. Instead of trying to listen to muffled sounds through a stethoscope it is now possible to use either a finger unit (for portability) or an arm cuff that will read out both systolic and diastolic pressure along with your pulse. We have reviewed many machines over the years, and we have been most impressed with those manufactured by Omron Marshall Products, Inc. They are compact, easy to use, and accurate. Prices range from $60 for a simple pump-up model (**Marshall 80**) to $140 for the finger model (**Marshall F89**) or the self-inflating model with a built-in printer—**Marshall 97**). For order information call (800) 634–4350.

Chemcard   R_x

☐ *Chemcard*
R_x

This do-it-yourself cholesterol test requires a drop of blood from a fingerprick. You won't learn your HDL or LDL, but you can get a general idea of your total cholesterol level. At the time of this writing, **Chemcard** is available by prescription only, but the company anticipates approval for OTC sale. Pharmacies can order from Chematics, P. O. Box 293, North Webster, IN 46555.

Mini-Wright Peak Flow Meter   OTC

☐ *Mini-Wright*
OTC *Peak Flow Meter*

Asthma patients, especially children, can't always tell how serious their lung conditions are. A simple device called a peak flow meter allows measurement of lung capacity (see p. 392). Parents can keep a numerical record and plot it on a chart to keep track of response to asthma medication. (This is essential for children whose asthma reacts to exercise, since it shows whether they are ready for an athletic event.) You can order the **Mini-Wright Peak Flow Meter** from Mothers of Asthmatics, 10875 Main Street, Suite 210, Fairfax, VA 22030 (800) 878–4403.

Urine Tests   OTC

☐ *Biotel u.t.i.,*
OTC *Chemstrip LN for Bladder Infection, or Microstix-Nitrite Reagent Strips*

Urinary tract infections can be hard to detect, especially in young children. These home diagnostic test strips can tell if infection is present. They can also help determine if antibiotic treatment was successful at eradicating the bacteria. Ask your pharmacist for **Biotel u.t.i.** home screening test, **Chemstrip LN for Bladder Infection**, or **Microstix-Nitrite Reagent Strips**.

THE EXPANDED HOME FORMULARY

If we knew we might be stranded on a desert island, there are some additional medications we would want to take along. You will have to select the ones that are appropriate for your household.

> If you would like to do your self-care shopping by mail we recommend the *SelfCare Catalog*. You can order everything from exercise equipment and a stocked first aid kit to an ear scope or water tester. For a free catalog call (800) 345-3371.

Aspirin (acetylsalicylic acid)   OTC

Aspirin goes with us wherever we go. It is still the standard by which other pain relievers are measured and it works well against inflammation. In addition, aspirin appears to help reduce the risk of heart attack and thrombotic stroke (caused by a blood clot). It may also diminish migraine frequency. Side effects and interactions may limit regular use. Sniff the open container periodically and replace the medication when it starts to smell of vinegar.

☐ *Aspirin*
OTC

Bactroban R_X

This prescription antibiotic ointment is a breakthrough in the treatment of impetigo and other staph infections of the skin. It will require a consultation with your physician.

☐ *Bactroban*
R_X

Beconase (beclomethasone) R_X

This steroid nasal spray helps prevent nasal congestion due to allergy. It will not provide immediate relief, but may be useful in overcoming symptoms and can also help break a nasal spray addiction caused by overreliance on decongestant sprays. Be patient, since it may take several days to produce benefits.
Alternate brand: **Vancenase**

☐ *Beconase*
R_X *or Vancenase*

Benadryl (Diphenhydramine)   OTC

This highly sedating antihistamine can serve double-duty against allergy symptoms and insomnia. In a pinch it may also help control a cough. Be careful about giving it to children since antihistamines may stimulate their nervous systems. Don't drive or operate machinery after taking diphenhydramine.

☐ *Benadryl*
OTC

Carafate (sucralfate) R_X

This prescription ulcer medicine helps protect the stomach lining from damage due to arthritis medications. It has few side effects, but questions remain about long-term aluminum absorption.

Chlor-Trimeton (chlorpheniramine)   OTC

This classic nonprescription antihistamine helps relieve symptoms of hay fever or other allergies. It may cause drowsiness or loss of alertness, so don't drive or operate machinery after taking it. Chlorpheniramine is not appropriate for those with glaucoma, prostate enlargement, or any of several other conditions.

Coenzyme Q$_{10}$ OTC

This nutritional supplement looks promising for the treatment of heart failure. It apparently improves the pumping ability of the heart, and may increase the effectiveness of other heart-failure medications. Another possible benefit is in the treatment of gum disease. Some researchers are even suggesting it may play a role in delaying the onset of Alzheimer's disease. For more information check *The Miracle Nutrient Coenzyme Q$_{10}$* by Dr. Emile G. Bliznakov and Gerald L. Hunt (published by Bantam Books).

Didronel (etidronate) R_X

New research shows that this prescription drug prevents bone loss and may even help reverse osteoporosis. It reduces the risk of spinal fractures. Side effects are minimal when it is used according to cyclical protocol (two weeks treatment, then thirteen weeks without). It will require discussion with a specialist in osteoporosis prevention. **Didronel** must be taken on an empty stomach to maximize absorption.

Dry Eye Product   OTC

This artificial tear solution does not have a brand name as of this writing. Dr. Jeffrey Gilbard, an opthalmologist at the Eye Research Institute, has dedicated his life to investigating such products.

He shook up the medical establishment when he discovered that most brands currently on the market do little, if anything, for dry eyes. In some cases he has shown these artificial tear solutions may even make matters worse. Dr. Gilbard has come up with what he believes is a better alternative. It will be available from Advanced Vision Research, Inc., Suite 358, 295 Cambridge Street, Boston, Massachusetts 02114.

EpiPen Auto-Injector (epinephrine injectable) R_X

People who are highly allergic to insect stings (bees, wasps, yellow jackets, etc.) should talk to an allergist about an emergency kit containing epinephrine. It can be injected immediately upon onset of anaphylactic symptoms to counteract a potentially lethal reaction. Of course emergency medical treatment is also essential. For children there is **EpiPen Jr.**
Alternate brand: **Ana-Kit**

☐ *EpiPen,*
R_X *EpiPen Jr.,*
or Ana-Kit

Hismanal (astemizole) R_X

This long-acting prescription antihistamine provides symptom relief from allergies without causing drowsiness. In addition it works against hives and itching.

☐ *Hismanal*
R_X

Intal (cromolyn sodium) R_X

Our allergy and asthma specialists sing the praises of this aerosol as a first-line treatment in preventing asthma attacks, including exercise-induced asthma. It is especially helpful for children. **Intal** must be used daily and is not useful in an acute attack.

☐ *Intal*
R_X

Lactaid (lactase) OTC

This enzyme digests the sugar in milk, which causes gastrointestinal discomfort to lactose-intolerant people. It is available as drops to be added to the milk several hours before it is consumed or as a pill that may be taken at the same meal as the milk, cheese, ice cream, or other dairy product.
Alternate brand: **Lactrase**

☐ *Lactaid*
OTC *or Lactrase*

Lotrimin AF (clotrimazole) OTC

This is the latest prescription antifungal agent to become available over the counter. It is effective against athlete's foot and other fungal infections. Patience and persistence are essential in clearing up athlete's foot infections.

Magnesium   OTC

This mineral supplement appears helpful for the heart and cardiovascular system. Magnesium may help lower blood pressure and is potentially beneficial against certain forms of angina, congestive heart failure, and irregular heart rhythms. Discuss the correct dose with your doctor.

Micatin (miconazole)   OTC

This antifungal agent is effective against skin infections (athlete's foot or jock itch). With a doctor's diagnosis and supervision, it may be used with a **Monistat** applicator for vaginal yeast infection.

Nasalcrom (cromolyn sodium) R_X

This nasal spray is safe and effective against allergy symptoms in the nose. It won't work like a decongestant to provide instant relief, but when used daily it can control nasal stuffiness.

Opticrom (cromolyn sodium) R_X

These eye drops contain the same ingredient as Nasalcrom and **Intal**. Used regularly during hay fever season, they can prevent redness and itching.

Prepulsid (cisapride)   Abroad

This experimental medicine is available abroad. It is our first choice for severe heartburn because it treats the cause of the problem, rather than the symptoms.

Proscar (finasteride)   Experimental

This exciting new compound has not yet been approved by the FDA. It looks promising for its ability to shrink enlarged

---

Lotrimin AF
OTC

Magnesium
OTC

Micatin
OTC

Nasalcrom
R_X

Opticrom
R_X

Prepulsid
Abroad

prostate glands, possibly providing an alternative to surgery in some cases.

Valerian Root   Herbal

This herbal tea has a history of use for mild anxiety and sleeping problems. It should not be used if someone has liver or kidney problems. As with any sedative, do not drive or operate heavy machinery.

☐ *Valerian Root*
Herbal

Zaditen (ketotifen)   Abroad

This oral asthma medicine acts preventively, much as cromolyn does. It is long-acting and is more convenient than an inhaler. It requires patience, however, since benefits may take weeks to appear. Although **Zaditen** is one of the more popular asthma medicines used around the world, it is not yet available in the United States. It can cause drowsiness in some people and alcohol is a no-no.

☐ *Zatiden*
Abroad

Zantac (ranitidine) R_X

There is talk that **Zantac** may become available over the counter. If it does, it will provide consumers with an effective medicine for severe heartburn and ulcers. It is less likely to interact with other medications than is its chemical cousin, **Tagamet**.

☐ *Zantac*
R_X

Zostrix (capsaicin) OTC

This ointment may help relieve pain after shingles and perhaps even certain other kinds of nerve pain. Keep it out of eyes, nose, mouth, and other sensitive tissues, since **Zostrix** is made from hot peppers.

☐ *Zostrix*
OTC

Zovirax (acyclovir) R_X

This antiviral medicine may abort an attack of genital herpes or cold sores if it is used before the lesions grab a foothold. Although not a cure, **Zovirax** can prevent frequent genital herpes outbreaks if the medicine is used prophylactically. The FDA has approved **Zovirax** for the treatment of shingles. To work it must be used shortly after the infection begins.

☐ *Zovirax*
R_X

References

[1] "Safeguards Needed for Carbamazepine." *FDA Drug Bulletin* 1990; April 5.

[2] Kabara, Jon J. "Bar Soap and Liquid Soap." *JAMA* 1985; 253:1560–1561.

[3] "Soaping Up." *Consumer Reports* 1990; 55(10):644–647.

[4] Frosch, Peter J., and Kligman, Albert M. "The Soap Chamber Test." *J. Am. Acad. Dermatol.* 1979; 1:35–41.

[5] "Soaping Up," op. cit.

[6] "Shampoos." *Consumer Reports* 1989; 54(2):95–99.

[7] "Q&A on Photoaging: An Interview with Albert M. Kligman." Presented at the conference Cosmeceuticals: The Science of Beauty and Aging, hosted by Boston University Medical Center, April 21, 1986.

[8] "All-purpose Moisturizers." *Consumer Reports* 1986; 51:733–738.

[9] Arora, Anil, and Sharma, M.P. "Use of Banana in Non-ulcer Dyspepsia." *Lancet* 1990; 335:612–613.

[10] Mowrey, Daniel B., and Clayson, Dennis E. "Motion Sickness, Ginger and Psychophysics." *Lancet* 1982; i:655–657.

Index

A

About the Authors

Joe and Terry Graedon have been writing as a team for over a decade, collaborating on books, articles, and a syndicated newspaper column called *The People's Pharmacy*. They are also co-hosts of a weekly radio talk show that focuses on health issues. In all their efforts, they strive to empower their readers and listeners to become active participants in their own health care.

They met in Ann Arbor, Michigan while Joe was working on a master's degree in pharmacology and Terry was studying for a doctoral degree in anthropology at The University of Michigan. Prior to graduate school Joe worked in the neuropharmacology laboratory at the New Jersey Neuropsychiatric Institute in Princeton, studying basic brain physiology, sleep disorders, and mental illness.

From Ann Arbor, Joe and Terry went to Oaxaca, Mexico, where Terry did her dissertation research on health and nutrition while Joe taught pharmacology to second year medical students at the medical school of the Universidad Autonoma "Benito Juarez." During those two years he started work on the *The People's Pharmacy*. The success of that book led to a newspaper column syndicated by King Features and additional books, including *The People's Pharmacy-2*, *The New People's Pharmacy-3: Drug Breakthroughs of the '80s*, *Totally New and Revised The People's Pharmacy*, and *50+: The Graedons' People's Pharmacy for Older Adults*.

Joe belongs to the American Association for the Advancement of Science, the Society for Neuroscience, and the New York Academy of Science. He has served as a consultant to the Federal Trade Commission on nonprescription drug advertising. He has also been a member of the Advisory Board of the University of California, San Francisco, Drug Studies Unit and the Board of Visitors for the School of Pharmacy, The University of North Carolina at Chapel Hill.

Terry has taught medical anthropology at the School of Nursing and Department of Anthropology at Duke University. She is a member of the American Anthropological Association, the American Public Health Association, the Society for Applied Anthropology, and the Society for Medical Anthropology. In addition, Joe and Terry collaborate on raising their two children.

The Graedons hope you have found this book helpful and fun to read. They trust you will never be stranded on a desert island, but will use the information to work toward collaborative relationships with your physician, pharmacist, and other health care providers.

The Graedons may not be able to answer your correspondence personally (they receive hundreds of letters weekly), but they welcome comments, suggestions, questions, and home remedies. All mail will be forwarded to them if you address it to:

Joe and Terry Graedon
Graedons' Best Medicine
Bantam Books
666 Fifth Avenue
New York, NY 10103